Workplace solutions for childcare

Workplace solutions
for childcare

Catherine Hein and Naomi Cassirer

INTERNATIONAL LABOUR OFFICE • GENEVA

Hein, C.; Cassirer, N.

Workplace solutions for childcare
Geneva, International Labour Office, 2010

Child care, child care facilities, employers role, trade union role, state intervention, local government, Brazil, Chile, France, Hungary, India, Kenya, South Africa, Thailand, UK, USA.
02.09

ISBN 978-92-2-122035-0

ILO Cataloguing in Publication Data

The designations employed in ILO publications, which are in conformity with United Nations practice, and the presentation of material therein do not imply the expression of any opinion whatsoever on the part of the International Labour Office concerning the legal status of any country, area or territory or of its authorities, or concerning the delimitation of its frontiers.

The responsibility for opinions expressed in signed articles, studies and other contributions rests solely with their authors, and publication does not constitute an endorsement by the International Labour Office of the opinions expressed in them.

Reference to names of firms and commercial products and processes does not imply their endorsement by the International Labour Office, and any failure to mention a particular firm, commercial product or process is not a sign of disapproval.

ILO publications and electronic products can be obtained through major booksellers or ILO local offices in many countries, or direct from ILO Publications, International Labour Office, CH-1211 Geneva 22, Switzerland. Catalogues or lists of new publications are available free of charge from the above address, or by email: pubvente@ilo.org

Visit our website: www.ilo.org/publns

Photocomposed in Switzerland   WEI
Printed in Switzerland   STA

Contents

Part II

Tables

Figures

Boxes

Preface

Finding appropriate childcare for their children while they work is a problem faced by working parents around the world. Access to childcare is sometimes thought to be an issue mainly in industrialized countries, but parents in developing countries are facing similar problems as family structures change and more women join the labour market either through choice or necessity. The repercussions of childcare difficulties for the workplace, the economy, gender equality, the education of children and society in general have yet to be well integrated into national policies in many countries, both developed and developing.

Almost 30 years ago, in 1981, the International Labour Organization (ILO) adopted the Workers with Family Responsibilities Convention (No. 156), which seeks to promote policies to reduce work–family conflict and combat the labour market discrimination resulting from family responsibilities. The Convention calls for measures "to develop or promote community services, public or private, such as childcare ...". Today, while far from meeting demand, many examples exist from around the world of governments, trade unions and employers' organizations actively working at policy level to promote and improve workers' access to childcare. Many examples also exist of actors taking action at the workplace, adopting programmes to help workers cope with their childcare responsibilities.

This book was conceived because it was felt that not enough was known about how workplace actors are working to promote childcare for working parents and what they are doing, particularly in developing countries where there has been less documentation. Why have employers as well as trade unions become involved in the childcare problems of workers? What sorts of solutions have been found? What is the link to government policies for childcare? To help answer these questions, this book not only reviews the existing literature but also provides overviews of childcare policies and programmes in ten countries (four industrialized and six developing countries) as well as case studies of workplace initiatives for childcare support in these countries.

It is hoped that the practical approach of this book with its many concrete workplace examples will provide governments, employers and workers' organizations with useful ideas that they might be able to adapt in their own contexts in order to reduce the impact of childcare problems on workers and on the workplace.

I would like to congratulate the two authors, Catherine Hein and Naomi Cassirer, for this excellent work, and thank the chapter authors for their rich contributions to the book. I am grateful to the International Organization of Employers, particularly Brent Wilton and Bárbara León, and to the International Trade Union Confederation, particularly P. Kamalam, for their assistance in mobilizing their networks to find the interesting workplace examples featured in the book, and for their encouragement of the project. I would also like to thank Eric Boulte and Nathalie Renaudin for their ideas and support for this work. Many ILO colleagues provided valuable assistance or inputs, in particular Anna Biondi, Adrienne Cruz, Can Dogan, Raphaela Egg, Deborah France-Massin, Nelien Haspels, Judica Makhetha, Sipho Ndlovu, Pedro Américo Furtado De Oliveira, Solange Sanches, Amrita Sietaram, Reiko Tsushima, Petra Ulshoefer and María Elena Valenzuela. Laura Addati provided expert research assistance and inputs throughout the book in addition to the chapters she authored. Charlotte Beauchamp, Kris Falciola, José Garcia and Claire Piper provided invaluable support on the administrative and production aspects of the book.

MANUELA TOMEI
Chief
Conditions of Work and Employment Programme

Part I

Introduction

1

For parents who work for income or would like to work, childcare is a concern that is almost universal. One way that workers have been receiving various kinds of assistance with childcare is through support that they can access through their workplace. Workplace programmes are not the only, nor even the primary, means of accessing assistance with childcare. However, they are nevertheless helping many working parents and are attracting increasing interest as a way of meeting the overall societal challenge of finding mechanisms for making childcare more accessible and available to working parents.

1.1 Objectives

This book seeks to explore why the workplace has become involved in childcare support and what programmes have been implemented, based on concrete examples of childcare support that can be found in workplaces around the world. Even a quick look at the Internet reveals that there are a number of enterprises, government departments, parastatals, universities and other organizations that have adopted measures to help their workers with childcare. These measures include not only the traditional workplace nursery but many other innovative ways of helping workers access care for their children.

While the role of the employer is often important, other partners such as trade unions, non-governmental organizations (NGOs) and organizations specializing in childcare, as well as government departments, are increasingly becoming involved in workplace-related programmes. Unions are providing advice to their affiliates on collective bargaining for childcare support and, in some cases, are involved directly in childcare provision. Governments in a number of countries (such as Australia, Singapore, the United Kingdom) specifically encourage and help employers to provide some form of childcare support, in some cases backed by incentives. National reports have been prepared in a number of countries, such as Australia, Canada, Singapore, the United Kingdom and the United States, giving examples of companies which are providing some childcare assistance.

Despite all the documentation and information available on web sites concerning industrialized countries, relatively little is known about workplace initiatives for childcare in the developing world. Also, awareness of the possibilities for workplace support and of the variety of ways that have been found for helping workers with childcare problems is not widespread globally. The present book thus tries to fill this gap by providing a review of how various partners have become involved and of the types of solutions they have found in both industrialized and developing countries.

The book draws heavily on concrete examples. Many such examples are derived from secondary sources, which tend to relate to industrialized countries. In addition, a number of case studies were prepared specifically for this publication with particular emphasis on the developing countries for which there is less information already available. The case studies were taken from a limited number of countries in order to allow for a more detailed assessment of national policies and programmes for childcare and to be able to situate the workplace initiatives within this context.

Part II of this publication consists of country chapters which provide a national overview followed by workplace examples. Six developing countries are included (Brazil, Chile, India, Kenya, South Africa and Thailand) and four industrialized countries (France, Hungary, the United Kingdom and the United States). The workplace case studies provide considerable detail on why the childcare support was started, how it is funded and managed, how various partners are involved, and the limitations and benefits of the support provided. In this way, the reader can better understand why and how the childcare solution was put in place and how it is working.

By providing and analysing examples of workplace solutions for childcare, the present book aims at:

- increasing awareness of the possibilities for workplace programmes as well as their benefits and limitations;

- providing insight into the reasons why various actors, in particular employers and trade unions, have become involved; and

- offering greater understanding on how support for childcare has been organized and funded in a variety of workplaces.

1.2 What is childcare?

At any particular time, a child can be in the care of (i) a family member, (ii) someone from outside the family or (iii) no one. This simple schema is represented in figure 1.1.

Figure 1.1 Childcare schema

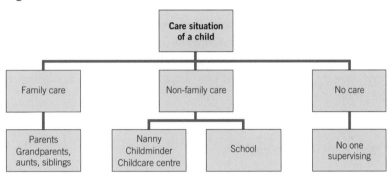

Family care

Families are the main providers of care for their children. At birth, usually the round-the-clock care needed is provided by the family and a baby is not normally left with no one responsible. Someone has to ensure their basic needs are met (fed, washed, clothed, housed and so on) as well as to provide a loving and stimulating environment that will foster their social and psychological development. Much of this is done by the parents themselves. Many countries facilitate parental care by providing paid entitlements for working parents to temporarily leave their jobs to care for young children. Most countries have legislated maternity leave for working mothers and some also provide for a short paternity leave for fathers and/or more extended parental leaves for either father or mother after maternity leave.[1]

From the end of maternity leave (the ILO norm is 14 weeks)[2] until the age at which a child can go to school, working parents need someone to look after their child during the time they are working. In virtually all countries, some working parents receive help from grandparents or other family members who may be able

---

[1] See Öun and Trujillo, 2005, for a review of national legislation.

[2] For more information on the Maternity Protection Convention, 2000 (No. 183), and Recommendation, 2000 (No. 191), see http://www.ilo.org/public/english/standards [11 June 2009].

to cover at least part of their childcare needs. This solution usually has the advantage of being without financial cost. Depending on the circumstances (such as where the grandparents reside, their health) this may or may not be a good solution. When the family member is a young child removed from school to look after a baby, this is clearly not the ideal solution from the point of view of society.

Once children attend school, working parents still have to make care arrangements for before or after school, lunch breaks and the school holidays. Family members may be able to cover at least a portion of this time. Also, as children get older, there may be less need for a care arrangement and they can be left to look after themselves with no one responsible for their care. Local contexts and norms influence perceptions of the age at which children do not need out-of-school care. However, leaving them in "no care", as "latchkey" children without supervision, may be problematic even for adolescents.

Non-family childcare

Non-family care is needed to look after children during the working hours of parents when there is no family member available. Evidence suggests that traditional family supports are weakening, particularly with the rise of nuclear and single-parent households, and with migration to cities and overseas such that many working parents in both industrialized and developing countries need non-family care for both preschool and school-age children. This non-family childcare is the focus of this book and the term "childcare" henceforth refers to non-family care.

School can be seen as a form of childcare but is usually perceived rather as "education" and so is shown separately in figure 1.1. As children get older, most societies agree that they should go out of the family to school, and in virtually all countries, attendance at primary school is obligatory as from the age of 5 or 6.

Box 1.1 describes in more detail the three main types of childcare arrangements proposed in figure 1.1: "nannies", "childminders" and childcare centres. The category "childcare centres" includes pre-primary schools (kindergartens, early childhood education) which might be categorized as schools, but since they are not part of compulsory schooling, are usually considered as part of childcare. For children of preschool age, it is difficult to make the distinction between childcare and education and, in fact, both care and education are needed and often occur simultaneously, as reflected in the use of the term "early childhood care and education" (ECCE).

For school-age children, childcare may be needed before or after school, during a lunch break or during school holidays. The types of childcare in box 1.1 also apply

---

Box 1.1 Main types of childcare

In the child's home. Someone who cares for children in their own home, in some cases living in the child's home, is variously called a "nanny", babysitter or au pair. This person is usually an employee of the parents. Care can be for children of any age.

In the home of a childminder. A childminder (day mother, family daycare) offers private care for children of all ages, usually in her own home. Childminders are normally self-employed and may have children of their own at home so that childminding provides a way for them to earn income while looking after their own child. The number of children that can be looked after by a childminder is in some countries limited by legislation.

Childcare centres. The terms used to refer to childcare centres differ considerably from country to country, as well as the age groups of the children attending. Centres that take very young children are sometimes called daycare centres, nurseries, crèches. Some centres may focus on pre-primary education for children aged 3 to 5 years and are variously called kindergarten, pre-primary school, nursery school, école maternelle or early childhood education centre. Sometimes, particularly in developing countries, childcare centres may take children from 3 months to school age.

---

to this age group, with nannies and childminders being possible providers, as well as various types of group arrangements, from summer camps to school canteens.

Childcare provision needs to balance the needs of children and the needs of working parents. At one extreme, leaving young children in non-parental care for 14 hours per day because of the work of parents is clearly not the ideal for the child or the parents. At the other extreme, providing preschool education for two hours a day may complicate considerably the lives of working parents.

1.3 Why childcare for working parents is important

In most countries, looking after children was traditionally considered to be a responsibility of families alone – mainly the women. It was not an issue of concern to trade unions or employers. As for governments, childcare was often regarded as mainly a matter of providing welfare assistance for poor families. The assumption was that most families can look after their children, which was perceived as "their responsibility anyhow".

Apart from a few welfare cases, childcare usually has to be paid for by the parents, so that it is mainly well-off parents who can find arrangements for ensuring that their children are well looked after while they work. Paying a reliable nanny or childminder or putting a toddler into quality daycare can be quite expensive and often out of the reach of low-income and even middle-income parents. So they are faced with a no-win choice. They can use parental time to fill in the childcare gap by, for example, working at different times in the case of dual-parent households or reducing their work activity (typically that of the mother) and consequently their income. Or they can leave the child with poor-quality care or no care at all. Whatever their choice, the child will probably suffer, as will the parents.

The consequences of lack of access to affordable, good-quality childcare go beyond the welfare of individual children and their families and affect the social and economic development of the whole society. For society, benefits of childcare include the following.[3]

Promoting gender equality

As women are often the parent with major responsibility for children, lack of access to affordable, reliable childcare can be a major factor in gender inequality, undermining women's ability to work and their opportunities for employment. In the European Union, childcare is recognized as a critical factor in meeting its goal of full employment and a concrete way of eliminating barriers to women's participation in the labour market. As a result, at the Barcelona summit in 2002, EU governments set childcare targets for the year 2010: 33 per cent coverage for children under 3 and 90 per cent coverage for children between 3 years and compulsory school age.

Evidence from Europe suggests that where governments support the costs of widely available childcare, these countries tend to have higher rates of women's labour force participation and fertility and lower gender inequality, as is particularly the case in Nordic countries.[4]

Childcare can help parents, particularly mothers, ensure continuity in their careers. If they are compelled to resign for lack of affordable, quality childcare and do not work at all for a long period, they tend to have difficulty re-entering work, particularly at the same level as they were when they left.

---

[3] For more details on how society benefits from childcare see http://www.ilo.org/travail.

[4] Del Boca and Locatelli, 2007; Den Dulk and Van Doorne-Huiskes, 2007.

In countries where girls continue to be removed from school to look after younger siblings, lack of childcare can be a factor in the lower educational level of girls.

While childcare is particularly useful for women, this does not mean that it is basically a women's issue: the whole family benefits if women have a fairer deal on the labour market. Men also benefit from childcare support and, as will be seen in the cases in this book, they also use and appreciate it when available.

Promoting the rights and development of children

The UN Convention on the Rights of the Child explicitly recognizes the need for parents to receive assistance in their childcare responsibilities as well as the rights of children to benefit from childcare facilities. Stories of harm coming to young children who have been left on their own while parents work have made headlines in a number of countries. In the Republic of Korea, for example, the grassroots movement for childcare was reinforced by an incident in 1990 when two children died in a fire, locked in the house while their parents worked.[5]

Improving the access of vulnerable and disadvantaged groups to quality care for preschoolers can provide opportunities for these children to begin primary education on a more equal footing with more privileged children. In the United Kingdom, for example, disadvantaged children already lag behind their middle-class contemporaries in terms of cognitive development at the age of 3, so the provision of high-quality early years education is clearly one very important way to counter this.[6] In developing countries, it is likely that a similar or even greater deficit might be found for disadvantaged children.

Contributing to the national economy

Well-structured childcare support policies can pay for themselves, according to a report from the Organisation for Economic Co-operation and Development (OECD): without support, parents can face a more difficult time participating in the labour force, which can lead to "higher welfare expenditure, lost tax revenues, inhibited growth and wasted human capital".[7]

---

[5] Kim and Kim, 2004.

[6] Daycare Trust/National Centre for Social Research, 2007.

[7] Immervoll and Barber, 2005, p. 48.

Childcare not only increases women's access to employment, but also increases employment opportunities in childcare, and contributes to job creation in the service sector to replace some of the unpaid household work such as cleaning and food preparation. One estimate of the job creation effects of women's employment is that ten jobs are created for every hundred additional women in work.[8] Indeed, in most industrialized countries, there has been an increase in employment in childcare. In the Netherlands, for example, the childcare sector has evolved since 1990 from a small sector with 8,000 employees into a mature sector employing over 60,000 employees in 2003.[9] Similarly in France, the number of childminders (*assistantes maternelles*) more than tripled during the 1990s: the number approved and directly employed by parents increased from about 70,000 in 1990 to 232,000 in 2000, reaching 264,000 in 2005.[10]

Helping to break the vicious circle of inter-generational poverty

For disadvantaged families, access to childcare can help prevent the perpetuation of social disadvantage by:

- increasing the family income, often through women's labour force participation; and

- fostering the physical, social and cognitive development of children, and improving their life chances.

Often as a result of research and political pressure from civil society, governments are increasingly realizing that many families are having difficulties ensuring that their children are well looked after while the parents work, and that lack of childcare is leading to the inefficient functioning of labour markets, under-utilization of public investments in human resources and insufficient care of the next generation. Thus it is increasingly accepted that it is in the public interest for governments to support and facilitate access to childcare. As will be seen in Chapter 2, the actual extent of government support for childcare varies considerably from country to country, as do government policies concerning workplace solutions.

---

[8] Esping-Andersen, quoted in Party of European Socialists, 2006.
[9] Statistics Netherlands, 2001, 2005, quoted in Platinga, 2006.
[10] Blanpain and Momic, 2007.

1.4 International guidance:
Conventions and labour standards

A number of international conventions recognize the fact that working parents need outside support in coping with childcare and call for the provision of childcare facilities.

The Convention on the Elimination of All Forms of Discrimination against Women (CEDAW), adopted in 1979 by the UN General Assembly, sets out an agenda for national action to end discrimination against women. Among the measures foreseen to prevent discrimination and ensure women's effective right to work is Article 11 2(c):

> States Parties shall take appropriate measures to encourage the provision of the necessary supporting social services to enable parents to combine family obligations with work responsibilities and participation in public life, *in particular through promoting the establishment and development of a network of child-care facilities.* (authors' italics)

Similarly, with a view to creating effective equality of opportunity and treatment for men and women workers, the ILO Convention on Workers with Family Responsibilities, 1981 (No. 156),[11] also calls for childcare measures:

> All measures compatible with national conditions and possibilities shall further be taken to develop or promote community services, public or private, such as childcare and family services and facilities. (Article 5(b))

Both these Conventions indicate that the public authorities should "promote" childcare facilities, but there is no compulsion for the government itself to provide. The ILO Convention No. 156 specifically mentions the possibility of public or private provision. Nevertheless both conventions recognize the key role of government in promoting and encouraging the development of family or social services and specifically mention the need for childcare for working parents.

It is important to note that both these instruments call for childcare for working *parents* and not just working *mothers*, implicitly recognizing the family responsibilities of men as well as women.

---

[11] For the text and ratifications of ILO Convention No. 156 and the text of Recommendation No. 165, see http://www.ilo.org/public/english/standards [11 June 2009].

As discussed above, the issue of childcare concerns not only the well-being of working parents but also of their children and how they are cared for. The UN Convention on the Rights of the Child (CRC), which has been ratified by 191 countries, specifies:

> 2. For the purpose of guaranteeing and promoting the rights set forth in the present Convention, States Parties shall render appropriate assistance to parents and legal guardians in the performance of their child-rearing responsibilities and shall *ensure the development of institutions, facilities and services for the care of children.*
>
> 3. States Parties shall take all appropriate measures to ensure that children of working parents have the right to benefit from child-care services and facilities for which they are eligible. (Article 18) (authors' italics)

The CRC thus also recognizes the need for parents to receive assistance in their childcare responsibilities and specifically asserts the rights of the children of working parents to benefit from childcare facilities. The responsibility lies with "States Parties" to ensure the development of services; however, this does not mean they necessarily provide these services themselves.

1.5 What are "workplace solutions"?

The present book focuses on childcare supports that working parents can access through their employment. Workplace solutions may be contrasted with the more common source of childcare support – community services – which have no link to any particular workplace. Municipalities may run childcare centres or have a service providing information on existing private and public centres and approved childminders in the locality. Religious organizations may run after-school clubs. Private daycare centres and childminders who look after children in their homes exist in many communities. In these cases, the access to childcare support is provided, irrespective of where the parent works, or indeed, in some cases, irrespective of whether one or both parents work for income at all. These existing community programmes (unrelated to the workplace) and their availability are not the focus of this book. However, they are covered indirectly, mainly as an important part of the context for "workplace solutions".

The workplaces covered in this book are those where there is an employer. The many workers who do not work in formal workplaces, particularly in developing countries, where the majority are often found in informal employment (self-employment and employment in small informal businesses), are thus not covered. The childcare problems of workers in informal settings, who are usually among the poorest, are even more acute and the childcare solutions found in these types of workplaces have been examined elsewhere.[12] It is nevertheless interesting to note that some of the childcare programmes initiated in formal workplaces which are documented in this book are open to other workers from the informal economy (see the case studies of Medley, Brazil, and the Phra Pradaeng Industrial Zone and Network of Nawanakhon Labour Unions in Thailand).

Types of measures

At the level of the workplace, there are basically two types of measures which can help employed parents cope with their childcare responsibilities:[13]

● measures which concern the working conditions of parents so that they can themselves look after their children when they need attention; and

● measures which help parents access care by others.

Box 1.2 presents some of the main measures of the first type which can help working parents themselves to care for their children. Working time and leave measures are not covered in this book but are often part of "family-friendly" policies and can be an important complement to childcare assistance as they help working parents to find time to be with their children.[14]

The second category – measures that help workers access non-family childcare – is the focus of this book. These measures can be very diverse and innovative, ranging from an on-site crèche for babies to financial subsidies to discounts negotiated with holiday camps for the schoolchildren of workers. In some cases, a relatively cheap solution can make an enormous difference to working parents, for example providing a room where schoolchildren can do their homework while waiting for their parent to finish work.

---

[12] See, for example, Cassirer and Addati, 2007.

[13] These same types of measures can help workers to cope with care of elderly dependants. In some workplaces, measures that help with childcare are also available for those with responsibility for elderly dependants. For more information on elderly care see Hein, 2005.

[14] More information can be found on working time measures in Hein, 2005, and at http://www.ilo.org/public/english/protection/condtrav [11 June 2009].

Box 1.2 Measures facilitating parental care

Measures related to working conditions that can help working parents have time to look after their children include:

- maternity leave, paternity leave, parental leave (often included in labour legislation but the employer can go beyond statutory provisions);
- emergency leave or sick leave which can be used to care for sick children (or other relative);
- reduction of long working hours and overtime for all workers;
- flexitime options which give some choice on arrival and departure times;
- the possibility of temporary switch to part-time or reduced hours;
- compressed working week;
- the possibility of shift switching; and
- teleworking.

See http://www.ilo.org/travail for fact sheets on leave policies and family-friendly working time arrangements.

Childcare needs and types of solutions

The care services needed by workers depend on the ages of their children and also on the ages covered by the school system as well as school hours and holidays in the country or region concerned. The childcare needs of parents also depend on their working conditions. For parents who work nights, on shifts or at unusual times, the difficulties in finding childcare can be even greater. Parents who work long hours and have little vacation have more time away from the family that needs to be covered by childcare.

Three main types of childcare needs are identified in figure 1.2. The first is care for young children until the start of formal schooling, which is probably the most obvious need. Workplace assistance for this age group is the most common. Nevertheless, the second need – out-of-school care for children of school age – can be a major problem for parents, and some workplaces provide help for this age group.

The need for emergency, back-up care can occur for children of all ages, as even the best arrangements can go wrong when a carer doesn't show up, a grandmother is sick or there is a special school holiday. Help at the workplace so parents can access emergency "back-up" care is becoming increasingly common.

Various types of arrangements can help workers find affordable childcare at the times they need and of the quality they want. As shown in figure 1.2, workplace solutions may be categorized into four main types:

- a childcare centre of the company (companies) or on-site;

- a facility in the community which is linked to the workplace (through arrangements such as negotiated discounts, reserved places, subsidized places);

- some form of financial support (childcare vouchers, funds or subsidies); and

- advice and referral services.

Each type of solution can, in principle, be used for any of the three basic childcare needs, namely care for preschool children, out-of-school care for schoolchildren and back-up care. Advice and referral services, for example, can help parents to find care for babies, for children after school or for a child whose usual carer is sick. Similarly, workplace arrangements with community facilities can help workers access daycare for babies, holiday camps for schoolchildren or babysitters for back-up care. In some workplaces, these solutions are also available to help workers access care for elderly dependants, particularly advice and referral and some financial support.

The four types of solutions in figure 1.2 are not mutually exclusive: for example, an on-site facility often involves some financial subsidy from the employer. Advice and referral services to help find a childcare provider may also be accompanied by some form of financial help to pay the provider.

Figure 1.2 Childcare needs of workers and types of workplace assistance

Workers' childcare needs
- Care for young children until the start of formal schooling
- Out-of-school care for children of school age (before and after school, lunch breaks, holidays)
- Back-up care for emergencies (child of any age)

Types of solutions found through workplace
- Company or on-site childcare centre
- Facility in the community which is linked to the workplace
- Some form of financial support (childcare vouchers, funds or subsidies)
- Advice and referral services

The role of partnerships

The fact that this book deals with formal workplaces does not mean that employers alone are providing or completely funding childcare solutions. On the contrary, workplace solutions typically involve innovative partnerships, often, but not always, including employers.

In most situations, ways are being found to share the costs and responsibilities among various partners such as workers' organizations, employers' organizations, local and national governments, organizations specializing in providing

15

childcare, religious organizations and other NGOs as well as, of course, the parents themselves. Parents are typically major partners since they often pay a high proportion of the costs, in some cases receiving some financial help from governments and their employers. Diverse systems for sharing the costs, including, in some cases, government grants or tax exemptions, mean that the actual costs of childcare to parents and employers are highly variable.

Partnership is a key theme of this book since it is mainly through combining resources and capabilities that effective programmes for childcare support have emerged in workplace settings. In order to obtain details on how partnerships for childcare have developed and worked in different workplaces and countries, the case studies have been designed to collect information on the partnerships involved: who provides what resources and who is responsible for organizing or operating the different programmes.

1.6 Case studies and examples

As already indicated in section 1.1 above, Part II of this book presents country reviews and workplace case studies from ten different countries. In each country chapter, there is first a review of government policies and the national situation concerning childcare, followed by the case studies, so that workplace solutions are situated within their national context.

Countries selected for the case studies

In the few industrialized countries where there is extensive public provision of childcare for children of all ages, there is little need for workplace involvement and indeed it is practically non-existent in countries like Sweden or Denmark.[15] Such countries were not considered for inclusion in the current study.

Countries were chosen in an effort to show a variety of public approaches to childcare and to the role of the workplace in childcare. They were also chosen to ensure some representation from the major regions.

The industrialized countries chosen are France, Hungary, the United Kingdom and the United States. Each of these countries has very different histories and approaches to childcare. Two countries, France and Hungary, have

---

[15] Plantenga and Remery, 2005, p. 72.

relatively long histories of public concern with childcare provision, although for different reasons and with different types of measures. The United Kingdom is interesting since the Government's efforts to improve access to childcare are relatively recent – starting in 1999 and including a role for the workplace. The case of the United States, where a low level of government involvement has left childcare to a large extent to the private sector, provides examples of the active roles played by trade unions, employers' groups, individual companies, academics, research organizations, childcare NGOs and the childcare business.

The developing countries selected tend to be larger countries with a relatively high proportion of their populations in urban areas and a significant number of workers in formal employment – Brazil and Chile from Latin America, India and Thailand from Asia and Kenya and South Africa from Africa. Urbanization is important, since for workplace programmes to exist, there must be some sort of workplace with a certain concentration of workers, which is most likely in urban areas – although plantations are a major exception in rural areas. For most of these countries, preliminary investigations suggested that interesting innovations were taking place at some workplaces which could provide ideas for others in similar circumstances.

Selection of examples within the case study countries

In the countries selected, there were many examples of childcare programmes. For the purposes of this book, only workplace examples were selected: that is, the childcare assistance had to be available to parents by virtue of where they worked. The many instances where childcare services are used by working parents, but had no link to their workplace, were excluded.

The examples tend to be successful programmes as these are easier to find than those which collapsed. Nevertheless, the case studies do try to bring out problems and practical lessons learned from the experience and are not necessarily examples of "best practice".

In order to find the examples in each country, trade unions and employer organizations were contacted for their suggestions and any information they could provide on the national situation.

In selecting the workplace examples to be documented for the book, the classification system presented in figure 1.2 was used to try to ensure that all the childcare needs of workers were represented and that different types of solutions for helping with each need were included. It was not always easy to find a variety of examples, particularly in developing countries, where those that were best known were typically nurseries for preschoolers in large corporations such as banks and telecommunication and IT companies.

Examples of programmes for school-age children or for back-up care in developing countries were harder to find – perhaps because there aren't very many. Similarly, it was more difficult to find solutions other than setting up an on-site facility. The table in the Annex lists the cases presented in the book, indicating the types of childcare support they are providing.

A special effort has also been made to identify programmes which help more vulnerable, lower-income workers who do not have the same capacity to pay for childcare as highly skilled, highly paid workers working for large corporations. Workplace programmes may tend to favour these fortunate few. Understanding why and how workplace programmes have been set up for lower-wage workers, who are the ones most in need of help, may be useful for encouraging others to initiate programmes for such workers.

1.7 Organization of the book

Part I provides a broad overview of workplace solutions for childcare, drawing on the relevant literature and providing numerous examples available from secondary sources as well as from the country case studies in Part II. It has four chapters, dealing with the following:

- national childcare issues and government approaches (Chapter 2);
- the perspectives and motivations of various partners that have been involved in workplace programmes (Chapter 3);
- the diverse types of solutions that have been found at workplaces to help parents to meet their different childcare needs, including their advantages and disadvantages (Chapter 4); and
- some conclusions and lessons learned regarding workplace initiatives for childcare from the point of view of policy-makers, of enterprises and sectoral and enterprise trade unions, and of regional and national-level workers' and employers' organizations (Chapter 5).

Part II presents the detailed case studies of existing workplace programmes by country (Chapters 6 to 15). In each country chapter, there is first a review of government policies and the national situation concerning childcare, followed by the case studies of specific workplaces in the country.

National contexts of workplace solutions

2

Workplace programmes for childcare are situated in and adapted to the national and local contexts in which they are located. In an ideal world, there would be free public childcare of quality for all children needing it and so little need for workplace programmes. However, this ideal is far from reality in many countries. To some extent, workplace programmes for childcare are helping to fill in the gaps not covered by public programmes.

As a background to understanding how and why workplace programmes have developed, this chapter begins by reviewing the concerns which arise with respect to care for children at different ages and the childcare needs of working parents. It goes on to consider childcare options in various countries and the different approaches of governments to childcare provision and their strategies for funding and organizing childcare. Challenges in funding childcare are nearly universal and the final section addresses the tensions that arise between minimizing costs and ensuring the quality of childcare, including ensuring decent working conditions for childcare workers, who are at the centre of the struggle between affordability and quality.

2.1 Ages of children and issues

The needs of children at different ages are to some extent similar in all countries, but perceptions of childcare needs are affected by local norms and conditions. Children's needs are very different from one age to another and raise different concerns about the types of care that are most appropriate.

Children under 3: What is best for the child?

The need for care facilities for children under age 3 depends to some extent on the duration of maternity leave and other parental leaves (particularly those which are paid). In the European countries, paid maternity leave is much longer (in France 16 weeks for first child and 26 for others, in Hungary 24 weeks and in the United Kingdom 26 weeks) compared to many developing countries or the United States (12 weeks, unpaid). Where maternity and parental leaves are more generous, the need for non-parental care during the baby's first year or two would be less frequent.

In some European countries, policy has been to facilitate parental (mainly maternal) care through long parental leaves after maternity leave. In Hungary, for example, concerns about low fertility coupled with traditional views regarding women's roles as mothers[1] have led to leaves which can last until the child is 3 years old, while the childcare services of the socialist era for children under age 3 have rapidly diminished. Similarly in Austria and Germany, the ideal of mother-care for young children has also resulted in policies for lengthy leaves and little development of childcare services for young children.[2] Such policies have been criticized as a trap for women, whose workforce participation is disrupted and who find re-entry after leave very difficult.[3]

In some countries, there has been considerable debate about whether very young children are best cared for by their mothers and whether putting children in childcare at an early age is harmful. For children age 2 or more, most evidence suggests that good-quality childcare can contribute to child development.[4] However, for very young children, the effects of non-parental care are less clear and depend on many intervening factors related to the cultural context, the quality of the substitute care, the duration of the care, the nature of the mother's work and her control over the use of the income earned. There is some evidence from industrialized countries that maternal *full-time* employment during the *first year* after birth is harmful to children's health, thus pointing to the need for more flexible schedules and longer maternity leaves.[5]

As concerns physical growth and nutrition, studies in developing countries have tended to find that, for children over 2 years, those with working mothers

---

[1] See Chapter 9 and Open Society Institute, 2002, pp. 284–285.
[2] Morgan and Zippel, 2003, p. 49.
[3] See Morgan and Zippel, 2003, and Chapter 9 on Hungary.
[4] Adema, 2007, p. 118.
[5] Immervoll and Barber, 2005, p. 10.

have a better nutritional status than similar children whose mothers do not work. But for children under one year, their nutritional status may be less good. The negative effect of mothers' work on the growth of children under 1 year may be related to the challenges that many women, in developing and developed countries, face in continuing to breastfeed after returning to work in view of a lack of support and facilities. In contrast, for children aged 2 to 5 years, purchased foods (and parental income to buy them) would be relatively more important to nutritional status.[6]

Much also depends on the quality of the substitute care. Evidence from developing countries consistently shows, for example, that when children are used as substitute caregivers, the association of maternal work and child nutrition is either negative or less favourable than when the care is provided by another adult.[7] A study in the United States which followed children over a long period found that children who received higher-quality childcare before kindergarten scored better on vocabulary tests in the fifth grade than children who received poor-quality care.[8]

The results of the same US study underlined the importance of the quality of parenting, which was found to be a much more important predictor of child development than was the type, quantity or quality, of childcare. So the results on the effects of non-parental care of young children are complex, but the key issue is the quality of the care, whether it be by parents or by someone else.

Given the importance of the quality of the care, there is also some concern that childcare for under-3s may be seen mainly as a service for looking after children while parents work, and thus the overriding priority is to keep them safe and clean, while the needs of the child for stimulation and affection may be overlooked. The OECD notes, "Services for children under 3 have often been seen as an adjunct to labour market policies, with infants and toddlers assigned to services with weak developmental agendas."[9] Ensuring that children have the necessary interaction and stimulation needed for their development is an important aspect of these services which depends greatly on the availability of trained and motivated staff.

There is some consensus among those who have studied the effects of care arrangements on very young children that, for the period immediately following birth, the most effective policies are those that provide flexibility and choice

---

[6] Glick, 2002, p. 10.
[7] Glick, 2002, p. 11.
[8] United States Department of Health and Human Services, 2007.
[9] OECD, 2006b, p. 207.

offering a combination of maternity/paternity leaves and part-time jobs/flexible work arrangements and childcare facilities for the following years. Such a combination is actually provided in Denmark, France, Norway and Sweden.[10] However, most countries would be unable or unwilling to finance such extensive provisions.

Age 3 to school age: The role of pre-primary education

For children from age 3 years until the start of compulsory primary schooling (usually at age 5/6 years), both parents and governments are increasingly aware of the benefits of preschool education. Early childhood is well known to be a critical period for physical, cognitive and socio-emotional development. Numerous studies have assessed the effects of early childhood education (ECE) interventions from about age 3 years on the development and future outcomes of children. Results show that such interventions have positive results on school readiness, retention and success in primary school. Effective programmes enhance children's physical well-being, cognitive and language skills, and social and emotional development.[11] Even parents who do not need childcare often put their children into pre-primary education, given the benefits for the child.

For children from disadvantaged backgrounds, attending preschool education is particularly significant. Early education programmes are important for providing young children, especially those from low-income and second-language groups, with a strong foundation for their growth and development.[12]

The evidence of the significant benefits to children of early childhood education, as well as pressures from citizens, have led many governments to expand access to pre-primary education (for details concerning the countries in this book see section 2.5 below). The World Bank and UNICEF both have extensive programmes to support this process in a number of developing countries.

For working parents with children of this age group, the situation can be rather complicated, as in many countries the opening hours of public pre-primary schools are limited, such as half a day in the United States or 12.5 hours per week in the United Kingdom. UNESCO notes that, in many countries, preschool programmes run for even less than 10 hours per week.[13] When public programmes cover very few hours, working parents must find additional ways of caring for

---

[10] Chapter 8 and Da Roit and Sabatinelli, 2007.
[11] UNESCO, 2006.
[12] OECD, 2006b, p. 12.
[13] UNESCO, 2006, p. 131.

children in order to cover their working hours, or may alter their working arrangements, working part time or in flexible or informal economy jobs.[14] For poorer workers, taking advantage of public preschool programmes which run for few hours may be difficult (even though they are free or relatively low cost), given the logistical problems of dropping off and picking up children and arranging additional care to cover their working hours.

School-age children

Public concern about childcare tends to focus on preschool children, often overlooking the major problems which working parents may have in finding care for school-age children before and after school, during lunch breaks and during school holidays. Normal school hours can be more-or-less problematic for working parents. For example, in France, there is no school on Wednesdays. In Brazil, primary school operates on half-day shifts.

In the EU, childcare policy was initially developed for children of preschool age. However, over the past decade, Member States have been addressing the need for childcare for school-age children through the development of a range of strategies and programmes. Nevertheless, a report in 2006 notes that only a few Member States are addressing the need for childcare services for school-age children.[15]

In developing countries, out-of-school care for children seems rarely to be perceived as a public concern. In those countries covered in this book, public programmes to look after children after school or during school holidays are virtually non-existent. And parents do not seem to expect governments to provide any help in coping with out-of-school care for children.

Government initiatives for out-of-school programmes are often driven by concerns about children in disadvantaged areas who are more likely to be left to their own devices than those of better-off families. The long hours of unsupervised time for children between the end of school hours and the time parents get home from work has been linked to anti-social youth behaviour,[16] and out-of-school programmes can be effective ways of addressing the needs of working parents, the needs of youths and public safety concerns.

---

[14] See, for example, Cassirer and Addati, 2007.

[15] Reid and White, 2007, p. 13.

[16] For example, see WHO, 2002, p. 44.

The age at which children can be left on their own after school or during summer holidays is highly debatable and parents are often worried even about adolescent children who are left on their own. Recognizing that childcare problems persist even when children are teenagers, some government supports for childcare expenses can be used for this age group. For example, in the United Kingdom, tax-free childcare vouchers can be used for children up to age 15 years. There has been a growing trend in the United Kingdom towards providing out-of-school care to older children aged 12 and above, recognizing that their needs and aspirations are different and that care needs to be provided in a different format (and with a different name).[17]

In theory, the cost of providing out-of-school care is much lower for older children than for younger children as child-to-staff ratios for this older age group are relatively high and no new capital investment is necessary if existing school buildings can be used.

2.2 Concerns of working parents

The childcare solutions available within their locality can facilitate parents' (mainly mothers') employment or act as a barrier to employment. For parents, the critical aspects of childcare which influence whether they use it are:

- affordability in relation to their earnings;
- convenience in terms of opening hours and location; and
- the quality of care the child will receive.

Even when childcare is available in theory, its cost to parents can be a major barrier to paid work for many families, leaving little option but parental care. As one new mother working in the UK National Health Service put it: "What's the point in going back to work when you're paying out more for your childcare than what you're actually earning?"[18]

Similarly, a study in Kenya found that high costs of childcare discourage households from using formal childcare and have a negative effect on the level of mothers' participation in market work.[19] A study by the OECD suggests that

---

[17] Reid and White, 2007, p. 19.
[18] Frew, 2004.
[19] Lokshin et al., 2000.

childcare costs particularly affect the employment rates of low-skilled women or low-income families, mothers of younger children and lone parents.[20] The cost problem for parents is particularly acute in countries where most childcare is provided privately, as in the United States (see box 2.1).

Box 2.1 Cost of childcare in the United States

In the United States, childcare can be very expensive with the average annual cost of childcare for a 4-year-old child ranging from $3,016 to $9,628. In 2001, 40 per cent of poor, single working mothers who paid for childcare spent at least half of their cash income for childcare; an additional 25 per cent of these families paid 40 to 50 per cent of their cash income for childcare.

Source: Matthews, 2006.

In some countries, publicly subsidized childcare centres do exist for low-income families but the number of places is insufficient. In Rio de Janeiro, for example, long waiting lists for public daycare centres in slum areas testify to the insufficient number of places compared to the needs of parents. As a result, for-profit centres, whose quality cannot be guaranteed, have sprung up (see Chapter 6 on Brazil).

Convenience is another factor affecting whether parents use childcare. Parents need childcare which is not too far from either their work or their home and which is available to cover the hours during which they are working. In a study of 30 European countries, a problem identified by the majority of countries was the incompatibility of the childcare services on offer with the working hours of parents. Even those that provide care over the course of a day from 9 a.m. until 5 p.m. no longer fit the flexibility firms are requiring from working parents.[21] Similarly in Thailand, the Women Workers Unity Group feels that the opening hours of existing childcare centres do not cater to the needs of workers and it has been advocating for childcare centres to be set up in industrial communities (see Chapter 13). When parents need to juggle a multiplicity of care arrangements for children in order to be able to cover their working hours, this can discourage the use of childcare.

For working parents who may have unexpected meetings or need to work overtime, the flexibility of childcare arrangements is an important aspect of

---

[20] Immervoll and Barber, 2005, p. 32.
[21] Fagan and Hebson, 2006, p. 109.

convenience. The rigid hours of childcare centres can be problematic when parents' working times are variable.

Apart from cost and convenience, a major childcare concern of parents is that their child is being well cared for while they work. The poor quality of available non-parental care is often cited as a major reason why women with young children who would like to work are not able to do so. For example, a report by the European Commission found that parents will be less likely to use childcare if they feel that there are problems with its quality – as is the case with childcare in the United Kingdom, where staff recruitment and retention are issues.[22] In Thailand, a report suggests that the low quality of a number of daycare centres and newspaper reports of accidents or mistreatment of children discourage the use of daycare by parents.[23]

There is an inherent conflict between the affordability and quality of childcare. Parents are looking for affordable childcare of quality, but quality has a cost. When there is little public financial support for childcare, finding a childcare arrangement that is affordable often means sacrificing on the quality by, for example, using an overcrowded childcare centre or hiring a young, inexperienced girl as a nanny, as many workers did on the Red Lands Roses plantation in Kenya, prior to the establishment of the workplace centre.

Workplace programmes have been helping employed parents by addressing these key aspects of childcare: mitigating the costs; making it more convenient; and/or helping ensure that childcare arrangements are providing adequate care for workers' children. In some cases, particularly in rural areas where there are no childcare facilities, workplace programmes have established a much-needed service.

2.3 Childcare options

As noted in the Introduction, there are basically three main categories of childcare which parents can use: care in the child's home (a nanny); care in a childminder's home; and centre-based care. Childcare centres tend to cater for specific age groups whereas nannies and childminders can be used for children of any age. This section looks at the use of these three types of arrangements.

---

[22] European Commission, 2006b, p. 110.
[23] Kusakabe, 2006, p. 56.

Employing nannies

Employing a nanny has been a popular childcare solution in both developed and developing countries for those families that can afford the cost. The actual numbers involved are difficult to determine since nannies are usually assimilated to domestic workers whose duties may involve more or less childcare. In countries where income disparities are great and there are large pools of unemployed or under-employed women, the employment of domestic workers is frequent, as in the cases of Latin America and South Africa in box 2.2. In other countries, migrant workers have been a major source of domestic workers, as in the cases of Singapore and Spain (box 2.2).

Children of all ages can be looked after by a nanny and this solution can be advantageous when there are a number of children to be cared for. Government policies concerning nannies usually relate to their conditions of work under the labour laws that apply to them, often being classified as domestic workers. Legislation concerning child labour may also be relevant when there is a tendency to hire very young girls as nannies, as can be seen in the case examples from Kenya. Immigration policies may also affect the availability of migrant women for this kind of work.

An ILO review of legislation related to domestic workers in 60 countries found that they are often afforded lower protection than other workers and

---

Box 2.2 Employment of domestic workers

Latin America. 13.5 per cent of employed women in urban areas and 10.7 per cent in rural areas work as domestic workers.

Singapore. Approximately 170,000 migrant women are currently employed in Singapore as domestic workers and one in six Singapore families currently hire one.

South Africa. 16 per cent of working women are employed in households as domestic workers, many of whom provide childcare among other services.

Spain. The 2005 Survey of the Active Population shows that more than half of the women who work in domestic services are non-Spanish citizens, mainly from South America. The greater demand for domestic services, along with the legalization of immigrants in domestic services, explain the increase in the number of non-national domestic workers.

Sources: For Latin America, Comisión Económica para América Latina y el Caribe, 2007. For Singapore, "UNIFEM Singapore, HOME and TWC2 launch national campaign 'day off'", Press Release April 2008, available at http://www.unifem.org.sg [17 June 2009]. For South Africa, Statistics South Africa, *Labour Force Survey September 2007*, table 3.4.1, at http://www.statssa.gov.za/PublicationsHTML/P0210September2007/html/P0210September2007_7.html [17 June 2009]. For Spain, Artiles, 2006.

tend by law to have longer hours and sometimes fewer holidays.[24] A major issue is the registration of domestic workers so they can benefit from social security. In some developing countries, legislative efforts have been made to improve the legal rights of domestic workers. In South Africa, for example, since 2002, domestic workers have had the right to minimum wages, paid leave, overtime payments and severance pay and employers are required to register them with the Unemployment Insurance Fund and pay contributions, thus making them eligible for unemployment and maternity benefits.[25]

While in some countries salaries of domestic workers are subject to minimum wages, the isolation of domestic workers in households makes it difficult to ensure that legislation related to wages and also working hours is respected. Wages depend basically on supply and demand and what the worker can negotiate with the employing household.

Using a childminder

Paying a person, almost always a woman (variously called childminder, family daycare, day mother), to look after a child in her home is often an informal arrangement that parents make with neighbours, in which case it is impossible to know the numbers involved. In the United States, where there is more specific information on childcare workers, the total number of jobs was estimated at about 1.4 million in 2006, of which about 35 per cent were self-employed; mostly as family childcare providers.[26]

Increasingly governments are seeking to formalize this type of care by registering childminders and setting standards. In a number of countries (such as France, Singapore and the United Kingdom), there is a system for their registration and some minimum of training required, as well as local (often municipal) information services which can help parents to find local childminders. In Hungary, there is now the possibility for licensed family daycare services but they have been slow to develop, perhaps because they are less subsidized than nurseries and thus much more expensive for parents.

For children under the age of 3 who require childcare, there seems to be a preference in some countries for care that is in homes rather than centres. In France, for example, 18 per cent of this age group were cared for by childminders

---

[24] See Ramirez-Machado, 2003, for details.

[25] Hertz, 2004.

[26] United States Bureau of Labor Statistics, 2008a.

("assistantes maternelles") while 8 per cent attended crèches (see table 2.1). Research results suggest that working parents appreciate the convenience of a childminder whose hours are often more flexible than those of a centre.[27]

In Singapore, family daycare has been promoted by government as being particularly suitable for children from 2 to 18 months since they need more individual care and there is felt to be less risk of catching infectious diseases than in a centre with many children.[28]

For parents with atypical working schedules who need childcare when centres are closed, some form of home-based care may be the only solution (although finding childminders willing to work evenings or weekends may not always be easy; see Chapter 14 on the United Kingdom for an example).

In some countries of Latin America, government programmes for the care of poor children have also used an approach which is home based. In Colombia, the Government set up the *Hogares Comunitarios* programme in the mid-1980s for poor children from birth to age 6 years. The programme now serves more than one million children. Households eligible for the programme form parent associations that elect a "community mother", who must meet minimal requirements set by the authorities. The community mother opens her home (*hogar*) to as many as 15 children. She gives them three meals a day.[29] (See also the Bolivian case in box 2.6.)

A major disadvantage of using childminders is that they often have little training and may not provide the stimulation and educational opportunities that children are more likely to receive in centre-based care.

The earnings of childminders depend on the number of children in their care and the hours worked. In France, for example, a collective agreement fixes the minimum hourly salary to be paid by parents. In 2005, it was estimated that a full-time childminder earned 815 euro per month, which amounts to only 56 per cent of the average salary of full-time women workers in the private sector.[30] The OECD estimates that unless family day carers operate in a market with weak supply and high demand, compensation in this field is considerably less than an average family wage and tends to be considered by the woman as a supplement to the main salary earned by a working spouse.[31]

---

[27] Leprince, 2003.
[28] Singapore, Ministry of Community Development and Sports, 2004.
[29] Attanasio and Vera-Hernandez, 2004, quoted in UNESCO, 2006, p. 157.
[30] Blanpain and Momic, 2007.
[31] OECD, 2006b, p. 169.

Using a childcare centre

This section considers available national information on childcare centres for children of different age groups. Table 2.1 summarizes available information on the ten countries in Part II relating to the care of preschool children, including the coverage and opening hours of existing facilities, who provides them and how they are paid for. Given the different methods of collection, the figures cannot be compared across countries.

Children under age 3

UNESCO estimates suggest that government programmes for the care of babies and toddlers are not available in many countries; just 53 per cent of countries have at least one formal early childhood programme before pre-primary education, accepting very young children (from birth or age 1). These programmes typically provide organized custodial care and, in some cases, health services and educational activities.[32] They often have limited coverage, targeting a small proportion of very poor families, with most families left to pay for whatever private facilities they can find and afford. In countries with no government programmes, any available services would be private.

As can be seen in table 2.1, figures on the proportion of children under age 3 that use a childcare facility do not seem to be available for a number of the developing countries, the exceptions being Brazil (15.5 per cent) and Chile (4 per cent). In Chile, about two-thirds of the children attending centres are in free public centres. The Chilean Government is currently working aggressively to expand the number of childcare places for children under 3 (see Chapter 7).

Among the industrialized countries, the proportion is particularly low (7 per cent) in Hungary where maternity leave combined with parental leave can last until the child turns 3 (see Chapter 9). Estimates for France, the United Kingdom and the United States are much higher (27 per cent, 26 per cent and 30 per cent respectively), although it should be noted that these figures include childminders as well as childcare centres.[33]

A review of childcare provision in 30 countries of Europe notes the poor level of provision for under-3s and the insufficient availability in all countries.[34]

---

[32] UNESCO, 2006, p. 126.

[33] The total number of children involved is difficult to estimate and estimates are not necessarily comparable among countries. In France, for example, one young child may go to the crèche but also spend regular time with a childminder so it is difficult to know the percentage using some kind of care.

[34] Fagan and Hebson, 2006.

In Hungary, the case studies in this volume reflect the pressure on childcare centres to accept children under age 3, given the lack of facilities officially accepting younger children. In France, about one-third of 2-year-olds are already enrolled in the free "maternelle" schools, which officially start at age 3.

Table 2.1 also provides some information on who is providing the childcare and how it is being financed. In France and Hungary, there is greater public subsidization of childcare for under-3s compared to the United Kingdom and the United States, where most facilities are private, with parents, except for some poor parents, paying the full cost, although they may be able to claim some tax exemptions.

Childcare centres for children under age 3 are expensive to provide since this age group needs much more attention and each carer can look after fewer children at a time than is the case with older children. Fees often reflect the higher cost for younger children as seen in the workplace case studies. In countries where there is little government support for daycare centres, the costs for working parents can be particularly high between the end of maternity leave and the start of pre-primary school. In the United Kingdom, for example, a full-time private nursery school costs over £8,000 a year, more than double the fees for university (see Chapter 14).

Staff in childcare centres tend to include a few professionals (often trained nurses) managing the majority of auxiliary staff who care for and interact with the children. The hiring of a high proportion of unskilled, low-paid women is common in childcare perhaps because the work is seen as being primarily a question of physical care which can be carried out by women without training.[35]

Children from age 3 to primary school

According to UNESCO, all countries have one or more programmes at pre-primary level (from age 3 to the age of primary school enrolment) to prepare children for primary school.[36] For each country covered in Part II, table 2.1 provides information on the age group targeted for pre-primary education as well as estimates of the proportion attending, how it is financed and the typical opening hours.

If one considers the coverage of 3–5-year-olds, the champion in our group of countries is France with 100 per cent of each age group. For other countries, enrolment rates in preschool increase with age, with more than 90 per cent of 5-year-

---

[35] OECD, 2006b, p. 163.
[36] UNESCO, 2006, p. 129.

old children enrolled in preschool in Chile, Hungary and the United Kingdom. In the other industrialized country, the United States, coverage is much lower: 42 per cent of 3-year-olds and 77 per cent of 5-year-olds are in preschool. In the other developing countries in table 2.1, coverage is highest in Thailand, where by age 4, 74 per cent of children are already in pre-primary school. Coverage seems to be particularly low in South Africa (21 per cent of 5-year-olds) and India (30 per cent of 3–5-year-olds), while in Brazil, more than 50 per cent of 5-year-olds are in preschool programmes.

As can be seen in the country chapters, India, Kenya, South Africa, the United Kingdom and some US states have all been extending the number of children attending pre-primary school. South Africa is aiming by 2010 to provide universal access of 6-year-olds to Grade R, which prepares children for primary school.

It is interesting to note that in countries with a higher government commitment to childcare (such as France, Hungary and Thailand), pre-primary schooling tends to have longer hours covering the full day, and thus is more useful to working parents. In Kenya, programmes run a full nine hours a day, although they are closed for three months of the year, posing problems for working parents in arranging care during the break (see Chapter 11).

Pre-primary education is much more likely to receive some public support than care for younger children. In France, Hungary and the United Kingdom, more than 90 per cent of all funding comes from public sources. In Brazil, 71.5 per cent of children in pre-primary are in free public schools. In Chile, private sources account for one-third of expenditures on pre-primary education, almost all of which comes from households.[37] Reliance on private funds is much greater in the United States, where two-thirds of expenditure on pre-primary school for children aged 3 to 6 comes from private sources, half of which comes from households.[38] When considering childcare (rather than early childhood education), public expenditure tends to be much lower, with parents assuming a much greater share of the costs.[39]

Governments may provide classes directly through the Ministry of Education or through local authorities or by voluntary or private organizations that receive some funding from government and have agreed to run services according to government regulations or specific contractual obligations.[40] In most countries, some

---

[37] OECD, 2006a, p. 219, table B3.2.
[38] OECD, 2006b, p. 431, Annex E.
[39] OECD, 2006b, p. 110.
[40] OECD, 2006b.

government provision exists alongside private pre-primary schools, which may have the advantage of longer opening hours.

In countries such as the United States and India, public provision of pre-primary education is not general but rather targeted at disadvantaged groups, in the States through the Head Start programme (although there is free pre-kindergarten for 4-year-olds in some localities) and, in India, through the Integrated Child Development Services (ICDS) programme, which targets children in rural and tribal areas and urban slums.

Staff in pre-primary schools, particularly when they are government employees, are more likely to be qualified as teachers and earning higher salaries than those in childcare for younger children. Earnings for teachers in pre-primary and primary education are usually not high but are more than those of childcare workers, who are often near minimum wages. In the United Kingdom, for example, the full-time weekly income of workers in childcare services and nurseries in 2004 was about 378 euro, less than half of the 842 euro of professionals working in primary and nursery education.[41] In Kenya, although the ECD centres are public, many teachers are actually employed by the Parent–Teacher Association using funds from parental fees, which results in low and sometimes irregular pay (see Chapter 11).

Out-of-school care for schoolchildren

Out-of-school care or supervision can be needed for school-age children before and after school, during the holidays and during lunch breaks. Out-of-school programmes can take a variety of forms and involve various types of activities including education, play, sports or physical supervision.

After-school care is a traditional public service in both France and Hungary, usually provided at the same school that the child attends. In Hungary, the after-school daycare service is open from the end of the teaching hours to 5.30 p.m. with no charge except for snacks. About 42 per cent of the primary school population attends after-school care. In Portugal, there has been a dramatic increase in after-school care due to new legislation passed in 2006, making it compulsory for all primary schools to deliver after-school activities between the hours of 3.00 p.m. and 5.30 p.m.[42]

---

[41] European Foundation, 2006, table 2.
[42] Reid and White, 2007, p. 19.

Table 2.1 Care provision, coverage, hours and financing by age of children [1]

Country (Date)	Coverage by age	% in care	Types of care	Provision	Financing	Hours
Brazil (2003)	Under 3 years	15.5% (2006)	Private daycare, community-based and public daycare centres	48% of daycare centres private and 52% public (municipal)	N/A	N/A
	4 years	26%	Pre-primary schooling	71.5% of enrolled children in public schools and 28.5% in private schools	Free for public institutions	3 hr/day
	5 years	54%				
Chile (2003)	Under 3 years	4%	Day nurseries	69% Public	Free for public nurseries	N/A
			Workplace crèches	31% Private		
	3 years	25.9%	Kindergartens	Mixed: • State funded • Public/private community centres • Private subsidized Municipalities administer public centres and subsidies to private centres	Free public kindergartens State subsidizes private kindergartens via monthly allowance per child Tuition fees of parents represent about one-third of expenditure	N/A
	4 years	51.3%				
	5 years	92.6%				
France (2002)	Under 3 years	26%	Crèches 8% [2]	Public	Subsidized	N/A
			Early entry "maternelle" 10%	Public	Free for parents	
			Childminders 18%	Private but registered	Subsidized through social security to parents	

Country (Date)	Coverage by age	% in care	Types of care	Provision	Financing	Hours
	3–5 years	100%	Pre-primary schooling "maternelle"	Public by National Ministry of Education with municipalities providing physical infrastructure	Free except meals	8–10 hr/day, 4 days/week
Hungary (2004)	Under 3 years	7%	Nurseries	94% run by municipalities	Central and local governments cover 85–90%, parents pay for meals	N/A
	3 years	71%	Pre-primary school	88% run by municipalities	50% covered by central government subsidies, rest by municipalities, parents pay for meals	7.30–17.30, 4-week summer break
	4 years	92%				
	5 years	98%				
India (2008)	Under 3 years	N/A	Crèche and daycare	• Central government scheme mainly for below poverty line families has very low coverage • Private organizations • NGOs	Small user charge for government crèche	N/A
	3–5 years	30%	Pre-primary school, daycare	• Integrated Child Development Services (ICDS) by central government for disadvantaged areas include preschool education for 3–6-year-olds • Voluntary organizations and private sector	ICDS is financed mainly by central government – free for users	4 hr

Country (Date)	Coverage by age	% in care	Types of care	Provision	Financing	Hours
Kenya (2004)	Under 3 years	N/A	Day nurseries, home-based care centres, play groups	No public provision	NGOs, private	N/A
	3–6 years	35%	Nursery school, kindergarten, day nurseries, Madrassa religious schools	• Policy guidance and registration by Ministry of Education, Science and Technology • Primarily run by local/district councils, municipalities and Parent–Teacher Associations	• Fees paid by parents, except in the case of Madrassas which are free • Parental fees depend on locality • Donations from churches; NGOs are key source of support	8.00–17.00, nine months/year
South Africa (2000)	Under 3 years	N/A	Community-, home- and school-based early childhood development centres	Public, NGO and private	Mainly private. Some subsidies for poor areas through Department of Social Development	N/A
	3–4 years	15%	Early childhood development centres	About 50% community based. Key role of NGOs training organizations, community and faith-based organizations	Government subsidies targeted at community organizations operating facilities for poor children	12% < 5 hr/day 68% 5–10 hr/day 20% > 10 hr/day
	5 years	21%	Focus on attendance at Reception class for 1 year prior to primary school which starts at age 7			
Thailand (2005)	Under 3 years	N/A	Private daycare, public child development centres	Private, public (sub-district administration organizations)	Government funding and parents' contributions	N/A
	3 years	48%	Pre-primary school	Mostly public by Ministry of Education	Government, free of charge	7.30 (8.00) to 16.00 (16.30)
	4 years	74%				

Country (Date)	Coverage by age	% in care	Types of care	Provision	Financing	Hours
United Kingdom (2004)	Under 3 years	26%	Of 1- and 2-year-olds, 30% are in the care of private nurseries and childminders	Private and public	Parents pay fees; some government credits for low-income parents	N/A
	3 years	50%	Pre-primary school for ages 3 and 4	Local authorities and private	Free	12.5 hr/week for 38 weeks
	4 years	92%				
	5 years	98%	Primary school starts at age 5			
United States (2005)	Under 3 years	30%	Family daycare centre	90% private	Fees paid by parents (which may be partly offset by tax exemptions)	N/A
	3 years	42%	7% in Head Start 3% in state pre-kindergarten	High role of private sector Provision of pre-kindergartens by state and local governments varies greatly	Head Start (targeted at low-income families) and state pre-kindergartens are free. Other care paid for by parents	Often half-day
	4 years	64%	11% in Head Start 20% in state pre-kindergarten		About one-third expenditure on preschool (3–6 years) from public sources	
	5 years	77%	Kindergarten starts at age 5 in a number of states		Public free of charge	

Sources: See country chapters. Also for France, Hungary, the UK and the US, OECD, *Family and Education databases*, table PF11.1: Participation rates in day-care and preschool for children under 6 years, 2004. Available at http://www.oecd.org/dataoecd/46/13/37864698.pdf [15 July 2008].
Notes: 1. Information in this table is not comparable across countries. Date for country relates to coverage information. 2. Some children are in multiple types of care so total is more than 26 per cent. N/A = not available/applicable.

In the United Kingdom and the United States, the need for after-school care is well recognized but services are relatively rare and often at the cost of parents. In the United Kingdom, evidence shows that only 16 per cent of children in primary schools and 6 per cent of 12–14-year-olds use after-school clubs.[43] In the United States, a survey of parents with children of primary school age found that 13 per cent were in "self care" after school.[44] In South Africa, where primary school finishes at 2.30 p.m., there have been some recent efforts by government to extend extracurricular activities for children without adult supervision but these appear to be limited (see Chapter 12).

Canteens for children who cannot return home during lunch breaks also offer important supports for working parents. In France, care facilities and meals are provided at lunchtime for primary school students, and more than half of primary school students use this service, for which fees are means-tested. Even if the child has to bring a meal from home, a service for supervision during the lunch break can greatly help working parents.

Summer camps offering activities for children during school holidays also receive some public support in certain industrialized countries. Daily activities during school holidays are typically organized at primary schools or municipal centres. In Hungary, for example, daycare summer camps are often offered by public schools and local municipalities, at much lower rates than private camps (see Chapter 9). In the United Kingdom, "holiday clubs" are organized in sports centres, youth clubs and churches but some can be quite expensive. The cost may be reduced somewhat in countries where expenses on holiday camps can be tax exempt as in the United Kingdom and United States (see section 3.1).

In developing countries, out-of-school programmes tend to be rare and are mainly NGO activities for disadvantaged youth or private facilities unaffordable for most. Little information is available on how the vast majority of working parents are coping with the care needs of school-age children. In Thailand, Petrat suggests that, for school holidays, most children stay at home or are sent back to rural areas (see Chapter 13). One interesting type of service provider for workers is found in Brazil, where industries are legally bound to contribute 1.5 per cent of payroll to the Serviço Social da Indústria (SESI) which has a wide variety of programmes for workers, including activities for their children after school and during school holidays (see Chapter 6).

---

[43] Daycare Trust/National Centre for Social Research, 2007.
[44] Kleiner et al., 2004.

2.4 Government approaches to childcare

Government policies and involvement in childcare tend to reflect the prevailing ideologies in society about who is responsible for childcare and about the labour force participation of women. This section looks at differences in the extent to which childcare is seen as a public responsibility and at the reasons motivating government programmes for childcare.

Perceptions of government responsibility

There are big differences among countries in how much governments and their citizens consider that supporting childcare for working parents is a public responsibility. At one extreme, childcare may be considered to be the responsibility of families, in which case government involvement should be minimal and laissez-faire, leaving it to parents to pay for non-family care bought on the market from a private provider if they need it.

At the other extreme are countries that view childcare as a public entitlement and a responsibility of government. Most countries are in between, with very different approaches to the questions of whether and how to finance childcare and how to provide it. National policies can, of course, change depending on the political party which is in power, as witnessed by the cases of Chile and the United Kingdom, where childcare has recently moved up the political agenda. Childcare and other work–family policies have moved higher on the policy agendas of many countries in response to major social changes, such as the increasing entry of women into the labour force and changes in family structure, resulting in a lack of family support for childcare. Economic concerns to increase the labour force participation of women are also driving governments to improve access to childcare, as in the EU (see section 1.3).

Among the countries in the current study, France and Hungary are the closest to considering childcare as a public entitlement and both provide considerable public services, as seen in the previous section. In such countries, the childcare "gaps" left by public services and the resulting problems for working parents and their employers tend to be less than in countries where there is less government intervention. In France and Hungary, estimated public expenditure on early childhood care and education constitutes a much larger proportion of GDP (1.0 per cent and 0.8 per cent respectively) than in the United Kingdom and the United States (0.5 and 0.48 per cent).[45]

---

[45] OECD, 2006b, p. 246.

In some of the developing countries in this study, there is also a declared government commitment to universal childcare provision for children before they start school. India and Thailand have declared a strong government role in childcare along the lines of children's rights and children's development (see box 2.3). Chile and Thailand have made considerable progress in extending the number of public preschool facilities. In India, criticisms have been levelled at the Government for failing to move beyond the rhetoric;[46] however, there has been considerable expansion of public programmes for early childhood education for the disadvantaged in recent years (see Chapter 10).

Box 2.3 Government commitments to childcare

India. The Constitution states that the "State shall endeavour to provide early childhood care and education to all children until they complete the age of six years" (Article 45 under the Directive Principles of State Policies).

Thailand. The 1997 Constitution states that government must provide basic services, including care and development for young children and families.

Sources: For India, see Chapter 10. For Thailand, see UNESCO, IBE, 2006c.

Even in countries where there has been little government interest in childcare, pre-primary education is increasingly being seen as a government responsibility to be provided, often free, as an extension of the educational system in order to prepare children for school – as seen in section 2.3.

Government objectives

In many countries, government does not have "a" childcare policy but a multitude of policies with each involved ministry having its own objectives, plans and programmes related to children or childcare. In the country reviews, the number of different ministries mentioned as having some responsibility in relation to childcare is impressive: for example, Ministries of Education for the development of preschool education, Ministries of Social Welfare for support to NGOs providing childcare to the disadvantaged, or Ministries of Youth and Sports for after-school activities for children.

---

[46] For example, see Wazir, 2001.

The various government services involved in childcare often tend to be focusing on the well-being of children in terms of health, nutrition, education and safety and may overlook the needs of working parents. In some countries, early childhood education programmes have grown dramatically in recent years, but the primary preoccupation is to prepare children for primary school, with little consideration for the needs of working parents in terms of the hours and duration of programmes. In other countries such as France, Hungary, Kenya and Thailand, full-day programmes at pre-primary level are more helpful to working parents (as seen in section 2.3 and table 2.1). Where public policy stems from concerns regarding employment growth, women's labour force participation and gender equality, public supports for childcare tend to be more closely aligned to the needs of working parents.

Ministries of Labour in some countries recognize the problems of working parents but often have many other priorities that take precedence. Moreover, they do not usually have any expertise or mandate concerning childcare, the exception being where crèches are required by labour law (as in Brazil, Chile or India) and can be subject to labour inspections. Nevertheless, these ministries can and sometimes do play decisive roles in inserting the care needs of working parents into the policy agenda for childcare and education.

The case of Brazil is interesting since there is an ongoing effort to provide integrated services and coordinate efforts for childcare. But in recent consultations, there was no participation of the labour sector (Ministry of Labour, employers or trade unions) in discussions despite legislation requiring workplace support (see Chapter 6). Therefore the needs of working parents and of employers concerning childcare provision would not seem to be represented in decisions about childcare reform.

2.5 Government funding strategies

Basically, there are two main strategies for government funding of childcare:

- funding the supply of childcare by giving subsidies to facilities or supplying services directly; and

- funding the demand for childcare by providing subsidies to parents.

These strategies are not mutually exclusive and can be combined. For example, the UK Government does both. On the demand side, it supports parents through tax exemptions and the childcare element of the Working Tax Credit for low-income parents. On the supply side, it has a system of grants to providers, as well as directly setting up children's centres in poor areas.

Financing facilities

By financing childcare facilities, government helps to ensure that there is a supply of childcare available. Direct government funding and provision of facilities is most common for early childhood education for children over age 3, although hours may be short and the coverage far from complete as seen in section 2.3. Providing or subsidizing childcare for children under age 3 is more rare.

Responsibility for childcare provision is often decentralized, with funds going to local governments, which have the major task of ensuring childcare provision (which sometimes but not always includes pre-primary education) within a framework of government standards, regulations and oversight. Thus municipalities can have a major role in organizing childcare (as can be seen in table 2.1 in the cases of Brazil, France, Hungary, Kenya, Thailand and the United Kingdom) and may also contribute some of the funding.

Decentralizing the funding and provision of childcare to the local level has the potential advantage of making services more responsive to local needs – including those of local workplaces. The roles of municipalities as partners for workplace programmes are discussed in section 3.4.

Apart from direct public provision of services, government funding to facilities may be in the form of subcontracts to childcare service organizations or grants. These contracts or grants may be the responsibility of municipalities or of a line ministry. Grants to providers can sometimes be used for capital expenditure to encourage start-ups, and at other times may apply to recurrent expenditures such as staff salaries, rent or meals.

In some countries (such as Hungary, Singapore or Thailand), workplace childcare centres can benefit from public grants to providers. In Thailand, the crèches organized by the trade unions (see Chapter 13) were receiving some support from the municipalities in terms of milk subsidies which, given their limited budgets, was a welcome assistance. Singapore provides grants to licensed centres for children of working mothers (see box 2.4).

To conserve resources and target those most in need, governments may concentrate on creating or subsidizing facilities in specific disadvantaged regions, so that the poor in that area may benefit. However, such programmes may fail to benefit the equally poor in other regions that have no facility. This has been a criticism of the children's centres in the United Kingdom, where fully one-half of at-risk children live outside the disadvantaged areas designated for setting up these centres.[47] Another problem of targeted facilities is the potential segregation of low-income children.

Governments sometimes provide subsidies to registered facilities based on the income of parents – the subsidy being only for low-income parents or more for them. Box 2.4 provides examples from Singapore and South Africa of regular subsidies paid to providers on this basis. In South Africa, the subsidy for low-income families has been a problem for some centres since these parents cannot always pay their part of the fee and so the centres are not receiving the full fees and quality is suffering (see Chapter 12).

Box 2.4 Subsidies to providers for low-income parents

Singapore. A centre-based childcare subsidy of up to $150 or $75 per month per child (depending on residency status) is available for children below 7 years of age attending licensed childcare centres whose mothers are working. A higher amount is given for infants aged 2 to 18 months. An additional subsidy is available for low-income families.

South Africa. The government pays a fixed daily subsidy to providers for each child that is eligible for support as a result of low family income.

Sources: For Singapore, see http://www.childcarelink.gov.sg/ccls/uploads/HIH-Issue-04_2008.pdf [17 June 2009]. For South Africa, see Chapter 12.

Funding parents

In countries with a more market-based approach to childcare, governments tend to prefer to give funding support for childcare to parents, who can then decide what facility they want to use. Financing demand for childcare rather than providing public facilities or public support to facilities has been viewed as a means to rapidly stimulate the creation of childcare services (mainly private), allowing greater sensitivity to parents' needs, bringing innovation and efficiency to the sector, and reducing government expenditures. An additional advantage of programmes providing subsidies to parents is that they can offer governments a way of targeting support to those most in need and can make support contingent on certain factors such as income, ages of children, employment and number

---

[47] PricewaterhouseCoopers, 2004.

of hours worked, like the childcare element of the Working Tax Credit in the United Kingdom.

A common form of government subsidy to parents is through tax systems whereby working parents can claim reductions based on childcare expenses. In the United States, this is one of the main ways the federal government provides support to working parents for childcare (as well as elder care). However, the poor who do not pay tax do not benefit and those in higher tax brackets would benefit more than those in lower ones. Other governments have systems for financial transfers to parents using registered childcare – the amount being greater for lower-income parents (see the examples of Australia and France in box 2.5).

Box 2.5 Government financial transfers to parents

Australia. Fee support (the Child Care Benefit) is available to 98 per cent of parents who use childcare and low-income parents receive a higher benefit. This means that approximately 60 per cent of expenditure on all early childhood services is public, with parents contributing in total about 38 per cent of costs.

France. The National Family Allowance Fund provides a payment for working parents to help offset the costs of home-based childcare (mainly childminders) for children up to 6 years (Complement de Libre Choix du Mode de Garde, CMG). The amount varies from 160 euro to 370 euro monthly depending on family income.

Sources: For Australia, see OECD, 2006b, p. 270. For France, see Chapter 8.

However, parental subsidies also have their shortcomings. The amount of the subsidies is often low compared to the cost of good-quality care and so recipients may tend to choose cheaper, poorer-quality care options. In the United States, where some states provide vouchers for poor families, programmes have been criticized because the value of the vouchers is so small that receiving families cannot pay for high-quality care.[48] The OECD suggests that funding childcare through parental subsidies weakens the steering capacity of government services and tends to lead to the proliferation of family daycare, characterized by lower standards and quality than professional childcare centres.[49]

A further problem with providing subsidies to parents is that they may have difficulty in judging the quality of the services proposed, particularly in countries

---

[48] Folbre, 2001, p. 189.

[49] For a full discussion of private market versus public provisioning models, see OECD, 2006b, pp. 115–119.

where there is a weak or non-existent official system for registering or licensing childminders. In addition, when low-income parents must cope with bureaucratic difficulties to make their claim for the subsidy, many who are eligible may not actually profit. In the United Kingdom the recent experience with the Working Tax Credit shows that low-income families often have difficulty claiming their due and take-up has, so far, been low (see Chapter 14).

Whether through support to parents or to facilities, there seems to be general agreement that substantial government funding and interventions are needed in order for parents – particularly less affluent ones – to have access to childcare they can afford that is of a reasonable quality. The OECD has concluded from a review of experience in 20 countries that sustained public investment is needed in childcare (either directly to services or indirectly through parent subsidies) in order to ensure both affordability to parents and quality of services.[50] But even among OECD countries, it is considered that investment by many governments is inadequate.

2.6 Balancing quality and cost

Those who pay for childcare, whether they be parents, national governments, municipalities, NGOs, employers, private providers or some other entity, are caught in the inherent conflict between ensuring the quality of the care as well as its affordability. Cutting costs tends to mean reducing the quality while ensuring quality increases the cost. This dilemma raises important policy questions about the setting of quality standards and the conditions of work of childcare workers.

Setting quality standards

In order to ensure that childcare environments are safe and healthy and that practices promote children's development and learning, most governments have regulations or standards that relate to childcare centres (including those that are employer sponsored). In some countries, regulations or standards relating to childminders also exist. Childcare quality is usually assessed by indicators such as:

● staff-to-child ratios;

● group size;

---

[50] OECD, 2006b, p. 118.

- premises and space;

- age-appropriate curricula and settings;

- hygiene and safety standards;

- staff qualifications and training; and

- staff salaries and turnover.

Each indicator has major implications for the cost of providing childcare which will be greater when there are fewer children per staff member, smaller groups, more spacious and better equipped facilities, and highly qualified and well-paid staff.

Concern about quality raises major issues for poorer countries and locations where resources are scarce. What are the key elements of "high-quality" care? As an Indian writer remarks: "If high quality is defined as the use of highly trained and motivated teachers or care-givers, a scientifically tested curriculum, a rich variety of educational and other stimulation materials and a stress on staffing ratios and good physical structures, then what does this imply for poor countries?"[51]

Importing standards from developed countries may be unrealistic for many developing country settings where facilities that do not meet standards of "high quality" may nevertheless improve the situation for children at risk. Experience from developing countries suggests that low-cost community-based initiatives can have a positive impact on child development indicators, as shown in the case of Bolivia in box 2.6. The example also shows how childminding can provide job opportunities for local women who are given very basic training.

Similarly, some of the workplace examples in this book also suggest that relatively low-cost childcare centres can still bring an improvement to the well-being of workers' children compared to the care they would otherwise receive. The case of Mobile Creches in India (see Chapter 10) illustrates how even a relatively low-cost crèche can be a vast improvement in the situation of the children of construction workers who would otherwise be left to their own devices on the construction site. In Thailand, workers appreciated the workplace crèche run by the Network of Nawanakhon Labour Unions and, despite its shortcomings, felt that their children were developing better than those who were sent back to the countryside to stay with grandparents (see Chapter 13).

---

[51] Wazir, 2001, p. 94.

Box 2.6 Positive effects of home-based daycare for poor children in Bolivia

Bolivia has undertaken a large-scale home-based early childhood development and nutrition programme, PIDI (Proyecto Integral de Desarrollo Infantil), that provides daycare, nutrition and educational services to children who live in poor, predominantly urban areas. Under the programme, children from 6 months to 6 years of age are cared for in groups of 15 in homes in their own neighbourhood. The community selects local women to become home daycare mothers. These non-formal, home-based daycare centres, with two or three caregivers, provide integrated child development services (play, nutrition, growth screening and health referrals). The women receive child development training prior to becoming educators but are usually not highly trained.

When children participating in the programme were compared with others on bulk motor skills, fine motor skills, language skills and psychosocial skills, participation in PIDI had a positive impact on all test scores for children age 37–54 months. Impacts were almost always positive for children who had participated in the programme for at least 13 months.

Source: World Bank ECD Program Evaluations in the Developing Countries; see: http://go.worldbank.org/S2GDFFHOB0 [3 November 2008].

For those making standards in contexts where resources are limited, an alternative approach could be to establish and strictly enforce minimums below which the children's development may be compromised rather than ideals which few can reach, which make childcare unaffordable for many and which may discourage the establishment of childcare centres.

Nevertheless, ensuring standards while maintaining affordability for parents is difficult in all contexts and, for low-income parents, some form of government financial support is inevitably needed.

Conditions of work of childcare workers

In efforts to provide childcare which is affordable and also of high quality, it is often the childcare workers who are "squeezed" by low salaries or high numbers of children per worker, or both. As noted by the UK trade union UNISON, "It is important that affordable childcare is not provided at the expense of childcare workers."[52]

---

[52] UNISON, 2004, p. 7.

An interesting finding about the quality of childcare is that the well-being of the children is particularly related to the nature of the interaction between the staff and the children. One of the key aspects of quality is a consistent and warm childcarer.[53] UNESCO notes that the importance of the relationship between the adult caregiver and the child is encouraging for those working in resource-poor situations where physical features are hard to address.[54] But this finding also underlines the importance of careful selection of childcare workers, adequate levels of staffing (staff-to-child ratios), and working conditions that permit this kind of interaction and promote continuity of their employment.

Although childcare workers and their relationship with the children are at the heart of childcare quality, evidence shows that they are often very poorly paid and over-stretched by their work.[55] In interviews collected for this book, a number of teachers indicated that while they are very motivated about their work with children, they are not very satisfied with their working conditions, in particular their salary. One respondent, a head teacher at a nursery in Kenya, reported earning a lower salary than that of some unskilled public officials at the government level (see Chapter 11). A number of workers also noted that insufficient staffing and very long working hours were important sources of stress. Low salaries, inadequate staffing and poor working conditions may reduce the cost of childcare, but they make it very difficult to attract and retain the trained and motivated staff needed for the well-being of the children.

In virtually all countries, turnover of childcare staff is high. In Kenya, the annual turnover rate of 40 per cent of trained ECD teachers is attributed to the poor remuneration and lack of supports.[56] A 2004 survey of the childcare workforce in Australia reported a turnover rate of 32 per cent and suggested that priorities for retention should be better pay, status, paid in-service training and more time for preparation. As the US Department of Labor notes in its career guide concerning future opportunities in child daycare services:

> Job openings should be numerous because dissatisfaction with benefits, pay, and stressful working conditions causes many to leave the industry. Replacement needs are substantial, reflecting the low wages and relatively meagre benefits provided to most workers.[57]

---

[53] Daycare Trust/National Centre for Social Research, 2007.
[54] UNESCO, 2006, p. 178.
[55] See Wallet, 2006, for a global overview.
[56] Kenya, MOEST, 2005, p. 13.
[57] United States Bureau of Labor Statistics, 2008b.

Since most workers in childcare for preschool children are women, it is not really seen as a profession and the skills involved tend to be undervalued. Looking after children is perceived as a capacity possessed by all women and training is not really necessary – 'any woman can watch children' is the assumption. The OECD notes the need for a new vision recognizing the requirements for well-trained professionals who can support the language and social development of young children and the child-rearing skills of parents.[58] If parents and society in general were more aware of the skills needed, they might be more willing to pay better wages for the service.

2.7 Conclusions

In most countries, both industrialized and developing, parents who work or would like to work have difficulty finding childcare that is affordable, convenient and of a quality such that they feel their child is well looked after. Difficulties are particularly great in countries where there is little public provision of childcare or financial support for costs. When parents have to pay most of the costs of childcare, the resulting differences in quality of care received by children reinforce existing inequalities into the next generation.

Government support in both developing and developed countries has focused mainly on preschool education for children about to start school, but coverage is highly variable and hours are not always convenient for working parents. Facilities for children under age 3 are much more rare and more likely to be privately run. Out-of-school care for children of school age (such as after-school clubs, summer camps) is increasingly a concern in some industrialized countries but provision remains limited and the needs of school-age children continue to be unrecognized in many countries despite the problems experienced by parents.

The shortfall of public support for childcare, even in many industrialized countries, means that the childcare gaps and difficulties for working parents are considerable, with implications for their ability to work and to work productively. However, the willingness of employers to help fill in the gaps is highly variable. It would be wrong to expect that in countries where little is done by government (and thus the childcare gaps are greater), more is done by employers. In some countries where there is very little government support for childcare, there is also

---

[58] OECD, 2006b.

very little employer support if childcare is generally perceived within the society as the responsibility of the family, apart from welfare cases.

In order to increase the resources available for childcare, governments in both industrialized and developing countries have been searching for ways to leverage existing resources and to mobilize additional resources, both internally (through partnerships with NGOs, employers and the private sector) and, in the case of developing countries, externally through aid programmes – although UNESCO notes that donor support for early childhood care and education has been limited and that increased support is essential.[59]

Given the repercussions for the workplace, some governments in both developing and industrialized countries have been trying to extend the resources available for childcare through measures to increase the involvement of employers. Chapter 3 considers government policies which target employers and looks at the roles and motivations of various partners who have been involved in promoting and providing workplace programmes – whether in response to government measures or as independent initiatives.

Details on the different types of workplace programmes and how they are functioning are provided in Chapter 4.

---

[59] UNESCO, 2006, pp. 185–187.

Key points

Childcare needs of children and parents

- For children under age 2, the effects of non-parental care are complex and depend on many intervening factors, including the cultural context and the quality and duration of the substitute care.

- Effective preschool programmes enhance children's physical well-being, cognitive and language skills, and social and emotional development.

- Public concern about childcare often overlooks the major problems of working parents in finding care for school-age children.

- For parents, the critical aspects of childcare which influence whether they use it are:
  - affordability in relation to their earnings;
  - convenience in terms of opening hours and location; and
  - quality concerning the well-being of the child.

Facilities for different ages, and costs, often fall short of workers' needs

- For working parents with children under age 3, there is a serious lack of affordable, quality childcare facilities in most countries.

- Employing a nanny is a popular childcare solution among the better off in both developed and, particularly, developing countries, where income differentials are high.

- Paying a woman to look after a child in her home (variously called child-minder, family daycare, day mother) is often an informal arrangement that parents make with neighbours but is increasingly being formalized.

- Pre-primary schooling (3–5-year-olds) is becoming more common in most countries but hours are often limited and coverage far from complete.

- Out-of-school care for school-age children is not well developed except in the few countries where childcare is seen as a public responsibility.

- Childcare is often expensive and full-time care of a young child can cost more than university.

Government approaches to childcare differ greatly

- A few countries view childcare as a public entitlement and a responsibility of government (France and Hungary being the closest examples in this study).

- Many governments leave parents to pay for non-family care bought on the market from a private provider.

- Various government systems exist for subsidizing parents and/or subsidizing facilities, particularly targeted at low-income parents.

- Many childcare programmes focus on the needs of children and neglect those of working parents.

Balancing quality and affordability is difficult

- In efforts to provide affordable childcare of high quality, it is often the childcare workers who are "squeezed" by low salaries or high numbers of children per worker, or both.

- The quality of interaction between staff and children is the most important factor affecting the well-being of children.

- Childcare workers are among the lowest paid in all countries and turnover is notoriously high.

- Importing ideal standards from developed countries may be unrealistic for many developing country settings where facilities that do not meet standards of "high quality" may nevertheless improve the situation for children at risk.

- For low-income parents, some form of government financial support is needed.

Perspectives
of workplace partners

3

Drawing on the case studies in this book as well as secondary sources, this chapter looks at the points of view of the various partners who have been involved in putting in place workplace measures to help workers with child-care – their motivations and how they have been involved. The chapter starts by looking at government measures which seek to increase employer involvement in childcare and their results. It then goes on to consider the motivations and roles of the various partners who have been helping to find workplace solutions for childcare, including:

- employers and their organizations;

- trade unions;

- municipalities and local governments;

- specialized childcare providers;

- childcare workers; and

- international donors.

3.1 Government measures targeting employers

In countries with more market-based approaches and less public provision of childcare, public authorities are more likely to look to employers as a source of childcare support for employees. This section focuses on the main types of measures which governments have taken to try to increase the involvement of employers in childcare: legislation, financial incentives, and advocacy and technical support.

Legal dispositions for employer childcare support

In some developing countries, as a way of ensuring childcare facilities for at least some working women, governments have legislated that employers must provide childcare once they have a certain number of women employees. There are three such countries covered in this book – Brazil, Chile and India, for which legislation is described in box 3.1.

Legislation providing childcare for women workers in Brazil is linked specifically to the breastfeeding period so that women can return to work and continue to breastfeed. Breastfeeding was historically the motivating reason for Chile's legislation as well. In more recent years, there has been more attention to the need for childcare, and in that context it is noteworthy that some unions in Brazil have succeeded in extending the right to childcare to include fathers as well. Similarly in India, some companies allow men as well as women employees to use the childcare centre. In the case of BHEL, which falls under the legislation requiring a crèche for women workers, both men and women can use it and some men are, in fact, using it.

Box 3.1 Legislation requiring employer childcare provision

Brazil. Establishments employing at least 30 women over the age of 16 should provide an appropriate place where they can leave their children during the breastfeeding period. The company can make agreements for provision by public or private crèches or operate a crèche reimbursement system, granting payment of expenses on a crèche chosen freely by the mother-employee, at least for the first six months of the child's life.

Chile. The law requires employers with more than 20 women workers aged at least 18 years to provide childcare facilities for children under the age of 2 by creating their own nursery, sharing a nursery with other employers in their location or paying for an approved nursery.

India. Various sectoral labour acts stipulate that a crèche must be provided once the number of women workers exceeds a certain number – 30 in the case of factories, and 50 for plantations and beedi and cigar workers.

Source: See country chapters.

Compared to India, the systems in Brazil and Chile provide more flexibility by allowing employers the possibility of reimbursement of payment for a community facility rather than having their own crèche.

In Brazil, companies often opt for a system of reimbursement, as in the case example of FURNAS. However, in other companies, the crèche reimbursement may be a minimal amount (the equivalent of around US$50 per month) that is not enough to ensure quality daycare. The fact that many women are not represented by trade unions and that trade unions may not be strong enough to negotiate for their full rights means that many women potentially covered by this provision do not fully benefit. The benefit of a crèche is more common in large enterprises and where the trade union is more active. As well as including men, some agreements also increase the minimum benefit period to cover older pre-school children, as in the case of the Oswaldo Cruz Foundation.

In Chile, only 5.1 per cent of the companies obliged to provide childcare support actually operate their own facility: most subcontract childcare provision or provide vouchers (69.2 per cent) and 14.5 per cent provide direct payment, although the latter is not strictly in compliance with the law. A number of companies have also exceeded legal requirements, introducing back-up childcare when regular arrangements fall through, and after-school and holiday care support.

In her chapter on India, Hamsa notes that, despite the legislation, there are few enterprise crèches. "Employers either refrain from employing women if it is mandatory for them to provide daycare for their children or they avoid the obligation by failing to show the employment of women in their official records." This legislation, which puts a penalty on employers who hire women, seems to be hindering women's employment opportunities in India.

Similarly in Chile, Kremerman Strajilevich reports that just 5.4 per cent of working women with children under the age of 2 have access to childcare through their workplace, since most do not work in companies with more than 20 female employees, and suggests that the law may be discouraging employers from hiring women. However, in Brazil, Linhales Barker does not indicate a similar effect.

It is questionable whether legislation providing the crèche benefit for women workers in companies employing a certain number of women is promoting equality in the labour market since it increases the cost of hiring young women. The position of the ILO Committee of Experts, which reviews legislation related to the Workers with Family Responsibilities Convention, is that "measures designed to promote harmonization of work and family responsibilities, such as childcare services, should not be specific to women".[1] As the

---

[1] ILO, 1999, paragraph 3.

Committee has noted, legislation on workplace provisions for childcare that excludes fathers' access perpetuates the idea that women alone are responsible for their children's care, and raises the possibility that employers will discriminate against women in order to avoid legal obligations linked to the numbers of female workers in their employ.[2]

One country with specific legislation on workplace childcare which does not limit the scope only to women workers is the Netherlands. Here, parents, employers and the Government jointly bear the costs of formal childcare for preschool and primary school-age children. An employer contribution was, in fact, often included in collective agreements even before the Childcare Act which took effect in 2005. Since then, employers are supposed, but not obliged, to pay one-third of the childcare bill (the employer of each parent paying one-sixth).[3] As of January 2007, the employer contribution has become mandatory.[4] The government contribution is related to income, being higher for low-income families. Parents buy the amount of childcare they need and are reimbursed through the tax system. To receive the benefit, both parents must be in work or education.

For parents, both fathers and mothers, the Dutch system has the advantage of covering care of children up to age 13 and allows them to choose the registered provider they want. This is a much more flexible arrangement than workplace facilities, which tend to cover limited age groups and provide no alternatives if the facility is not convenient to the parents. Also, working parents are paying only about one-third of childcare costs, making childcare more accessible to all income groups.

France provides another interesting model of a compulsory employer contribution to childcare support, in this case through the social security system. The family branch of social security (Caisse Nationale des Allocations Familiales, CNAF) is the major national provider of childcare financial support and almost 60 per cent of its funds come from employer contributions.[5] This system has the major advantage that the employer payment is not based on the sex composition of the company personnel nor their specific childcare needs and thus there is no possibility of inducing bias against the hiring of women or parents.

---

[2] ILO, 2000, paragraph 3.

[3] http://www.pes.org/downloads/Campaign_Childcare_Discussion_Paper.pdf [11 June 2009].

[4] http://www.cbs.nl/en-GB/menu/methoden/toelichtingen/alfabet/r/revised-childcare-legislation.htm [11 June 2009].

[5] Sénat, rapport 3384, tome 3: cited in Daune-Richard et al., 2008, p. 62.

Financial incentives for workplace initiatives

A number of industrialized countries have schemes that are meant to encourage employers to provide childcare support using grants or direct subsidies and/or fiscal incentives. In developing countries, such incentives are rare and none of the employers with workplace nurseries in such countries in the present study reported any financial support from governments. The nature of the incentives offered by governments has a major impact on whether employers offer any support and the type of support which they offer.

Grants and subsidies

In some countries, there are government grants to encourage employers to set up a childcare facility. Often the grants are to help with the capital expenditure to set up the childcare centre. Support for capital expenses does not seem to be very attractive for employers. In Canada, for example, the provinces of Manitoba, New Brunswick and Saskatchewan had a grant programme in place in the 1990s. The grants ranged from $5,000 per childcare centre in New Brunswick to $75,000 in Manitoba. Childcare advocates indicate that there was little take-up from employers and the programmes were discontinued.[6] One of the reasons for the low take-up may be the fact that once the facility is set up, funding must be found to run it. Also the grants may be insufficient compared to the expenses involved.

In France, since 2004, there has been a major effort to encourage employers to set up an enterprise crèche or a multi-enterprise crèche (*crèche inter-entreprise*) given the need for more places for children under age 3. The CNAF (mentioned above) offers subsidies for both the investment costs and the operational costs, available through its local branches, which have "enterprise units" to advise and support companies interested in childcare projects. Depending on the project, some 50 to 70 per cent of the total costs for a new crèche place are subsidized. In particular, under the 'childhood-youth contracts' (*contrats enfance-jeunesse*), which encourage local partnerships between local branches of the CNAF, local authorities, public institutions and/or companies, 55 per cent of the operational costs for a new crèche place are subsidized by social security under a renewable cost-sharing agreement of 3 to 5 years.[7] As shown in the case example of SNPE, companies are expected to contribute around 15 per cent of the cost of a new childcare place.

---

[6] Code Blue for Child Care, 2007.
[7] Caisse Nationale des Allocations Familiales, 2006.

In a few countries, there is a government subsidy for the operation of childcare centres which is paid to licensed providers, often according to the number of eligible children attending. In these countries, workplace crèches that are registered can sometimes also receive the subsidy. In Hungary, for example, a private company which sets up a workplace kindergarten is entitled to 30 per cent of the subsidy the state normally pays for a community kindergarten. In the case of Gedeon Richter Plc in Chapter 9, the state subsidy represents approximately 5 per cent of the kindergarten's yearly costs. In Singapore, a state subsidy is paid for children under 7 in a licensed childcare centre, so an enterprise centre would presumably be able to receive this subsidy.

Tax exemptions

In some countries, governments have been using fiscal incentives specifically for encouraging employers to set up their own childcare centres. In Malaysia, expenditures on the provision and maintenance of a childcare centre for employees are allowable expenses for the employer and, for employees, the benefit is treated as tax exempt. For other types of childcare support, no tax benefits are provided. The response from employers, especially those in the private sector, has apparently been very slow. Of the 166 childcare centres that have been established at the workplace, 140 are in public and statutory bodies and 26 in private organizations. The Malaysian Employers' Federation explains the low take-up by the high cost of setting up and operating a childcare centre and the difficulties in finding suitable space, particularly in urban areas.

In Australia, similar legislation making employer-sponsored childcare exempt from fringe benefits tax only when it is provided on business premises has been the cause of considerable controversy since any other form of employer support for childcare would be taxed as a fringe benefit. A report of a parliamentary inquiry criticizes the current system, noting that on-site facilities are rare and affordable mainly for large employers, such as the major banks, that are able to build or lease childcare centres. And even in the few enterprises that offer on-site facilities, only parents who can actually use them benefit from the tax exemption. The committee found that employers were interested in helping employees with childcare and noted: "It is contradictory to the best interests of government, business and workers that employers continue to decide against childcare assistance due to tax penalties."[8]

---

[8] Australia, House Standing Committee on Family and Human Services, 2006, p. 252.

Three of the industrialized countries in the present study (France, the United Kingdom and the United States) provide that a certain amount of salary can be set aside for childcare expenses and thus be exempted from tax or social security payments for both employers and employees. The systems can be rather complicated and are embedded in the overall fiscal and social security systems of the country. Table 3.1 provides some details and more are available in the country chapters.

Basically the systems make childcare expenses exempt from social security and tax payments for employers and employees up to a certain limit. The system is implemented mainly through vouchers in the case of France and the United Kingdom and special accounts set up by the employer in the United States. In the United Kingdom, the system is only for childcare expenses whereas, in the United States, elderly care is also included. In France, the vouchers (*Chèques d'Emploi Service Universel*, CESU) can be used by employees for any kind of registered childcare as well as many kinds of household services, including for the elderly. In all systems, the financial contribution of the employer to the tax sheltered funds of the employee can vary from nothing to 100 per cent.

When the legislation making employer-sponsored childcare a non-taxable benefit was passed in 1981 in the United States, it had been expected that employers would provide some of the funds in addition to the worker's salary. But the main trend has been to offer funds coming out of salary.[9] Similarly in the United Kingdom, an employer survey in 2006 found that childcare vouchers were primarily offered to employees through salary sacrifice and only a minority of organizations offered them as additional salary.[10] In France, an employer addition seems to be more likely (as in the case of the Caisse d'Epargne Auvergne Limousin, which contributes one-third – see box 4.6), perhaps because employers benefit from a 25 per cent tax credit on their contribution.

In the United States, where the possibility of tax-exempt reimbursement accounts has existed since the mid-1980s, about 45 per cent of employers with more than 50 employees have such a system in place.[11] In the United Kingdom, the system was started by government in 2005 and a study in early 2006 found that take-up was relatively good among large organizations (almost 50 per cent of those with over 1,000 employees) but less in small ones (about 20 per cent of those with 175–249 employees).[12] In France, take-up of the CESU by employers since it was initiated in mid-2005 seems, so far, to be low (see Chapter 8).

---

[9] Kelly, 2003.
[10] Kazimirski et al., 2006.
[11] Bond et al., 2005, table 9.
[12] Kazimirski et al., 2006, table 3.5.

Table 3.1 Government fiscal incentives for childcare support by employers

	France	United Kingdom	United States
Government objective	Create declared jobs in home services and childcare Encourage employers to facilitate work–family balance for parents	Increase use of registered childcare Encourage parents to work	Encourage employers to contribute to care costs
Government measure	For enterprises family tax credit (crédit d'impôt famille) of 25 per cent on expenses to facilitate work–family balance, including crèche and CESU (vouchers), up to an annual ceiling of 500,000 euro On CESU, employers do not pay social security and have 25% tax credit on their contribution (up to an annual ceiling of 1,830 euro per employee). For employees, no income tax on up to 1,830 euro yearly	Three types of childcare provision are exempt from tax and national insurance contributions: • use of a workplace nursery or play scheme; • employer payments to a registered childcare provider up to maximum of £55 per week; • childcare vouchers up to £55 per week Provision can be in addition to salary or instead of salary, which is officially reduced ("salary sacrifice"). Each working parent is eligible	Employees can allocate up to $5,000 pre-tax dollars towards a Dependent Care Reimbursement Account if both spouses (or lone parent) are working. Funds can all come from the employees' salary or the employer can also make a contribution Employers can receive a tax credit of 25% of their spending on the construction or rehabilitation of a childcare facility or on contracts with a third-party childcare facility to provide childcare services to employees. In addition, employers can receive a credit of 10% of their spending on resource and referral services for employees. The total credit cannot exceed $150,000 annually

	France	United Kingdom	United States
What care is covered?	CESU (universal cheque for service employment) can be used for childcare at home and registered childcare outside home, services for elderly and handicapped, domestic workers, gardeners	Vouchers can be used for any registered childcare for children under 16 including childminders, nannies, holiday play schemes, out-of-school clubs, nurseries	Funds can be used for caring for the elderly, children under age 13 and dependants with special needs, including payments to adult family members
How implemented?	The employer sets up a voucher (CESU) system through an approved voucher-providing company	The employer sets up a voucher system using a voucher-providing company. It must be available to all employees	The employer sets up a system that allows employees to be reimbursed childcare expenses from a Dependent Care Reimbursement Account
Employer incentive	No social security contribution and a tax credit of 25% on the employer contribution	Does not pay national insurance contribution on the salary given in childcare vouchers	No payroll charges on amounts in accounts
Employee advantage	Does not pay social charges or income tax on an amount up to 1,830 euro per year	Does not pay any tax or national insurance contribution on vouchers up to £55 per week (£2,860 per year)	Tax savings on the $5,000 per year per household depend on the income bracket

Sources: For France, see Tabarot and Lépine, 2008. For the United Kingdom, see HM Revenue and Customs, 2007b. For the United States, see Economic Growth and Tax Reconciliation Act of 2001, http://www.irs.gov/pub/irs-utl/egtrra_law.pdf, and https://www.fsafeds.com/fsafeds/SummaryofBenefits.asp#DCFSA [both 16 June 2009].

A major advantage of these systems is that they go beyond workplace nurseries for preschool children as the focus for employer incentives and provide much more choice for working parents. The systems also cover school-age children. In France and the United States, the schemes have the further advantage of covering care for elderly dependants.

While these systems have the advantage of flexibility in terms of the choice of childcare, the parents are still paying a high proportion of the cost. The savings for employees using "salary sacrifice" in the United Kingdom could amount to about £1,000 per year, which is a small proportion of the cost of full-time daycare, which is about £8,000 per year (see Chapter 14). Also it can be quite difficult for employees to understand how they can gain and how to cope with the bureaucratic procedures required.

From the government point of view, there is considerable debate about tax incentives for employers and employees. While the arguments in favour include the flexibility of choice for parents and the coverage of various types of care expenses, the argument against is basically that those who profit tend to be workers who are already better off and employees of large enterprises.[13] The person in the highest tax bracket will benefit the most from a tax-deductible benefit while the low-income worker who needs it most derives little benefit. Workers earning near-minimum salary cannot even set aside tax-free money for care expenses because their salary would go below the legal minimum. Schemes available to employers tend to be used mainly by larger companies, those whose employees are already in a higher pay bracket, while those working for smaller employers or in self-employment are left out. It could be felt that government money (or loss in tax earnings) would be better spent being targeted to low-income workers who need it most.

France, the United Kingdom and the United States have other schemes to help low-income workers pay for childcare. The UK system provides a direct tax credit to low-income parents based on their childcare arrangement, hours worked and income. In France, the non-parental childcare supplement (CMG; see box 2.5) is an allowance intended to support low- and middle-income working parents purchase care for their children, although in practice it is primarily higher-income families that use it, as the cost of childcare remains too high for lower-income families, even after the benefit (see Chapter 8).

---

[13] See for example, Masters and Pilkauskas, 2004, p. 39.

Advocacy

With or without financial incentives, governments have been trying to encourage employers to support childcare for employees, and in general to become more family-friendly.

When government incentives for childcare support exist, making employers aware of their existence is a major task for government, often at the local as well as national level. Enterprises, particularly small ones, do not necessarily follow the latest government policies. In a UK survey of employers in early 2006, only around half of medium-sized employers and a minority of smaller employers even knew about the new exemption rules.[14]

In the United Kingdom, the Government has web sites that explain the system and encourage employers to support the childcare needs of their employees.[15] In France, a proactive approach by the local branch of social security responsible, the regional authorities and the municipalities has been found to be a key factor in the use of the new incentives for enterprise and inter-enterprise crèches.[16]

Government advocacy toward employers often promotes work–life balance more generally, of which childcare is one component, as for example in Singapore.[17] Some governments provide legislative information, research, tools and advocacy materials to assist enterprises in understanding legal obligations and encourage voluntary initiatives regarding work–family balance, including childcare, as in the case of Australia's Workplace Relations service and Saskatchewan's Work and Family Unit under the Ministry of Advanced Education, Employment and Labour.[18]

One advocacy strategy tried by governments to encourage employers is offering awards for work/family policies (see box 3.2). To the extent that these awards are well researched and then publicized, they give good publicity to firms that are making efforts and provide examples for others.

---

[14] Kazimirski et al., 2006.

[15] See, for example, the brochure Sure Start, 2006.

[16] Daune-Richard et al., 2008, p. 67.

[17] See, for example, the web site of the Singapore Ministry of Manpower: http://www.mom.gov.sg [11 June 2009].

[18] For Australia, see http://www.workplace.gov.au; for Saskatchewan, Canada, see: http://www.workandfamilybalance.com [6 November 2008].

Box 3.2 Government awards for work–family programmes

Hungary. A Family-Friendly Employer competition was launched in 2000 by the Ministry of Labour. Each year, award-winning companies are identified in small, medium and large company categories. The awards ceremony is accompanied by high media coverage.

Singapore. The Work-Life Excellence Award is organized biennially by the Tripartite Committee on Work-Life Strategy (chaired by the Ministry of Manpower). The award pays tribute to employers that are committed to helping employees harmonize work and personal commitments. The Award serves to encourage other employers to implement Work-Life Strategies for the benefit of their organizations and employees.

Thailand. The Ministry of Labour has included having a childcare centre among the criteria for the prizes given to enterprises that provide good conditions for workers.

Sources: For Hungary and Thailand, see country chapters. For Singapore, see Ministry of Manpower: http://www.mom.gov.sg/publish/momportal/en/communities/workplace_standards/work-life_harmony/ Work-Life_Excellence_Award.html [17 June 2009].

3.2 Employers and their organizations

The involvement of employers in workplace programmes varies considerably from country to country and among organizations within countries. This section first looks at information about the frequency of workplace programmes and which employers tend to be involved. It then looks at why some employers have been reticent and why other employers have been providing childcare support and the benefits they have experienced. Finally the roles of employers' organizations and employer partnerships are considered.

How common are workplace programmes for childcare?

It is difficult to have a precise idea of what proportion of work organizations provide childcare benefits and what proportion of workers would have access. Even in countries where there are surveys, these are often restricted to certain types of enterprises and the questions asked are not the same. So data are not comparable from one survey to another nor from one country to another. Nevertheless, this section takes a brief look at some survey results.

For the European Union, a study of establishments with ten or more employees in 2004–05 found that, on average, only 3 per cent of all establishments offer an own-company childcare centre; a further 2 per cent offer, partly in addition to a company facility, other forms of childcare help such as a babysitting service organized and/or paid for by the company.[19] Establishments providing childcare facilities are most frequent in the Netherlands, with 12 per cent having their own childcare facility and 17 per cent offering other forms of childcare assistance. The frequency of company childcare facilities is also above the EU average in Ireland (6 per cent) and the United Kingdom (7 per cent).

The authors note that in Ireland, the Netherlands and the United Kingdom the supply of public childcare facilities is relatively weak, especially for children aged 3 years or under. Nevertheless, in other countries such as Germany, the relatively poor public supply of childcare facilities for this age group is not supplemented to a comparable degree by services from the employer's side. So even within Europe, countries differ in respect to whether employers are likely to take childcare measures in the face of a weak public supply.

In developing countries, very little information seems to have been collected about workplace support for childcare. Even in countries where there is legislation requiring certain employers to provide a crèche, there is little information on compliance and the number of enterprises falling under the law. In Brazil, a survey by the human resources consulting firm Hewitt reported that, in 2007, only 2 per cent of 120 companies with industrial plants had a crèche or childcare centre in their workplace (see Chapter 6).

As seen in section 3.1, government programmes for payment of childcare are available through the workplace in France, the United Kingdom and the United States. Thus this type of financial support tends to predominate in these countries. In France, the proportion of organizations with 20 or more employees offering crèche facilities was a low 2 per cent according to a study in 2005. However, 18 per cent of organizations were offering some financial help to cover childcare expenses, meaning that this benefit was potentially available to 29 per cent of employees.[20]

In the United Kingdom, there is some indication that the 2005 reforms providing tax exemptions may mean that more parents are receiving some financial help from employers. Among parents paying for childcare, the percentage receiving help from their employer more than tripled between 2004 and 2007 from 1 per cent to 3.4 per cent.[21]

---

[19] Riedmann et al., 2006, p. 40.

[20] Lefèvre et al., 2008, table 1.

[21] Calculated from Kazimirski et al., 2008, pp. 78–79.

In the United States, the results of a nationally representative sample of employers with 50 or more employees indicated that by far the most frequent type of childcare support is putting aside pre-tax salary for care expenses (which has no cost for the employer; 45 per cent provide this). The next most frequent type of support is access to information about childcare in the community (34 per cent). About 7 per cent of employers have a facility at or near the workplace, about the same as in the United Kingdom. About 7 per cent contribute financial support, and 6 per cent offer back-up care support.[22]

Various studies indicate that the employers who provide support for childcare tend to be large establishments in the services sector and the public sector. The EU survey found that establishments offering their own childcare facility were more than twice as frequent in the services sector as in industry and also more likely to be in the public sector than in the private sector. Such services were also far more common in larger establishments than in smaller ones, with 13 per cent of companies with more than 500 employees having their own childcare facility compared to 3 per cent overall. Similarly in the US study, large companies were much more likely to provide childcare at or near the worksite, reaching 17 per cent of companies with more than 1,000 workers.

Reasons for employer reticence

For some employers, childcare is not seen as their responsibility but that of individual workers or government and so no childcare support is envisaged. In a UK employer survey, about half of those not offering any support gave this as a reason.[23]

Another major reason why employers are reticent to help with childcare is the perceived cost of creating and operating a workplace facility, which is seen as the only option. It is clear that even partially financing a workplace childcare facility is not realistic for many employers. Also, as will be seen in Chapter 4, a workplace childcare facility is often not the best solution for helping employees with their childcare needs. There are other ways that employers can help, such as resource and referral services, negotiating discounts with community facilities or providing some form of financial help, and these may even meet employees' needs better than a workplace childcare centre. Such possibilities tend to be overlooked. Chapter 4 presents these options in detail.

---

[22] Bond et al., 2005, table 9.
[23] Kazimirski et al., 2006.

Employers often feel that they are not in the childcare business and that providing any support for childcare would distract company staff from their main work. As noted by an official of the Irish Business and Employers' Confederation (IBEC): "For many businesses childcare is not their core competence and there is genuine concern that involvement in such projects will become time and resource consuming taking the focus away from business priorities."[24] For employers, finding effective ways of supporting without unduly increasing the administrative work of their staff would make childcare support more attractive.

Employers sometimes hesitate to provide childcare support since the limited number of employees who benefit may cause resentment among those employees who do not. Indeed, only a small proportion of an organization's staff is likely to need childcare at any particular point in time. In box 3.3, this is estimated at about 5 per cent at Ford. So providing a benefit for this minority would not seem to be fair to the rest of the workers, who might feel they were not getting their share. In the cases of Ford and CIBC (box 3.3) management was somewhat worried about this reaction, but finally found there was not a problem. In firms that have a cafeteria system of benefits whereby workers can choose the benefits that they prefer (as in the case of Magyar Telekom), there would be no issue of parents of young children getting preferential treatment.

Small employers are particularly hesitant to offer childcare support. Since so few employees would be potentially interested, they do not feel it would be

---

Box 3.3 What about those who don't need childcare?

Heather McAllister, Senior Director of Strategic Initiatives, CIBC. The message that everyone benefits is the one that CIBC consistently gave when it rolled out the new (childcare) service. "If your colleague isn't able to show up for the day, someone else has to fill the void. That has resonated very well with our employees."

Richard Freeman, Ford Director, Family Service and Learning Center. "We expected a disconnect between the older workforce who are finished with child rearing and those who have young children. Only about 5 per cent or less of the workforce need to use the childcare centers at any one time. Despite this, we have not seen a rise in demand for direct wage increases, instead of these services. This may be because a lot of our members understand what collective bargaining is all about – negotiating things for the future. It means opening doors for future generations."

Sources: For CIBC, see Lowe, 2007. For Ford, see Corey and Freeman, 2003.

---

[24] Cronin, n.d.

worthwhile putting any system in place. In the UK employer survey, many employers not providing support felt that they had too few employees who wanted a childcare scheme or had too few employees in the organization in general.[25]

Yet keeping trained staff and reducing absenteeism are concerns of small as well as large enterprises. For small businesses, every employee is often a key worker and so absences or loss of employees because of childcare problems can be even more disruptive and costly. When smaller organizations were offering some support, the UK survey found that the reason was often that there had been requests from employees. In cases where a worksite facility would be appropriate, some small employers can pool resources but often it is an outside organization such as a mall or industrial zone administration which takes the initiative from which smaller companies can benefit (see section 4.1).

Benefits of childcare support

Among the employers who are helping employees with childcare, motivations are varied. For some it is seen as a charitable gesture; a gift to help employees. For others, helping employees with childcare may be seen as a way of improving their image in the community and showing that they are socially responsible. But for most employers who provide help, it is part of a business strategy. For IBM, one of the pioneers in providing childcare support, this is considered "a strategic business initiative, not charitable dollars".[26]

Childcare support is often, although not always, part of a more general strategy for work–life balance as can be seen in the examples of the British National Health Service (NHS) and of IBM in box 3.4. Other measures for work–life balance include leave policies and working hours, such as flexible work schedules, pay during childcare leave and a general effort by management to develop a culture that accepts that workers have responsibilities and a life beyond the workplace.[27] Since childcare is part of a package, it is sometimes difficult to say whether any positive changes were the result of the childcare assistance or of the whole package.

Childcare is considered a strategic initiative for organizations because of the benefits which have been perceived in relation to:

---

[25] Kazimirski et al., 2006.
[26] Shapiro, 2005.
[27] See Hein, 2005, for more details on other types of measures.

- reducing turnover and retaining employees, including women who go on maternity leave;

- attracting new employees;

- reducing absenteeism and lateness;

- increasing productivity and focus; and

- enhancing employees' morale, commitment, motivation and job satisfaction, while reducing stress and stress-related disorders in the workplace.

Box 3.4 Childcare as part of a package of measures

An HR Director, National Health Service (NHS), UK. "Childcare forms part of a whole package of measures that help to retain people. It is not the only thing in the package, but we can't have the package without it."

Ted Childs, Vice President of Workforce Diversity, IBM. "Our centers complement IBM's other business practices that come under the concept of work/life, for example, our workplace flexibility programs, where employees can arrive to work two hours earlier and leave earlier in the day. Or our telework programs that allow employees to work at home, a customer site or other non-IBM locations."

Sources: For the NHS, see Frew, 2004, p. 20. For IBM, see Bright Horizons Family Solutions. December 2002. "Executive spotlight on Ted Childs, Vice President of Workforce Diversity, IBM." Available at http://www.brighthorizons.com/SolutionsAtWork/article.aspx?articleid=143 [16 June 2009].

Reducing turnover

One of the major reasons why employers provide childcare help is to retain their employees. Losing employees can be expensive considering the costs of replacing an employee in terms of recruitment, advertising, selection and training. As can be seen in box 3.6, HSBC in the United Kingdom estimates that replacing an experienced employee costs the equivalent of about one year's salary.

When employees need extensive training, it becomes even more important for the company to retain them. There is nothing more frustrating for a company than to see its employees, trained at high expense, being attracted to the competitor next door for a small salary increase, as noted in the case of Pranda Jewelry in box 3.5. In the case of Wipro in Bangalore, the management attributes a higher rate of employee retention to the fact that the company crèche services have been very well received by those of its employees who have young children.

Box 3.5 Childcare for reducing turnover

Pranda Jewelry, Thailand. The childcare centre at Pranda Jewelry in Bangkok opened over 15 years ago. "In the jewelry business, artisans are the king. We need to do everything for them to stay with us," says Mr. Pramote Tiasuwan, vice president of Pranda Jewelry. It requires three years of training for artisans to become skilled enough to work on their own. In Thailand, companies need to be competitive in terms of design and quality so experienced artisans are a must. Earlier, artisans would leave the company if another company gave them 500 baht more as salary. Given the other benefits that Pranda provides, if another company does not provide their artisans with salaries at least 2,000 baht higher than Pranda's, there will be no additional gain. Due to this, Pranda enjoys a very low turnover rate – only 2 per cent.

Red Lands Roses, Kenya. The Director notes that childcare has an impact on employees' loyalty and commitment. "If they feel that we take care of them and their children, they would not leave the company after investment in their training."

Infosys, India. Management believes that many employees who have completed their technical training on the job and accumulated sufficient work experience to move on to other jobs decide not to leave because of the crèche. They see the crèche service as one of the major contributors to the company's relatively low attrition rate.

NCR Corporation's Retail Solutions Group, Duluth, US. "The daycare program helps the company hold on to 'high-potential' female employees, especially difficult to find female engineers," said Martin Healiss, human resources strategic partner with the Retail Solutions Division of NCR. "Many of these women have said that they are staying with the company primarily because of its childcare center," he added.

Sources: For Pranda Jewelry, see Kusakabe, 2006. For Red Lands Roses and Infosys, see Chapters 11 and 10 respectively. For NCR, see "Company daycare gets high marks." August 2003. Available at http://www.wikigwinnett.com/content.cfm?Action=wiki&WikiID=2668 [16 June 2009].

For some organizations, such as those in box 3.6, a major concern is the loss of valuable women workers who do not return after maternity leave: for these firms, increasing the proportion of women who return is a key concern. Childcare support is often a key component of efforts to encourage women to return. For HSBC, childcare support is felt to have had a marked impact on reducing the number of women leaving after the birth of a baby. Research in the United Kingdom indicates that women are twice as likely to return to work for an employer who gives some help with their childcare than one who gives none.[28]

---

[28] Forth et al., 1997. *Family friendly working arrangements in Britain 1997*, DfEE Research Report No. 16, cited in UNISON, 2004.

Other measures, complementary to childcare, also are taken to encourage the return of employees after childbirth. At Magyar Telekom in Hungary there is a reorientation programme for women on maternity leave and the possibility of flexible working hours. At IBM Hungary, there is also a maternity leave and return programme, including a "maternity buddy system" whereby mothers-to-be are matched with a mother who has already gone through the experience of maternity leave and returned to IBM (see Chapter 9).

Box 3.6 Childcare to encourage the return of new mothers

HSBC, UK. A childcare programme has been operating since 1989 and provides some 850 nursery places, 300 of them on the bank's premises. The Group Head of Diversity notes: "Providing a childcare programme has contributed considerably to reducing the number of women who leave after having a baby, from 70 per cent to 15 per cent in 13 years. This represents a massive budget saving – the average service of a maternity leaver is 11 years and the cost to the bank of replacing each one is estimated at around a year's salary."

Alston & Bird LLP, Atlanta. "Anecdotally, we know that we have retained associates who would have left if not for the support that the childcare facility has given them in trying to balance a legal career and a family."

Areva, France. This French energy giant opened its first crèche in 2002. It has been noticed that the crèche means that women can return sooner to work after maternity leave as they are reassured that they are near the child.

Sources: For HSBC, see UK Department for Education and Skills, 2006a, p. 5. For Alston & Bird, see Bright Horizons family solutions, 2006. "An interview with Ben Johnson, Managing Partner, Alston & Bird LLP." Available at http://www.brighthorizons.com/SolutionsAtWork/article.aspx?articleid=14 [16 June 2009]. For Areva, see Platat, 2007.

Attracting staff

For companies that are competing to recruit highly trained staff, childcare support can help improve their competitive position, helping them become "an employer of choice". The Canadian Imperial Bank of Commerce (CIBC), for example, cites the very competitive labour market as one of the primary reasons for creating programmes like back-up childcare. "We are very aware that for the younger generation whom we are trying to recruit, we are all going after the same people," says the Senior Director of Strategic Initiatives at CIBC. "These are savvy young people here who look very carefully at what is offered. It doesn't take long if you're a parent, once you've had one childcare crisis, to intuitively recognize that if your employer has something to help you out in this area, it would be a big benefit."[29] For similar reasons of attracting and retaining highly qualified staff, in South Africa, financial groups are major leaders for the creation of childcare facilities in a country where such facilities are relatively rare (see cases of FNB and Old Mutual in Chapter 12).

At the NHS in the United Kingdom, the childcare strategy was also seen as a way of improving the retention of staff as well as attracting personnel (see Chapter 14). The general perception is that the childcare strategy has made a bigger impact on the retention of staff than on their initial recruitment. This was partly because it was much easier for parents who were in the service to know about the programme, while for potential recruits the programme was, in fact, not well publicized in recruitment notices.[30] Even the best programme will not help in attracting staff if it is not well publicized.

Absenteeism

More than half of employers in the United Kingdom think that childcare problems result in late attendance and leaving work early.[31] Childcare problems can also be a reason for not coming to work at all. An Australian consulting firm notes that the reasons for absenteeism among nurses, teachers and police officers are often linked to difficulties with childcare and that the costs to the state can be considerable when replacements have to be found.[32] In the United States, employed mothers of children under 6 miss an average of 8.5 days and fathers an average of 5 days per year due to family-related issues.[33]

It is not surprising, therefore, that childcare support has been found to reduce absenteeism and loss of work time (see box 3.7). This is sometimes because the support means that employees have more reliable arrangements for childcare. For example, since the opening of the crèche at Red Lands Roses in Kenya in 2006, unplanned leave has declined by 25 per cent (see Chapter 11). Previously, workers had tended to leave their children in the care of rather unreliable teenage maids.

Reducing the absenteeism resulting from childcare problems is the main objective of emergency back-up care, which is sometimes the main type of support offered by the employer. This type of childcare is considered in detail in section 4.4.

---

[29] Lowe, 2007.

[30] Frew, 2004, p. 19.

[31] Daycare Trust, 2002.

[32] Australia, House Standing Committee on Family and Human Services, 2006, p. 249.

[33] Shore, 1998.

Box 3.7 Effects of childcare support on absenteeism

Gokaldas Images Private Ltd, India. The management reported that their child-care facility has translated into better productivity and greater regularity at work, as seen in part by a decrease in the number of days that employees are taking off.

SOCFINAF, Kenya. The general manager notes: "Childcare is an inexpensive but at the same time a pivotal part of SOCFINAF workers' welfare policy. Thanks to the crèches and the related health care service that SOCFINAF provides free of charge to its employees, absences or leaves related to family responsibilities are virtually non-existent in our company."

Ford Motor Company, US. Ford provides extensive childcare services for chil-dren of all ages. A director notes that "the programme could end up paying for itself in terms of lower absenteeism and retention, but this is difficult to track. Among the people who participate, the only group that we have been able to measure is the group with young dependents. The absenteeism among that group has dropped."

Sources: For Gokaldas and SOCFINAF, see Chapters 10 and 11 respectively. For Ford Motor Company, see Corey and Freeman, 2003, p. 9.

Productivity

In addition to reducing absenteeism, childcare support has also been found to improve productivity in various ways. Some employers talk about better relations with the staff and about increased loyalty and commitment, which make for better performance on the job. Others mention the reduction in stress and better ability to concentrate on the job, as in the examples in box 3.8. The SOCFINAF man-ager links the better ability to concentrate with the reduction of workplace injuries.

For some organizations, childcare problems of workers affect productivity very directly because the children actually come to work. They may come regularly after school to wait for their parents or when there is a problem with the usual childcare arrangement. The presence of children can have a disruptive effect on the work of parents. If the presence of children is infrequent, many employers tolerate the problem since otherwise the employee might be absent. The childcare centre at Telecom Union TOT Corporation Plc (currently TOT Plc) in Bangkok origi-nated from the needs of employees who took their children to their work during the school break because there was no one to take care of them at home.[34]

---

[34] Kusakabe, 2006.

> ## Box 3.8 Childcare and the ability to concentrate on work
>
> **Aguas Andinas, Chile.** Management noted the benefits of providing childcare support, saying "Mothers who are at ease are more productive", a sentiment clearly shared by the workers in their statement that "This [childcare support] clearly has implications on labour productivity, thus decreasing the stress that this situation [of lacking childcare] causes. One knows that the children are safe and sound in the kindergarten so I don't have to worry about my son all day."
>
> **Nong Nooch Tropical Botanical Garden, Thailand.** The Human Resources section notes that before the daycare was established, some workers left their children at home. This is not safe and so they were worried and could not concentrate on their work. Since they have the daycare centre, parents have become more disciplined, there is less absenteeism and tardiness and both fathers and mothers can concentrate on their work.
>
> **National Centre for Biological Sciences, India.** Management notes: "If the kids are happy the parents will automatically be happy and the parents can devote more time to the research work."
>
> **SOCFINAF coffee plantations, Kenya.** A manager notes: "Mental comfort is key to workers' safety at work, but also to employers, enabling them to reduce costs coming from workplace injuries and health claims."
>
> Sources: See country chapters.

Employers' organizations

Many employers' organizations bring recognition and guidance for their members on the issue of childcare and other family-friendly policies. The International Organisation of Employers' (IOE) 2008 survey of workplace trends calls attention to the need for family-friendly policies, including childcare, to facilitate female labour force participation.[35] National employer organizations can provide guidance and services to their members, and can lobby for stronger government interventions. The Swiss employers' organization (Union Patronale Suisse), for example, has provided its members with information on laws and on workplace work–family initiatives, has promoted collective bargaining as an effective means for addressing the work–family needs of workers and employers, and has called on government to take steps to meet workers' and employers' needs related to family

---

[35] International Organisation of Employers, 2008.

services, for example by making school hours more compatible with working parents' hours and providing after-school programmes.[36]

In some countries, there have been organizations set up by employers to promote work–life balance. In the cases of Singapore and the United Kingdom, the role of the employer group is basically promotional, creating awareness of work–life balance issues among employers (see box 3.9). In New Zealand, the Equal Employment Opportunities (EEO) Trust, claiming more than 400 organizations as members, provides information and training tools for businesses to encourage workplace diversity and equality, including work–life initiatives.

Box 3.9 Employer groups responding to needs for work–life balance

New Zealand. The EEO Trust Employers' Group provides its membership of more than 400 organizations with a wide range of research and resources to assist businesses to achieve success through managing workplace diversity. It offers tools, research and recognition for workplace practices and initiatives on work–life balance, including its annual Work & Life best practice awards. It is funded by membership fees and government contributions.

Singapore. The Employer Alliance is a network of corporations committed to create an enabling work environment to enhance work–life integration. The Employer Alliance exists to help and support organizations committed to work–life strategies. Their vision is for corporations to be aware of the contribution of work–life balancing to their business outcomes.

United Kingdom. Employers for Work–Life Balance was set up by an alliance of employers, big and small, who believed that work–life balance was a relevant and valuable business concept. Having achieved its objective of awareness raising, its web site, which provides resources for employers, has been taken over by the Work Foundation.

United States. Corporate Voices for Working Families is a leading national organization of 50 partner companies providing a private sector voice in the dialogue on public policy issues involving working families. A non-profit, non-partisan organization, Corporate Voices aims to improve the lives of all working families and the competitiveness of American businesses by developing and advancing policies that have bipartisan support built through collaboration among the private sector, government and other stakeholders.

Sources: For New Zealand, see http://www.eeotrust.org.nz; for Singapore, http://www.employeralliance.sg/ea_mission.html; for the UK, http://www.employersforwork-lifebalance.org.uk; for the US, http://www.cvworkingfamilies.org/about-us [all 16 June 2009].

---

[36] See http://www.arbeitgeber.ch/f/webexplorer.cfm?ddid=6C2EA591-F59C-408C-9C037F11 F360292B&id=31&tlid=1 [10 November 2008].

In contrast, the US organization Corporate Voices for Working Families seeks to provide a private sector voice in discussions of public policy that affect working families including childcare (see box 3.9). Corporate Voices has linked up with another employer group, the American Business Collaboration (see below), for a campaign to lobby government for an increase in the amount of pre-tax salary which employees can put aside for care expenses and its indexing to inflation.[37] Similarly in Australia, Deloitte and 37 other corporate partners lodged a submission with the Federal Treasurer appealing for reform of the fringe benefits tax treatment of childcare.[38]

A somewhat different type of employer group is the American Business Collaboration (ABC) for Quality Dependent Care, in which a few large US companies (champions) partner to ensure that their employees have access to quality care services. Current ABC Champion companies are: Deloitte & Touche, Exxon Mobil Corporation, IBM Corporation, Johnson & Johnson and Texas Instruments. Working in about 65 communities throughout the country, more than 1,500 childcare and eldercare projects have been funded through ABC's efforts.[39] In general, the initiatives of ABC have been based on the belief that, through collaboration, companies can accomplish more to improve and expand dependent care resources for employees and make a positive contribution in local communities. Another example of an employer group helping upgrade the qualifications of staff in local childcare centres used by employees is the Employers' Child Care Alliance in Alabama (see box 4.4).

Given that employers in many countries are increasingly affected by the difficulties of working parents in accessing childcare, it may be that, in the future, more examples will emerge like these of employers' organizations and groups taking action and putting pressure on governments to improve childcare services and make them more affordable for workers.

3.3 Trade unions

Trade unions are also concerned about the childcare options available for working parents who are their members or potential members. As increasing numbers of women are joining the workforce, work and family issues have become more

---

[37] http://www.cvworkingfamilies.org/our-work/family-economic-stability [19 June 2009].

[38] Australia, House Standing Committee on Family and Human Services, 2006, p. 235.

[39] See http://www.abcdependentcare.com [11 June 2009].

important not only for women but also for the increasing numbers of men who are part of a dual-earner couple. Parents who are working atypical hours have particular difficulties. In the case of the inter-enterprise crèche at Rennes Atalante Park (France), which serves low-income parents with atypical working hours, a CFDT delegate explains the trade union's involvement:

> It was the difficulty of working parents in finding a childcare arrangement that pushed our trade union to support this project. When a worker starts at 5.00 or finishes at 22.00 nobody will accept to take care of his/her baby. So a lot of women, in particular, were in trouble and often the only solution was to take sick leave, which had an impact on absenteeism.

Responding to the evolving needs of workers helps unions to show their relevance in a changing world and their ability to make gains to improve the lives of workers. Childcare for working parents is one of a number of work–family issues such as maternity and paternity leaves that have been on the agendas of trade unions.

Trade unions have found various ways of helping working parents access quality childcare:

- advocacy and participation in policy dialogue on childcare;
- negotiation of collective bargaining agreements that include childcare support;
- collaboration with an employer to help set up childcare support;
- setting up childcare facilities for workers; and
- organization of childcare workers to improve their conditions of work and training opportunities.

Policy dialogue and advocacy

In some countries, trade unions have been a major voice in promoting government measures that will improve the availability of childcare support for working parents (see box 3.10). These actions help not only their members but all workers and can give considerable visibility to the unions.

Sometimes unions join with other organizations to put pressure on governments, as in the case of SEIU Kids First, which partnered with parents, advocates, educators, elected officials and business leaders to stop state cuts in childcare budgets in the US states of California, Illinois, Rhode Island and Washington. In Illinois, they succeeded in obtaining $315 million over four years to expand preschool provision and secured a commitment to universal preschool for all 3- and 4-year-old children.[40]

In other instances, unions may be called upon by governments to participate in policy consultations. In Ireland, for example, SIPTU has participated actively in the work of a group set up under *Sustaining Progress* to examine, among other things, the potential and possibilities for further development of workplace childcare. SIPTU has published its own view of the directions which it thinks childcare policy should be taking, noting that the first trade union submission to government on this issue was made in the mid-1970s, and it has been raised in negotiations on every national agreement since 1987.[41]

Providing voice and collective bargaining

A major way in which unions have been involved in improving childcare access for workers is by making the request to the employer, sometimes as part of a collective bargaining process.

In Brazil, legislation concerning the provision of childcare for women workers (see section 3.1) has given considerable importance to collective bargaining since

---

[40] See http://www.seiu.org/a/publicservices/seiu-kids-first.php [19 June 2009].

[41] Services, Industrial, Professional and Technical Union (SIPTU), 2005.

provisions have to be included in collective agreements in order to be effective. Indeed, all of the case studies in Brazil feature a prominent role of trade unions in collective bargaining agreements with employers on the availability and design of childcare benefits for workers. As described in Chapter 6, in Brazil the reliance on collective bargaining to give effect to the law has the tendency to favour workers in companies with strong unions which can negotiate good conditions.

In other developing countries as well, requests from the trade union have been a critical factor in initiating a workplace programme. In a number of the case studies in Part II, including BOWT in Thailand, BMW South Africa and, in Chile, Aguas Andinas and the Childcare Centres for Seasonal Working Mothers, the union played a key role in articulating a request for childcare which individual workers might have been too shy to make individually and which made an impact on the employer.

In the Netherlands, employer contributions to the cost of childcare have long been incorporated into collective bargaining agreements. To illustrate, in 2002, three-quarters of Dutch employees were covered by collective agreements that included childcare provision as a fringe benefit. New legislation has formalized the practice of employer co-funding by directing that the cost of childcare should be shared on an equal basis between parents, employers and government (see section 3.2 for details).

Collective bargaining has played a key role in gains for workers in the United States, the case of the Child Care Fund negotiated by Local 1199 of the Service Employees International Union (SEIU) in New York City in Chapter 15 being just one example. In this case, a sectoral union negotiating with many health-care providers in the region was able to put together the combined contributions of a number of employers to create the childcare fund and the number of contributing employers continued to grow subsequently.

In industrialized countries, many large trade union federations provide support for their member unions on collective bargaining, including collective bargaining for childcare. Bargaining for childcare has been the focus of various publications, which provide detailed advice on how to develop the case for childcare and examples of what provisions have been included in existing agreements. In the United Kingdom, for example, both the TUC and UNISON have produced documents with extensive advice and explanations concerning childcare needs and options.[42]

In the United States, the labour unions have set up a special unit, the Labor Project for Working Families, which provides support for bargaining on measures

---

[42] TUC, 2006; UNISON, 2004.

to improve work and family balance. Started by California unions in 1992 to address the issue of childcare, it has since grown to become a national resource and advocacy organization thanks to funding by various foundations as well as contributions by many unions and individuals, including the Institute of Research on Labor and Employment of Berkeley University, which provides in-kind support by housing the project. The project encourages unions to include work–family benefits in their agreements and has produced a comprehensive guide on organizing and bargaining for work and family issues.[43] Box 3.11 presents an example showing how it has helped a local trade union.

Box 3.11 Improving work–family balance for bus drivers

In the US state of California, the Amalgamated Transit Union Local 192 (whose 2,000 members are mainly bus drivers) and the Alameda-Contra Costa Transit District ratified in 2000 a collective bargaining agreement that, inter alia, established a trust fund to help support dependent care.

The new contract was the result of many factors including judicious use of research. After the results of an earlier survey on the impact of family responsibilities on bus drivers were presented to AC Transit's joint labour-management committee by the Labor Project for Working Families, the committee established a dependant care subcommittee and a new childcare needs assessment survey was undertaken. The survey identified the problems employees were facing and how these problems were being resolved by taking time off, arriving late or leaving early – with high cost implications for the company.

Source: Dones, 2001.

Collaboration at the workplace

Union leaders have joined with employers at the workplace to help find childcare solutions. Most cases are no doubt undocumented. Box 3.12 presents one case where the trade union helped management find an appropriate solution to the childcare needs of employees.

In Thailand, also, two of the cases in this book (AEROTHAI and BOWT, the Secretariat Office of the Teachers' Council of Thailand) provide examples

---

[43] The guide called *A job and a life* was published in 2005. In 2009, an online database of language used in contracts will be launched. More information is available at http://www.working-families.org/about/index.html [11 June 2009].

> ## Box 3.12 UNISON in the UK helps address recruitment and retention
>
> **Graham Cuffley, secretary of Cambridge Branch, tells his story.** "The UNISON branch was first approached from the personnel department of Cambridge City Council in 1990 in relation to staffing problems. We were offered £100,000 by the local authority for initiatives to address recruitment and retention issues. Childcare was quickly identified as a key barrier to staff.
>
> "A meeting of women activists decided to convene two lunchtime meetings. These created great interest and around 100 women attended to discuss how to address the childcare issue. Since 60 per cent of those with children were commuters, a crèche at the main council offices was going to be no use. Instead, they decided to use the money for a childcare allowance, so parents could arrange childcare closer to home. The whole campaign was extremely successful and greatly strengthened the branch organization."
>
> Source: UNISON, 2004, p. 19.

where the trade union is helping with childcare solutions and is on the management committee for the childcare centre. In the latter case, the idea of the childcare centre originated with the trade union. Similarly, at BMW in South Africa, it was the National Union of Metalworkers of South Africa (NUMSA) that first approached the company regarding on-site childcare facilities. It continues to be consulted on any changes or problems at the facility.

In France, the trade union representatives on the Works Council at SNPE raised the problems in finding childcare in the company's rural setting as a priority for use of the welfare funds available to it. It was through the trade union's initial efforts that the employer, municipalities and workers came together to develop a full range of childcare services to serve the diverse needs of children from 3 months to 14 years which has now become one of the models for private–public partnerships for childcare in France.

Union childcare facilities

It is rare that trade unions set up their own childcare facilities. In this book, there are two examples from Thailand where unions active in an industrial zone took the initiative to set up a childcare centre. In both Nawanakhon and Phra Pradaeng industrial areas, the unions took the initiative, mainly because of the difficulties being experienced by the many working parents who were migrants with no family support nearby for childcare. In the case of Nawanakhon, the fact that the Network of Nawanakhon Labour Unions, composed of about 30 labour unions, already existed facilitated cooperation among trade unions.

A well-known example of a trade union which has become heavily involved in childcare provision is the National Trade Union Confederation (NTUC) of Singapore. NTUC has been involved in childcare since 1977, when the Ministry of Social Affairs asked it to take over two crèches that it was running. NTUC Childcare has been a cooperative since 1992. Today, it is a large provider of childcare in Singapore with 39 centres and a total intake of almost 4,000 children.[44] In Singapore, part of the finance for childcare comes from a state subsidy to children under age 7 whose mothers are working; this is paid through the registered childcare provider.

Organizing childcare workers

Trade unions in a few countries have been organizing childcare workers in an effort to improve the quality of childcare and the conditions of work of childcare workers. "The quality or, too often, lack of quality of services offered to our children is directly related to staff-to-child ratios and training and wages of early childhood workers," notes the National Secretary of the Liquor, Hospitality and Miscellaneous Union (LHMU) in Australia. "Quality of childcare cannot and will not improve without improving training and career structures for early childhood workers and without appropriate pay for their work."[45]

The LHMU, which represents early childhood workers, launched its childcare campaign, BIG STEPS, in June 2008 to push for a strategy that develops the skills of the entire early childhood workforce and creates the career paths needed to stop massive rates of turnover in the sector. It is fighting for better ratios and working conditions, for recognition of childcare professionals' skills and for financial support for training.[46] Similarly, in the United Kingdom, UNISON works to promote improvements in the pay, status, training and development of childcare workers, in order to attract and retain them as the cornerstone of quality childcare provision.[47]

In the United States, the Service Employees International Union (SEIU) has developed a new model for organizing home-based care workers which has recently

---

[44] Information found at http://www.ntuc-childcare.com [11 June 2009].
[45] LHMU, 2007.
[46] See http://www.lhmu.org.au/campaigns/big-steps-in-childcare [7 November 2008].
[47] See http://www.unison.org.uk/women/pages_view.asp?did=102 [31 October 2008].

been extended to include home childcare providers. Since these workers are self-employed and do not have an employer, this model uses their relationship with the state – receipt of payment from the state under a programme administered by the state – as the nexus to find an "employer of record" with whom to bargain. In 2005, Illinois was the first state to allow subsidized childcare providers to organize and require the state to engage in "collective negotiations" with their representative.[48]

Negotiations between SEIU and the State of Illinois resulted in childcare providers receiving four subsidy rate increases in base rates totalling 35 per cent over three years, and a state contribution to health-care premiums. Providers who meet certain training or quality standards receive an additional 5–20 per cent increase on top of the base rate under a new tiered reimbursement programme. These training incentives are expected to encourage more providers to become regulated.[49]

3.4 Municipalities or local government

As seen in Chapter 2, many national governments have decentralized responsibility for providing childcare services to the local or municipal levels, and in some cases responsibility for funding as well. Childcare initiatives are often at the local level and coordinating facilities at this level is most likely to make them relevant to workers' needs. Most childcare programmes in municipalities are not linked to any particular workplace but do provide a useful service to workers within the community.

Workplace partnerships with local authorities can take many forms depending on the attributions of the local authority concerning childcare as well as the dynamism of its personnel. In Thailand, for example, municipalities are providing a milk allowance per child to the two childcare centres run by trade unions (see Chapter 13). Although not very much, it was still an important help for keeping these centres operational in tight financial circumstances.

In the United Kingdom, municipalities can be a key partner for employers (as seen in the case of the Royal Marsden) since they have a legal duty to ensure that there is sufficient childcare in their area and are responsible for commissioning and supporting the delivery of early years education, childcare and play. In addition, every local authority is required to have a Children's Information Service which can provide parents with details of local providers of registered childcare.

---

[48] At least six other states have authorized similar arrangements. See Chalfie et al., 2007, for details on the organizing strategy.

[49] Chalfie et al., 2007, p. 14.

In France, municipalities, together with the family branch of social security (CNAF), play a key role in funding and managing childcare services. Municipalities cover around 30 per cent of France's annual spending on childcare and are the main national providers of these services. Today, more than 60 per cent of centre-based childcare services are managed by municipalities and inter-municipality institutions, although the share of crèches run by associations, and more recently by crèche companies, has consistently increased over the last years. A recent study reports that municipalities are also playing a key role in mobilizing and facilitating the setting up of company crèches and multi-enterprise crèches.[50]

However, the French experience also shows that partnerships for the creation of crèches between municipalities and enterprises are not always easy. In one case, a multi-enterprise crèche ran into financial difficulties when the municipality decided to stop its subsidy for the crèche because, although the children's parents worked in the town, they did not live there. In another case, tension arose because an enterprise was constrained by an agreement with the municipality to provide places in the crèche for the local community, while there was a lack of places for its own personnel. It is difficult to establish partnership agreements that have some flexibility, encourage employers and also ensure the sustainability of the crèche.[51]

Similarly in the United Kingdom, joint funding of childcare schemes can be complicated. In the case of the NHS, difficulties arose in some cases because each source of funding had its own criteria and rules. There were also issues around who employed the staff, took ownership of the project and assumed the risks.[52] These experiences point to the need for careful design of partnerships between municipalities and employers to ensure clear responsibilities and shared benefits.

3.5 Specialized childcare providers

Specialized childcare providers, be they for-profit companies or NGOs that are not working for profit, are frequent partners for workplace support to childcare. NGOs have in some cases been the actual originators of workplace childcare such as Mobile Creches in India (see Chapter 10) but this is rare. Typically, these specialized organizations are already running childcare centres and have extended their services to workplace clients. They sometimes help with setting up and/or

---

[50] OECD, 2004a.
[51] Daune-Richard et al., 2008, p. 68.
[52] Frew, 2004, p. 16.

managing a company childcare centre or their centres may be used by employees of companies that make special arrangements with them, such as reserving places or negotiating discounts.

In the examples in this book, there are a number of establishments which have used the services of childcare specialist organizations to help set up a work-place childcare centre. These childcare organizations have played various roles from advising on spatial set-up and equipment to helping with the recruitment of staff and providing training. This professional advice helps ensure the quality of the centre and that government standards are met in countries where registration or approval is required. In France, since 2007, crèche enterprises can be mandated by companies to undertake the administrative procedures necessary for obtaining subsidies for an inter-enterprise or enterprise crèche. This is expected to encourage greater participation of small and medium enterprises who might otherwise be discouraged by the bureaucratic process.[53]

In some cases, a professional childcare organization has been given the responsibility for actually managing a company or on-site childcare centre (see box 3.13). For-profit childcare companies may be more common in industrialized countries and they have been extending their services (as in the case of Dédy-sitter in Hungary in box 3.13) in order to respond to enterprise needs. In developing countries as well, there are examples of childcare organizations that manage work-place facilities for companies (see the examples of Brazil and India in box 3.13).

Box 3.13 Childcare organizations managing company childcare centres

Brazil. The Centre for Professional Training and Education runs various childcare centres, including centres for a number of companies including Natura.

France. The services of the crèche company Les Petits Chaperons Rouges were used for the creation and management of the inter-company crèche of Aix-les-Milles, which involves 18 private and public partners from the worksite.

Hungary. Dédy-sitter & Baby-sitter is a nanny agency which was selected by IBM Hungary to provide a babysitting service for staff who have childcare emergencies. It is building up a database of childcare centres and childminders that offer back-up care for those employees who prefer out-of-home care.

India. The specialized NGO Nirale helped to design the childcare programme at Wipro in Bangalore and is also running it.

Sources: See country chapters.

---

[53] Daune-Richard et al., 2008.

Another possible type of partnership with specialized providers (be they for-profit or NGOs) is for enterprises to make arrangements to use the providers' existing facilities in the community. As will be seen in more detail in section 4.2, these types of arrangements can be useful not only for preschool children, but also for care of school-age children after school or during holidays. For providers, arrangements with companies may be more secure and long term than their usual arrangements with parents. When companies check out the quality of the providers used by their employees (as in the case of FURNAS in Brazil), this can be an incentive for providers to improve their services.

Childcare NGOs tend to work in the community rather than being workplace focused but their services are still a considerable help to workers. Often they are located in poor areas to serve disadvantaged children. In such cases, the links of NGOs with employers may be more related to requesting charitable donations. The case of Mobile Creches, which specifically targeted a workplace for childcare provision, is rare and it took considerable effort to convince the employers of construction workers to contribute to the crèches. Nevertheless, for NGOs that are running crèches, if the children's parents work in enterprises, these would be a logical source of support given the benefits to the employer.

3.6 Childcare workers

Workplace support for childcare does not always involve any direct relation with childcare workers, as in the case of vouchers or of arrangements with community facilities. Direct partnerships and involvement with childcare workers occur mainly in the case of an on-site facility or one that is operated by the employer, rather than being outsourced as in a number of the examples in this book.

The childcare workers in the cases in Part II vary enormously from those with little education and no training who are working for barely minimum wages in the Nong Nooch Garden in Thailand to the highly trained and well-paid workers in state-of-the-art facilities such as BMW South Africa or the Oswaldo Cruz Foundation in Brazil.

But whatever the level of qualifications of the childcare workers, the success of a facility depends highly on their motivation and skills. A number of case studies emphasized the need not only for qualifications related to childcare but also a real motivation for working with children if the person is going to be able to enjoy their work and give good care to the children. In the case of Melsetter Farm in South Africa, a major lesson learned is that "despite educational limitations in resource-limited settings, childcare workers should be carefully selected to ensure that they are genuinely passionate about children and hence their jobs" (see Chapter 12).

Some of the examples in this book are clearly only continuing to operate because of the devotion of poorly paid workers (such as in Thailand, with the childcare centres at Phra Pradaeng and Nawanakhon industrial zones). As noted in the case of the Zuid-Afrikaans Hospital, "[t]he success of such a facility lies in employing qualified, experienced but most importantly passionate employees to take care of children. It is important that those taking care of children love what they do and do not just see it as a job" (see Chapter 12).

Careful selection of staff was seen in some cases. At BMW South Africa, for example, the company first recruited a well-qualified manager to guide the selection of the other staff. In other cases, the company has taken a childcare consultant to assist or called on the services of an outside specialist organization, as in the case of BHEL in India, which has partnered with the Indian Council for Child Welfare to engage competent staff.

In contrast, in other cases, women with no particular childcare qualification have been taken on as childcare workers: agricultural workers at SOCFINAF in Kenya and trade union committee members at Phra Pradaeng and Nawanakhon industrial zones in Thailand. However, it seems that in these cases the women had at least some secondary education (this was a criterion in Kenya) and received some in-service training. In another case, a number of care workers with low educational levels had refused to attend training (BOWT in Thailand) and parents were complaining about their low level of qualification and also motivation.

In-service training is not only a way of upgrading the skills of the workers but also a source of satisfaction for them as they feel that the company appreciates the importance of their job and they feel themselves better equipped. At the Hungarian Academy of Sciences, a staff member of the crèche expressed her appreciation for the emphasis of management on self-development and continuous learning. An employee at the Phra Pradaeng Metal and Steel Workers Centre in Thailand noted, "Getting to train helps to give me skills I can apply personally and in my work."

Workers who do not receive in-service training feel the need for it. At the Nawanakhon Centre in Thailand, workers with no background in childcare were anxious to improve since they received only one short training session at the beginning. Most of them acquired knowledge through reading and asking teachers in other schools, then applied the knowledge in their teaching. Similarly, at the Nong Nooch Botanical Garden Centre, low-qualified employees who had received no training expressed interest in receiving some.

In cases where in-service training was given, the provider was usually an outside agency. The examples in box 3.14 illustrate the variety of organizations, both public and often NGOs, that are providing this technical assistance to workplace centres. Bringing in a specialist for on-the-job training is another alternative adopted by the Melsetter Farm in South Africa, where workers were being trained by a childcare consultant who visited the facility weekly and was very involved with the day-to-day decisions and training and support for the childcare workers.

Box 3.14 Partnerships for training childcare workers of workplace crèches

Gokaldas, India. At Gokaldas, the training of the workers was undertaken by the NGO, the Indian Council for Child Welfare, and the Karnataka State Council for Child Welfare.

SOCFINAF, Kenya. With company support, caregivers participate in training schemes, such as the national Occupational Safety and Health Environment Programme (OSHEP), or other internal training organized by the SOCFINAF human resources department in collaboration with external facilitators, such as courses on nursing care and ECD programmes, first aid, health and safety at the workplace, social equality and HIV/AIDS at work. In addition, ECD teachers receive support from the company to attend short courses (five weeks) at the District Centres for Early Childhood Education (DICECEs), the decentralized institutions created by the Ministry of Education of Kenya to develop ECD training programmes at the local level.

Zuid-Afrikaans Hospital, South Africa. The principal reports that ongoing development and training of staff is a priority. Teachers belong to the Nursery School Association and attend up to two courses a year to stay abreast with developments.

Phra Pradaeng Metal and Steel Workers Childcare Centre, Thailand. One to three times per year, each member of the teaching staff gets the chance to attend training organized by the Ministry of Social Development and Human Security; once a year, they attend training on nutrition and child development.

Sources: See country chapters.

3.7 International donors

In some of the cases documented in this book, there has been an international partner who has provided some form of support for the childcare initiative. Initiatives by NGOs and trade unions have been more likely to attract outside support than those by employers.

In Thailand, the efforts of the trade unions to set up childcare facilities in industrial areas were supported by outside trade union organizations. In both Nawanakhon and Phra Pradaeng industrial areas, the American trade union federation AFL-CIO provided an interest-free loan to help establish the early childhood centres. The centre in Phra Pradaeng also received some help from Terre des Hommes for initial operating costs.

The example of Red Lands Roses in Kenya is particularly interesting since an employer with relatively low-paid staff on an agricultural plantation producing roses for export, in partnership with another local company, was able to access funds from a German development bank (DEG) to help set up the childcare centre (see box 3.15).

Box 3.15 Donor partnership for enterprise childcare in Kenya

The Gitothua Children & Community Centre was built and run by Red Lands Roses and Pollen Syngenta in the framework of a partnership initiative co-funded by DEG, a German development bank, under its Public Private Partnership (PPP) programme. Its co-funding mechanism provided an initial investment (150,000 euro in this case) to build a community-run project and the companies involved committed to finance the corresponding amount of the initial investment to run the project. The project is managed by a steering committee composed of workers' representatives from the community, Red Lands Roses, Pollen Syngenta and the Max Havelaar Foundation, which awards a fair trade label to the companies.

Source: See Chapter 11.

3.8 Conclusions

This chapter has covered the many partners that are engaged in workplace partnerships for childcare solutions, and has shared examples showing a range of ways that partners engage and work with each other. In both industrialized and developing countries, the involvement of the partners is partly shaped by the framework set by government: whether it legally obliges childcare support on the part of the employer as in the cases of Brazil, Chile and India, or offers fiscal incentives for employers to undertake initiatives as in the cases of France, the United Kingdom and the United States, or has other ways of subsidizing either facilities or parents.

Beyond that context, however, there is considerable scope for the partners to better leverage their unique positions and constituencies for childcare solutions that meet the needs of employers and workers. Relatively few examples were found of trade union or employer action at the national level to shape laws, policies and programmes related to childcare and early education. And while a number of employers, trade unions, municipalities and childcare providers are experimenting with innovative ways of solving workers' needs for childcare, for the most part these are not yet widespread.

Partners in childcare solutions often come to the table with very different objectives and contributions: this can be a great source of strength but can also pose some challenges. For example, municipalities come with funds and a mandate for providing community services that can complement well employers' efforts to provide childcare supports for workers. But municipalities using tax dollars need to serve their residents while enterprises often hire from broader geographical pools, and the logistics of meeting all needs can become complicated. As another example, all partners aim for quality care, but employers and working parents wish to keep costs reasonable, while childcare workers require adequate pay and training opportunities, and these needs must be balanced.

Successful partnerships often bring together actors that offer complementary financial, human and technical contributions, but the sustainability of the entire initiative can be threatened when one partner must withdraw. Finding ways to nurture partnerships and strengthen their sustainability is an important project that would benefit from strong policy frameworks and clear agreements among partnering organizations. In the words of a trade union representative involved in the SNPE partnership in France:

> A key lesson learned is that difficulties [in partnering] should not discourage action, especially if the project is solid. It is important to accurately identify the actual needs and put together all partners' competences and strengths in order to provide high-quality services to both children and parents.

Key points

A number of actors are involved in childcare, bringing different motivations, needs and resources:

Governments

- In countries with more market-based approaches to childcare, public authorities are more likely to look to employers as a source of childcare support.

- It is questionable whether legislation providing a crèche benefit for women workers in companies employing a certain number of women (as exists in some countries) is promoting equality in the labour market.

- Employer contributions to childcare through social security systems are less likely to lead to discrimination against women or parents.

- A number of governments in developed countries offer subsidies or tax exemptions to encourage workplace support to childcare with varying degrees of success.

- Systems whereby a part of workers' salary which is used for care expenses can be tax exempted have relatively high take-up among large companies since there is no cost to the employer.

Employers and their organizations

- Employers provide childcare support often for reasons of business strategy because they recognize benefits in attracting and retaining staff, reducing absenteeism and generally improving productivity.

- Employers are sometimes reticent about childcare because they perceive workplace facilities as costly while overlooking other alternatives.

- Employer organizations and groups in some countries have engaged in policy advocacy to improve government measures for workers' childcare.

Trade unions

- Some trade unions have played a major role in raising the issue of childcare and obtaining childcare benefits, through collective bargaining and also directly with individual employers.

- Some trade union federations have publications providing guidance on bargaining for childcare.

- Trade unions have been involved in policy dialogue and have helped improve childcare accessibility for all workers.

- Trade unions have been organizing childcare workers in an effort to improve their conditions of work as well as the quality of childcare.

- Although rare, a few trade unions have set up their own childcare facilities.

Municipalities

- In many countries, responsibility for childcare provision has been decentralized to municipalities, thus making them useful partners for workplace initiatives.

Professional childcare organizations

- Organizations specializing in childcare provision are increasingly providing professional support to the establishment and/or operation of workplace facilities.

- In some cases, employers negotiate with childcare providers so staff can use existing facilities under advantageous conditions.

Childcare workers

- The success of a workplace centre depends not only on the qualifications of its staff but their motivation and love of their job.

- Careful recruitment, decent wages and working conditions and opportunities for training are critical factors for retaining childcare workers and improving childcare quality.

International donors

- The support of international donors for workplace-linked childcare seems to be rare but there are some examples in the book.

Workplace solutions 4

This chapter reviews how workplaces are responding to the various childcare needs of working parents using numerous examples from secondary sources and also the chapters in Part II. The types of assistance are presented according to the categories given in the Introduction:

- company or on-site facility;

- facility in the community which is linked to the workplace;

- monetary support through allowances, reimbursements, vouchers or tax savings; and

- advice and referral services.

These types of assistance typically help parents access regular childcare for children of different ages. However, they can also be used to help parents access back-up care when their child is sick or their regular arrangement breaks down. However, since back-up care requires different measures from regular childcare, a final separate section on back-up care is included.

For each type of childcare assistance, examples are given for children of both preschool and school age and its advantages and disadvantages are discussed from the points of view of employers and workers. At the end of the chapter, table 4.2 summarizes the advantages and disadvantages of the different types of workplace support, indicating when they are most appropriate.

4.1 Company or on-site facilities

This section starts by looking at company childcare facilities, at or near the workplace. It continues by considering workplace facilities for older children, since company facilities at the workplace are not always limited to preschool children. And finally, because on-site facilities for workers' children are not always at the initiative of their employer, initiatives being taken by other partners (trade unions, municipalities, zone authorities, NGOs) to provide on-site childcare for workers are considered.

Facilities for preschoolers

A company facility at or near the workplace for the care of workers' preschool children (variously called crèche, nursery, daycare, kindergarten or childcare centre) is probably the best-known form of workplace support. In the search for cases for this book, workplace centres provided by a company were the easiest examples to find, particularly in the developing countries where other types of arrangements seemed to be rare.

The age of the children covered by company childcare centres is highly variable. In Brazil, France, India, Kenya, South Africa and Thailand, for example, a number of the facilities documented take babies. This can be particularly important for women workers to be able to return to work and continue breast-feeding after maternity leave. In France, the maximum age accepted is often 4, perhaps because full-day public pre-primary schooling is freely available at this age. In contrast, BMW South Africa provides an early learning centre for children age 3–5 as a way of helping employees with the education and school preparation of their children.

Apart from regular care for enrolled children, some workplace centres can also be used for emergency back-up care, although this service seems to be relatively rare and mainly informal when it exists. The crèches being set up recently in France seem to be the most flexible in terms of offering regular, occasional and part-time care. Most workplace centres run on a fixed full-day basis to fit the working hours of parents. Nevertheless, in a number of cases, staff of the centre complained of problems of parents coming late to pick up their children.

Which companies?

Company childcare centres, either on-site or close to the workplace, tend to be found in companies that have a large number of workers concentrated at one site. Some of the examples in this book are large businesses which have located the crèche at or near their headquarters where many workers are employed, such as Infosys in India and the First National Bank headquarters in South Africa.

When organizations with large numbers of workers are located in relatively isolated rural areas where there are few services, the benefits of a crèche can be considerable. In this book, there is the SNPE case in a rural area of France where residential growth has outpaced growth in services, including childcare. Also there are cases of on-site crèches for agricultural workers on two plantations in Kenya, Melsetter Wine Farm in South Africa and Nong Nooch Botanical Garden in Thailand.

Companies where many workers are working atypical hours which do not correspond to the opening hours of community facilities are also more likely to set up their own crèche. In the case of the inter-enterprise crèche at Rennes Atalante, the needs of low-income workers with irregular and atypical hours such as office cleaners, nurses and bus drivers were a major driving factor for the initiative. In the United States, for example, hospitals have been the pioneers for workplace facilities given the need to ensure continuous 24-hour services. That a high proportion of staff are women is also a likely factor.[1] Two hospitals are among the cases for South Africa and the United Kingdom.

Employer partnerships

In some cases, a number of employers in the same locality have shared a child-care centre in order to achieve economies of scale, given that none of them would have enough demand to justify a company nursery. In countries where governments encourage enterprise initiatives, employers in partnerships can usually benefit from the same incentives or tax exemptions as a company on its own. In the United Kingdom, for example, employers who join with other employers and help to finance and run a shared nursery get the same tax rebates as for a company crèche.

In France, recent legislative measures have sought to encourage enterprise crèches as well as "inter-enterprise" crèches where different employers in a locality

---

[1] Friedman, n.d.

reserve places. According to a French specialist in crèche management, even large enterprises often prefer to be part of a group as this is more reassuring for sustainability.[2] He notes that, for an inter-enterprise project, it is good to have one or two large enterprises which drive the project, reserve a substantial number of places and motivate smaller enterprises in the locality to join. The case study at Rennes Atalante in France provides an example of a group of enterprises in the transportation, health and information and communication technology (ICT) sectors that established a crèche together with local authorities.

While the benefits of employers joining together to create a crèche are evident, in practice examples of joint employer initiatives seem to be rare both in the literature and in our case studies. The only examples in this book are in France, where *inter-entreprise* crèches are a recent phenomenon encouraged by government measures but are still quite rare. These are interesting experiences but it is too soon to assess the extent to which enterprises are willing to participate in inter-enterprise crèches and the sustainability of the partnerships on which they are based. In other countries, where a number of employers are using the same crèche, it is often an outside organization that has set up the crèche such as a zone authority, a trade union or an employers' organization rather than being a partnership of employers (see the examples below under *On-site childcare organized by others*).

Financing

In financial terms, workplace centres require space and can be expensive to set up and run. The cost for the employer depends on the public assistance available for the capital investment and operating expenses, the amount of fees paid by employees and the requirements of the national standards for such facilities. Operating costs can be high and careful analysis of the initial and operating costs, worker needs and demand, income and benefits is necessary.

The country in this study with the most advantageous government incentives for creating workplace centres (crèches) is France, where measures are recent, dating from 2004. Taking the case of the enterprises that have reserved places in the Calaïs crèche at Rennes Atalante Science and Technology Park (Beaulieu), the gross annual employer contribution for each childcare place is 5,000 euro, about one-third of total cost. Parents' contributions cover about 20 per cent while the remainder is covered mainly by the family branch of social security (CAF, to which

---

[2] Interview with Jean-Emmanuel Rodocanachi, Directeur General, Les Petits Chaperons Rouges, in *CE Actualités*, No. 59, July 2006.

all employers contribute) as well as contributions from local authorities. Since the employers benefit from a tax credit on their contribution and from other subsidies, the actual annual cost to them is 2,200 euro, only 14 per cent of the actual cost.

Workers tend to pay somewhat lower fees for an enterprise crèche than for similar facilities available in the community because there is usually some enterprise subsidy. However, for workers on low salaries, this may still be too much of their earnings and they will not use it. In countries such as the United Kingdom and the United States, government subsidies for low-income workers operate side-by-side with tax exemptions for better-paid workers, extending public support for both groups. Some employers establish fees on a sliding scale that sets lower fees for low-income workers. Barts and the London NHS Trust, for example, use the employer savings resulting from the salary sacrifice system (see Chapter 14) to subsidize fees for low earners.[3] The rules governing subsidized enterprise crèches in France also provide for sliding fee scales.

In some cases, almost all of the cost of the childcare centre is assumed by the employer, with employees paying little or no fee, such as the SOCFINAF coffee plantations in Kenya. When there is a legal obligation for employers to provide a crèche, it is usually free for workers. In Brazil, for example, workers do not usually contribute financially to the crèche, as in the cases of Natura Company and the Oswaldo Cruz Foundation. Similarly at Gokaldas Images and Bharat Heavy Electricals Ltd (BHEL) in India, both of which come under the legal requirement to provide a crèche, workers pay virtually no fee.

Some companies increase the income of their nursery by allowing children from the community to attend if there is excess space, as in the case of the Hungarian Academy of Sciences which charges a higher fee to outsiders.

Management

For the management of workplace crèches, some employers run the facilities themselves while others outsource the management to a specialized organization.

In industrialized countries such as France, the United Kingdom and the United States, there are increasing numbers of professional providers of childcare, both for-profit and not-for-profit, offering management services to employers. Outsourcing relieves the company of the responsibility for managing the crèche, an undertaking that they typically know little about and which is not related

---

[3] UNISON, 2004.

to their core business. Nevertheless, there still has to be some mechanism for oversight of the provider.

The cases from developing countries suggest that outsourcing the management of a workplace nursery is less common – perhaps because there are fewer organizations proposing this service. Nevertheless, examples do exist, such as Natura in Brazil, the University of Concepción in Chile and Wipro in India in this book. Similarly, Johnson & Johnson in the Philippines, which provides a full-time daycare centre on its premises, delegates the management to a private service provider.[4]

Among the examples of company childcare facilities in this book, the company is managing the childcare facility itself in the majority of cases. Some employers, like hospitals, may feel they have the internal resources and services to cope. Where a company or organization runs its own childcare centre, it can use its own staff and resources on an ongoing basis to support the childcare centre. In a number of cases, existing canteen and medical facilities at the company were used by the nursery. Companies also have services that can help set up, operate and maintain the nursery, such as purchasing, maintenance, gardening, accounting/auditing, counselling, hiring, training, legal services and engineering.

Such establishments (the Royal Marsden Hospital, United Kingdom, for example) prefer to run the nursery themselves, concerned that outsourcing would lead to lower-quality care and higher costs for the workers. In contrast, others may see outsourcing to professionals as a way of improving quality. An intermediate model, as seen in the cases of the Melsetter Farm in South Africa and Infosys in India, is to have a childcare consultant who monitors and advises on the facility which is run by the company.

In the cases in this book, it is usually the human resources department (HRD) which is responsible for the operation of the childcare centre whether it is outsourced or internally run. In some cases the HRD relies on advisory boards for direction and input. This is the case at the Oswaldo Cruz Foundation in Brazil, where HRD consults with a Parents' Advisory Council on discussions and decisions for the crèche, and at Melsetter Farm in South Africa, where HR consults a board comprised of parents and management. At Infosys in India, a committee including management, parents, a childcare consultant and the crèche director meets weekly.

In some cases, the actual management of the crèche is by a committee. At AEROTHAI in Thailand, the crèche is managed by the Welfare Management Committee, composed of managers, union nominees and members elected by

---

[4] Caparas, 2008, p. 40.

employees. At the National Centre for Biological Sciences in Bangalore, a committee made up of crèche users and management oversees the budget of the facility, including the employment of staff.

Another management formula is to create a separate legal entity which is responsible for the crèche and its operation. A study of work-related childcare centres in Canada found that the sponsoring employer was rarely the legal entity running the centre and most were independent organizations with their own board of directors.[5] Such cases are rare in the examples in this book, one being the University of Concepción in Chile, which relies on an independent unit to provide the childcare services for its staff through coordination with its HR department.

Advantages of company nursery

For an overview of the advantages and disadvantages of each type of childcare assistance, see table 4.2 at the end of this chapter. Working parents appreciate workplace childcare for a number of reasons (see box 4.1). They can be close to their children and can come quickly in the case of emergency. They are able to spend more time with their children and avoid the time lost in dropping them somewhere before work and picking them up after work. Workplace nurseries are particularly helpful for mothers who are breastfeeding and want to continue to do so after their return to work. In communities where childcare is difficult to find, a workplace nursery makes it much easier for parents to find a childcare solution. Indeed, in some of the case studies, workers indicated that they or their spouses would have had to quit their jobs had there not been the workplace crèche (Gokaldas and Infosys, India; Nong Nooch, Thailand). In Thailand, the crèche at the Nawanakhon industrial area made it possible for workers to keep their children with them rather than sending them back to grandparents in the provinces.

Workers were also appreciative of the effects of the childcare facility on their children's development. In Thailand, workers using the Metal and Steel Workers Union's daycare in the Phra Pradaeng Industrial Zone noted that they felt that the children's development was better than when they were left with grandparents. At Wipro in India, employees felt that, in addition to being looked after, the children benefited from all-round development due to the educational activities organized at the crèche. Teachers and parents of children enrolled in the Melsetter Wine Farm in South Africa found that the children were well prepared once they started primary education and progressed faster than other students.

---

[5] Barbeau, 2001, p. 17.

Box 4.1 Parents' reasons for appreciating on-site care

National Health Service, UK. In a study of parents working in the NHS, many parents said that they preferred to have childcare provided at their place of work, particularly because if there was an emergency or their child was sick they could get there quickly.

NCR Corporation Retail Solutions Group, Georgia, US. For most parents, the convenience and security of having their children play in the same building are the most popular reasons that employees use the on-site daycare centre. The centre has workstations for mothers with newborns, so that they can work just steps away from their baby and nurse them throughout the day. It is felt that the centre has improved NCR's return rate among mothers out on maternity leave.

Gedeon Richter, Hungary. A parent notes that the crèche helps communication at work as parents get to know each other. The parents also note that they feel secure knowing their children are nearby.

Sources: For NHS, see Frew, 2004, p. 13. For NCR, see "Company daycare gets high marks." August 2003. Available at http://www.wikigwinnett.com/content.cfm?Action=wiki&WikiID=2668 [16 June 2009]. For Gedeon Richter, see Chapter 9.

When a significant number of staff work shifts or atypical hours during which it is difficult to find childcare in the community, a company crèche can make a big difference to them. Billie, a single mother of a 6-year-old, used to work the early shift on Toyota's assembly line in the United States, but when she was promoted, she had to work nights. Toyota's 24-hour childcare centre enabled her to accept the position as no other childcare in the area covered these hours.[6] The Rennes Atalante Science and Technology Park inter-enterprise crèche example from Chapter 8 was a response to the needs of working parents whose atypical working hours posed serious challenges for finding care.

From the point of view of managers, the main benefits of on-site nurseries include decreased stress and better concentration on the part of workers, improved loyalty and commitment, lower turnover and less absenteeism. Managers also see benefits from a positive image, better industrial relations and a positive workplace environment and culture.

Few employers with childcare centres seem to have actually made a cost–benefit analysis. Possible benefits like less stress and greater commitment to the firm are understandably difficult to estimate. However, absenteeism is easier to

---

[6] Public Broadcasting Service, n.d. Corporate Childcare on *That Money Show* at http://www.pbs.org/wnet/moneyshow/cover/011201.html [11 June 2009].

measure. In the case of Red Lands Roses in Kenya, for example, since the crèche opened in May 2006, unplanned leave had decreased by 25 per cent in the year following its opening in 2006, and was continuing to decrease. While managers at Nong Nooch Botanical Garden in Thailand did not have specific estimates, they also reported a strong link between the childcare facility and lower absentee rates and less tardiness. Managers in other companies in the current study reported that the childcare facility was playing a role in attracting and retaining staff, as in the cases of Infosys in India and Old Mutual Bank in South Africa.

In order to compare the effects of an on-site crèche with other types of child-care support, a survey of human resource professionals in the United States asked what impact they thought various types of childcare support had on the attraction and retention of employees. As can be seen in table 4.1, 41 per cent of those whose company had on-site childcare thought it had a high impact on attraction of staff compared to only 5 per cent of those with referral and resource services and 9 per cent of those with emergency back-up care services. For retention of employees, the result was similar. This result suggests that although the on-site facility can be expensive, it can also have more impact on turnover and on attracting new employees than other less expensive options.

Table 4.1 Perceived impact of care support on the attraction and retention of employees: US survey of human resource professionals

		Degree of impact (per cent of those with programme)			
		None	Low	Moderate	High
On-site childcare	Attraction	7	16	37	41
	Retention	5	19	33	43
Dependent care referral and resource services	Attraction	28	52	16	5
	Retention	29	47	20	4
Emergency back-up dependent care services	Attraction	16	42	33	9
	Retention	17	31	39	12

Source: World at Work, 2007, p. 2.

In some cases, the management feels that a workplace childcare facility creates a good atmosphere at the workplace. One CEO remarks: "It's nice to see groups of children walking around outside the building on sunny days and in the cafeteria having lunch with their parents. It's surprising how much good feeling this creates."[7]

---

[7] Bright Horizons, 2003. Ron Sargent, President and CEO of Staples, Inc. Found at http://www.brighthorizons.com/SolutionsAtWork/article.aspx?articleid=140 [10 August 2008].

Some companies seem to be less concerned about financial benefits, seeing the crèche as part of fulfilling their corporate social responsibility. For example, BMW in South Africa feels it is providing the children of its workers with better educational opportunities than they would otherwise have.

Disadvantages

For workers, possible disadvantages of a workplace childcare centre include the logistics of commuting with children to work, pressures to stay at work longer and being tied to the employer when other alternatives are lacking.

Commuting to work with children can be difficult when the commute is long, unsafe or uncomfortable, for example taking a number of hot and dusty buses, walking long distances or going through polluted or unsafe areas. Many parents prefer care that is close to home. The experience of the Royal Marsden in England, for example, suggests that, compared to a suburban context, there is less demand for workplace nurseries in large cities like London where many workers have long commuting times and it is more difficult to travel to work with the child. Also when parents work at night, they sometimes prefer home care rather than bringing the child to a centre.

Another possible disadvantage is that when employers have helped finance a crèche near the workplace which closes late, employees with young children may face direct or indirect pressure from managers to stay beyond normal working hours, to the detriment of the child who spends too long in the crèche away from parents. Also, for parents using a workplace nursery, it may be difficult to change jobs if alternative care arrangements are not easily available, with the result that they become tied to the employer.

For employers, on-site care is usually (though not always) expensive and it is difficult to predict demand as the demographic profile of the workforce changes. In a few of our case studies, nursery facilities were under capacity, either because workers' needs and demographics had changed, or because other alternatives were emerging that were more attractive (for example, Gokaldas and BHEL, India; BMW, South Africa; BOWT, Thailand). Nurseries that do not have sufficient places for all the eligible children of staff may end up with long waiting lists, resulting in frustration for those whose children do not get in. Or if demand from staff is far below capacity, the financial sustainability may be in question. One of the advantages of sharing with other employers can be to have some flexibility on the number of places that each company subsidizes in any particular year. All these considerations point to the need for careful needs and impact assessments, an issue discussed further in Chapter 5.

For companies with a workforce spread over several sites, a nursery may be conveniently located only for a limited number of staff and this could create internal feelings of injustice since some get assistance while others do not. At Wipro in India as well as the First National Bank in Johannesburg, pressure was being put on the company to provide facilities in more locations, given that existing facilities were not accessible for many staff. Some companies with on-site facilities make provision for those who cannot use it by reserving places in other nurseries (see, for example, Magyar Telekom), providing daycare stipends (Oswaldo Cruz Foundation, Brazil) or having some sort of voucher system (NHS, United Kingdom).

For employers, setting up their own centre may be seen as too complicated because of legal issues, insurance matters or standards. An employer study in the United Kingdom found that among the most common reasons for not offering direct provision of childcare was reluctance to take responsibility for a childcare provider.[8] In Australia, Deloitte has asserted:

> The cost of an [on-site childcare facility] and the associated administration costs will usually outweigh the benefits for most employers. ... The administration and risks associated with government regulations and industry accreditations in operating and managing a child care facility are significant.[9]

Outsourcing may be a way of avoiding this risk depending on the legal provisions in each country.

In countries with strong regulations for nursery facilities, it can be quite complicated to find and set up appropriate premises near the workplace. In Vancouver, Canada, there was considerable controversy when Syscon Justice Systems, a software company, was permitted to set up an on-site crèche which did not have an outside play area as required by regulations.[10] In the United Kingdom, the Brighton and Sussex University Hospitals NHS Trust found that setting up a nursery was complicated due to tight regulations around the quality of buildings, the range of activities provided, training the staff, and regulated staff-to-child ratios.[11] And a study of workplace childcare centres in Canada found that, in the majority of the cases studied, childcare centres took between 18 months and three years to complete.[12] Magyar Telekom in Hungary has circumvented this problem by buying an already operational nursery.

---

[8] Kazimirski et al., 2006.

[9] Australia, House Standing Committee on Family and Human Services, 2006, p. 240.

[10] Woolley, 2007.

[11] UNISON, 2004.

[12] Barbeau, 2001, p. 14.

Company facilities for school-age children

On-site facilities for schoolchildren are less common than for preschoolers but do exist, particularly for after-school hours or for covering emergencies. In some cases, it is the on-site nursery facility itself that looks after young schoolchildren after school or in emergencies. At Wipro in India, for example, the after-school scheme has proved to be quite popular as parents find it difficult to find reliable caregivers to look after their children at home and the company is thinking of expanding activities to include school vacation times. However, in some cases, providing care for school-age children using nursery facilities may not be effective. For example, BMW South Africa found that allowing older children to come to the childcare centre after school was too disruptive for the younger children and the practice was stopped.

In countries where after-school care is not readily available, children may turn up at work to wait for parents or parents may leave work early to look after their children. To help solve such problems and show some understanding for the predicament of employees, some companies have set aside a room where children can go after school while they wait for their parents (see box 4.2).

Saturday work by parents may also pose a childcare problem. In Mumbai, the bank ICICI started a Saturday Kids Club at its Bandra Kurla office to attend to the children of employees who come to work on Saturdays. Average attendance in 2002 was over 25 children.[13]

Some companies open their childcare centres to schoolchildren during school holidays. In Thailand, few workers seem to use this possibility, perhaps because there is a fee, and thus they prefer to leave children in the care of older siblings. The crèche at the National Centre for Biological Sciences in India organizes activities for the school-age children of workers during summer holidays, which are very popular with employees. In the Philippines, Johnson & Johnson offers a summer programme on company premises for children of employees, in which children participate in art lessons, dance and other activities.[14]

A few companies actually run camps for the children of employees during school holidays, as in the cases of Hungarian Post and IBM in Hungary. As described in the IBM Hungary case study, this large multinational even has international camps for children of employees from different countries. In the case of Hungarian Post, the idea of having a camp is inherited from the socialist era, but the camp has been kept while trying to put it on a more sustainable financial

---

[13] Chakravorty, 2002.
[14] Caparas, 2008, p. 41.

Box 4.2 A children's room at the workplace

Computer Associates, Denmark. This company has a special room available where children can play computer games and do other activities. By having this room available, the company aims to signal to its employees that it is legitimate to bring their children to work if there is a problem with childcare.

SP Consulting International Pte Ltd, Singapore. Following an informal discussion, SP Consulting, which has eight employees, chose to convert office space into a family room, allowing staff to bring their young children to the office when home care is not available. Older children can also use the room for before- or after-school activities, where parents can supervise their homework. Employees feel good that senior management show keen interest in the well-being of their children. SP Consulting saw a 12 per cent improvement in their quota-based revenue generation in 2005.

Sources: Denmark, Family and Work Commission, 2007; Singapore, Ministry of Manpower, 2006, p. 81.

---

footing. The company tendered to find a hotel to house the camp and has a special relationship with a local school for finding staff among teachers.

Companies are more likely, however, to link up with community facilities and camps to provide support during school holidays than to run their own programmes. Establishing summer programmes can be challenging, as found by childcare coordinators in the NHS, United Kingdom, who tried to set up in-house play schemes for the holidays: recruiting staff, getting official registration and other official requirements proved hard work.[15]

On-site childcare organized by others

Childcare facilities at or near the workplace are not always the responsibility of the employer. A number of examples have been found of workplace childcare centres initiated by trade unions, employers' organizations or NGOs. These examples tend to be located where there is a concentration of enterprises, like industrial zones, business parks, airports or shopping malls.

Among the cases in this book are two trade union initiatives from Thailand to open childcare centres in the industrial zones with heavy concentrations of factories and workers' residences. In both Nawanakhon and Phra Pradaeng

---

[15] Frew, 2004.

industrial areas in Thailand, the unions mobilized considerable funds from the workers as well as from local and international organizations. Currently, these centres are filled beyond capacity. A considerable portion of operating expenses comes from parents' fees, so there is a tendency to accept a high number of children. Funding the centres primarily on the basis of parental fees is difficult in any context, and in these cases, the devotion of poorly paid staff has been a major factor sustaining these centres.

Employers' organizations have also organized childcare in industrial zones: an example in this book comes from the Peenya Industries Association of the Peenya industrial complex in India. In this case, the crèche was constructed as part of a large project to improve the infrastructure in the complex, with funding from the national and state governments as well as a contribution from the zone employers.

In some cases, it is the promoter or the authority responsible for the zone which has taken the lead in providing childcare facilities. In Ireland, for example, the IDA, which develops business and technological parks, has incorporated a crèche in the plans of some sites, as a way of enhancing the sites' attraction for companies (see box 4.3). Similarly, the company which owns the Business Park near Orly airport in Paris considers the crèche to be a basic facility which companies would expect to find in such a zone (see box 4.3).

Airports are a very special kind of area where there are workers from a number of companies or administrations, many working on shifts with atypical hours. On-site childcare for workers' children is increasingly being made available at airports: the example of the childcare centre organized by the Civil Aviation Authority of Singapore is given in box 4.3.

Commercial centres and malls also may incorporate crèches for those working in the shops. In the Canadian example in box 4.3, the nursery is a somewhat philanthropic project of the owner of the commercial centre. Despite contributions by the owner and the childcare NGO, the centre has had difficulty surviving financially on the fees the parents can pay. In Chile, the law requiring employers of 20 or more women to provide childcare for children under age 2 years was extended to include shopping malls in 1995. One of the Chile examples is the Plaza Vespucio Mall facility, set up to comply with this law.

There are also cases of non-profit organizations that have developed childcare facilities near to the workplace so low-income parents can work while being assured that their children are in a safe, healthy environment. Usually the workers involved are low paid and in informal activities such as street vending or market selling. Their children are suffering from poor care while their parents work and, in some cases, become child labourers once they are old enough to help their

---

Box 4.3 On-site crèches in zones and centres

The Industrial Development Agency (IDA), Ireland. As part of the basic infra-structure of some of its more recent Business and Technological Parks, the IDA has built on-site crèches, one in each park. The crèches are run by private provider companies that liaise with employers and workers. The existence of an operational crèche is advertised as one of the advantages for businesses to locate in the parks.

Business Park, Orly-Rungis, France. M. Vene, regional director of SILIC, the company which owns the business park next to Orly airport, notes in an inter-view that the crèche is part of the facilities required to attract new businesses to the park and satisfy the needs of the current clients. The crèche is run by a professional organization, Les Petits Chaperons Rouges, in a locale owned by SILIC, for which the installation costs were subsidized by the CAF and the regional government. The crèche is used by Aeroports de Paris, Corsair and the Préfecture (regional administration) of Val-de-Marne.

The Civil Aviation Authority of Singapore (CAAS). The authority has a child-care centre located within the airport to cater for the airport community, which includes about 30,000 workers. The centre, which is operated by the private com-pany Learning Vision, provides comprehensive services ranging from toddler pro-grammes, nursery, kindergarten and enrichment programmes. While the centre operates on a typical pattern of 7.00 a.m.–7.00 p.m. (Mondays to Fridays) and 7.00 a.m.–1.00 p.m. (Saturdays), it also operates on extended hours as it provides back-up care services for parents who may need such a quality childcare service.

Owner of 401 Richmond Inc., Toronto, Canada. When the owner of this ware-house in downtown Toronto converted it into a leased cultural and commercial centre, she included a childcare centre. Most of the 130 tenants were self-employed women, mainly in the arts and culture fields, who did not qualify for Employment Insurance when they took maternity leave and faced the challenge of having to return to work within a few months after childbirth. The centre was set up and run by an NGO, the Canadian Mothercraft Society (CMS).

Sources: For Ireland, see http://www.idaireland.com/locations/business-technology-parks/athlone [29 June 2009]. For SILIC Orly, see http://www.planetefacility.com/index.php?id=676 [16 June 2009]. For Singapore, see Sharif, 2007. For Toronto, see Barbeau, 2001.

---

parents. An NGO childcare programme for workers with an employer is that of Mobile Creches in India, which has created on-site childcare for the children of construction workers, of which about 30 per cent are women (see box 10.2 in Chapter 10). Strong and persistent fund-raising, both locally and internationally, has been a major factor in the survival of Mobile Creches.

On-site childcare centres in industrial zones, business parks or malls provide access to childcare for workers in companies that would not normally provide any on-site childcare on their own. The enterprises or organizations in the zone benefit from childcare facilities without the risks and hassles of organizing a facility. Their financial contribution may be more-or-less voluntary depending on the modalities set up by the organizer. This type of joint on-site childcare can be a key way for small and medium enterprises to help support workers with childcare needs. As with company on-site childcare, the interest of workers will depend on their travel arrangements for bringing children to work as well as the cost, convenience, suitability and quality of the care compared to any other options available to them.

4.2 Linking with facilities in the community

Rather than childcare at or near the workplace, workers often prefer to use childcare that is close to home. There are many different ways that enterprises can help workers access the childcare they need in the community.

Preschool children

Negotiating discounts for their workers with local providers is a common strategy used by employers in many industrialized countries (see the example of the Royal Marsden Hospital, United Kingdom, in Chapter 14). Just as some companies may negotiate discounts for employees for health facilities or restaurants, discounts can also be negotiated with childcare providers. Discounts tend to be in the range of 10 to 15 per cent. Companies with many employees are likely to be in a stronger bargaining position but this could still be feasible for smaller companies.

Reserving or buying places with a nursery in the locality is another option for employers. For example, a childcare centre in Dearborn, Michigan, receives seed money from Ford Motor Co. for staff, educational materials, extended operating hours and preferential enrolment for Ford families. Six open slots are also reserved for Ford-salaried employees for back-up childcare in emergencies.[16] In the Philippines, Indo Phil Textile Manufacturing arranged with a local childcare centre for employees, particularly those on the night shift, to drop off children and provided fee subsidies.[17] Among the cases in this book, Magyar Telekom in Hungary has signed an agreement with four private kindergartens to reserve

---

[16] Information found at http://www.mycareer.ford.com [20 August 2008].
[17] Employers' Confederation of the Philippines (ECOP), 2004.

places for Telekom children who are not able to use its main nursery. Employees are required to make official applications for childcare places well in advance in an effort to avoid reserving (or having to pay for) places that are not used.

Improving the availability and quality of facilities in the community seems an unlikely concern of employers, but a number of companies have taken such initiatives (see box 4.4). The Employers' Child Care Alliance of 17 employers in the US state of Alabama has developed programmes to upgrade the qualifications of staff in childcare centres used by employees and helped centres progress towards accreditation. Apart from the contributions of member employers, the Alliance has also been able to attract grants and support from the State of Alabama and from private foundations.[18] In Brazil, FURNAS, which provides childcare subsidies, has a system of accreditation for crèches to be eligible and assesses the quality of services provided. Since workers must use accredited crèches to be eligible for daycare reimbursement, the quality of childcare centres in the region has improved.

Box 4.4 Employers' efforts to improve the quality of childcare

Employers' Child Care Alliance, Alabama, US. Based on a needs assessment survey and with the assistance of the local Child Care Resource Center, the Alliance has worked to develop programmes to enhance the quality of childcare options in the local community. The Quality Enhancement Partnership (QEP) matches a local business/employer sponsor with a childcare programme where employees' children spend the day. The programme consists of child development training for teachers and staff and an innovative STEPS to Accreditation programme that provides support and assistance to help them advance towards national accreditation.

Ford Motor Co., Michigan, US. To improve the quality of family daycare homes in south-eastern Michigan, Ford has a programme which loans educational materials, toys and games to daycare homes and centres providing childcare for Ford families.

Sources: For the Employers' Child Care Alliance, information found at http://www.auburnalabama.org/childsurvey/ChildCareTaskForceReport.pdf [29 June 2009]. For Ford, information found at http://www.mycareer.ford.com [20 August 2008].

Texas Instruments in the United States also decided to invest its childcare support funds to improve the quality of existing centres by underwriting health and safety training programmes and offering free management consulting expertise. Since its 11,000 workers were spread among three separate areas, the company

---

[18] Valdejão and Purvinni, 2008.

felt more workers would profit from support to community childcare than from a company centre that wouldn't be conveniently located for everyone. The company also worked with local community colleges to recruit students to alleviate the chronic shortage of daycare workers.[19]

In the United Kingdom, organizations and companies such as NHS trusts and police authorities have linked with local authorities to improve the quality of care provided by childminders. For organizations with many staff on shifts, childminders can be a useful childcare option. These organizations have been developing networks of childminders which are managed by a coordinator who gives advice and training to build skills and monitors regularly their work. Some NHS trusts provide short training programmes for childminder networks on health concerns.[20]

Thus, employers have been linking to care facilities in the community in a great variety of ways, both to improve access for their employees and to improve the quality of the care that is locally available. The next section looks at links to help with the care of school-age children.

School-age children

To help with care during school holidays and before- and after-school care, linking up with community facilities can be a cost-effective strategy for workplace support.

School holiday camps

For school holidays, one of the most common types of community facilities is camps, with some being residential and others being on a daily basis, often based in schools. Employers have sometimes negotiated with camps to make special arrangements for the children of their staff, often negotiating discounts as in the case of Magyar Telekom in box 4.5. In Bangalore, BHEL made arrangements with the Sports Authority of India for employees' children to attend activities during the school holidays and provided transport to and from the crèche. Similarly, the Royal Marsden has made arrangements with a local holiday play scheme (box 4.5).

---

[19] Kiger, 2004, pp. 34–40.
[20] Sure Start/National Childminding Association, 2005.

Box 4.5 Linking with existing camps

Magyar Telekom, Hungary. The company looked for good-quality operating camps and signed a general contract with selected camps on the level of discount for its employees in relation to regular prices. The average discount was about 10–15 per cent. It then provided information about camps to employees. Parents decided on the camp and made their own payments. A system to provide a subsidy is currently being put in place.

Royal Marsden Hospital, UK. For school holidays, the childcare coordinator has a special arrangement with a holiday play scheme run at a school near the hospital by Kensington and Chelsea Community Play, a service of the borough. In addition, discounts at various summer camps are available to staff.

Sources: See country chapters.

Before- and after-school programmes

Lack of before- and after-school care is a difficult problem to address directly through workplace strategies. In the case of the NHS, United Kingdom, lack of after-school care was acknowledged as a reason why some parents were forced to change their working hours or to rely on informal support. But it was difficult to envisage any particular NHS facility which would meet this need since staff tend to be from a wide geographical area and any service would need to be near the child's home or school rather than the workplace.[21]

Poor families are particularly affected as they cannot afford the multiple coping strategies used by middle-income families, such as child-sitters before school and after school, extra-curricular activities or vacation camps. An interesting example of an employer promoting after-school care in a poor community is the case of BHP Billiton in Trinidad and Tobago. The company established a homework centre in a rural area, Toco, as part of its community outreach programme. The centre employs five people, three of whom are teachers. It is available to children of the community, from all school levels, from 3.30 p.m. to 6.00 p.m. on school days.[22]

In Brazil, it is interesting that Serviço Social da Indústria (SESI), a worker welfare organization funded by obligatory contributions from industries, has recognized the need for after-school care and summer camps and provides these services to workers employed by businesses that contribute. The electricity company

---

[21] Frew, 2004.

[22] Reddock and Bobb-Smith, 2008, p. 54.

FURNAS, for example, holds a contract with SESI to provide its workers with after-school activities and they can also attend its summer holiday camps.

For individual employers, it may be difficult to link up with community services such as schools to start or improve after-school care. According to the American Business Collaboration, one of the key lessons learned in addressing the need for out-of-school programmes is that solutions get the most leverage when coordinated within the community. No single entity can do it all, and the entire community benefits when schools can establish collaborative relationships with other community agencies and providers to deliver care.[23]

Advantages and disadvantages

In general, while some examples were found of employers' linking with the community, this appears to be a fairly limited type of childcare support. Nevertheless, partnering with community facilities holds considerable promise and potential for addressing the childcare needs of workers and employers. The actual cost to the employer is highly variable – from nothing in the case of a discount negotiated for employees to considerable in the case of a reserved place in a local crèche which is not used.

For employers, linking with community services can be a way of supporting employees that, unlike a company childcare centre, does not require a large capital investment nor a major management effort to run it. Also many workplaces are not in locations suitable for childcare facilities for health and safety reasons and may be located in areas where real estate costs are particularly high. Arrangements with community facilities provide greater flexibility to adapt to changing needs of staff and to the varying numbers needing different types of care for their children. Usually all who are eligible can take advantage of the care support, unlike a company facility, which typically has a fixed number of places. The local community may also benefit from improvements in the quality and quantity of childcare available, leading to an enhanced reputation of the company in its locality.

For employers, a major disadvantage of the community approach is the staff time that may be needed to negotiate agreements with different providers. It may also be time-consuming to try to ensure the quality, if the company feels it needs to do this, as in the case of FURNAS in Brazil.

---

[23] See http://www.abcdependentcare.com/docs/communities.shtml [4 December 2008].

For employees, using childcare that is available in the community may be a more convenient and flexible solution than bringing children to a workplace centre. Depending on their nature, arrangements with community facilities may give parents some choice on childcare provider. Even when most of the cost is paid by employees, they appreciate any efforts by employers, however minimal, which help make childcare more affordable or of better quality, or more convenient with respect to their working hours.

4.3 Financial support

Rather than being directly involved in providing childcare or dealing with childcare providers, another option for employers is to provide some sort of financial support for employees so they can choose their own provider. A great variety of systems has been found for financial support for childcare needs – so much so that it is difficult to make a simple classification.

The actual financial contribution of the employer can be virtually nothing as in the case of tax sheltering of care expenses or can be considerable when a proportion of payroll is paid to a fund. In some cases, the financial support is an additional benefit only for those with care expenses, whereas in other cases it may be part of a "cafeteria" benefits system whereby workers with no care expenses can choose other benefits.

Most systems have built-in methods to ensure that the support is in fact used for childcare rather than just giving an allowance to employees with young children, for example by using vouchers or reimbursing a proportion based on receipts. The financial support often covers a proportion of the costs not only for the care of preschool children but also school-age children. And in the United States, dependent savings accounts and some of the funds set up with employer contributions can be used for care expenses for elderly dependants as well.

Tax sheltering of care expenses

Tax sheltering of care expenses is only an alternative for employers in countries where national law permits employees to put aside some of their salary for this purpose – France, the United Kingdom and the United States being examples in this book (see section 3.1 on government incentives for details). Income used for care expenses (up to a certain limit) is not considered to be part of the employee's salary (which is officially less as a result) and so the employee does not pay the income tax or social security contributions on these earnings and the employer does not pay social security contributions.

For employees to be able to benefit, their company or organization must have in place the appropriate system: in the United States, the company must create a dependent care spending account system so that workers' childcare expenses can be paid by the employer from this account. In France and the United Kingdom, the company must have instituted a voucher system (see below for more on vouchers).

In some cases, employers may provide additional funds for dependent care expenses rather than just utilizing the part of employees' salary which has been put aside for care expenses. For example, when Providian Financial in the United States was looking for ways to help employee parents access care, of the different options considered, offering company-matching funds through a Dependent Care Spending Account was chosen as the preferred solution. Employees who contributed pre-tax dollars to such an account were matched dollar for dollar by the company up to $2,000 (the maximum amount which can be tax-free being $5,000).[24] In France, an employer contribution seems to be more likely, as in the case of the Caisse d'Epargne Auvergne Limousin, perhaps because employers can claim a tax credit of 25 per cent on their contribution (see box 4.6).

Box 4.6 Employer contributions to the cost of care vouchers

Caisse d'Epargne Auvergne Limousin, France. The bank started participating in the CESU voucher scheme in 2007 following a request presented by the company's trade unions at the annual collective bargaining session. CESU vouchers are given to any of the Caisse's 1,450 employees who submit an order.

For each 15 euro CESU voucher, the employee pays two-thirds of the cost (10.50 euro), with the remainder funded by the employer (4.50 euro). Each of its 1,450 workers is entitled to up to 600 euro per year in CESU vouchers to offset the purchase of personal services. Workers with dependants who are disabled or under age 6 are entitled to up to an additional 300 euro.

Source: Based on a telephone interview with the Caisse's human resources department, June 2008.

---

[24] Litchfield et al., 2004.

Advantages and disadvantages

Government systems that allow part of the salary to be used tax-free for care expenses give employers a flexible way of providing some support to employees, as the amount which is from salary and the amount which is in addition is at their discretion. When the entire amount is from the employee's salary there is no cost to the employer. In fact, since their payroll officially becomes less, they actually save money on whatever charges are normally applied to the payroll. Any costs of administering the tax sheltering programme (such as paying a voucher provider) are usually more than covered by these savings.

Although the tax savings that employees make in tax sheltered programmes may not cover a high proportion of the actual cost of childcare, employees generally appreciate any help provided. In the case of the NHS in England, an assessment [25] found that parents were mainly positive about voucher schemes operated on a salary sacrifice basis. A parent is quoted as saying: "I have a bit more income now and I feel a bit more appreciated."

However, it is not always easy for employees to understand how the tax reduction scheme works and its potential benefits. Even when a scheme exists in an enterprise, it may be underutilized by eligible employees. Communication and explanation are required on the part of employers using the system to explain to staff how it works and how they might benefit. In the case of vouchers, the voucher providers often help with communication (see below).

A major disadvantage of systems based on tax sheltering of care expenses is that they are of no help to employees whose earnings are close to the minimum wage and cannot be legally reduced. In all three countries, there are other possible arrangements for low-income workers, for example tax credits in the United Kingdom, which provide considerably more support than the salary sacrifice system. Nevertheless, this means that there are sometimes problems effectively coordinating different types of support, which can be confusing for parents.

Funds

Ways of generating a "pot of money" which can be used to help employees pay for the costs of childcare have been particularly common in the United States, often as a result of collective bargaining. Chapter 15 describes an example of the 1199 SEIU/Employer Child Care Fund in New York City which was created as

---

[25] Frew, 2004, p. 20.

a result of a collective agreement between the 1199 New York City chapter of the Service Employees International Union (SEIU) and health-care employers (hospitals, nursing homes).

These funds created for dependent care are usually based on an employer contribution which permits the fund, typically an independent organization, to subsidize the care used by the union members and employees of participating employers. The amount of the contribution has been based on total payroll, as in the case of the 1199 SEIU/Employer Child Care Fund, or on hours worked, as in the case of AC Transit in box 4.7. Employees using care services typically pay a certain proportion of the expenses with a subsidy from the fund. As can be seen in the case study of the 1199/Employer Child Care Fund, the fund manages the care provision, from finding childcare providers and negotiating discounts to operating the subsidy system.

In some countries, there are general funds for workers' welfare that have been used to help finance childcare. The Serviço Social da Indústria (SESI) in Brazil, noted above for its after-school programmes, is a worker welfare system funded by industry payroll and run by the National Confederation of Industry with representation from government and trade unions.

In Mauritius, there is a tripartite fund created by government to finance social services for workers in the Export Processing Zone (EPZ Labour Welfare Fund). Around 1998, for example, employees contributed 1 rupee and employers contributed 3 rupees per employee per month and, annually, the Government

---

Box 4.7 Care funds for bus drivers and hotel workers

Child and Elder Care Fund, Alameda County (AC) Transit, California, US. In 2000, AC Transit and ATU Local 192 negotiated that AC Transit would contribute to the fund 3 cents for every hour worked, including overtime. This amounts to a minimum of $125,000 per year for 2,000 employees, most of whom are bus drivers. A Dependent Care Committee was formed to decide how the money would be spent.

Hotel Employees and Restaurant Employees (HERE) Union Local 2 and the San Francisco Union Hotels, US. HERE Local 2 negotiated for a Child and Elder Care Fund with the San Francisco Union Hotels, thus providing a unique benefit to hotel workers. The employers contribute 15 cents per qualified employee-hour worked. Since 1994, a labour-management committee has worked cooperatively to design a programme that best suits the needs of Local 2 hotel workers.

Sources: For Alameda County, see "Family benefits for bus drivers", in *Labor Family News*, Vol. IX, No. 2, Spring 2001. For HERE Local 2, see http://www.working-families.org/contractlanguage/childcare.html [16 June 2009].

contributed 2 million rupees. One of the fund's programmes involves giving start-up and operating grants to non-governmental organizations to create and run day-care centres in areas with many factory workers and subsidizing preschool fees for the children of EPZ workers.[26]

Financial help for care expenses may also be part of a cafeteria of benefits from which employees can choose those which best meet their needs. For example, "perk" accounts at Microsoft Singapore can be used to cover costs related to health club membership, childcare, maid levy and holidays.[27] In the case of Magyar Telekom in Hungary, one way found for subsidizing childcare was to include the childcare subsidy in the cafeteria of benefits offered by the Dimenzió Insurance and Self-Supporting Association, to which employee members contribute 1 per cent of salary and the employer 2.3 per cent.

Advantages and disadvantages

The fact that most funds cover a variety of care needs means that they are useful for a wider group of employees than just, for example, workers with young children. For workers, flexibility concerning the type of care for which they can use the funds can be a major advantage of financial support as compared to an on-site crèche. Funds can give more options to the worker to choose the kind of care they need to fit their specific needs. For example, a housekeeper at the Marriott Hotel in San Francisco who had no one to look after her 90-year-old mother-in-law during the early morning shift received help from the hotel employees' fund (described in box 4.7) which paid for a caregiver.[28]

For employers, most fund arrangements have the advantage that they require little administrative work related to the childcare benefit, as the fund is a separate entity which sets out the rules for eligibility and benefits, deals with providers, communicates with staff and keeps accounts in relation to staff, providers and tax requirements. When a number of employers are contributing to a fund, it is possible to achieve economies of scale for service provision. On the other hand, employers may feel they have insufficient control over how the funds are used and get little credit from employees for the contribution they are making.

It is important that the use of the funds is seen as fair and that support is spread over all workers whose employers are contributing, rather than focusing

---

[26] Information found at http://www.webofmauritius.com/epzlwf/about.htm and http://siteresources.worldbank.org/INTECD/Resources/mauritiuscasestudy2.htm [11 June 2009].

[27] Singapore, Ministry of Manpower, 2006, p. 45.

[28] Johnson, 2008.

on a specific site or benefiting only a very small proportion of those with child-care needs. The budget of the fund may not be able to cover all eligible workers, so clear and fair rules on who has priority and their transparent implementation is important.

Vouchers

Childcare vouchers are a way for employers to help workers pay for childcare, just like meal vouchers have been a well-known way for companies to subsidize the meals of employees.[29] In some cases, the employer or a fund might issue its own vouchers to workers, who then use them towards the cost of childcare. To redeem the vouchers, the childcare provider would have to present them to the company or fund that issued them. Since issuing vouchers involves considerable work (such as printing vouchers, negotiating with providers to take them, reimbursing providers) companies typically use an outside specialized company to administer the voucher system.

Figure 4.1 illustrates the basic operation of a voucher scheme. The employer pays the voucher company, which then provides the vouchers to eligible employees. Employees use the vouchers to pay a childcare provider, who then redeems them from the voucher company. Since voucher schemes are usually part of government social benefits and involve tax exemptions, government sets the legal framework, specifying the tax exemptions, who is eligible, which dependants they can be used for and which types of childcare providers can be used. In this way, government tries to ensure that the voucher scheme is serving its objectives.

Of the countries covered in the current study, three have some form of voucher system in place for childcare needs: Chile, France and the United Kingdom. In France and the United Kingdom, the systems are linked to legislation exempting certain expenses from social security and income tax (see section on tax sheltering above and in section 3.1). In Chile, childcare vouchers are only used as a way for companies employing 20 or more women but with no nursery to fulfil their legal obligation to provide childcare to mothers with children under age 2.

The widest coverage of expenses is probably in France, where the service employment voucher called Cheque Emploi Service Universel (CESU) can be used for childcare in and outside the home, as well as for elder care, care for the disabled, and domestic services (see also box 4.6 on the use of the voucher system

---

[29] See Wanjek, 2005, for information on food vouchers.

Figure 4.1 Operation of a voucher scheme

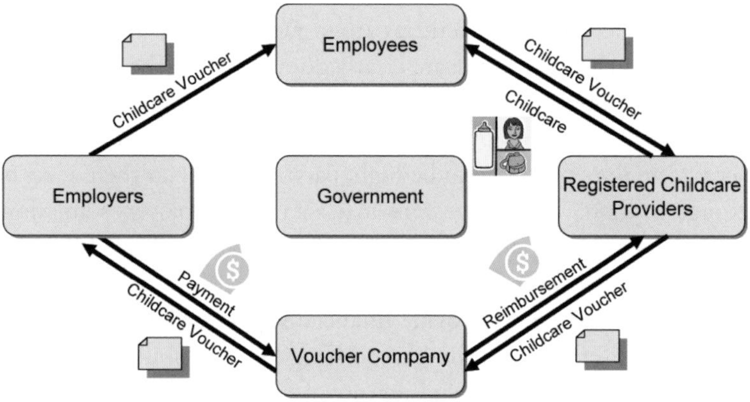

Source: Adapted from Accor Services at http://www.ticket-cesu.fr

in a bank). In both France and the United Kingdom, vouchers are being used as a means of pushing childcare providers out of the "grey" economy since child-minders must be registered in order to be paid by vouchers.

In the United Kingdom, employers can offer the benefit of up to £55 per week, either on the basis of salary sacrifice, in addition to salary, or as part of a wider flexible benefits scheme. On-line systems set up by the voucher provider facilitate the payment process and mean that childcare providers can be paid automatically. A senior finance manager at Airedale NHS Trust in the United Kingdom explains how it works for her:

> I have registered to receive Accor vouchers, through my employer, and I have taken the maximum value available. I have found the process easy to set up and the Accor website easy to use. I send the total voucher value automatically to my childcare provider each month, which means that I don't need to remember to do this after the initial set up. The voucher value is deducted from my total invoice to be paid to my childcare provider. Because the vouchers are deducted from my salary before I pay tax, I have seen a significant saving in my total tax deducted, which is in the region of £80.[30]

---

[30] *Childcare Summer*, 2006, p. 3: Staff newsletter of the Childcare Support Service NHS Bradford and Airedale Trust.

Advantages and disadvantages

Vouchers can be a convenient way for employers to help employees with childcare costs as long as childcare facilities are in fact available in the community. For employers, vouchers for childcare clearly do not involve the same investment costs as a company facility nor the risks related to predicting the eventual usage of a company facility by employees. Staff time needed for the administration of a voucher system does not seem to be high, particularly when there is an outside provider organization. Voucher systems may also give employers some flexibility to decide on how much support will be given for various kinds of childcare needs within the rules set by government.

For employees, vouchers provide financial support which makes childcare more affordable. In France and the United Kingdom, the ability to use vouchers for various kinds of childcare, including care of school-age children, makes them more useful to a larger group of parents and provides greater flexibility than some other types of support, such as a workplace nursery.

Vouchers are not useful if there is no care available to pay for. For some parents, finding and accessing a childcare place of the quality they want may be a problem. It has been suggested that if more and more employers offer vouchers instead of workplace nurseries, there might be a danger that more parents will face difficulties in finding childcare.[31] However, vouchers may stimulate the supply of childcare, encouraging the establishment of more places and the registration of more providers when registration is required to be able to accept vouchers.

For childcare providers, a major concern with vouchers is to be able to redeem them quickly and with a minimum of problems. On-line services are streamlining the payment systems in industrialized countries. Providers may prefer to deal with only a few voucher companies in order to simplify this process. Knowing that the parents of children receive vouchers has been reported as reassuring for the childcare provider, who consequently has less worry about the client being able to pay.

Subsidy schemes

Subsidy schemes seem to be rare, perhaps because in a number of countries childcare subsidies would be taxable benefits for employees. Among our case studies, the only example is FURNAS in Brazil, which provides a daycare reimbursement valued at US$750 a month for women employees with children aged

---

[31] TUC, 2006.

0 to 7 years. Employees can only receive the reimbursement for childcare centres accredited by the company.

Most systems which provide financial support for childcare costs also offer a referral service which helps parents to find the childcare they need. The next section looks at how this is done.

4.4 Advice and referral services

Often employees are not familiar with the childcare services that exist in their locality and it can be quite useful to provide some basic information on options and help them link up with existing services. Also, in countries like France, the United Kingdom and the United States where workers may be eligible for various government benefits or tax exemptions, advice can be very useful to help them benefit from these provisions. Many workers who are eligible for government benefits do not profit because they are unaware or do not know how to apply. Thus referral services can usually also give advice on various questions related to paying for childcare.

In industrialized countries, advice and referral services linked to the workplace have become quite common and are often the only type of assistance provided at the workplace, often covering care for elderly as well as children. In the United States, a survey of employers found that 34 per cent offered referral services.[32] Providing referrals can be relatively low cost, particularly if employees can be referred to reliable information services in the community. In the United Kingdom, every local authority has to have a Children's Information Service to provide parents with details of local providers of registered childcare, including day nurseries, childminders, play schemes and after-school provision. In Australia, there is a federal government information service on childcare options and location of services.[33]

In the developing countries, this study found no examples of employers providing workers with advice and referral services and there are none in the case studies. The reason is not clear. Perhaps larger firms with HR departments are providing referrals on childcare but this is done very informally and not really known. Or perhaps there are just too few childcare facilities available and/or most are nannies or childminders working in informal employment.

---

[32] Bond et al., 2005, table 9.
[33] http://www.mychild.gov.au [20 October 2009].

Some companies provide referral services in-house, often by someone in the HR department. In the case of the NHS in the United Kingdom, internal childcare coordinators are responsible for advising staff on care options (see Chapter 14). Having someone within the organization to advise and help staff has the advantage that this person knows the working environment and understands the needs of employees better than an outsider. In the case of childcare coordinators in the NHS, a study found that parents emphasized the value of their advice on issues such as leave entitlements and the coordinator's ability to act as an advocate where the parent was having difficulties with the line manager over a childcare issue.[34]

Many companies choose to contract outside providers of referral and advisory services. In the United States, the recent growth in private companies which offer referral services would seem to indicate that employers are interested in contracting this type of service. Employees can call the service free of charge in order to get advice and find out about childcare options in their area (see the cases of the US Postal Service and IBM Philippines in box 4.8). In the United Kingdom, voucher providers sometimes offer advice and referral services as part of the package: Accor, for example, has a free childcare helpline, which provides help on everything from finding emergency childcare to advice on returning to work after maternity leave.[35]

Box 4.8 Helping employees find childcare

IBM Philippines. The company subscribes to a global online resource and referral centre through http://www.worklifeessentials.com, which serves over 30 countries. IBM workers in the Philippines can use the online resource centre to access location maps of local daycare centres and preschools.

US Postal Service. Under the terms of a memorandum of understanding with the American Postal Workers Union (APWU), the Postal Service maintains a contract with a vendor to provide a dependent care resource and referral service to management and APWU-represented employees. The service allows employees to get assistance in locating dependent and elder care resources, as well as offering a variety of options to help balance work and home life.

Source: For IBM Philippines, see Caparas, 2008, p. 25. For US Postal Service, see 2006 Comprehensive Statement on Postal Operations, http://www.usps.com/strategicplanning/cs06/chp1_011.html [16 June 2009].

[34] Frew, 2004.
[35] Accor Services, n.d.

Advantages and disadvantages

For employees, finding childcare that fits their needs can be a major difficulty and, if there are various choices in the community, a referral service could be very helpful and save considerable time. An example of the advantages is an employee looking for elder care at Pfizer UK, which subscribes to the Employee Advisory Resource providing workers with online and personal support for a range of needs, including child and elder care:

> I now have dossiers of information on elder care accommodation and have narrowed my search considerably. The saving to my time has been incalculable as I would never have been able to compile such a comprehensive pack of information for myself.[36]

For employers, providing an advice and referral service can reduce the time employees need to spend looking for childcare and help them find viable options. It shows that the employer recognizes that they have family problems and is trying to help. To justify the expense, the service needs to be used, and to be used it must demonstrate its usefulness in addressing the problems of workers.

4.5 Back-up emergency care

Even the best childcare arrangements can break down and those that are less reliable are even more likely to break down. In the United States, for example, it is estimated that the average parent-employee misses five to eight days of work due to childcare arrangement breakdowns.[37] Companies and organizations are increasingly putting in place ways for parents to find a quick solution in order to avoid unnecessary absences. According to a US survey by the Society for Human Resource Management, 14 per cent of 373 employers offered emergency or sick-child care services in 2006, up 6 per cent from the previous year.[38] In this book, the main example of a company providing back-up childcare services is IBM Hungary.

A referral service is often a key component of the back-up support since a major problem for parents is knowing where to turn to find someone to look

---

[36] http://www.ear.co.uk/eaps_case.asp [4 December 2008].
[37] Durham-Vichr, 2000.
[38] Hope, 2008.

after their child when there is a problem. This can be provided either as part of a general referral service or as a specific service for emergency care. The service is sometimes provided in-house. Employers can maintain a register of child-minders who work locally and have offered care to employees of the company. This practice helps to ensure the quality of the service provided. The Hereford and Worcester Ambulance Service NHS Trust (United Kingdom), for example, has a list of registered childminders who will take children at short notice and at unsocial hours in an emergency.[39]

Other companies prefer to outsource. There has been a considerable growth in some industrialized countries in the number of private companies which specialize in providing services to find emergency childcare for employees.[40] These agencies have a local or sometimes national network of childminder agencies and daycare providers through which they find an emergency care solution for the employees of their client companies. The service often includes a round-the-clock phone service and the hiring of the carer for the employee as in the case of IBM Hungary.

Many firms that provide employees with help in finding emergency child-care also include some financial support for the payment. Usually there is a yearly ceiling on the payments by the company in terms of the number of days or the amount paid. For example, the Royal Marsden (Chapter 14) covers the cost of staff's use of an emergency baby-sitting service on up to three occasions in a 12-month period, an occasion being for up to two consecutive days. In the case of IBM Hungary, the company reimburses 30 per cent of the cost. Box 4.9 gives some other examples of company policies for providing financial support.

Like other kinds of childcare, emergency care can be at the child's home, at a childminder's home or in a centre. Having a carer come to the house can be a convenient solution in an emergency, such as when a child is not well but parents may understandably be hesitant to allow strangers into their house to look after their child. Careful checking of the backgrounds of carers and monitoring their work can be an important function of the agency providing the service.

Often in an emergency, parents prefer to call on help from relatives or friends. Recognizing this, Citigroup in New York City felt it should support these arrangements and asked its provider of back-up care services to include the option of payment to a relative or friend. People find it easier to ask a neighbour or even their own family members to help them if they can tell them that their company will pay them for their services.[41]

---

[39] UNISON, 2004.

[40] For details concerning some companies in the United States, see Harty, 2005.

[41] Harty, 2005.

Box 4.9 Financial support for back-up care

SEIU Locals 535, 616 and 790 and the County of Alameda, California, US. These SEIU Locals negotiated a fund with Alameda County to provide reimbursement for parents whose children are mildly sick or who, for some other emergency reason, are unable to use their regular provider. Employees receive reimbursement for 90 per cent or up to $80 a day, to a maximum of $350 a year. The employer also provides resource and referral services for families who need sick or emergency care.

Trafford Healthcare NHS Trust, UK. The Trust has retained places with registered childminders for parents where care arrangements have broken down. These can be accessed for up to three days a year. The Trust pays half of the fees.

Ford Motor Company, Detroit, US. "Safe-At-Home" provides up to 80 per cent of the cost of a trained caregiver, for up to 24 hours a day, for dependent children of full-time salaried employees when the child is too sick to attend school or daycare, when regular childcare arrangements fail or for other unexpected business-related reasons such as travel or overtime on short notice. The programme subsidizes costs for up to 80 hours per year per Ford family with one child and 120 hours for families with more than one child.

Source: For Alameda, California, see http://www.working-families.org/contractlanguage/childcare.html [16 June 2009]. For Trafford NHS, see UNISON, 2004. For Ford, see http://www.mycareer.ford.com [16 June 2009]

In addition to back-up care in the home, places in daycare centres or with childminders are sometimes available for back-up care. In some cases, a company pays a yearly fee for reserving a place. Some daycare centres in the United States now only provide back-up care with various employers buying in for reserved places.[42] Similarly in Ottawa, Canada, the Short Term Child Care Program, run by Andrew Fleck Child Care Services, provides an example of a consortium model where a number of companies finance the facility. At one time, it had been a government subsidized programme, but when that money ran out, area companies and unions, ranging from Canada Post to the Ottawa-Carleton District School Board, developed a consortium.[43]

Few employers would have sufficient need to justify having their own back-up care centre. Some exceptions found include the Brigham and Women's Hospital, a teaching affiliate of Harvard medical school, and the Canadian Imperial Bank of Commerce (CIBC) in Toronto (see box 4.11).

---

[42] Durham-Vichr, 2000.

[43] Information found at the web site of the Short Term Child Care Program, http://www.afchildcare.on.ca/STCC/program.html [20 December 2008].

In most back-up care schemes, parents must have registered their children in advance so all the information on the child is available immediately for the childcare provider and the employer knows how many children are potential users of the back-up care.

Advantages and disadvantages

For employees, back-up care for children in an emergency can be difficult to find, and stressful and expensive when they can find it. Knowing that they will be able to find a quick solution that is not too expensive can be one less source of worry for parents. This benefit can be so important to parents that they may feel tied to their job and hesitate to change (see box 4.10). Similarly, the testimony of an employee at IBM Hungary in box 4.10 reflects the appreciation of employees for rapid help in providing emergency care.

Parents often worry about how their children will react to the back-up care situation and need to feel confident that the carer or the daycare centre used is properly screened for quality. In the case of IBM Hungary, an employee noted his appreciation of the fact that a reliable company had been chosen and that the carer coped well with the children.

Compared to other regular forms of childcare support, the benefits of back-up care are more directly obvious for employers since it can make the difference between an employee being absent or at work. Absenteeism can be expensive when the employee is a surgeon scheduled for an operation that has to be cancelled or the operator of an expensive machine that goes unused. Even with the

---

Box 4.10 The value of back-up care to employees

Journalist in New York, US. "When I left my previous job for this one, I was excited about the new work, but there was one corporate perk I was leaving behind that made me think twice: a free, on-site back-up childcare centre that employees could use up to 20 days per year. It was perfect for unexpected daycare closures and odd school holidays. Colleagues cited the centre as a reason for staying with the company."

Employee at IBM Hungary. "On one occasion we were in real trouble. What I really liked was that the babysitter company was ready to respond to urgent needs, as I telephoned in the evening and the babysitter was there in the morning on time."

Sources: Merritt, 2008, and Chapter 9.

---

large investment made for an on-site childcare centre as in the case of CIBC, the company still estimates that the investment is paying off (see box 4.11). Similarly KPMG, which uses an external service to organize the care and offers it free of charge, calculates that it is profitable.

Also, back-up care benefits more staff than the traditional on-site centre. "You can cover a far greater number of people than with conventional on-site care because they're not going to be using the center every day," says Kathie Lingle, the former work/life director for KPFG Insurance. At KPFG, the return on investing in back-up care is high, calculated at $5.50 in saved productivity for each $1 spent.[44]

Box 4.11 Back-up care pays off for employers

Canadian Imperial Bank of Commerce, Toronto. To offer back-up care for employees' children, CIBC paid a well-known childcare provider company to set up a purpose-built childcare centre centrally located in downtown Toronto in one of CIBC's office towers. There are no full-time spaces and children cannot attend if they are sick. The Centre can accommodate a maximum of 40 children aged from 3 months up to the 13th birthday. There is a limit of 20 days per child per year. The benefit is taxable for employees that use it. CIBC estimates that, since it opened, the Children's Centre has saved CIBC about CAN$1.5 million in productivity costs. These are the direct savings from the parent being at work when the service is used.

KPMG, US. Every KPMG partner and employee is eligible for 20 days of 100 per cent subsidized back-up care per year for child and elderly dependants. KPMG estimates that its back-up care initiative saves the company approximately $3.36 million annually. The programme has grown so popular with some workers that KPMG began offering what it calls "back-up sharing", allowing employees to donate unused back-up "usages" to others who had exceeded their 20-day limit.

Sources: For CIBC, see Lowe, 2007. For KPMG, see Hope, 2008.

Managing the provision of emergency back-up care can be difficult as the demand is by definition unpredictable and often with little notice. Companies that have a specific number of emergency childcare places reserved may find they are sometimes underused while, at other times, high demand means there are not sufficient places for all those who need them which can be a source of annoyance and stress for those who must search elsewhere.

---

[44] Kiger, 2004.

Take-up of emergency care may be less than originally expected. For example, in the case of some NHS areas, surveys had identified the provision of emergency childcare as a priority, but in practice the take-up was often low. In one area, four emergency places were set aside and these were used only twice in one year.[45] The reason may be that, in an emergency, parents often preferred to take carer's leave, particularly when their child was sick. There was also a reluctance to leave a child with a childminder that the child did not know.

For employers, it is important to ensure that the benefit is well publicized and that parents are well informed about how to use the system, how to register a child in advance and the guarantees concerning the quality.

4.6 Conclusions

This chapter has sought to illustrate the many ways that workplaces have found to provide concrete support for the childcare needs of workers. Each situation requires a careful assessment of workers' needs and the local possibilities in order to determine what kinds of solutions would be appropriate. Table 4.2 summarizes the specific advantages and disadvantages of various types of workplace support and the sorts of circumstances in which they may be appropriate.

---

[45] Frew, 2004.

Table 4.2 Evaluation of different types of workplace support

Type of support	When appropriate	Advantages	Disadvantages
1. Company or on-site facilities	• many workers at the same location • feasible for most workers to bring children to work • lack of daycare facilities in community • atypical hours or shifts so community facilities are inadequate • focus on the breastfeeding needs of new mothers	*For workers:* • appreciate having children nearby • opening hours are often more convenient in relation to working hours • solves often difficult problem of finding childcare • can save on travel time to childcare • facilitates breastfeeding *For employers:* • can be useful for attracting staff • helps retain staff and the return of women after maternity leave	*For workers:* • may be difficult to bring the child to work • little choice of provider • can be waiting lists in order to access • may mean the employer can put pressure for more hours of work *For employers:* • can be expensive • may be difficult to manage • number of places is fixed so may be too many or not enough
2. Linking with facilities in the community (reserving or buying places, discounts)	• when workforce is scattered • when it is difficult to bring children to work • when the workplace and surroundings are not a good environment for children • when facilities exist in community • often useful for school-age children (camps, play schemes)	*For workers:* • may offer more choice of provider than on-site and be more convenient • any discounts are always welcome *For employers:* • avoids investment in own site • gives more flexibility to adapt to the changing needs of staff • ensures all eligible staff have access	*For workers:* • choices are often limited to specific providers • financial advantage may be less than with a company facility *For employers:* • may be time consuming to negotiate with different providers • may be difficult to ensure the quality of partner facilities

Type of support	When appropriate	Advantages	Disadvantages
3. Financial support (income tax sheltering, funds, vouchers)	• when a company is small, with insufficient staff to justify more complex system, a voucher-type system could be appropriate • in contrast, funds as established in some US companies require significant number of employees of one employer or of a group of employers • possibilities and advantages are influenced by national fiscal policies affecting the employer and employee	*For workers:* • allows choice of childcare arrangement • often includes school-age children • not limited by waiting lists (available to all who are eligible) *For employers:* • less administrative effort is needed • can modulate the amount of support and cover all who are eligible • can actually gain when on salary reduction basis	*For workers:* • financial gain may be limited when based on salary reduction • still must find an appropriate care facility *For employers:* • have less control on how money is spent
4. Advice and referral	• when different types of facilities are available in the community • when workers may be eligible for government benefits but do not profit • when workers are having difficulty finding facilities and wasting time looking	*For workers:* • can help when it is difficult to find or choose childcare • useful when they may need advice on government benefits *For employers:* • can be low cost • less work time lost finding solutions	*For workers:* • may not help with the cost of care nor with ensuring that care facilities are available *For employers:* • may not be useful for employees and therefore underused and an unnecessary expense

Type of support	When appropriate	Advantages	Disadvantages
5. Emergency back-up care (proportion of cost paid by employee varies considerably)	• when absenteeism due to childcare breakdowns is high • when children are often brought to office because of problems • when employee absence can lead to extensive costs to the organization	*For workers:* • avoids considerable worry and hassle in finding arrangements • when homecare is available, it can also help when the child is sick *For employers:* • quick solutions can be found to avoid lateness, absenteeism	*For workers:* • may prefer to stay with the child rather than bring a stranger to the house • child may be upset by an unknown carer *For employers:* • depends on the cost of care in relation to the cost of absence

Conclusions and lessons learned

5

Access to quality, affordable childcare is an important determinant of parents' employment opportunities and workplace productivity. Poor access to work, lower earnings, lower productivity and higher absenteeism are just a few of the consequences of the lack of suitable childcare, all of which jeopardize families' income security and company success. Existing public policies, programmes and services are rarely adequate to meet workers' and employers' needs for childcare even in many industrialized countries; in developing countries, the problem is greater yet. To help fill the gaps, workplace initiatives to find suitable childcare solutions have been taken by employers, trade unions, NGOs and workers in countries around the world, in some countries with government encouragement and in others with little or no government involvement.

This book has reviewed national policy frameworks and case examples of workplace partnerships with particular emphasis on the ten countries covered in Part II, in an effort to understand when, why and how different partners have come together to develop workplace solutions for childcare and with what effect. Although each national and workplace situation has its own opportunities and constraints, this chapter summarizes some of the insights and considerations that can guide policy-makers and workplace partners in making decisions appropriate to their own contexts.

5.1 Lessons for governments and public policy

This section considers how public policy affects the emergence of workplace initiatives. It discusses the potential benefits that can be gained by public support for workplace initiatives and it raises several issues from a societal point of view about the role and design of workplace initiatives within the broader public policy framework.

How does public policy affect workplace initiatives?

The broad framework of public support to childcare services is a major determinant of working parents' needs and thus of the potential role for workplace programmes. Workplace initiatives for childcare are particularly rare in countries where public policy ensures that parents' needs are well met by leave policies and extensive publicly provided childcare, as in Denmark and Sweden. Nevertheless, even in countries where there is considerable government provision for childcare, workplace initiatives can still be found in an effort to fill in the remaining gaps, such as crèches for children under age 3 in France (where government incentives for workplace measures also exist) and summer camps and back-up care in Hungary. The same social ideology which is driving government programmes for childcare is also influencing some workplace actors.

However, while extensive public support for childcare might reduce the need for the workplace to get involved, the reverse – that *low* public support may lead to *more* workplace involvement – is not necessarily true. Where low government involvement in childcare stems from cultural norms and a prevailing social premise that the family should look after its own children, it follows that workplace involvement in childcare may also be low. In fact, workplace programmes seem to be rare in countries where there are very few public childcare services and, at the same time, where cultural norms or economic circumstances mean that there is little pressure on employers or trade unions to facilitate the formal employment of women.

Spontaneous workplace initiatives for childcare seem to occur more often in countries where government services are patchy and where, in addition, employers and trade unions perceive a need for greater labour force participation of women and/or are under some pressure to find ways to improve work–family balance such as in Thailand, the United Kingdom and the United States. The reasons why some employers have taken initiatives, as well as the benefits they report, are reviewed in section 3.2. As seen in a number of examples in this book, trade unions have also played a key role in pushing for childcare support at some work-places by providing voice for expressing workers' need for childcare and having it included in collective bargaining agreements (see section 3.3).

Governments in some countries have taken childcare measures targeted specifically at workplaces and these have a major influence on the frequency and nature of workplace programmes, as seen in section 3.1. Government measures that have little or no cost to the employer, such as tax sheltering of childcare expenses in the United Kingdom and the United States, are understandably the most popular type of childcare support in those countries and tend to increase the number of companies which are providing some form of childcare support (see section 3.2). In countries such as Brazil, Chile and India, where legislation requires that employers of a certain number of women must provide childcare, the legislation is more-or-less followed. Typically, however, very few employed women are actually in establishments covered by such legislation and such legislation itself has raised concerns about the willingness of employers to officially hire women, and the implications for gender equality.

Evidence from industrialized countries where there have been surveys (see section 3.2) suggests that workplace initiatives for childcare are limited. In the United Kingdom, a survey of establishments with ten or more employees in 2004–05 found that, on average, 7 per cent of establishments offered an own-company childcare centre, which is much higher than the 3 per cent average for European countries. In the United States, a similar 7 per cent of employers with 50 or more employees provided a childcare facility while 45 per cent offered the possibility of putting aside pre-tax salary for care expenses. Organizations which provide childcare support for employees tend to be large organizations, often in services (banks, hospitals), and are more likely to be public than private.

Some general considerations for designing public support for workplace initiatives from a societal point of view can help frame national and local discussions of the role of workplace initiatives.

Potential benefits of public support for workplace initiatives

If well designed and targeted, public measures supporting workplace initiatives can achieve the following:

- **Increase resources available for childcare.** In an ideal world, governments would have the resources to provide free community facilities for childcare for all children that need it. In a world of financial constraints and limited resources, leveraging employer resources may help expand the availability of the childcare needed by working parents (see section 3.1 on government measures).

In France, employers contribute to public childcare through their contribution to social security, the National Family Allowance Fund (Caisse National des Allocations Familiales, CNAF), which provides childcare allowances to parents and subsidies to providers. In this way, all employers are contributing, not just those whose staff need childcare or are women. A more common approach is for governments to put in place incentives to encourage workplace initiatives and greater private investment in childcare services. This is the case, for example, in the United Kingdom, where the full cost of a nursery place provided by the employer is exempt from national insurance contributions (and income tax for the employee) as compared to a limit of £55 per week if vouchers are given.

However, the overall resources devoted to childcare will increase only if policy measures provide sufficient incentives for raising contributions: in the United Kingdom and the United States, for example, tax incentive systems through the workplace have somewhat decreased the amount that parents pay on childcare by shifting some of the costs to government, but few employers have themselves stepped up contributions. Similarly, take-up of grants and subsidies for childcare services has been low when the grant offered is small compared to the additional investment required.

- **Encourage partnership and innovation.** Appropriately designed public incentive programmes can do much to encourage organizations to work together, bringing together diverse perspectives, resources and expertise, or simply pooling financial resources to bolster financial stability. In France and the United Kingdom, recent legislative measures provide financial incentives for groups of employers to collaborate on childcare, putting the establishment of crèches within the financial reach of smaller companies who work together. Similarly for malls in Chile which are required to provide childcare, it has become part of the common services which are paid by all enterprises, spreading the costs over all companies and not just those whose employees are using it at a particular time.

- **Help ensure that provision is responsive to needs of working parents.** Even where public services are readily available, workplace initiatives can help fill gaps in responding to the needs of working parents. Workers in rural areas and workers with atypical shifts or long hours have needs that are not often me even where public services are relatively good. Workplace initiatives in some countries are helping address these gaps, although the needs remain far greater than existing solutions.

- **Encourage greater labour force participation of women.** Since it is mainly women who are responsible for childcare, childcare services impact directly on the labour force participation of women and can be a key factor in promoting gender equality. The availability of childcare and its cost, convenience and quality are major factors influencing whether mothers can be economically active, as discussed in section 2.2. Various forms of workplace support have been affecting the ability of companies to attract and retain women workers and the ability of mothers to take employment or return to the same employer after the birth of a child. Even when it is the father who is accessing childcare support at his workplace, this can free the mother for employment, as reported in the case of SOCFINAF in Kenya.

Issues in designing public policy

Despite the potential benefits of workplace initiatives, possible disadvantages or limitations can also arise. From a societal perspective, some considerations in designing workplace initiatives and in defining their role within a broader public policy framework include the following:

- **Workplace initiatives alone are unlikely to contribute to societal goals of poverty reduction and social equity.** Workplace initiatives can supplement but cannot substitute for efforts to improve the availability, quality and affordability of community services for all families. As seen in section 3.2, most workplace initiatives for childcare can be found in large companies, often in financial or business services, and thus tend to reach workers in middle or upper levels of occupational skills and income ladders. This book contains some examples of workplaces where many of the workers have relatively low qualifications and incomes, but these tend to be less common and were more difficult to find. Workplace initiatives are less likely to reach lower-income employees and also do not cover the many women and men who work in the informal economy, often self-employed. For lower-income families for whom the costs of childcare are usually high compared to their earnings, access to some form of public support is necessary for childcare to be affordable. Rather than workplace initiatives, public support for childcare may be better invested in programmes targeting low-income and other vulnerable groups for whom access to childcare can make enormous differences in access to paid work, family income, child development and child health.

- **Public measures obliging employers to provide childcare support can have negative consequences for workers and employers.** In the face of overwhelming demand, tight public budgets or assumptions that childcare is an isolated need not requiring broad public responses, the temptation to relegate solutions entirely to employers and the workplace can be high. Placing the financial responsibilities for childcare, which is a public good, on employers can undermine their key objectives of profitability and competitiveness.

In a number of countries, employers are required to provide nursery supports on the basis of the number of women they employ. In the current book, there are examples of three countries – Brazil, Chile and India – where laws require certain employers to provide childcare for their female employees once they have a certain number of female employees. These laws reflect a very legitimate concern for enabling working mothers to breastfeed their babies, a major issue when maternity leaves are short. However, once children have passed the breastfeeding stage, the reason for excluding men no longer exists and there is a real concern that such provisions can lead to discrimination against hiring women. Public policies for workplace childcare that are based on sex-stereotyped assumptions that women alone are responsible for childcare tend to perpetuate gender biases in society and may limit women's employment opportunities.

- **Workplace initiatives should be linked to broader childcare strategies.** Workplace initiatives are most useful when they fit within a broader public strategy for the provision of childcare services and follow national standards related to the qualifications of the staff and the content of the programmes. Workplace initiatives for childcare that are linked to general measures promoting child education and development help to ensure that workplace childcare is more than just childminding and contributes to the development of children. Several cases in this book highlight the benefits in terms of quality of care that result from linkages and partnerships between workplace initiatives and national and local government agencies responsible for the registration and standards of childcare and education provision.

- **The design of workplace initiatives should take into account the working conditions of caregivers.** Problems of labour market shortages in experienced and qualified caregivers, high rates of staff turnover and the quality of care for children are all interrelated. A number of countries are experimenting with systems to monitor and regulate the qualifications, training and working conditions of caregivers, and this includes efforts to design workplace supports for childcare in ways that encourage decent working conditions for caregivers. For example, vouchers that can be used only to purchase the services of registered childminders can bring childminders into the formal economy and provide possibilities for improving their qualifications, training opportunities, pay and other working conditions. Case examples in this book also suggest that opportunities to participate in training and qualification programmes offered by relevant national agencies are highly appreciated by caregivers at corporate childcare centres.

Public financial incentives for workplace initiatives are mainly found in some industrialized countries. Other non-financial types of government support can however be found, mainly in the form of technical assistance for setting up and running on-site childcare centres and for providing training for caregivers. Public oversight and support for the quality and content of workplace centres can help avoid some of their disadvantages. In the case studies in Part II, a number of workplace childcare centres were benefiting from some government services to improve their quality, such as centre registration and inspection, staff training, health checkups and vaccinations of children.

5.2 Lessons for workplace partners

The examples of workplace initiatives reported in this book are those that still exist. Several workplaces known to have programmes were contacted only to find that they had collapsed, whether because of corporate takeovers, mergers, financial problems, shifting management priorities or withdrawals of key partners. Even among those that still exist, some face uncertain futures and struggle to continue.

A number of lessons concerning practical steps that can greatly affect the success of an initiative (including its financial stability and how well it is used) have emerged from the experiences in this book and are shared below. More details concerning specific types of measures can be found in Chapter 4.

Linking to business plans

Whether childcare assistance for employees might help an organization reach its objectives is a question that cannot be answered without investigation. As noted by the human relations manager in the Grant Medical Center in Ohio, "Sometimes people put programmes in to get publicized and it serves no strategic need. It may look good for *Working Mother* magazine, but if it doesn't meet employees' needs, deliver return on investment, and fit into the strategic plan, then don't do it. Be thoughtful."[1] A representative of the Irish Business and Employers Confederation advises that childcare "needs to be a strategic initiative, in line with your business strategy".[2]

Assessing the needs

In order to decide on a workplace solution that will be effective, a key first step is to find out the needs and preferences of workers: the ages and numbers of workers' children, the distance and modes of transport between work and where workers live, current childcare arrangements and the availability of alternatives, costs and quality of childcare and so on. Initiatives can fail if they do not adequately take into account and accommodate the needs and constraints of workers that will affect the extent to which they use any services. Many of the cases in the book involved surveys of workers before deciding on the childcare initiative. Companies like Wipro in India and the Rennes Atalante Park in France undertook careful preparatory consultations and research to design solutions that were responsive to workers' needs and have become very popular. Magyar Telekom in Hungary scrapped its original plans to subcontract kindergarten care during summer holidays when a needs assessment survey indicated that workers preferred holiday activities for school-age children. The willingness of the company to change direction led to a highly successful programme for summer camp.

Good assessments and consultations explore not only needs and current arrangements but also preferences for various options with respect to fees, location, opening hours, registration options and services.[3] Not only can consultation and research ensure that solutions will be used, they can also lay the groundwork for positive relations and productive partnerships.

Partnering for success

The case studies in this book offer a number of innovative examples of maximizing resources and expertise through partnerships. Partnerships can achieve the following:

---

[1] Friedman, n.d.

[2] Cronin, n.d.

[3] An example of a questionnaire for a childcare survey can be found at UNISON, 2004, p. 26.

- **Bring together diverse capabilities and resources.** In the example of the childcare centres for seasonal agricultural workers (CAHMT) in Chile, the unions raised the idea and continue to monitor the programme, the employers provide voluntary financial contributions, the parents contribute fees, the national government administers the programme, the municipalities provide the facilities and manage the programme, and different government agencies provide staffing and food; the end result is a rich and integrated programme that has run for 15 years.

- **Take advantage of existing facilities and services.** A range of services and facilities are already available in many communities, and workplace initiatives have found different ways of taking advantage of what already exists. For example, FURNAS in Brazil, IBM in Hungary, the Royal Marsden in the United Kingdom and BHEL in India were able to offer needed holiday activities for workers' children by identifying and entering into agreements with existing community programmes. The staff of some workplace centres have been able to improve their skills by attending training courses offered by various government services and NGOs. To enrich the educational component of the childcare programme at the Phra Pradaeng childcare centre in Thailand, staff regularly attend government courses on child development.

- **Pool resources.** In a number of cases, enterprises and trade unions in zones or geographical areas are coming together to work out collective solutions for childcare and pool resources. The Peenya Industrial Area in India and the Network of Nawanakhon Labour Unions in Thailand are key examples. In France, the Aix-la-Duranne crèche highlights how, in the context of government incentives, partnership between small, medium and large enterprises operating in an area brings mutual benefits, enabling small and large enterprises alike to benefit from economies of scale and to share the costs and risks.

Ensuring quality

Throughout the case studies, a common theme in the reactions of parents to the childcare programme is their concern about the quality of the care that their children are receiving. Their appreciation tends to be linked to how the programme has affected their children's development (for example, in childcare centres in the Thailand cases and BMW South Africa) or how well their children have reacted (for example, to emergency care at IBM Hungary or to summer camps at Hungarian Post). Criticisms and lack of use of facilities are also often linked to quality issues such as training of staff or insufficient space. Attention to ensuring the quality of any facilities offered to employees seems to pay off by encouraging use by employees.

The strategies used to ensure quality vary depending on the type of programme involved. In the cases of support provided for use of community facilities, the facilities may be pre-selected as in the case of FURNAS in Brazil, or the use of financial support may be restricted for use only with those providers that are registered, as in France or the United Kingdom where there is a public registration system.

For on-site childcare centres, public institutions can help improve the quality of workplace facilities through establishing national guidelines, providing curricula, undertaking inspections and providing training opportunities for staff. Box 3.14 in section 3.6 provides some examples of how outside partners are helping with training of staff of workplace childcare centres.

For workplace facilities, efforts to ensure quality have included:

- registering the centre with the appropriate national body;
- careful selection of staff, in particular the director;
- appointment of childcare consultants to help with the design of the space, recruitment of staff, monitoring of operations and linking to registering or accrediting bodies;
- in-service training for staff;
- attention to staff's working conditions, including hours, wages, needs for predictable schedules and time off for their own family responsibilities; and
- establishing mechanisms for feedback from parents.

Monitoring the results and measuring the benefits

Monitoring the use of workplace measures by employees with children is important in order to be able to deal with shortcomings that discourage use and to anticipate future use. For childcare centres where capacity tends to be fixed over a long period, monitoring can be particularly important to ensure that the capacity available is utilized and to understand any reasons for underutilization which can threaten the financial sustainability of the facility.

Several of the workplace initiatives documented in Part II have built-in formalized mechanisms to monitor the use of programmes and encourage feedback. Sometimes these are welfare committees or works councils as in France, which allow partners to discuss concerns related to benefits or welfare programmes, but more often they are advisory committees formed specifically to be consulted on the running of an on-site childcare centre (as at Melsetter Farm in South Africa, the Oswaldo Cruz Foundation in Brazil and Infosys in India). Surveys of parents to get feedback from users or find out why they are not using a workplace programme were rare.

Sometimes general worker satisfaction surveys can help situate the role of the childcare programme within the range of benefits proposed by a company. For example, at Natura in Brazil, where almost two-thirds of the workers are women, surveys carried out by external auditors have regularly identified the company crèche as one of the best benefits offered by the company, partly because of the quality of the centre.

Initiatives for childcare solutions are often started by a few motivated persons, including typically a human resource manager or CEO, as noted in the case of South Africa. When these people leave, the new managers may be less convinced about the benefits of investing in childcare. Thus for the sustainability of a programme, documenting the benefits can help to convince management of the usefulness of a childcare programme. Such documentation would seem to be rare, leaving programmes with little defence when faced with sceptical managers.

Communicating about the programme

Involvement of employee representatives in the development of the programme not only helps ensure its usefulness but also facilitates later communication to employees. If employees are going to use the facility, they must know it exists, who is eligible and how it works. Rules need to be clear, and their implementation transparent. Information related to guarantees concerning quality is also crucial for parents in making their decisions. If the programme is meant to attract new staff, it is important to mention it in recruitment notices and also provide details in information for new recruits.

Moreover, many workplace initiatives can have complex rules and requirements, which may not be well understood, and therefore not fully used by workers. In some cases, service providers, such as those providing vouchers or establishing workplace crèches, offer support in providing information for clients' workers.

Meeting the costs

Quality childcare can be expensive. In workplace programmes, there are basically three main contributors to paying costs: the parents, the employer and government. The many examples throughout the book have illustrated diverse types of arrangements in different countries for sharing the cost of childcare among these three actors.

In the many countries where parents must pay most of the cost of childcare themselves, they are generally appreciative of any financial help from employers through subsidies, negotiated discounts, tax-sheltered care expenses and so on. In these types of programmes, the employer can decide on the amount of the contribution, which may be little or considerable.

For workplace childcare centres, parents usually pay some part of the cost (and sometimes most of the cost) and find this normal. Even the poor workers at Red Lands Roses in Kenya, for example, seem to be quite willing to pay a small fee for the company nursery, noting that it is much less than the cost of a young maid, who may not be reliable.

Where the employer is required by legislation to provide childcare, eligible parents (usually only mothers) typically do not pay fees. Also in some cases, employers with workers on very low wages are charging no fee, such as SOCFINAF in Kenya, while others prefer to charge at least a token amount.

Among the countries of focus in this book, any public support for workplace childcare centres is a very small proportion of the cost (except for the inter-enterprise crèches in France). It should be noted however that public childcare support paid directly to workers can also help subsidize the use of workplace programmes. But basically, it is the parents and the employer who pay most of the costs.

The cost of childcare is a major barrier to employer initiatives and also to use by employees. For low-wage workers who cannot contribute much to the costs, employers may be particularly reluctant to shoulder a cost which may be a significant proportion of the worker's salary. Making childcare more affordable may often involve sacrifices on the quality. In the cases in Part II, most of the facilities for low-wage workers are not of the same standard as those for highly skilled professionals. Yet they seem to be useful for workers, and imposing high public standards concerning workplace facilities may not be in the interest of these workers. At the same time, a certain minimum needs to be ensured. As discussed in section 2.6, finding a reasonable balance between affordability and quality is a major challenge, especially in contexts where resources are limited.

Expanding the possibilities

The search for examples of workplace programmes supporting childcare undertaken for this book suggests that the range of examples is fairly limited. It was not easy to find programmes other than the traditional workplace childcare centre nor was it easy to find examples that reached lower-income workers. Workplace partners could be more innovative and expand the possibilities considered in the search for workplace solutions to help with childcare.

- **Beyond regular care for preschool children:** Most workplace initiatives focus primarily on regular care for children of preschool age. Preschool care is indeed a pressing problem for workers in virtually every country. But care for school-age children before and after school hours and during holidays can also pose considerable logistic and financial problems for parents, as can back-up care for emergencies. These other types of care needs tend to be overlooked despite the difficulties they can pose for parents trying to focus on work priorities. IBM in Hungary, for example, found that summer care during school holidays was the top stressor that working parents wanted support for and the after-school care available at Wipro in Bangalore is quite popular with parent employees.

  Some initiatives, such as the childcare centre at the SNPE Le Bouchet in France, provide supports that can be used for a wide range of childcare needs, including preschool care, care during school holidays, and reserved places for care in the case of emergencies. Other workplaces have partnered with community services to help workers find out-of-school care such as summer camps. Chapter 4 provides details on programmes that are helping parents with out-of-school care and emergency care.

- **Beyond the workplace childcare centres:** Most workplace initiatives fall into one category – on-site childcare centres. Workplace centres are extremely useful when workers need services for young children during their working hours. But they are not the best solution in every situation (see table 4.2 at the end of Chapter 4).

  Other options for support may be better for addressing the needs of a wider range of workers, providing workers with more flexibility or a greater range of care services while being less costly and risky for the employer. Beyond direct provision, many possibilities exist to provide childcare support through linking to existing community facilities, providing financial supports (including taking advantage of existing government incentive schemes) and assisting workers with information and resources on care options in the community. By considering a wider range of solutions and "thinking out of the box", workplace partners may be able to better leverage the opportunities and resources that already exist. The result could be a more cost-effective way of providing workplace assistance for childcare to all employees who need it.

- **Beyond high-income workers:** Childcare support at the workplace is more common in organizations such as banks, IT companies or academic institutions that are concerned with retaining highly skilled employees than in those where most workers are in lower-paid, less-skilled jobs. Yet the examples of programmes for low-income workers in this book suggest that employer gains can be considerable.

The experiences of the coffee and rose exporters in Kenya and the Nong Nooch Botanical Garden in Thailand suggest tremendous returns on their investments in childcare centres for rural agricultural workers in terms of goodwill, productivity and lower absenteeism; workers would otherwise have few desirable alternatives for childcare. Hungarian Post, where many workers have low incomes, finds that workers greatly appreciate the good summer camp programmes for their children (which they otherwise could not afford) and views the camp benefit as an important means for bringing greater job satisfaction to this group of workers. Similarly at BMW in South Africa, the Early Learning Centres are seen as a means to help workers' children have a better start in life and part of fulfilling the company's corporate social responsibility.

To encourage workplace initiatives that benefit low-income workers, public policies might specifically target employer incentives (tax credits or exemptions, subsidies) at employees on low or minimum wages.

Within organizations, greater financial support is sometimes provided to those workers with lower incomes, sometimes involving sliding scales for a workplace centre as in the case of the inter-enterprise crèches in France. Similarly, the Royal Marsden in the United Kingdom provides greater childcare subsidies to its lower-income workers. And in Chile, the University of Concepción provides kindergarten scholarships for the children of lower-paid workers.

- **Beyond mothers:** Childcare benefits are sometimes reserved for female employees – this seems to be particularly the case in countries where laws require employers to provide childcare for their female employees. However, even in these countries, some workplaces offer childcare benefits to fathers, for example at the University of Concepción in Chile, the Oswaldo Cruz Foundation in Brazil, and in India, Bharat Heavy Electricals and Gokaldas Images (which fall under the law) as well as Wipro, Infosys and the National Centre for Biological Sciences. These companies thus explicitly recognize that men also have childcare responsibilities and fathers interviewed for the case studies expressed appreciation for these benefits. In all the other countries, none of the workplace examples of childcare support was restricted to women workers: both fathers and mothers were eligible and used the benefit.

5.3 Lessons for employers' and workers' organizations

For the most part, the workplace examples in Part II of this book involve individual employers and show how they have taken measures for improving employees' access to childcare. In a number of workplace examples, trade unions at enterprise or sectoral levels were also instrumental in pushing for workplace support, often through collective bargaining, or in some cases even providing childcare directly. These examples show that efforts by workplace actors can make an important difference for working parents who are often struggling with their childcare needs.

At the national level, workers' and employers' organizations could do more to encourage and facilitate childcare initiatives, by influencing government policies and programmes. This book has presented a number of examples to show the different ways that regional and national level employers' and workers' organizations have been promoting policies to help workers cope with their family responsibilities and improve their access to childcare (see Chapter 3). Some of the ways that workers' and employers' organizations (or sometimes associations or coalitions) have been promoting childcare at regional and national levels include:

- engaging in national policy debates;
- mounting or supporting campaigns for policy changes;
- setting up enterprise awards;
- compiling good practices; and
- providing tools, services, information.

The general impression is that in many countries, employers' and workers' organizations could play a much stronger role, particularly through advocacy for the improvement of public policies, including measures to improve community childcare services and to encourage workplace assistance. Advocacy efforts seem to be rare despite the fact that lack of childcare that is affordable, convenient and of good quality is a problem that negatively affects both workers and employers around the world. The workplace disruptions and the worker stress caused by childcare inadequacies are too often perceived as resulting from personal problems of workers rather than from the organization of society and a lack of childcare services.

Since childcare services have major implications for the welfare of workers and of businesses, trade unions and employers' organizations have every interest in participating in policy debates and government consultations related to childcare policy and provision, yet this is far from being the case in a number of countries. With greater engagement of the social partners, public policies would be more realistic and take into account not only the needs of children but also those of working parents and employers. By participating in national policy discussions, workers' and employers' organizations could stress the relevance of the childcare issue not only for their members but more generally for the economy and the welfare of workers.

While it is clear that access to childcare is a major problem for many working parents, the answers to the problem are complex and constitute a major challenge for governments, employers and workers. As this book shows, workplace initiatives have been very helpful in addressing the problems of some workers. However, governments need to take the lead by integrating workers' needs into childcare policies and programmes and also by providing the enabling framework for collaboration with and technical support of workplace initiatives. The very existence of workplace solutions for childcare points to the urgent need for more action and better policies and measures that take greater account of the needs of working parents.

Part II

Photo © gettyimages

Brazil 6

Suyanna Linhales Barker [1]

National overview

As a result of social movements for women's and workers' rights, the provision of childcare for working mothers during the breastfeeding period has been guaranteed in Brazilian law since 1988. Many of the companies falling under the legislation prefer the option of providing a childcare subsidy rather than a workplace crèche, but the amount is often less than needed for quality childcare. There has also been considerable public effort to provide preschool education for children aged 4 to 6 years, although this operates on a half-day basis. Nevertheless, few public facilities are available for children under age 3 or for primary schoolchildren, whose school hours are just four hours per day, a situation that particularly poses problems for poor families.

[1] Suyanna Linhales Barker is a psychologist and researcher specializing in the health effects of child labour and in youth development and adolescent health policy. She holds a doctorate in public health. She would like to thank Silvia Lacouth and Yvone Souza of Oswaldo Cruz Foundation, Ricardo Furlan of Natura and Alcenir Portela of FURNAS for their collaboration. She would also like to express her appreciation to Marianna Olinger of Promundo and to Denise Maria Cesario and Tatiana Pardo of the Foundation of the Toy Manufacturers' Association–Abrinq for their important cooperation.

Childcare and workers' rights

The first workplace-based crèche in Brazil was inaugurated in 1899 by the Spinning and Fabrics Corcovado Company in Rio de Janeiro. Despite industrialization in twentieth-century Brazil, which brought a considerable increase in women's labour force participation, the care of workers' children was mostly neglected. Often it was delegated to philanthropic entities whose main function was to mitigate the poverty of the working classes. Only in the 1960s and 1970s did crèches come to be seen as a right for all, as a result of the women's rights and workers' movements. However, given the political repression in the country, it was only at the end of the 1980s, with the return of democracy, that legislation provided for childcare for working mothers during the breastfeeding period as part of workers' rights.[2] Also since the 1980s, there has been a considerable increase in the labour market participation of women aged 24 to 54 – the age group with most young children – from 44 per cent in 1982 to almost 66 per cent in 2004.[3]

Workers' rights in Brazil are set out in the *Consolidation of Labour Laws*[4] which affirm:

1) maternity leave of 120 days for women;

2) five days of paternity leave for men after the birth of a child;

3) that any company with 30 or more women over 16 years of age must have an appropriate place for employees to place their children during the period of breastfeeding. The text does not specify the duration of this period, and states that the firm itself can offer this space or can provide it via subcontracted nurseries;

4) that crèches available to companies through such an agreement should be close to the workplace;

5) that until a child is 6 months old, female workers are entitled to two paid breastfeeding periods of half an hour each during the working day. When the health of the child necessitates it, the period can be extended beyond six months; and

6) a company that has no daycare or other arrangement can adopt the system of daycare reimbursement for payment of institutional or other forms of childcare, chosen by the worker. Periods and values are stipulated in collective bargaining agreements.

---

[2] Joia, 2008.
[3] De Mello et al., 2006, table 1.
[4] Carrion, 1997.

It is important to note that workplace initiatives serve only a small number of relatively privileged families in Brazil. In 2007, only 2 per cent of 120 companies with industrial plants had a crèche or childcare centre in their workplace.[5] The same survey also found that most employers prefer to provide daycare vouchers, which normally cover only part of the cost spent on childcare by workers. The solution for many workers in the formal labour market is to pay private crèches or to employ domestic servants in their homes to care for their children while they are at work.

The payment of daycare reimbursement has been the most recurrent means used by Brazilian companies to comply with labour laws, which require every company without an on-site crèche to adopt a system of reimbursement for the payment of private daycare or another method of providing for childcare for workers. The amount of this reimbursement is a non-taxable benefit for employees; its duration and amount are set by a collective agreement between the employer and the trade unions. Some companies with workplace crèches also provide reimbursement if there is no room for an employee's child.

Legislation initially focused on the need for working mothers to breastfeed babies and to have crèches in or near the workplace for this purpose. However, some companies are going well beyond the legal requirements by agreeing to provisions for children well beyond the breastfeeding stage and by offering the benefit to male as well as female employees, as seen in the first case which follows. Unions have played an important role in ensuring these additional rights.

In some settings, agreements may ensure childcare reimbursement for children up to 6 years of age, while in other settings they provide daycare only for children up to 2 years of age. However, in many cases, this benefit is provided without a careful planning process and in many collective agreements this benefit is more a matter of form – for example, employers may pay only a minimal amount (around US$50 per month), which is not enough to secure quality daycare. A review of collective bargaining agreements in Brazil between 1996 and 2000 found that childcare is relatively low on the list of agreements; only 11 per cent of the clauses in collective agreements included childcare.[6]

The institution responsible for ensuring the implementation of childcare agreements is the Ministry of Labour and Employment, through its Inspection Sector. In the case of non-compliance, the company is given a warning and a timeframe to achieve compliance.

---

[5] Hewitt Associates, 2007. *Survey of worker benefits.* See http://www.hewittassociates.com [16 June 2009].

[6] Brazil, Departamento Intersindical de Estatística e Estudos Socioeconômico, 2003.

Many workers do not benefit from the childcare legislation. Changes in the structure of the labour force have led to diminishing benefits for workers who, in their collective agreements, are not able to negotiate for their full rights, including crèches in the workplace, as was seen above.[7] Brazil is currently facing a considerable loss of jobs in manufacturing and is also seeing a growth in women's labour force participation in the service sector. Women now represent approximately 45 per cent of the total labour force in the country.[8]

Given that manufacturing jobs were mostly men's employment, this loss of jobs in manufacturing has in some cases meant that men are more likely to be unemployed, or see wage losses. As a result, there has been an increase in households where women are the primary or sole providers.

About half of the active workforce in the country is in informal employment, where social security and legislated benefits do not extend.[9] Employment figures confirm that, in recent years, there has been a considerable increase in the proportion of men and women working in the informal economy, as a result of the restructuring of production processes caused by the neoliberal economic organization in the country (and worldwide). Thus work is taking forms that are not protected by labour laws, and collective agreements are applied only to the category of workers who negotiated the agreement, leaving behind the majority of workers.

In some countries, the legal provision of crèches for women workers has meant that employers sometimes avoid hiring the number of women which would require providing a crèche; however, in Brazil, this has not been the case. Because the cost in Brazil of providing daycare has been minimal (compared with the cost of other benefits), having childcare benefits does not seem to have had a negative impact on the hiring of women.

Public policies and provision of childcare

Increasingly, the crèche is being seen as more than a question of women's rights and workers' rights to have care for their children but also as part of children's rights to quality early childhood education. This combination of the labour rights and children's rights movements has pressured policy-makers to assume

---

[7] Sorj, 2004.

[8] Instituto de Pesquisa Econômica Aplicada (IPEA), http://www.ipea.gov.br/sites/000/2/boletim_mercado_de_trabalho/mt32/03_anexo_Populacao.pdf [11 June 2009].

[9] De Mello et al., 2006.

responsibility for providing healthy spaces and quality education for all children up to 6 years old in Brazil. Children's rights legislation passed in 1990 states that all children under the age of 6 should have access to publicly funded (but not necessarily publicly provided) daycare. The implementation of this law has been the focus of much advocacy in early childhood education – that is, seeking to ensure that, in fact, children under 6 have such services.[10]

In Brazil, daycare centres serve children from 0 to 3 years old and preschool children from 4 to 6 years old (although in 2007, the primary school age was lowered to age 6). Some private centres may take older children. In 2006, 15.5 per cent of children up to 3 years of age were attending crèches or daycare around the country.[11] It is important to keep in mind that most of these daycare centres are not workplace based, and that this number includes both children from middle- and upper-income families who pay for private daycare, as well as community- based or public daycare centres, which primarily service lower-income families. In total, Brazil has 28,055 daycare centres; 48 per cent of them are private. A report of a UNESCO visit to a public daycare centre in a slum of Rio de Janeiro notes that there is a long waiting list of children for whom there is no place. "In response to poor working parents' desperate need for childcare, a number of small for-profit centres have sprung up, whose quality cannot be warranted."[12]

Access to kindergartens and preschools is higher, and although still limited, reflects a considerable public effort. In 2002/2003, national data confirmed that 26 per cent of 4-year-olds, 54 per cent of 5-year-olds and 67.1 per cent of 6-year-olds were enrolled in preschool.[13] It is estimated that 72 per cent of pre- schools are public.[14] Public preschools are free of charge for parents and operate for three hours per day.

For children who are not enrolled in daycare centres or are in preschool with hours that do not cover parents' working time, families have three possible strategies:

1) **Employing a domestic worker:** Many better-off families employ domestic workers whose work includes childcare. In Brazil, according to data for 2005, there are about 6.6 million people in domestic work, of whom 93.4 per cent are

---

[10] Public education in Brazil is decentralized. It is funded by a mixture of federal, municipal and state government funds, with municipalities responsible for implementing preschool and primary education, and state and federal governments running secondary schools.

[11] Instituto Brasileiro de Geografia e Estatística (IBGE), *Pesquisa National por Amostra de Domicilios 2006*, Table 2.4. ftp://ftp.ibge.gov.br/Indicadores_Sociais/Sintese_de_Indicadores_Sociais_2007/Tabelas (select Educacao.zip) [9 June 2009].

[12] UNESCO and OECD, 2007.

[13] UNESCO, IBE, 2006a.

[14] Ibid.

girls or women. Of these, 55 per cent are black. Of all the women who work in the country, 17 per cent are domestic workers.[15] There is also a problem of child domestic workers. Brazil has an estimated 500,000 children and adolescents between the ages of 5 and 17 who work as domestic workers in family homes; the majority are girls, most of whom are Afro-Brazilian.[16]

2) **Relying on the extended family or older children:** In low-income families, as has been confirmed in child labour studies in Brazil, daughters may provide childcare along with other domestic work in their own homes, replacing their parents during the work day.

3) **Paying a *mãe-crecheira*:** These are women who take children into their home, sometimes caring for several children at a time. There is no quantitative research on this group and their number is not known.

Even when children start school at age 6, the childcare problems of parents do not end. Public and private schooling in Brazil is only four hours per day (either 8.00 to 12.00 in the morning or 1.00 to 5.00 in the afternoon); thus working parents also have to consider before- or after-school alternatives for their children over the age of 6. Since few public schools offer a full day of activities, children either have to be picked up by someone at 12.00 or taken to school at around 1.00 by someone. The vast majority of low-income parents rely on informal care and informal activities for their school-age children before or after school hours.

Workers in formal employment in commerce and industry may have access to after-school or holiday activities for their school-age children through social service organizations for workers and their families. Since 1966, industries are legally bound to contribute 1.5 per cent of their payroll to SESI (Serviço Social da Indústria), which runs a wide variety of programmes in health, education, leisure, culture and nutrition, and promotes socially responsible business. SESI is a quasi-governmental agency run by the National Confederation of Industry, but its council includes representatives of government and the trade unions. There is a regional branch in each state so programmes vary. Programmes for workers' children include early childhood education in addition to arts, leisure and sports activities after school and during school vacations. In 2006, there were approximately 35,000 children enrolled in SESI's early childhood education programmes.[17]

---

[15] Bruschini, 2007, p. 560.
[16] ANDI, 2003.
[17] http://tinyurl.com/klv6p3 [19 June 2009].

Another way that women may be coping with problems of childcare is to work reduced hours. In 2004, about 17.5 per cent of employed women worked less than 20 hours per week (compared to just 6.4 per cent of men), up from 13.5 per cent in 1982.[18] Some states and municipalities in Brazil are seeking to offer after-school (or before-school) programming, and a full school day is to be implemented in Brazil as part of national legislation. This measure would probably make it easier for mothers of young children to work or to work longer hours.

Efforts to increase quantity and quality

To develop strategies for increasing the coverage of preschools and kindergartens in the country, the Federal Government established a working group of representatives from the Ministries of Social Development, Education and Planning and from the Fome Zero (hunger alleviation) Initiative, and sought to create solutions for federal funding to meet the needs of children up to 6 years old.[19]

The inter-ministerial working group developed short-term budgetary policies to fund the care of children aged 0 to 6 and established a national policy of early childhood education. The Ministry of Education, which is responsible for implementing this policy,[20] provided guidelines and directives for its implementation and funding via the National Programme for Restructuring and Acquisition of Equipment for the Network of Early Childhood Education, called PROINFÂNCIA. This new action plan brings together various pre-existing initiatives of the Ministry of Education, which, through its programme on Early Childhood Development, had already been working to enhance the qualifications of childcare workers through the National Training Programme for Childcare Workers, called PROINFANTIL.

This transition meant that public funds for childcare that had previously been seen as welfare are now seen as part of the public education sector, and part of children's basic rights to free, high-quality education. This transition – of viewing early childhood education as a right – has been endorsed by various advocacy groups working on behalf of children's rights. Among the advocacy groups worth citing is the Inter-forum Movement for Child Education in Brazil – MIEIB,[21]

---

[18] De Mello et al., 2006, p. 12.

[19] Interministerial Ordinance No. 3219, 21 September 2005.

[20] Resolução nº 6, 24/4/2007, found at http://www.fnde.gov.br/home/index.jsp?arquivo= resolucoes_2007.html [25 May 2009].

[21] http://www.mieib.org.br [11 June 2009].

which has lobbied for more resources for early childhood education and whose members have actively participated in developing training and qualification standards for public early childhood education.

It is worth noting that neither the Ministry of Labour and Employment, the Amalgamated Workers' Union, nor the Employers' Associations of the country are participating directly in the process of restructuring early childhood education, although they are responsible for negotiating and reviewing workers' rights with regard to childcare in workplaces. In this context, the workplace-based daycare centres of large companies are excluded from the process of expansion and restructuring of publicly funded early childhood education in Brazil (with a few exceptions, such as the crèche of the Oswaldo Cruz Foundation, which follows the early childhood education curriculum of the Ministry of Education; see the case study which follows). Furthermore, these workplace-based daycare centres are nearly always excluded from studies on the quality of daycare in Brazil.[22] Better linkage of workplace provisions for childcare with policies for early childhood education and greater involvement of workplace actors in policy discussions might help make childcare more relevant for working parents.

Some corporations have been making a considerable effort to improve childcare and early childhood development facilities through their social responsibility activities. For example, the C&A Institute,[23] the foundation affiliated with the clothing company of the same name, and the Foundation of the Toy Manufacturers' Association – Abrinq,[24] have partnered on a programme called Early Childhood First. This initiative includes the creation of a Regional Advocates' Network for Early Childhood Education, which promotes early childhood education for all children, with a focus on infrastructure development, staff training and public–private partnerships to maintain and sustain early childhood education centres.

The Regional Advocates' Network for Early Childhood Education has established leadership in 25 Brazilian states and is in the process of organizing regional meetings with local partners, including representatives from business, trade unions and the public sector, and experts in early childhood education. The goal is to organize a group that can advise municipalities and states on the implementation of proposals for the inclusion of all children aged 0 to 6 in the public education system.

---

[22] Campanha Nacional pelo Direito à Educação/MIEIB, 2006.

[23] http://www.institutocea.org.br/instituto/site/content/home/default.aspx [11 June 2009].

[24] http://www.fundabrinq.org.br [11 June 2009].

There have been some small-scale examples of public–private collaboration. In the Southern state of Rio Grande do Sul, IBM and some other businesses have been working with the state government to implement high-quality daycare services. These services have been funded mostly with public funds, with technical and financial assistance from these businesses.[25]

Conclusion

The need for childcare has long been recognized in Brazil thanks to social movements promoting women's rights, workers' rights and, more recently, children's rights. Public authorities are clearly making a considerable effort to make childcare more available and to improve its quality despite public budget constraints. Private corporations, collectively and individually, as well as the labour unions and civil society groups, have been active in this effort. While there is still considerable progress to be made, the active involvement of both the public and private sectors as well as civil society would seem to bode well for the future of expanding and improving early childcare.

Oswaldo Cruz Foundation

Type of business. Public health institute.

Workplace. Headquarters, Manguinhos campus in the North Zone of Rio de Janeiro, including a vaccine factory, units in Belo Horizonte, Salvador, Recife and Manaus, and a second site in Rio de Janeiro.

Workers. 7,500 with varied professional training and educational levels, ranging from factory workers to medical researchers.

Working hours. Shiftwork; those using the crèche are entitled to work on the 8.00 a.m. to 5.00 p.m. shift.

Childcare solution. Crèche from age 4 months to 6 years for men and women workers at headquarters; daycare subsidy for children aged 4 months to 6 years for men and women workers.

Partners. Workers' Trade Union of the Oswaldo Cruz Foundation.

---

[25] Promundo, 2007.

The Oswaldo Cruz Foundation (Fiocruz), part of the Ministry of Health, is the largest science and technology institution of health in Latin America. Its basic principles are health promotion and social development through the production and dissemination of scientific knowledge.[26] The institution carries out diverse activities including: research; providing health reference services for hospitals and outpatients; manufacturing vaccines, drugs, reagents and diagnostic kits; educating and training human resources; and information and communication in health, science and technology.

Foundation workers' benefits are managed by the Department of Human Resources, including the Foundation's crèche.[27] The workers are represented by the Workers' Trade Union of the Oswaldo Cruz Foundation.[28] The union was founded in July 1978 and has served as the trade union entity since 1986.

The crèche was inaugurated in September 1989 and was the result of long negotiations between the Foundation's administration and the trade union. This "space" for the negotiation was made possible by the process of the new-found democratization in the country in the 1980s, which enabled both the return of a more democratic administration for the Foundation, as well as the political space for the trade union in a commission that defined the scope and quality of the daycare centre.[29]

Childcare facility

The crèche provides early childhood care and education for the Foundation employees' children up to 6 years of age. The crèche seeks to provide the child with knowledge of the surrounding world and encourages interaction at home, in the community, and as an active agent in his/her own learning.

The crèche has a capacity for 300 children and is open from Monday to Friday, 7.00 a.m. to 5.00 p.m., with a "grace time" of half an hour on arrival and departure. It is closed on weekends and holidays and during a vacation period in January.

Occupying an area of 5,553 m², with a built area of 734 m², there are three blocks of buildings, separated by outside courtyards, for an airy and open environment. The playground has a park with wooden toys, a dollhouse, a sandpit and a vegetable garden. The entire area is surrounded by a large number of trees comprising a green area.

---

[26] http://www.fiocruz.br/media/relatorio_2007.pdf [11 June 2009].

[27] http://www.fiocruz.br [11 June 2009].

[28] http://www.asfoc.fiocruz.br [11 June 2009].

[29] Fiocruz, 2008.

Today, 20 years after its foundation, the crèche is a successful example of caring for workers' children, and has also become established as a centre of research and training in the area of early childhood education.

Some workers with children aged 4 months to 6 years may not use the crèche if, for example, they work at other sites or have other arrangements. Such workers can receive a daycare stipend worth approximately US$56.00 per month. This allowance is paid even if the child is cared for by a relative and they actually have no direct childcare costs.

Eligibility and use

All male and female full-time workers and those belonging to the Oswaldo Cruz Foundation staff are entitled to use the daycare for their children and no fee is charged. There is no formal system for evaluating satisfaction with the crèche, but the high demand by the workers for this service speaks for its quality. The crèche is nearly always close to 100 per cent of its total capacity, and the children of medical researchers as well as vaccine factory workers can and do use the service.

Management and financing

The crèche is fully funded and maintained by the Oswaldo Cruz Foundation and the company's investment in this benefit is approximately US$625 per child, per month. Its management is under the Department of Human Resources and is supervised by a Parents' Advisory Council, which participates in discussions about the crèche. The Council does not set policy and practice, but is consulted on all decisions and develops the rules for the crèche.

Both the Department of Human Resources and the trade union actively participate in the maintenance of the crèche on the Manguinhos campus. The trade union – which includes the parents of the children enrolled in the crèche – participates from negotiations to evaluations of the quality of the services provided.

The state health control service and the municipality inspect the working environment, and the crèche follows the national parameters set out by the Ministry of Education's early childhood education curriculum.

Finally, it is worth noting that, as part of a foundation concerned with public health, this workplace-based facility gives paramount concern to providing early childhood education in a safe and healthy environment. Medical monitoring of the children also adds value to the quality of service.

Staff

The crèche's technical team consists of a coordinator, two psychologists, three teachers, a doctor, a nutritionist and a social worker. There are 14 teachers and 23 assistants, two music teachers, a drama teacher and a physical education instructor. Another 29 professionals take care of cooking, janitorial services and administrative and security functions.

The quality of its service, particularly the high level of qualification of its staff and its investment in infrastructure, has made the Oswaldo Cruz Foundation crèche a model for early childhood research and professional training. The staff provide training to early childcare and education workers from other centres. Through its Teaching and Research Centre, the crèche's staff advances human resources in child development and has influenced early childhood education policy at the national level. For example, the course Professional Development in Infant Education aims to develop human resources in infant education, ensuring the quality of training and promoting an understanding of the young child as a citizen deserving of respect, care and education.

Management perspective

For management, investment in childcare is in line with the importance they place on this type of service for employees, ensuring that workers can leave their children knowing they are cared for with utmost attention. In turn, this allows workers to achieve their highest potential and be motivated in their work. The Foundation has achieved a high degree of excellence precisely because it has invested in its employees by ensuring their right to have their children well cared for, protected and educated.

Conclusion

It is not by chance that the Oswaldo Cruz Foundation, which is recognized as the largest and one of the most renowned institutions of science and technology in health in Latin America, also has one of the most recognized centres of early childhood education in the country. The same level of competence and worker participation that goes into the public health actions of the Foundation are applied to the crèche.

Natura

Type of business. Manufacture and sales of cosmetics.

Workplace. Factory in Cajamar which is a centre of research, production and logistics and shopping mall in Itapecerica da Serra which is a sales and distribution centre.

Workers. 63 per cent women workers who occupy 52 per cent of leadership positions.

Working hours. The factory runs several shifts.

Childcare solution. Two crèches (running from 5.30 a.m. to 8.00 p.m. to cover the first two shifts) for children of women workers from age 4 months to fourth birthday.

Partners. Trade union, private childcare company.

Natura is the leading company in the domestic market of cosmetics, fragrances and personal hygiene in Brazil. Currently it manufactures about 900 products, including make up, perfume, sunscreen and creams for facial, body and hair care. It is an expanding business and also has operations in Argentina, Chile, France, Mexico, Peru and, more recently, in Colombia and Venezuela.[30] In Brazil, its manufacturing operations are concentrated in the area of Cajamar, São Paulo, with an integrated centre of research, production and logistics. It also has sales offices and distribution centres in Itapecerica da Serra, São Paulo State, and in Uberlândia and Mathias Barbosa, Minas Gerais State.

Natura views its workers as partners. Its commitment to the development of an organizational culture of worker well-being has led to a series of awards including recognition as one of the 50 Best Companies for Working Women in 2006; one of the 150 Best Companies to Work For in 2004, 2005 and 2006; and one of the 100 Best Companies to Work For in Latin America – 2005 and 2006.

Benefits and services for employees are designed to promote a healthy and productive work–life balance. In addition to the benefits stipulated by law, Natura offers all employees an extra year-end bonus (in addition to the 13 months of salary stipulated in Brazilian labour law), medical-dental benefits for workers and dependants and a programme to promote educational attainment and advancement (for employees and their children up to 21 years of age), called Natura Education. Prenatal services are provided for pregnant women employees and contractors and for wives of employees and contractors. These benefits are negotiated in annual collective bargaining between the company and the Chemists'

---

[30] http://natura.infoinvest.com.br/static/enu/perfil_organizacao.asp?language=enu [19 June 2009].

Union. Natura provides spaces and forums through which unions can provide information to employees and increase participation in the unions.

Childcare facility

Crèches are located in the cities of Cajamar and Itapecerica da Serra, in São Paulo State. The first is at the factory site and the second is in a shopping mall. Both crèches have existed for more than 17 years. The crèches were created to attend to mothers' needs and were set up so children could be breastfed on demand. Still today, mothers are called when their children cry to be fed during the breastfeeding period.

The crèche in Cajamar has 1,300 m², cares for 175 children and operates from 5.30 a.m. until 8.00 p.m. daily, serving the employees working the two first shifts in the factory. All women on other shifts who have children have the right to be moved to the first shift to be able to use the crèche. The factory is open two Saturdays a month, during which time the crèche is also open. The Itapecerica da Serra crèche has 400 m², serves 30 children and is open from 8.00 a.m. to 8.00 p.m. daily; since this is a business unit, it is not open on Saturdays.

Both crèches have open-air spaces, with a cafeteria and restrooms adapted for young children and different rooms for different age groups. The activities offered encourage child development and provide a safe and welcoming environment.

Eligibility and use

Natura's crèches provide services for children of women workers from the age of 4 months up to 3 years and 11 months – two years beyond legal requirements. Facilities are generally full to capacity.

Management and finance

Ten years ago the administration and staffing of the crèches was outsourced to a private company called the Centre for Professional Training and Education (CEDUC),[31] which has extensive experience in the organization of early

---

[31] http://www.crechesceduc.com.br [11 June 2009].

childhood education services and is responsible for other childcare institutions, including those provided to the employees of Avon and Unilever.

The investment of Natura in this benefit is US$800 per child per month and there is no fee for workers. This is a considerable benefit given that women's salaries range from US$1,600 to US$5,900 per month.

In total, approximately 50 professionals work in the two crèches, including teachers, breastfeeding specialists, nutritionists and nurses. The coordination of the crèche is divided into administrative and educational units. The crèches are regularly inspected by the health inspectors by the municipalities.

Management perspective

The crèches were created initially to meet the needs of breastfeeding women workers in response partly to legislation and partly to pressure from staff. It is part of Natura's effort to create an organizational culture supporting its workers, who are seen as partners in achieving company goals.

Worker perspective

In worker satisfaction surveys carried out by external auditors, the crèches are regularly identified as being among the best benefits offered by the company. In part, this is because the centres are based in the workplace, and are well maintained, well staffed and attractive for children and parents.

Lessons learned

Natura is a good example of a workplace crèche funded by a company but outsourced to a high-quality, specialist organization – CEDUC. Mothers clearly appreciate the quality of the childcare provided.

FURNAS

Type of business. State-owned electricity company.

Workplace. 11 hydroelectric plants, two thermoelectric plants and sales offices.

Workers. 6,500, of whom 30 per cent are women.

Working hours. From 8.00 a.m. to 8.00 p.m., in two eight-hour shifts.

Childcare solution. Daycare reimbursement for women workers with children aged 0–7 years; summer camp; after-school activities.

Partners. Trade unions (collective bargaining agreements); private daycare centres in the community; SESI (Serviço Social da Indústria).

FURNAS is a state-owned company managed by the Federal Government through the Ministry of Mines and Energy.[32] It was founded in 1957 to meet the energy demands of Brazil's rapid urbanization in the 1950s. It operates in the generation, transmission and marketing of electric power, ensuring the supply of energy to 51 per cent of Brazilian homes and to businesses accounting for 65 per cent of Brazilian GDP. Today, it consists of a complex of 11 hydroelectric plants, two thermoelectric plants, 19,278 km of transmission lines and 46 substations.

Most of its staff are technicians and clerical workers. Since 2003 the company has developed the Gender Working Group, coordinated by the Director of Social Responsibility, a body attached to the FURNAS Presidency, which creates mechanisms that ensure gender equity and women's empowerment, both inside the company and in the communities where it operates.[33]

Among the company's policies for childcare of employees, the following initiatives stand out:

- comprehensive health-care insurance for employees and their dependants under age 21 years for those attending university and up until age 18 for non-university-going youth;

- summer camp in January for employees' children aged 7 to 14 years;

- a contract with the Industry Social Service (SESI)[34] for after-school activities for children of employees;

- daycare reimbursement up to US$750 a month for women employees with children aged 0 to 7 years;

---

[32] http:// www.furnas.com.br [11 June 2009].

[33] http://www.furnas.com.br/links.asp?lnk=grupogenero/grupogenero.asp [11 June 2009].

[34] http://www.sesi.org.br [11 June 2009].

- payment of education aid valued at US$125 for male employees with children aged 0 to 14 and women employees with children between 8 and 14 years of age;

- payment of extra support for children with special needs, through health-care insurance, access to services for mental health, speech therapy, physical therapy, educational counselling, neurological services or others. These services are used to help improve the children's academic performance; and

- implementation of educational agreements offering discounts on tuition at private schools and private universities. FURNAS currently has agreements with 148 private educational institutions which provide tuition discounts for employees' children. Most of these schools are in neighbourhoods where the company is located or where a representative number of employees live. Workers can ask FURNAS to accredit an establishment for this benefit by presenting a concrete need on behalf of a significant number of employees.

These benefits are negotiated in annual collective agreements with trade unions. The Office of Trade Union Relations, linked to the Director of Human Resources, has the task of designing, on the basis of research with other companies, the type and scope of benefits to comply with union demands. This office's function is to find the best cost–benefit rate to meet the needs of workers. FURNAS has around 3,000 unionized employees and the annual collective bargaining agreement extends to the entire workforce. The company negotiates annually with approximately 14 unions, affiliated to the two largest labour unions in the country, CUT – Central Única do Trabalhadores – and CGT – Central Geral do Trabalhadores.

This case study focuses on the main childcare benefits: daycare reimbursement and after-school activities and summer camp for schoolchildren.

Daycare reimbursement

The payment of daycare reimbursement has been the most common way for Brazilian companies to comply with labour law, which requires every company which does not have a crèche on its premises to adopt a system of reimbursement for women employees. By providing reimbursement until the child is 7 years old, the programme at FURNAS goes well beyond the requirements of the legislation. To obtain reimbursement, women must show receipts for the money they spend for care.

The programme for daycare reimbursement includes a system of accreditation of private daycare institutions. Accreditation of crèches is carried out by

FURNAS human resource staff, who assess the quality of services provided. This assessment includes the capacity of the establishment, the adequacy of its health and safety standards for children and its educational curriculum. Only after assessing the daycare centre is the establishment offered to employees as a place for daycare services. All accredited establishments are close to the workplace and can be used after maternity leave to enable breastfeeding until the child is 6 months old. In company locations where there is no nearby daycare, workers may apply for reimbursement for domestic help in their homes.

The advanced accreditation process helps women workers to choose the daycare centre most appropriate for their needs, and also establishes a network between the company, the private daycare centres and the workers, which ensures the quality control of services provided. It should be noted that the amount reimbursed by FURNAS for care covers the market costs for daycare services. Thus the local, private daycare centres have much interest in being on the list of accredited institutions as it provides a steady source of business for them.

Reimbursement of daycare costs as a way of supporting childcare needs has interesting advantages for both workers and the company. For workers, the system means they can choose where and how to provide daycare for their children. It is efficient in that it gives flexibility for workers to find the best childcare arrangement for their needs. This is precisely the objective of the reimbursement programme at FURNAS. The cost for the company of this benefit is just 0.01 per cent of net revenues while the positive results are evident in studies on organizational climate, which report worker satisfaction with this benefit.

After-school activities and summer camp

FURNAS has a contract with SESI (Serviço Social da Indústria) in which SESI provides after-school activities for employees' children. As previously mentioned, SESI is part of what is called the S-system in Brazil, a quasi-public system funded by a tax paid by industries. All workers formally employed by a business that pays into the S-system (and their family members) are able to use these services, which include recreation, continuing education courses, literacy courses and art classes, among others.

In addition to the after-school activities, summer camps for the month of January (during the summer vacation in Brazil) are open to children of all FURNAS employees as well as employees of other companies that contribute to SESI. The cost is fully paid by the company through its tax contribution to SESI; there is no additional cost for workers.

Conclusion

The example of FURNAS shows how daycare reimbursement programmes can have major benefits both for workers and companies, with greater flexibility compared to providing workplace-based nurseries. For workers, the reimbursement covers the market cost, they have some choice in facilities, and provider accreditation by the company helps to ensure quality services for their children. For the employer, the cost is not likely to be greater than a workplace nursery. The accreditation system has the merit of offering an incentive for eligible daycare providers to improve their services.

The example of FURNAS also illustrates the usefulness of the services of SESI for workers' school-age children. This organization, which provides social services for workers, is a unique national agency created in Brazil 60 years ago to raise the standard of living of workers and their families, and it offers a wide range of activities including educational and leisure facilities.

Medley

Type of business. Manufacture and sales of pharmaceuticals.

Workplace. Factories in the cities of Campinas and Sumaré, in São Paulo State.

Workers. 1,609 employees, 42.4 per cent of whom are women.

Working hours. From 6.00 a.m. to 2.00 p.m. and from 8.30 a.m. to 5.30 p.m., according to the shift patterns of workers.

Childcare solution. A crèche for children of employees and children who live in the neighbourhood of the factory site aged 0–6 years.

Partners. Public municipal institutions, neighbourhood associations, NGOs, the Federation of Social Services Entities of Campinas, the Municipal Council of the Rights of Children and Adolescents.

Medley[35] is one of the largest pharmaceutical companies in Brazil, employing approximately 1,609 employees, with units in Campinas and Sumaré, in São Paulo State. Since 2002 the company has received awards for being one of the 100 best companies to work for in Brazil and it is on the list of the 50 best companies for women to work in.

---

[35] http://www.medley.com.br [11 June 2009].

Medley has a number of programmes which focus on the family including family visits to the company on Sunday mornings with special activities planned for children, a "baby kit" for newborn children of employees and a monthly food basket. It also has a daycare centre.

Childcare facility

Since 1999, Medley has maintained the Santa Genebra daycare centre, created to supply the needs of its employees in both the Campinas and Sumaré plants. Located in a neighbourhood called Geneva Garden, near the company's head-quarters in Campinas, the nursery also serves the low-income families who live near the factories. Around 30 per cent of the 150 places are reserved for children whose parents are not employees of Medley. The company's involvement with the surrounding community started with the establishment of the Santa Genebra daycare centre.

Children range from 0 months old to 6 years old in age. The company provides uniforms, meals and educational materials. In addition, the Santa Genebra daycare centre offers a tutoring programme, based on a constructivist approach that prepares children to enter elementary school without difficulties.

The daycare centre provides the following:

- five meals daily, with dishes prepared by nutritionists who offer special attention to children weighing above or below age-appropriate levels;
- educational activities appropriate to each age group, from the age of 3 months on;
- one caregiver for every three babies or eight older children;
- special attention to oral hygiene. From the first tooth, children learn to brush their teeth and a dentist visits periodically for routine examinations; and
- 1,500 square metres of enclosed space, plus gardens and playgrounds.

Following a constructivist pedagogical approach, the centre strives to reach the performance expected for child growth, offering encouragement, incentives and opportunities for full and harmonious development.

The 32 employees working at the centre are dedicated to the mission of guaranteeing the development of the children. All instructors have a teaching degree. The children participate in activities in painting, arts, poetry, theatre, music, dance, sports, walks, parties, commemorations, gymnastics, cooking, massage, games, research and group work.

Eligibility and use

For children aged from birth to 6 years of employees and families who live in the neighbourhoods where the centre is located.

Management and finance

The daycare centre is funded exclusively by Medley, with all activities offered free of charge. The estimated cost per child is US$350 per month.[36] In 2007, the company spent 2.03 per cent of its gross payroll – 0.34 per cent of its net revenues – on daycare and daycare reimbursement.[37] The crèche is seen not only as a benefit for workers but also as part of the social responsibility policy of the company and its efforts to promote community development. In developing this policy, its Social Responsibility Committee fosters the participation of a wide range of community partners – NGOs, municipal bodies and children's rights entities – including the Federation of Welfare Entities of Campinas, the Municipal Council of the Rights of the Children and Adolescents and representatives of NGOs and neighbourhood associations.

Management perspective

In Medley, investment in staff begins with careful selection and continues with policies intended to make the company a preferred employer, attracting talent. The company's annual reports describe the nursery as one of the benefits that is central to ensuring the quality of worker performance. All evaluations of managers indicate that the crèche is a source of quality of life and work enhancement of its employees.

Worker perspective

Medley is considered by its employees to be one of the best companies for working women. The crèche is always identified by employee ratings as one of the most important factors for this positive assessment.

---

[36] http://www.medley.com.br/pdf/relat_resp_social_2004.pdf [11 June 2009].
[37] http://www.medley.com.br/pdf/relat_resp_social_2007.pdf [11 June 2009].

Lessons learned

One of the key lessons learned from the Medley experience is the positive aspect of combining social responsibility – opening its daycare for children from neighbouring communities – with providing a key social service for workers' children. Furthermore, the proximity of the daycare centre to the factory helps create a sense of community within the factories and a positive link between work and family life.

Chile

7

Marco Kremerman Strajilevich [1]

National overview

Chile is currently working to improve its childcare system through new programmes and developments, although it is still struggling to meet its aspirations. Despite recent advances in the last decades, Chilean women still represent a low percentage of the national workforce compared to developed countries and other Latin American countries. Currently, only 40 per cent are either working or seeking a job.[2] Those that do participate are usually incorporated into more precarious jobs than men. As noted in a recent speech by President Bachelet:

> Almost 3 out of 4 women are employed in the trade or in personal services, social or communal, which are two of the industries with the lowest rates of pay, formality

---

[1] Marco Kremerman Strajilevich is a researcher at the Fundación Sol and an adviser of the Ministry of Labour and Social Security in Chile. He would like to acknowledge the valuable collaboration of Gonzalo Durán, Valentina Doniez and Karina Narbona on this work; they are all researchers at the Fundación Sol.

[2] National Institute of Statistics of Chile, Employment Survey, March to May 2008.

173

and job stability. Amongst all employees, the average income for women is 16 per cent below the average for male employees, despite the fact that working women have higher levels of education than men. In fact, the income gap is amplified with the increase of education levels, reaching 31 per cent amongst university students.[3]

A lack of childcare is partially responsible for these disparities, posing considerable barriers to the labour force participation of women with children. According to findings from the 2006 National Socio-Economic Characterization Survey (Encuesta de Caracterización Socioeconómica Nacional, CASEN), the rise in female labour participation has been observed mainly among married and unmarried women without children, suggesting that having children constrains women's labour market participation. The survey shows that one in three women between the ages of 30 and 39 is not seeking a job because they have no place to leave their children. Only women belonging to the richest 20 per cent of households experienced little difficulty in finding childcare solutions.

National policies

Chile has developed a number of commitments and policies on childcare, with early childhood policies developed as early as the 1920s, calling on all primary schools to offer early childhood sections.[4] In the 1940s, Chile developed a school to train early childhood educators, and the Ministry of Education incorporated early childhood education into its plans in 1948.[5] In 1965, the education system was modified to officially include early childhood, and in 1970, Chilean law established an autonomous public corporation, JUNJI, the first of its kind on the continent, to promote child development and women's participation in the labour force through early childhood education programmes. This led to an expansion of early childhood education for 4–6-year-olds, particularly in poor communities, although policies and efforts largely overlooked the care needs of parents with younger children.

The focus of early childhood programmes changed from the 1970s when the military regime (1973–1989) adopted a politically conservative approach and neoliberal economic policies, which affected the educational system as well. In 1990, the new democratically elected government inherited a system marked by

---

[3] Bachelet, 2008.
[4] Umayahara, 2006.
[5] Umayahara, 2006.

disjointed institutional coordination and considerable social inequalities in access to and outcomes of early child education.

In 1990, the new government prioritized improvements in the quality and equity of educational systems. It ratified the UN Convention on the Rights of the Child and undertook a six-year educational investment programme, the Programme of Education Quality and Equity Improvement (Programa de Mejoramiento de la Calidad y Equidad de la Educacion, MECE, 1990–1996), which included efforts to improve the quality of early childhood education and expand the poor's access to such programmes.[6] It also appointed a National Commission for Early Childhood Education to improve coordination among involved institutions from different sectors.

Since 2001, efforts have continued towards the creation of a basic national framework for early childhood education. Efforts have been made in:

- promoting multidimensional learning outcomes;

- extending programmes to vulnerable groups of children including those from indigenous and poor households;

- expanding coverage from ages 0 to 6 years;

- training greater numbers of early childhood educators;

- improving quality of programmes; and

- strengthening management and coordination systems.[7]

In 2006, efforts to expand childcare intensified as part of the agenda of the newly elected President, Michelle Bachelet. The President created a Technical Advisory Council to guide early childhood policies. A strong emphasis has since been placed on developing childcare services, not only to foster children's development, but also to improve women's labour force participation, providing them with access to better-quality jobs, enhancing their autonomy and self-actualization, and promoting gender equality and national development.[8]

Expenditure on pre-primary education (for children 3 years and older) constitutes 0.5 per cent of GDP in Chile.[9] However, reliance on private investment, primarily through tuition fees, is heavy, representing approximately one-third

---

[6] Umayahara, 2006.

[7] Umayahara, 2006.

[8] Bachelet, 2008.

[9] OECD, 2006a, p. 207, table B2.1c.

of expenditure, posing challenges for achieving equality of access for all.[10] Both private and public funds are controlled by individual municipalities, which manage and administer finances for public and subsidized private centres offering childcare.[11]

Service provision and use

The Ministry of Education and organizations such as JUNJI (the National Board for Kindergartens – Junta Nacional de Jardines Infantiles)[12] are in charge of organizing and supervising early childhood education. They also monitor early childhood educators, who are required to have a five-year university degree in education (*Licenciatura de Educacion Parvularia*), and auxiliary personnel, who should have received technical training from technical-professional or educational centres recognized by the state.[13]

Childcare and preschool education in Chile is divided into day nurseries for 0–2-year-olds and kindergartens for children aged 3 to 6 years. Kindergarten groups are divided into classes for children aged 2 to 3 years (lower medium), 3 to 4 years (upper medium), 4 to 5 years (transition 1 or pre-kinder) and 5 to 6 years (transition 2 or kinder). Childcare in Chile is provided through four main sectors as follows:

1) **Free public childcare institutions**, which are state funded and delegated to local communities that are part of both the JUNJI, which was established in 1970, and the INTEGRA Foundation, formed in 1990.[14]

2) **Private childcare and kindergartens** are comprised of private and subsidized establishments or paid individuals providing childcare services in schools and colleges or independently. Subsidized private kindergartens are privately owned and receive a monthly allowance per child from the state. In addition to the subsidies, parents or guardians are expected to co-finance the childcare

---

[10] OECD, 2006a, p. 219, table B3.2a.

[11] Umayahara, 2006.

[12] A state institution whose mission is to deliver integrated nursery education to children under age 6 living in poverty and social vulnerability, and to create and plan, coordinate, promote and supervise the organization and operation of kindergartens in Chile.

[13] Umayahara, 2006.

[14] A private non-profit institution that is part of the Network for Foundations of the Presidency of the Republic, whose role is to "achieve the comprehensive development of children, between three months and five years of age, living in poverty and social vulnerability"; http://www.integra.cl [11 June 2009].

place with a fee, which varies by establishment. This type of childcare solution usually benefits families of middle and higher socio-economic levels.

3) **Workplace crèches:** Employers recruiting 20 or more women workers are, according to the Chilean Labour Code, obliged to provide childcare for children younger than 2 years.

4) **Community kindergartens** are social initiatives creating public/private partnerships for working women who are not covered adequately by conventional means of childcare, such as seasonal workers.

The percentage of children between the ages of 0 and 5 who attend any establishment that provides early childhood education has increased from 15.9 per cent in 1990 to 36.9 per cent in 2006.[15] The major deficit in access to care is for children aged 0 to 2, where only 4 per cent of children attend nurseries. Slightly more than 18 per cent of 2–3-year-olds, 25.9 per cent of 3–4-year-olds, 51.3 per cent of 4–5-year-olds and 92.6 per cent of 5–6-year-olds are in early childhood care and education.[16] Significant gaps persist in socio-economic terms. Only three in ten children coming from the poorest 20 per cent of households are in childcare, compared to almost half of the children belonging to the richest 20 per cent of households.

In her recent speech, Chilean President Bachelet noted government efforts to improve access to care. She stated that, since 2005, the INTEGRA Foundation and JUNJI, which provide kindergartens and nurseries for the public sector, have substantially increased the number of free places for children between the ages of 3 months and 2 years who are living in the poorest areas of Chile. Numbers have risen from 14,400 in 2005 to 64,000 in 2008, with the number expected to reach 84,000 in 2009. In addition, for children aged 2 to 4 years, kindergarten places will have expanded from about 84,000 in 2005 to about 127,000 by 2009.[17]

Workplace obligations

Chilean law has long required employers to participate in childcare provision. The first obligation for companies to provide childcare was Law No. 3.186 of 1917. This legislation required employers in certain sectors with more than 50 women

---

[15] Calculated by the author from the national labour force survey – Encuesta de Caracterización Socioeconómica Nacional (CASEN), 2006.

[16] Umayahara, 2006.

[17] Bachelet, 2008.

workers aged 18 or over to have childcare facilities for children under the age of 1. The main objective of this provision was to facilitate breastfeeding. In 1925, Law No. 442 was passed, lowering the minimum number of female employees to 20 and expanding compulsory childcare provision to children up to 2 years old. This initiative remains part of the current system.[18]

Since only mothers are covered in this legislation, the ILO Committee of Experts on the Application of Conventions and Recommendations (CEACR) raised the concern that the law explicitly excludes working fathers from employer-provided access to childcare, noting that "section 195(2) of the Labour Code explicitly provides that fathers do not enjoy the employment protection set out in section 201 and 174 of the Labour Code".[19] Excluding fathers from access to childcare presumes that women alone are responsible for the care of children, and also raises the possibility that employers may seek to avoid hiring more than 19 women in order to avoid the costs of providing a crèche.

In 1998 the Government established sanctions for non-compliance with the law. In 2002, the regulations were extended beyond commercial centres to include companies in industrial and service sectors.[20] Finally, the legislation established that this benefit is inalienable and not transferable.

According to the Department of Labour, the obligation to provide nursery services may be fulfilled in three ways:

1) creating and maintaining a nursery;

2) through a collective nursery by a number of employers in the same geographical location, namely establishments that have been previously built or set up, following authorization by JUNJI; and

3) where circumstances permit, paying a designated nursery selected by the employer from those approved by JUNJI.

Since 1995, shopping malls are required to provide a solution for female workers with children under the age of 2, as are all "Centres for commercial and industrial services, which belong under a single umbrella or count as a juridical person, and which employ 20 or more workers".[21] Employers may provide crèches directly or may pay for nursery expenses for employees with children under the age of 2. The most common solution has been for companies to establish a relationship

---

[18] It was incorporated in Article 188 of the Labour Code of August 1995.
[19] ILO, 2007a.
[20] Currently these regulations are part of the Labour Code (Articles 203 and 208).
[21] Article 203 of the Labour Code in paragraph 1.

with one or more nurseries already in place. In some cases, the mother chooses an establishment near her home, for which she is later reimbursed.

Even though the law stipulates that companies are obliged to provide a solution for nursery care when employing 20 or more female workers, whether through on-site kindergartens or through voucher systems or external agreements, most women do not have access to this benefit since many work in small or informal enterprises not covered by the law, and because employers tend to keep the number of women to less than 20, to avoid the obligation of providing childcare services. Given that most female workers have the economic means to access only public or community childcare establishments, there have been public and private initiatives to improve workers' access to childcare.

Public and private initiatives for workers

Seasonal workers in agriculture, as well as those in isolated rural areas, have been the focus of public initiatives. In the case of temporary workers, the Servicio Nacional de la Mujer (National Women's Service, SERNAM)[22] has helped to create public programmes to address the needs of mothers carrying out temporary work, particularly in rural areas. These programmes are as follows:

- **Seasonal kindergartens by JUNJI:** This programme is part of the alternatives for kindergartens offered by JUNJI in alliance with SERNAM and JUNAEB (the National Board for School Assistance and Scholarships). It focuses on children of female workers who work in the fruit sector, the agricultural industry or tourism. It runs during the months of January and February.

- **Seasonal kindergartens by INTEGRA:** This programme was created in conjunction with SERNAM and concentrates on children aged 2 to 5 of temporary workers in fruit cultivation, the agro-industry, fishing and tourism. This programme usually runs for three to four months in a year, generally during summer.

- **Centre for children of temporary working mothers (Centro para Hijos de Mujeres Temporeras, CAHMT):** This programme seeks to promote intersectional partnerships and operations with various government agencies, communities and the private sector.

---

[22] SERNAM is the government body to promote equal opportunities between men and women, created by Law No. 19.023, 3 January 1991. SERNAM designs, proposes and coordinates policies, plans, measures and legal reforms for equal rights and opportunities, http://www.sernam.cl [11 June 2009].

In addition, the INTEGRA Foundation also runs a programme of rural community kindergartens which targets children living in isolated rural areas with low population density. Working hours are flexible according to the family's needs. This programme includes food aid, providing breakfast and lunch.

Finally, in recent years, there has been an emergence of initiatives by some companies which have expanded their commitment to childcare and gone beyond the minimum required by law. They provide not only the legally required nurseries, but also solutions such as:

- back-up care for children aged 0–6, providing support for mothers and fathers during the day for childcare due to an emergency or unexpected matter;

- after-school care, for children between the ages 6 and 12 who are attending school and require learning assistance through supportive tasks and activities;

- after-hour or special work, for children from ages 0 to 12 in need of care if their parents have to work overtime; and

- holiday care, which corresponds to programmes developed specifically for hosting and supporting children on holiday from school.

These types of solutions are starting to be developed in companies such as IBM, which works together with the company Chilena Vitamina[23] to provide these types of integrated care solutions, so workers have greater peace of mind and improve their performance and productivity at work.

Despite the fact that Chile has a full school-day system, meaning that children are usually in school between 8.00 a.m. and 4.30 p.m., many parents working full time do not return home until after 7.00 p.m. This means that many children between the ages of 6 and 12 are obliged to stay alone at home for two or more hours until their parents return home. In this regard, childcare solutions providing a fuller range of support is an important need.

Results of workplace obligations

In 2006, only 7,805 children attended kindergartens or nurseries provided by the workplace of a parent, comprising only 6.7 per cent of all children attending

---

[23] Vitamina is a Chilean company that provides educational and childcare solutions for working parents of different companies. According to its projections for the coming year, it is expected to have built more than 100 childcare centres.

nurseries.[24] Of these, 72.7 per cent belonged to the richest 40 per cent of households. In fact, few companies fall under the legislative requirement: just 12.9 per cent of a sample of 1,500 companies employ more than 20 female workers and therefore have an obligation to provide daycare nurseries.[25] The very low percentage of companies with more than 20 female workers suggests that the law discourages employers from hiring women, so they do not have to pay for childcare.

Of companies with 20 or more female employees, only 5.1 per cent have or co-manage their own nursery, while 69.2 per cent contract external nursery facilities or use a voucher system.[26] Finally 14.5 per cent of the companies that are obliged to deliver the benefit of childcare directly pay the mother for the care of their child – a practice which is generally illegal but meets some basic requirements and which has become more popular in recent years.[27] The percentage of companies that violate the legislation and do not comply with the rules is estimated at 11.1 per cent. One of the reasons companies do not comply with the legislation (or do not hire women) is the high cost of setting up and managing a crèche or contracting a third party, especially in some sectors such as agriculture.

According to the 2006 workforce survey, 8.4 per cent of working women have children under the age of 2, of which only 5.4 per cent had access to childcare facilities through their workplaces (that is, they were working in companies with 20 or more female employees).[28] Even when entitled, not all workers make use of the childcare benefit, because some are supported by family members, or have sufficient income to have their children taken care of at home and are reluctant to send them to a collective childcare facility.

Conclusion

Chile has long held commitments to early childhood education, although the primary concern, until recently, with child development and child rights, has come with a lack of attention to the needs of working parents for care services for

---

[24] Calculated by the author from the national labour force survey – Encuesta de Caracterización Socioeconómica Nacional (CASEN), 2006.

[25] Chile, Dirección del Trabajo, 2007a.

[26] Chile, Dirección del Trabajo, 2007a.

[27] Exceptionally, a payment for care may legally replace the right to a childcare nursery in the following cases: a) for women who work in an area where there is no adequate establishment approved by the JUNJI; b) where female workers engage in work placements away from urban areas such as camps, separated from their children during that time; c) when female workers work at night time or health issues prevent them from sending their child to a nursery. (See Chile, Dirección del Trabajo, 2007b.)

[28] Chile, Dirección del Trabajo, 2007a.

children aged 0 to 4, and particularly for children younger than 2. Laws requiring workplaces to provide childcare for working mothers with children under the age of 2 have limited effect because relatively few women work in companies covered by these laws. Moreover, legal obligations on employers to provide childcare are linked to the number of female workers employed by a firm, not the total number of workers, and can typically be used only by women employees, thereby overlooking fathers' needs for such facilities, and perpetuating the idea that women, not men, are responsible for parenting and childcare. They also introduce the possibility that firms may discriminate against hiring more women in order to avoid the legal obligations that come with 20 or more female employees. However, since 2006, efforts to expand childcare and child education for children from the ages of 0 to 6 have stepped up with renewed attention to concerns for women's labour force participation and children's development.

University of Concepción

Type of business. Tertiary education.

Workplace. University campus.

Workers. 3,257; 41.8 per cent are women.

Working hours. Full-time week: 45 hours; part-time week: 33 or 22 hours.

Childcare solution. Workplace nursery and kindergarten plus an agreement with three external kindergartens. Kindergarten scholarships for male and female employees.

Partners. Private childcare company which is part of the university holding corporation, three external kindergartens.

The University of Concepción is a tertiary education institution established in 1919 and managed by a non-profit private organization. With 20,929 undergraduate students registered in December 2007, the university was the fifth largest by student enrolment in Chile. The university is located in three Chilean cities: Concepción, Chillán and Los Ángeles. Concepción is the main site and employs 3,257 staff members, of which 41.8 per cent are women.

In 1969, a joint initiative between workers and the university led to the establishment of a workplace nursery, which also served as a training site for students of the Faculty of Education. In 1990, the nursery's management was transferred to a private company, the Centre for Comprehensive Child Development Limited (Centro de Desarrollo Integral del Niño Limitada, CEDIN), which is part of the University of Concepción holding corporation. CEDIN operates as an independent business unit offering a nursery and kindergarten programmes to children whether their parents are employed by the university or not.

Today, the University of Concepción provides childcare solutions through the CEDIN nursery and kindergarten and also has agreements with three external kindergartens (Montessori, Babylandia and High Scope), so parents can opt for alternative childcare solutions.

Childcare programme

The CEDIN nursery and childcare centre is located on the university headquarters premises and extends over 650 m^2. It has capacity for 58 infants and 155 children, with 47 infants and 98 children enrolled in its nursery and kindergarten at the time of writing. All infants but one are children of university staff members who do not pay a fee. The kindergarten section includes children of university staff (with or without university scholarships), but also children of workers from other companies. There is no waiting list for children whose parents are employed by the university. CEDIN operates from Monday to Friday between 7.45 a.m. and 7.30 p.m., from the end of February to the end of January.

CEDIN, a pioneer in innovative early childhood methodologies, has implemented a five-level or five-workstation system, with one educator and two assistant staff for each level. The methodology applies to both the nursery and kindergarten and is aimed at developing children's abilities.

CEDIN has recently been restructured and a covered courtyard for physical activities has been created. Another innovation is the introduction of the centre's internal rules and a calendar of activities, some of which parents may participate in.

As established by law, the childcare service is free of charge for all mothers employed by the university. The childcare benefit does not end when a child turns 2 years old, as stipulated by law, but at the end of the semester, which exceeds legal requirements. In special cases, parents' proposals for alternative childcare solutions can be approved for funding by the university. Furthermore, benefits are maintained while mothers are on sick leave or even when the mother opts, for valid reasons, for in-home childcare.

The university provides kindergarten scholarships for children aged 2 to 4, which also moves well beyond the requirements of the law. It is also innovative in that it reaches out to low-income parents and is extended to men as well as women. Parents are free to use these scholarships in the CEDIN centre or in other childcare facilities.

Eligibility, use and cost

In May 2008, 46 women employees were using the CEDIN childcare facilities, including teachers, secretaries, administrative accountants and workers from the laboratories and other offices. An additional 20 women employees use one of the three external childcare facilities which have agreements with the university.

Of the 100 kindergarten scholarships offered by the university, 74 are used at the CEDIN centre and the remainder are used at external centres; 46 per cent of scholarships go to male employees.

Scholarships fully or partially cover the costs of kindergarten. Currently, 31 per cent are full scholarships and 69 per cent are partial, covering between 25 and 95 per cent of the full costs of childcare. The university usually grants full scholarships to low-income officials, on a means-tested basis, while wealthier parents receive a partial scholarship. The university plans to offer more full scholarships in the coming years. Currently, a 50 per cent partial scholarship for the CEDIN childcare facility requires a parental contribution of 50,000 Chilean pesos (around 105 USD), which is equivalent to about 10 to 15 per cent of the average salary.

Nine per cent of the university's women employees use this benefit and all low-income female employees who need childcare are covered. Those who do not use the benefit do not have eligible children or do not meet the socio-economic criteria to receive a scholarship.

Organization, management and funding mechanism

The Social Development Unit of the Department of Human Resources manages the programme. It is responsible for informing potential beneficiaries about the service, selecting workers eligible for kindergarten scholarships, establishing agreements, and evaluating, monitoring and paying CEDIN and external childcare providers.

Since CEDIN operates as an individual company, the university pays for each child of a staff member. The centre is financed out of university funds, alongside the fees paid by workers employed by other companies.

Childcare staff

According to the internal rules, the overall objectives of the CEDIN centre are to: i) promote comprehensive child development; ii) encourage family involvement in child education; iii) foster and develop child relations with parents, family, staff and community; and iv) promote staff who encourage child development.

Interviewees from CEDIN noted that the centre operates in line with these objectives and highlighted the quality of the service, its teamwork and its organization. They also pointed out the importance of the educational model, attributed to an innovative process that began 25 years ago.

The staff team includes 47 people: a director, a manager, a secretary, 14 educators, 21 child assistants, a nutritionist (ten hours per week), an audiologist (ten hours per week), four cooks/kitchen assistants and three cleaners. The working week is 45 hours at full time and 33 hours on part time with a shift system in place. Salaries vary according to staff functions, working hours, seniority and staff evaluations, and range from 0.75 to 2.2 times the minimum wage. CEDIN is a self-financed company, and it is expected that greater financial stability could contribute to better staff salaries.

In addition to their salaries, CEDIN employees are covered by life insurance, and they receive transportation allowances, special bonuses for Christmas, national celebrations and anniversaries of the centre, and an annual grant as part of the company's profit-sharing plan.

Employer perspective

Management places value on supporting working parents and provides options enabling them to choose from a number of childcare solutions. The aim is to accommodate parents' preferences in schedules and locations. Thus, not only is a facility available on university premises, but the university also has agreements with external facilities and has supported parents' requests for alternative childcare solutions.

Moreover, the university has extended kindergarten scholarships to fathers, in recognition of their childcare responsibilities. It also introduced paternity leave, even before the law was enacted.[29]

Finally, the University of Concepción sees organizational benefits to the workplace childcare facility as workers can visit their children at any time, and can work better and more peacefully knowing their children are well cared for.

---

[29] In 2007, the University of Concepción was ranked sixth among the "10 Best Companies for working mothers and fathers", issued by the magazine *Revista Ya* and the Foundation Chile Unido, http://www.chileunido.cl [11 June 2009].

Management recognizes the links between the availability of quality childcare and staff productivity as well as more harmonious staff relations.

In conclusion, management views investments in early child development as key for both children and working parents, with direct and overall benefits for the organization.

Employee perspective

Employees have highlighted the excellent service the childcare delivers. In particular, its workplace location, the infrastructure, the quality of staff and the open-door policy has made CEDIN especially attractive for them. They especially appreciate the compatibility of its opening hours with their working hours. All these features of the service allow them to work more calmly, improving their performance and reducing their absenteeism at work.

In addition, parents highly value the methodology developed by CEDIN and the excellent relations they have with the educators. Most hope to receive scholarship benefits for their child to enter the CEDIN kindergarten after leaving the nursery. According to them, if CEDIN did not exist, most workers would have to ask family members or friends to take care of their children, a solution they do not consider desirable.

Lessons learned

In general, all participants highly value the childcare service. The quality is high and special care is given to both the learning process of children and active participation of parents. It seems the only concern relates to workers' wishes to extend the nursery benefit to working fathers, as is the case already for the kindergarten scholarships.

This case study highlights the importance of offering different childcare options, so parents can choose the most suitable for their childcare needs. The kindergarten scholarships greatly increase parents' options, since many could not afford this service from their own means alone. The university's support for children older than 2 and its extension of kindergarten scholarships to fathers as well as mothers is progressive in Chile, moving beyond the requirements of the law and recognizing that both men and women have childcare needs. This may offer a useful example for other companies in Chile.

Aguas Andinas S.A.

Type of business. Water supplier.

Workplace. From production to distribution.

Workers. 884 men and 244 women.

Working hours. 45 hours per week.

Childcare solution. Childcare Payment Scheme for female employees until child is age 5.

Partners. Three trade unions at Aguas Andinas S.A.

Aguas Andinas S.A. is a water supply company operating in more than 60 venues in various parts of Santiago's metropolitan area, with centres for water collection, drinking water plants, water treatment plants, agencies and corporate offices. Work at Aguas Andinas mainly includes physical work requiring technical knowledge and expertise, and most workers are men. Women working for the company are primarily found in administrative and customer services, which are clustered in one building.

Today's company has inherited a number of workplace benefits, many of which were trade union initiatives, from previous administrations. The childcare benefits that Aguas Andinas workers enjoy today are part of this legacy. Female employees are entitled to childcare benefits for their children through to the age of 5. This benefit goes well beyond legal requirements on the company to provide childcare through to the age of 2, and was established because the company and workers originally viewed the legal provisions as inadequate and because there was a strong demand for more support from the workers. Today, the company notes that good childcare solutions have positive benefits in the workplace, improving workers' productivity.

Before 1999, Aguas Andinas owned and operated their own facilities to provide childcare, with a pick-up service that transported children to and from childcare facilities. This system was transformed into a voucher scheme in 1999, due to the expansion of the company into different areas across the city and due to the employment of more female staff, which raised practical and financial challenges for offering on-site childcare. The voucher system gave mothers more choice and convenience for arranging childcare, while also increasing the usage rate of the benefits.

The company programme of childcare benefits

Aguas Andinas offers female employees a choice between three types of benefits:

1) **A direct agreement between the company and selected care centres/ kindergartens:** In this arrangement, the company directly pays the providing institution for the service. The female employee chooses the nursery or kindergarten, and Aguas Andinas makes the monthly payment. Currently, six employees use this system for nursery care and eight employees for kindergarten care.

2) **Refund of payments:** The company will provide a full refund to employees choosing to pay individually for nursery or kindergarten services not party to the company's direct agreement, provided adequate documentation is provided. Currently eight employees use this refund scheme.

3) **Home care grant:** This benefit is only available for care services for young children when a nursery is not available or convenient for a justifiable reason. The company pays female employees 92,126 Chilean pesos (CLP: approx. 145 USD) per child, per month, to offset the costs of in-home help with childcare. There are currently 11 employees who use the home-care grant.

In schemes 1 and 2, the company also pays a transportation allowance for the children.

Not including annual registration fees, the monthly maximum the company pays for nursery or kindergarten care, whether directly or through reimbursement, is CLP189,102 (about US$300), an equivalent of 1.3 times the minimum monthly salary of CLP144,000. The transportation bonus is not given in the case of the home-care grant, placing the maximum home-care grant at CLP92,126 per month, the equivalent to 0.64 of a minimum monthly salary.

Eligibility and use

Aguas Andinas's programme for childcare is a negotiated agreement between the company and the workers' union. The childcare benefits beyond the legal requirement are not a universal benefit, but are limited to unionized workers at the companies. Seventy per cent of women workers are union members. The remaining 30 per cent are not eligible, although because the majority of non-unionized workers are older women, this group of workers has less need for childcare for young children.

The compensation unit in charge of the benefit system reported in May 2008 that 35 children of female employees were covered by the benefit system, of which nine were in nurseries and 26 were in kindergarten. In all, 20 per cent of all unionized female workers were using the benefit at the time of the company's report. The remaining 80 per cent of women did not have eligible children.

Childcare centres used by Aguas Andinas employees

Play House is an example of a childcare facility used by employees. There are a total of nine employees: two nursery educators, four nursery technicians (two for each of the nursery/kindergarten sections), a nutritionist, a food manager and a cleaner. Staff and facilities are inspected and authorized by JUNJI. Salaries vary from CLP230,000 (US$489, 1.59 times the minimum wage) for educators and CLP130,000 (US$277, 0.9 times the minimum wage) for cleaners.

Working hours are 7.30 a.m. until 7.30 p.m., with four shifts, at five days a week, adding up to a total of 45 hours a week. This childcare facility is more than 200 m^2, with capacity for 22 infants and 31 older children. Currently, ten infants and 31 older children are enrolled. The facility offers four rooms for children (separated for infants and children), a secretariat, two courtyards, a kitchen, a special room to handle milk, a breastfeeding room and two bathrooms for infants and one for children with sinks and baby-changing facilities.

Play House also gives educational services required by the JUNJI curriculum, basic health care and English classes. Parents can participate in commission meetings, personal meetings, institutional activities and open days.

Other childcare facilities such as the Little Bee College offer similar services but on a larger scale with computer classes and more room for children. It has 24 employees and its 178 places are currently fully occupied.

Management perspective

Aguas Andinas S.A. recognizes the role of the trade unions in establishing good working relations. According to the company, "it is more convenient and useful to have a union spokesman, than the entire workforce at once". The company believes that the childcare benefit (beyond what is legally required) should be limited to unionized employees, as this affects their membership and incentives to affiliate to the union. The company also recognizes the importance of childcare services and other policies that help reconcile work and family. They noted that "mothers who are at ease are more productive".

Employee perspective

Mothers tend to report that they prefer the company's childcare benefits scheme over an on-site childcare facility at the company. They appreciate the flexibility to choose the most convenient childcare facility (in terms of proximity to home, quality of care) for themselves and their children. According to one of the interviewed female employees, "this is much more manageable, as it would be more complicated for me to carry my child to one specific kindergarten than to have the option of choosing the most convenient one, especially if you are in the centre of Santiago where there is lots of pollution".

Extending the benefit from the legal requirement of 2 years to the age of 5 has also been positive for family budgets, as well as for worker turnover and productivity. As one worker indicated, "This benefit is very important as I would not be able to pay for it myself and it should also be noted that early childhood education is crucial for the development of the children. I would have been obliged to the help and care of my family, if it was not for the benefit we receive." Some female employees specifically mentioned that the benefit played a crucial role in determining whether to stay at Aguas Andinas after receiving other job offers. Some spoke of the peace of mind that quality childcare has brought them, particularly given the high rate of domestic accidents that occur among young children: "This clearly has implications on labour productivity, thus decreasing the stress that this situation causes. One knows that the children are safe and sound in the kindergarten so I don't have to worry about my son all day."

Lessons learned

The childcare benefits scheme at Aguas Andinas clearly assists mothers with the costs of caring for their children while at work, and provides more generous benefits than the law requires. The mothers appreciate the flexibility of the system, which allows them to choose the appropriate childcare arrangement and location for their needs. However, while the benefits scheme is inspired by legal requirements and by the negotiations and agreements between the company and the union, many fathers would also like to receive such benefits as well.

This case study also highlights the potential for trade unions to participate in the demand and development of childcare solutions. In doing so, it is also important to achieve coverage for all workers. This is only possible with representative trade unions. In the case of Aguas Andinas, seven out of ten female employees are part of the union.

Childcare Centres for Seasonal Working Mothers (CAHMT), Melipilla

Type of business. Agricultural industry for export.

Workplace. Fruit fields and packaging factory.

Workers. Mothers who are seasonal agricultural workers.

Working period. Between October and March.

Childcare solution. Five seasonal childcare centres run by Municipality of Melipilla for children between 2 and 12 years.

Partners. The National Service for Women (SERNAM). Also, as of 2007, the Ministry of Planning (MIDEPLAN); the National Board for School Assistance and Scholarships (JUNAEB); the National Board for Kindergartens (JUNJI); the National Sports Institute (IND); employers (two entrepreneurial families in the agricultural sector: the González and Fernández families); trade union: the Association of Seasonal Women Workers of Melipilla Province.[1]

[1] This trade union organizes workshops on health care, cooking, leadership and economic self-management for its members (except during summer).

The Childcare Centres for Seasonal Working Mothers (Cuidado a Hijos de Mujeres Temporeras, CAHMT) provide temporary childcare for seasonal working mothers in agriculture. In line with the policy objectives of the Chilean Government, the programme promotes childcare services through inter-sectoral cooperation among a broad range of partners, including several co-implementing public institutions, local authorities, trade unions, community organizations and private entities.

The CAHMT programme was first initiated in 1991 following a request for childcare services during working hours by the inter-company trade union of permanent and seasonal workers of Talagante, called Fifth of October, which was addressed to the National Service for Women (SERNAM). The programme was organized and institutionalized between 2000 and 2006 in nine regions of Chile. The example of CAHMT analysed in this case study is located in the Chilean province of Melipilla.

This childcare initiative is specifically aimed at seasonal working women, who comprise around 52 per cent of the total seasonal workforce. Women's participation in agricultural work remains low and is constrained by their domestic responsibilities, particularly in rural areas, where households tend to have more dependants than in urban areas. Heavy responsibilities for childcare coupled with the fact that agricultural companies stand out for their lack of compliance with childcare regulations help explain the importance of a programme targeting working mothers in agriculture.[30]

The Melipilla programme began in 1993 with a request from the trade union Association of Seasonal Women Workers of Melipilla Province (Agrupación de Mujeres Temporeras de la Provincia de Melipilla) to SERNAM, after seeing the success of the Talagante programme. Two centres for 50 children were opened the same year. The founder and former director of the trade union established contacts with the private sector to mobilize employers' support.

About ten employers participated in the initial stages of the programme. As of 2006, only two remained: the González and the Fernández families. The González family enterprise, the focus of this study, operates three agricultural companies and one packing facility (Sociedad Empacadora Royal Limitada). The three companies (Sociedad los Huertos de Chocalán Limitada, Sociedad Agrícola el Pabellón Limitada and Agrícola La Vega) produce fruit for export (grape and other seed fruits) and employ 38 permanent workers and 103 seasonal workers working in the fields. Empacadora Royal employs five permanent and 115 seasonal workers. The latter are mostly hired by external companies (contractors).

Childcare programme

In 2008, there were five CAHMT centres operating in Melipilla: three main centres in the urban areas with a fixed number of places (Carol Urzúa, Los Jazmines, Jaime Larraín) and two centres in the rural areas with variable numbers of places (Bollenar and Pabellón). The CAHMT centres are provided by the Municipality of Melipilla and are usually set up in public schools during the summer holidays in January and February. While the structure and organization of facilities varies by centre, they are usually open between 7.30 a.m. and 7.30 p.m., Monday to Friday. Spaces and activities are organized to fit the different age needs of children from 2 to 12 years. All centres have been certified by JUNJI. Los Jazmines has capacity for 90 children while the other four centres can accommodate up to 60 children each. Enrolment is very high and all centres are almost fully booked.

---

[30] SERNAM/FAO, 2005.

Eligibility and use

In line with the definition of "seasonal agricultural workers" (Article 93 of the 1993 Labour Code),[31] the target group of the initiative has been identified as "mothers contracted in the period between October and March of each year, to work in the agricultural industry for exports", specifically women "who work in the harvest of fruits for external markets".[32] Seasonal workers making use of CAHMT are mainly those working in local fields for different agricultural companies, which in turn deliver their products to large enterprises such as Dole, Seminis, Andifrut and others. In order to enrol for the childcare programme, mothers have to show their child's birth certificate, and their work contract or the contact telephone number of their employer.

Organization and management

Setting up a childcare centre for seasonal working women (CAHMT) requires a joint request by women employees, at least 50 children under 12 needing childcare, and an adequate facility. When these requirements are met, MIDEPLAN, which assumed SERNAM's place in January 2007, takes responsibility for the overall administration of the programme. Since 1994, a general coordinator from the municipality level Department of Community Development has been in charge of the management of the centre. In the case of the Municipality of Melipilla, the general coordinator is a teacher working at Los Jazmines. The director of the childcare centre is in charge of the overall supervision of the services.

Costs and funding mechanisms

The programme funding and operation is the result of the participation of multiple partners as follows:

- **Municipality** – hires the director, cleaning staff, two sports instructors and, with the exception of the largest facilities in the area, two child educators. It also provides the school infrastructure during summer holidays.

---

[31] Article 93 of the 1993 Labour Code refers to "seasonal agricultural workers" as: "All those who carry out seasonal/temporary field work or seasonal activities in farming, commercial or industrial forms of agriculture and sawing mills and agricultural crops for the wood or other industries."

[32] Hernandez and Montero, 2004.

- **JUNJI** – hires childcare staff (two child educators) and provides food for the largest childcare centres in the area.

- **JUNAEB** – provides food for children between 6 and 12 years in the largest childcare centre in the area, and for all children in the other centres. It also employs two cooks.

- **IND** – provides resources for the recruitment of sports teachers (one sports teacher and one sports instructor).

- **Employers** – the González and the Fernández families make a joint voluntary contribution of 2,200,000 Chilean pesos per season (4,680 USD).

- **Employees** – they contribute voluntary seasonal fees of 3,000 Chilean pesos each (6.40 USD), which are used for extra-curricular activities.

Childcare staff

Staff members working at CAHMT centres are those who work in facilities that exist all year round, but which are expanded during the harvest season. The staff members appreciate their working environment and the relationship they have with the parents. Moreover, they appear to be very motivated with their pedagogical work, particularly with vulnerable children, such as those with serious educational deficits. In addition to recreational activities, the curriculum includes teaching social skills, in order to raise children's awareness of the risks they are exposed to in their social environment. Children can thus become agents of social change within their households and communities.

As regards working conditions, childcare workers in the same facility are hired by different institutions, according to their own wage policies, which creates a feeling of unfair treatment among childcare workers. This is particularly the case for teachers hired by the IND, whose wages are even lower than those the municipality pays to their instructors. A subsidy has been subsequently introduced to eliminate this difference.

Employer perspective

Entrepreneurs see two main problems related to access to childcare services. First, external agricultural contractors are employing an increasing number of workers, while major companies have reduced their internal recruitment, often to less than 20 women employees (minimum number that, by law, requires childcare services).

Second, they noted that, due to high workforce costs, it is very difficult to provide childcare services. Thus, many employers employing 20 women prefer to pay fines instead of complying with the law.

However, not all agricultural employers in the province hold this view. In particular, the González family stated that the CAHMT programme is very important for the childcare needs of seasonal workers and, through their contribution, they are fulfilling their social responsibilities in line with their economic capacities.

The González and the Fernández[33] families have been systematically contributing to the programme since it began; however, this service is not actually used by their workers. This could be related to the distance between their workplace and/or their households (usually rural areas near Melipilla) and the CAHMT centres. The employers also reported that most of their women employees are over the age of 40 and usually have children who do not need childcare services. Nevertheless, although their workers do not use it, they highlighted the value of the programme, which helps workers to better perform their tasks. In particular, they consider the public–private system, such as CAHMT, to fit the mechanisms of the agricultural industry particularly well.

Employee and trade union perspective

Trade union

The Association of Seasonal Women Workers considers the programme indispensable for both seasonal working mothers and their children, which was the reason why the trade union promoted this initiative. In the words of one member: "Children love it and, at the same time, it takes away a burden from mothers, which makes them more productive at work."

Originally, the unions were in charge of supervising and organizing the programme. Recently this responsibility has shifted to the municipality of Melipilla. Union members reported that this change has reduced the quality of the programme, and its ability to mobilize resources from the private sector. They also felt that their participation in the project had become lost. On the other hand, the municipality representative estimated that the cause of the companies' gradual withdrawal from the programme was the organizers' inability to keep employers committed to the initiative.

---

[33] The author was unable to get a direct statement from the Fernández family. However, a secondary source reported about this employer's satisfaction and his support to the project.

Moreover, the unions expressed concerns about the lack of control over the service users. Reportedly, all women have access to the facilities, not just seasonal workers. So far, the centres have had the capacity to meet local needs, but the unions fear this misuse may eventually jeopardize the quality of the service for the original beneficiaries. Finally, the process of recruitment of childcare staff has raised allegations that family or personal ties may play a major role in staff selection, leaving better trained people aside.

Beneficiary mothers

The women using these services were very satisfied and did not report any shortcomings. "Children are well looked after, they play and enjoy themselves. The caregivers are very young, which is very important, since they are more active and able to stimulate the kids." The existence of these facilities is a great benefit for working women, who otherwise would not be able to provide good childcare for their children and would be likely to rely instead on relatives or neighbours who are not always available. Lack of access to childcare would pose problems for mothers in finding jobs, directly affecting families' socio-economic well-being.

There are no childcare facilities in the area targeting younger kids. This is an enormous problem for a number of mothers as they cannot fully concentrate on their work, given the extra attention very young children require. Moreover, working mothers reported that they were not able to breastfeed their children, which represented a great source of distress.

Lessons learned

Despite declining participation by employers, this programme has been running for 15 years and continues to rely on the support of the private sector. This programme may be exceptional as it was not possible to identify similar initiatives elsewhere in Chile where the programme exists with the support of private companies. It would seem that the initial dynamism of the trade union leader was a major factor in mobilizing support from employers in the region.

A central concern for the programme relates to its sustainability and the lack of a local policy regulating seasonal childcare facilities in line with the national policy. Its continued operation depends on an annual vote of the municipal council, which has to approve and allocate resources for its functioning. This makes financing discretional and uncertain.

This case shows some of the difficulties of achieving a common vision on the objectives of a facility and how it should operate when partners come from different organizations such as municipalities and trade unions. Unions expressed concern that their initial aim to provide a service for seasonal women workers might be lost by the municipality. There appears to be no committee where partners can come together to discuss their concerns and perspectives.

Among the main lessons learned, trade unions report the importance of creating a climate of dialogue between employers and unions as a tool to address employee problems. However, this task seems very difficult given the number of obstacles workers' organizations face when unionizing.

Finally, despite the challenges, the participation of various actors has proven sustainable, operating successfully for the past 15 years. It appears to provide a relatively strong work methodology for developing quality childcare services, in general, creating a shared sense of responsibility and belonging in both providers and beneficiaries.

Plaza Vespucio Mall S.A.

Type of business. Retail sales.

Workplace. Shopping mall.

Workers. 11,210 shop assistants, security and cleaning personnel (about two-thirds women).

Working hours. 7 days a week from 7.30 a.m. to 9.00 p.m.

Childcare solution. Contracted childcare facilities nearby for children under age 2 whose mothers are employees.

Partners. Mall operators, contracted childcare centres nearby.

Plaza Vespucio Mall S.A. consists of nine establishments and is the largest chain of urban shopping centres in Chile. The company deals with real estate and also manages shopping centres. Plaza Mall generates its main source of income by charging companies (mall operators) rent for their businesses in the shopping malls. Like all other commercial centres, Plaza Mall operates seven days a week, between 10.00 a.m. and 9.00 p.m. It closes only during the five days of national holidays.

Plaza Mall began financing childcare services for working mothers in 1995, including mothers working in shops, security and the service sectors. Before 1995, only women working in department stores or other large companies had access to childcare benefits. Since then, Parliament extended the provisions of Article 203 of the Labour Code to make childcare services compulsory for commercial centres or complexes that are managed under the same corporate name or legal entity. As a result, commercial centres such as Plaza Mall, which employ 20 or more women under the same legal entity and facility, are now obliged to provide childcare services for the women employees including those of small companies in the mall, since they are part of one commercial entity and space, and share common expenses.

This case study focuses on childcare options that the company administration offers to employees of small businesses (shops, security and services). Other childcare solutions, provided to staff of department stores and direct employees of Plaza Mall, operate in a more traditional way, with the employer being directly responsible for providing childcare to comply with the regulations. The case study uses the example of Plaza Vespucio Mall, located in la Florida (Metropolitan Region), and one of the first commercial centres in Chile.

Childcare programme

Plaza Vespucio Mall has agreements with two childcare centres: Las Florcitas, situated one block from the commercial centre, and Chip y Dale, located several blocks away with a transportation service. Both establishments comply with the JUNJI regulations in terms of infrastructure, personnel, programme and so on.

As of March 2008, 42 women workers out of 1,250 were benefiting from one of these childcare services. In particular, Chip y Dale nursery has 13 children of women shop assistants, security and service personnel of Plaza Vespucio Mall. This facility was set up to meet the childcare demands of mall workers while Plaza Vespucio Mall was under construction. Afterwards, when regular demand for childcare by the mall was guaranteed, the facility was expanded to take more children.

Chip y Dale nursery offers childcare places for 40 infants and 60 children. In March 2008, 40 infants and 45 children were enrolled. The institution operates seven days a week from 7.30 a.m. to 9.00 p.m. The facility extends over 200 m^2 and includes two playgrounds, a video room, two kitchens, a breastfeeding room, bathrooms and one changing room. The service also includes food, recreational activities, basic health care and a transport service from the mall.

Eligibility and use

All working mothers with a child less than 2 are eligible and there are no quota restrictions, since a company has the legal requirement to provide childcare to every requesting mother. If childcare demand exceeds the available places, then the company would need to establish new agreements with other childcare centres.

Organization, management and funding mechanisms

The mall administration is responsible for addressing requests and selecting childcare facilities. The mall secretary, and more recently the communication manager, is in charge of arranging all the administrative operations, in particular contacting applicant mothers, establishing links with childcare facilities and coordinating procedures.

In order to qualify for childcare, mothers have to prove their eligibility by presenting their employment contract, the child's birth certificate and a letter from the mall operator, stating the name of the nursery and the duration of the service. The mother chooses a childcare facility that suits her needs and Plaza Mall headquarters processes payment directly to each childcare facility.

The costs are financed from the common expenses paid by mall operators, which cover cleaning, maintenance, childcare services and so on. Thus, costs are equally divided among all operators and do not depend on whether an operator's women employees use the childcare facility or not. Operators' contributions vary depending on the childcare facilities the mall company has agreements with, and on average co-payment amounts to 110,000 Chilean pesos per month (around 234 USD).

Childcare staff

Childcare staff members value their institution and believe it has a good working environment, in which they have the opportunity to actively participate. This compensates, to some extent, for the low wages they receive and their exhausting work with children. They also recognize the importance of their service, since it allows mothers to work with peace of mind.

The staff team is composed of 18 employees: three child educators, 11 technical child assistants, two cooks, one nutritionist and one cleaner. The institution operates seven days a week from 7.30 a.m. to 9.00 p.m. with four types of shifts (45 hours a week). During the weekend, temporary workers are hired.

In the case of Chip y Dale nursery, a child educator earns 230,000 Chilean pesos (1.59 times the minimum wage); a technical child assistant earns 160,000 Chilean pesos (1.1 times the minimum wage); while the cooks and the cleaner earn 130,000 Chilean pesos (0.9 times the minimum wage).

Employer perspective

Plaza Mall recognizes the importance of childcare policies in supporting mothers' working conditions and facilitating their integration into the workforce, especially in the retail sector, where they represent a large share of workers.

The company is promoting the importance of corporate social responsibility (CSR) and its varying modalities of implementation. The Human Resources Manager of Plaza Mall pointed out that the company is oriented towards people (both employees and customers), thus addressing workers' needs is part of the company's CSR policy. Good childcare policies help Plaza Mall further strengthen its corporate image and compete in the national CSR rankings. The management recognizes that the childcare programme is like a very valuable "gift" to its women employees, since they do not have to pay for it, and at the same time it results in an enormous benefit for them.

Employee perspective

Women workers appreciate the childcare provision, as they would not have the means to pay for a quality nursery themselves due to the low wages most of them receive. They also appreciate the proximity of the childcare facility to their workplace although they would prefer it to be in the mall. In fact, proximity is so important to working mothers that the closest childcare facility has the highest number of children enrolled, and at some points during the year it has a waiting list.

Employees are satisfied with the childcare facilities contracted by the mall. They appreciate the adequate infrastructure and the friendly staff, which reinforces their confidence. Women workers recognize that they can work better, knowing that their children are being well looked after.

Lessons learned

One of the problems encountered is the continuity of preschool education for children once the benefit ends. Many mothers lack the financial resources to support their children's preschool education themselves after their children turn 2. The educational upbringing of children is interrupted as they are not able to attend a quality kindergarten. Children are either looked after by family members or have to attend other, more affordable kindergartens, which lack the institutional accreditation.

Another problem is the incompatibility of the time schedule of the childcare facility Las Florcitas with mothers' working hours. There also appear to be no major linkages between the mall's management and the childcare facilities. Additionally, no formal evaluation or monitoring system, nor central database with information on the childcare programme, appears to exist. Plaza Mall attributes this shortcoming to the restructuring process and expects the programme to work better in a very short time.

Nevertheless, the childcare is a great support to mothers working in shopping malls, who would not be able to afford quality childcare on their own. Mothers value the quality and proximity of the childcare service provided, especially given the poor conditions of childcare facilities in their own communities.

The financing system is interesting since it spreads the cost of childcare over all employers in the mall as part of their expenses for common services and those whose employees use it do not pay more. Thus the cost of the legal obligation to provide childcare does not fall directly on the woman's employer, a situation which can discourage employers from hiring young women.

Photo © Laura Addati

France 8

Laura Addati[1]

National overview

Childcare policies in France are part of a broad set of family polices which have been driven by economic and social objectives, linked to fertility promotion, employment creation and social inclusion. Since the 1970s, French work–family measures have been shaped by the principle of parents' 'liberty of choice', combining provisions for long and well-paid maternity and parental leave with a number of supports for the costs of childcare as well as public provision of preschools from age 3

[1] Laura Addati is a Technical Officer in the Conditions of Work and Employment Programme, ILO, Geneva. She sincerely thanks the following people for their valuable collaboration on the three case studies in this chapter: Ms Jocelyne Cabanal, President, and Ms Emmanuelle Rousset, Director, of ParenBouge Association (Rennes); Mr Jean Pierre Viganego, Works Council Secretary, and Mr Rohmer Serge, Director, of the SNPE Le Bouchet Research Centre (Vert-le-Petit); Mr Claude Audrain, Secretary, of CFDT (Île-de-France); Ms Bénédicte Ranchon, Communication Manager, and Mr Jean-Emmanuel Rodocanachi, Director, of Les Petits Chaperons Rouges. She also expresses her appreciation to: the working parents; the childcare staff of "Charlie Chaplin" and Calaïs Crèche; the CAFs of Essonne and Ille-et-Vilaine; the Municipalities of Echarcon and Vert-le-Petit; and all company and trade union representatives interviewed during her visits to Vert-le-Petit and Rennes.

and low-cost after-school services. In 2003, the soaring demand for childcare for children under age 3 pushed the adoption of measures to increase private sector involvement in childcare provision in a budget-constrained environment, through partnership modalities with social security institutions and local authorities.

Policy orientations

France ratified the Convention on Workers with Family Responsibilities, 1981 (No. 156), in 1989 and is one of the leading European Union countries in public provision of childcare and in benefits aimed at reducing childcare costs for families. In 2003, France spent around 3.7 per cent of its GDP on family policies, 1.3 per cent more than the OECD-24 average.[2] Since the 1970s, France's family policy has gradually shifted from a 'male breadwinner' model to a more mixed and pragmatic system aimed at supporting the principle of parents' "liberty of choice" freedom to work or to withdraw from the labour market, as well as freedom to choose between different types of childcare options.[3]

Care policies during the 1980s and early 1990s were essentially marked by parenting incentives, with the side-effect of encouraging the labour force withdrawal of low-paid women with two or more children.[4] More recent reforms in the 2000s have taken a new orientation, putting more emphasis on work–life balance and gender equality objectives.[5] In addition, further to the 2006 law on equal pay, a more conducive legal environment for the introduction of work–family policies at the workplace has been established.

Service provision and use

France has a long-standing, state-subsidized system of childcare and preschool services. State intervention in childcare is linked to the traditional concept that family is a social institution playing a major part in the maintenance of social cohesion and children are seen as a "collective good" worthy of the wealth of the nation. Therefore, childcare is considered a state responsibility and a public concern.[6]

---

[2] OECD, 2007a.
[3] Morel, 2007; Morgan and Zippel, 2003.
[4] Fagnani, 2007.
[5] Klammer and Letablier, 2007; Gregory and Milner, 2008.
[6] Letablier, 2002.

Children under age 6

Although not compulsory, virtually 100 per cent of children aged 3 to 6 years and 20.9 per cent of 2-year-olds are enrolled in free public preschools (*écoles maternelles*). These are an integral part of the national education system and operate on a full-day basis from 8.30 a.m. to 4.30 p.m. four days a week (closed Wednesdays).

The organization of services outside school hours is the financial responsibility of municipalities and their cost is relatively low to parents.[7] Municipalities cater for children at lunch-time and frequently run out-of-school care services, before and after school hours, to help parents working full time. In 2002, 21 per cent of children aged 3 to 6 attended out-of-school services.[8] Other forms of nonparental care are mainly for children too young to attend preschool or for preschool children outside of school hours. The main options for parents are either centre-based or home-based care.

Centre-based services: For children between 4 months and 3 years, there are collective crèches, usually run by local authorities or by non-profit associations. Among them, the most common is the traditional neighbourhood crèche which can receive up to 60 children. Open about 11 hours per day, it closes on Sundays and public holidays. Due to the high demand, priority is given to children from low-income households and to children with special needs. Workplace or company crèches are more rare, with only 11,359 places in 2006.[9] In 2006, collective crèches represented 56 per cent of centre-based childcare arrangements, which totalled 265,000 places.[10]

For temporary or occasional care for children under 6 years, there are back-up crèches (*haltes-garderies*); this arrangement particularly suits the needs of parents working part time or atypical hours as well as preschoolers during non-school hours (Wednesdays and holidays). Waiting lists for these services are common.

Recent reforms have promoted the development of multi-care centres, a more flexible childcare arrangement combining regular, occasional, emergency and part-time care within the same structure, with the possibility of using the same crèche place for multiple childcare solutions. Over the last five years, there has been a steady growth of childcare places in multi-care centres, which increased by 13 per cent from 2002 to 2006.

Home-based services: These are often a complementary solution to a centre-based arrangement, including preschools, when these do not respond to

---

[7] OECD, 2007a.
[8] Ruault and Daniel, 2003.
[9] Bailleau, 2007.
[10] Ibid.

parents' care needs. In general, centre-based childcare ends between 4.30 p.m. and 7.00 p.m., while home-based caregivers can work later.

Home-based services include mainly licensed childminders *(assistantes maternelles)*, who provide regular childcare in their own home. They must be licensed by the Agency on Maternal and Child Protection (Protection Maternelle et Infantile), and are allowed to tend two or three children at the same time, depending on the age of the children. Registered childminders can belong to a municipal or agency scheme or network (family crèche) or operate as self-employed providers. In 2005, there were 288,000 active accredited childminders, caring for around 752,000 children.[11] Although parents can receive social security subsidies to hire an in-home caregiver, in 2004 less than 2 per cent of children under 6 were cared for by in-home caregivers.[12]

The 2006 Early Childhood Plan has introduced *micro-crèches*, a new flexible arrangement half way between collective and home-based childcare. This scheme allows three accredited childminders to join in a private home or premise and care for up to nine children under 6 years old. One place has to be reserved for emergency care. Micro-crèches can be managed by local authorities or by childminders themselves through an association or private company. The law provides details about childminders' training and qualification requirements and health and security regulations.[13] Preliminary results from pilot tests show that this flexible formula has potential for meeting the childcare needs of families living in rural or poor urban areas. On the other hand, some concerns have been raised on the accreditation and monitoring system and their impact on service quality.[14]

Finally, another component of the reform aims to develop referral and information services for parents such as the Family Info Points and the Registered Childminders Networks (Relais d'Assistantes Maternelles – RAM), which were first created in 1989 to help reduce the isolation of *assistantes maternelles*.[15] These services, some of which are offered on a mobile basis to reach small rural communities, target both parents and registered childminders to help match childcare supply and demand. While some initiatives are still at the pilot stage, RAMs have recently experienced strong development, with 61 per cent of all registered childminders belonging to such a network in 2006.[16]

---

[11] Blanpain and Momic, 2007.

[12] Tabarot and Lépine, 2008.

[13] Art. 24, Décret No. 2007-230, 20 February 2007, relatif aux établissements et services d'accueil des enfants de moins de six ans et modifiant le code de la santé publique.

[14] Centre d'Analyse Stratégique, 2007.

[15] Hetzel and Cahierre, 2007.

[16] Tabarot and Lépine, 2008.

For children under age 3, estimates show that, in 2005, parental care was still the most common primary arrangement in France (57 per cent). For non-parental care, licensed childminders were the most frequent solution (18.5 per cent), followed by collective crèches (8.7 per cent), preschools (5.5 per cent), grand-parents/family (5.1 per cent), family crèches (1.9 per cent), in-home caregivers (1.9 per cent) and undeclared childcare (1.4 per cent).[17] Although in France about 32 per cent of children under 3 have access to some form of childcare,[18] this is still insufficient to meet the existing demands of French parents.

School-age children

As of September 2008, school duration (including *écoles maternelles*) has been reduced from 26 to 24 hours per week over four days instead of five. Thus, Saturdays and Wednesdays are school-free days. To meet the demand for out-of-school care, the country has generated a network of accredited support services called Centres de Loisirs Sans Hébergement (CLSH: literally leisure-time centres without accommodation) for recreational activities and guided homework. These services are run by non-profit associations, municipalities, enterprises or their Works Councils (see the SNPE case study for an example). These services operate on Wednesdays, after school and during holiday breaks. The CLSH are financed by local authorities (45 per cent), families (25 per cent) and the CAF (Caisses d'Allocations Familiales – local social security agencies: 14.5 per cent) at a cost of about 25 euro per day per child.[19]

Alongside the CLSH, children can attend the *garderies périscolaires* (out-of-school childcare), run by municipalities and parents' associations, which operate immediately before (7.00 a.m. to 8.00 a.m.) and after (4.30 p.m. to 6.00 p.m. or 7.00 p.m.) school, generally on school premises. Moreover, care facilities and school meals are available during lunch time and are used by more than half of school-age children. Means-tested fees are usually charged for the set of services. Although their stated objective is to ensure equal opportunities for children, in practice these services also support work and family reconciliation. In fact, while on average 15 per cent of school-age children attended one out-of-school service in 2005, more than twice as many did so when their mother finished working between 4.00 p.m. and 6.00 p.m.[20]

---

[17] Ibid.

[18] Ibid., Annexe 7.

[19] OECD, 2004a. The OECD report is unclear about the remaining 15.5 per cent, but we understand it to be paid by central government.

[20] Ananian and Bauer, 2007.

Funding and cost to parents

The major financial supporter of childcare services for children under 3 is CNAF, the National Family Allowance Fund, which, through its local CAF offices, covers around 60 per cent of France's annual spending (7.7 billion euro in 2005). For the remainder, local authorities cover 27 per cent and the State provides the remaining 13 per cent. Local authorities are the main providers of childcare, with more than 60 per cent of centre-based childcare services managed by municipalities and inter-municipality institutions, although the share of crèches run by associations has increased to about 30 per cent over the last 20 years.[21] The cost of childcare varies by type and by family income.

Centre-based childcare fees are means tested and vary according to family composition, in line with the social security national scale. On average, childcare costs, after taxes and cash benefits, represent 11.3 per cent of the average French family's net income, which is lower than the average for all OECD countries (12.6 per cent).[22] However, while French families enjoy considerable public support for childcare costs, lower-income families face substantial challenges in covering their share of childcare costs. In-home caregiving is the most inequitable of childcare solutions, while centre-based care is the most equitable – largely due to the sliding scale fees with public support for low-income families.

Strengthening parents' "solvency"

In order to improve families' ability to meet the expense of both parental and non-parental childcare (parents' "solvency"), since 2004 the cash family allowance system has been simplified through the introduction of a unified childcare benefit, the early childhood benefit (Prestation d'Accueil du Jeune Enfant – PAJE). PAJE is a two-component mechanism:

1) A **unique basic childbirth benefit** (863 euro) received at the seventh month of pregnancy plus a monthly basic allowance (172 euro) from the birth of the child until 3 years of age. Although the basic benefit is means tested, around 80 per cent of newborns' families benefited in 2007.[23]

---

[21] OECD, 2004a.
[22] OECD, 2007a.
[23] Conseil de l'Emploi des Revenus et de la Cohésion Sociale, 2008.

2) A **complementary childcare benefit**, in which parents choose between:

    a. a **flat-rate parental care benefit (Free Choice of Activity Supplement – Complément de Libre Choix d'Activité – CLCA)**, which supports women or men with two or more children who choose to reduce or cease their paid work for three years, as a part of their parental leave entitlements.[24] Since January 2004, parents with only one child have also been entitled to CLCA for six months after the end of maternity leave.[25] This flat-rate benefit, in addition to the monthly childbirth benefit, represents around half of the French minimum wage, for a total monthly benefit of about 530 euro. As of July 2006, to promote employment reinsertion, a shorter (one-year) and better remunerated (750 euro) optional parental care benefit (COLCA) was introduced from the time of the birth of a third child.

    b. a **means-tested non-parental care benefit (Free Choice of Child Care Supplement – Complément de Libre Choix du Mode de Garde – CMG)**, which is intended to support low- and middle-income working parents of children up to 6 years old by helping with costs for selected home-based childcare services. The amount of the benefit varies between around 160 euro and 370 euro according to family income. In particular, the benefit makes home-based care more affordable, by eliminating or partially reducing the social contributions of parents hiring a licensed childminder (*assistante maternelle*) or an in-home caregiver and by providing a means-tested allowance to cover the childminder's salary.

At the end of 2006, there were 2,255,000 households benefiting from an early childhood allowance, including the new PAJE scheme (around 1.3 million families). Five times more families in 2006 than in 2004 were benefiting from the CMG to offset the cost of a licensed childminder. While designed to assist low- and middle-income working parents, the CMG remains an allowance mostly accessible to high-income parents, because, even with the benefit, the cost of childcare is too high a proportion of family income for lower-income workers. As a result, 70 per cent of allowances for licensed childminders and 96 per cent of allowances for in-home caregivers went to families in the fourth and fifth income quintiles.[26]

---

[24] Eligible parents include those with two children who have worked two of the past four years and those with three or more children who have worked two of the past five years: OECD, 2004a.

[25] Maternity leave lasts 16 weeks (26 from the third child) and is paid at full earnings. ILO, Database of Conditions of Work and Employment Laws. Available at http://www.ilo.org/public/english/protection/condtrav/database/index.htm [11 June 2009].

[26] Tabarot and Lépine, 2008.

Finally, as of 2007, active parents, either employed or seeking work, can benefit from a tax credit of 50 per cent of the cost of both centre- and home-based childcare up to a ceiling of 12,000 euro per year. This fiscal incentive is intended to benefit more than 3 million households with an average tax credit of about 750 euro. In addition to PAJE, this measure seeks to further reduce the final cost of childcare for families, including those exempted from income tax. However, two-parent households in which one parent is not active are still excluded from the fiscal benefit.[27]

Diversifying childcare providers through public–private partnerships

In order to meet the objective of the 2003 Family Conference of creating 72,000 new crèche places by 2008, an increase of more than 30 per cent,[28] priority has been placed on the creation of innovative and flexible childcare arrangements, such as multi-care centres and micro-crèches as well as on company and inter-company crèches.

Incentives for employers

Since 2004, three Childcare Investment Funds have been created to expand the supply of collective crèche places. Ten per cent of the budget of one of the funds, PAIPPE (Plan d'Aide à l'Investissement Pour la Petite Enfance), is reserved for the creation of company crèches.[29] In parallel, the CNAF Social Action Fund has allocated more funds to promote a more active childcare policy, with work–family balance objectives among the priorities.[30] In addition, the new childcare reform has broadened the eligible beneficiaries of CNAF social action funds to include private companies. The CNAF social action system on childcare operates under two main mechanisms:

---

[27] Conseil de l'Emploi des Revenus et de la Cohésion Sociale, 2008.

[28] Rapport relatif à la Convention 156 sur les travailleurs ayant des responsabilités familiales, 1981, présenté par le Gouvernement de la République Française conformément aux dispositions de l'article 22 de la Constitution de l'OIT (2007) [Report on Convention 156, Workers with Family Responsibilities, 1981, presented by the Government of France in accordance with article 22 of the Constitution of the ILO (2007)].

[29] Caizzi et al., 2008.

[30] Caisse Nationale des Allocations Familiales, 2008.

1) The **single service allowance** (*Prestation de service unique – PSU*), which the CAF provides to local childcare providers (local authorities, non-profit associations and recently companies) to support the operational costs of collective crèches, based on actual hours of service use.[31] One of its main objectives is to improve crèche utilization and management with funds tied to performance on these dimensions. Parents pay for actual hours of use, while the same place can cover the needs of more than one child, through the development of multi-care centres.

2) The **childhood-youth contracts** (*contrats enfance-jeunesse*), which encourage local partnerships between the CAF and local authorities, public institutions and/or companies, to cost-share crèche places. The CAF subsidizes 55 per cent of the operational costs for a new crèche place under a renewable agreement of 3 to 5 years. Childhood-youth contracts aim to encourage the development of childcare in under-served geographical areas, such as rural and vulnerable urban zones.[32]

Until recently, few French companies offered childcare facilities (224 in 2004, mostly hospitals and big companies);[33] however, CNAF subsidies have encouraged more companies to actively participate in childcare provision. Companies may be entitled to either childcare investment funds or the single service allowance (PSU) to cost-share start-up investments for collective crèches (including company crèches and inter-company crèches, for which, see next section) and to offset operating costs.

Also, as of 2006, companies can become part of childhood-youth contracts (then called childhood-company contracts) to support inter-company or inter-municipality collective crèches (see the Rennes Atalante Science and Technology Park case study). In 2007, 27 childhood-company contracts were signed; this number is expected to rise to 40 per year.[34]

To facilitate private companies' participation in childcare services, the CNAF has established a national department as well as local enterprise units in each CAF, with the task of advising and supporting companies' childcare projects. When accessing CNAF funding, enterprises or other childcare providers are

---

[31] PSU targets childcare services for less-than-six and covers up to 66 per cent of running costs, equipments and other childcare-related services. PSU is provided based on the actual cost that families pay for one hour of childcare service, instead of a daily flat-rate allowance, as previously. Tabarot and Lépine, 2008.

[32] Caisse Nationale des Allocations Familiales, 2006.

[33] Silvera, 2005.

[34] Tabarot and Lépine, 2008.

subject to national standards and regulations and the CNAF national fee scale, which takes into account families' incomes and composition.

Finally, the *family tax credit* (*crédit d'impôt famille*), set up in 2004, has allowed enterprises to claim a tax credit of 25 per cent, which increased to 50 per cent as of January 2009, of the expenses incurred to help employees harmonize work and family life, up to an annual ceiling of 500,000 euro.[35] Preliminary findings show that, in 2005, only 2.2 per cent of companies applying for a family tax credit had incurred expenditures for childcare while more than 90 per cent declared expenditures related to remuneration of workers on maternity, paternity or childcare leave.[36]

Emergence of childcare companies

As part of the follow-up to the 2003 Family Conference recommendations, the Government allocated funds for the development of crèche companies.[37] This subsidy, as well as the enterprise incentives noted above, has favoured the externalization[38] of crèche management functions to private entities, such as La Ronde des Crèches or Les Petits Chaperons Rouges (see the Aix-la-Duranne Employment Site case study). Crèche companies specialize in planning, establishing and operating collective crèches for single or groups of private and public workplaces which decide to offer childcare facilities to their employees, whether through a new company or inter-company crèche or through pre-booking a fixed number of places in a municipal crèche. In addition, since the direct provision of childcare services may prove less affordable and more challenging for small and medium enterprises (SMEs), the 2006 Early Childhood Plan encourages crèche companies to provide special support to SMEs in preparing and presenting childcare projects to CNAF.

Since 2005, the 15 crèche enterprises operating under the French Federation of Crèche Companies have supported the establishment and management of more than 6,000 new crèche places (1,500 between January and July 2008 alone), mostly in multi-care centres, which has created more than 2,000 new jobs in France.[39] Preliminary impact studies mention two key advantages of this new service provision: the partnership mechanism, which reduces costs

---

[35] Loi de Finance 2004 (No. 2003-1311 of 30 December 2003) and Loi de Finance 2009 (No. 2008-1443 of 30 December 2008).

[36] Tabarot and Lépine, 2008.

[37] Ortiz, 2008.

[38] Daune-Richard et al., 2008.

[39] Fédération Française des Entreprises de Crèches, http://www.ff-entreprises-creches.com/la_federation_en_chiffres.html [11 June 2009].

and duration of setting up a new crèche;[40] and the ability of crèche companies to achieve economies of scale, by optimizing crèche places and resources, and adjusting to both workers' and employers' needs for flexibility, suitable hours and affordable costs.[41]

Nevertheless, some concerns have been raised about the impacts of a progressive relegation of a service in the public interest to market institutions which operate under a for-profit rationale. Questions have also been raised about the ability of these new mechanisms to deliver quality services, while also responding to the needs of low-income working parents.[42]

Workplace financial support for personal services (services à la personne)

Over the last decade, policy-makers in France have perceived care work as an important job growth sector, in particular for the less skilled. In order to develop official employment in home-care services and encourage households to employ household help, a plan for the development of personal services jobs in July 2005 provided for the establishment of a "universal service employment voucher" (Chèque Emploi Service Universel – CESU). CESU cheques can be bought at the bank or received pre-financed from an employer.

1) A **bank CESU cheque** (*CESU bancaire*) is used by individuals, as a simplified way to formally hire and remunerate personal care providers, including their social security contributions, which are partly offset through tax reductions, and/or to pay for centre-based childcare. In 2006, 70 per cent of individuals hiring personal services were using bank CESU cheques to pay their providers.[43]

2) A **prefunded CESU** (*CESU préfinancé*) is paid by the employer as a salary complement for the employee, comparable to a food voucher. The employee can utilize the prefunded CESU to pay for personal services provided by either an organization or an individual. Prefunded CESUs are not treated as salary, so employers do not pay social security (up to an annual ceiling of 1,830 euro

---

[40] Crèche companies average 5 months to set up a crèche compared to 26 by other childcare providers, because they use and adapt existing infrastructure made available by the employer.

[41] Tabarot and Lépine, 2008.

[42] Daune-Richard et al., 2007.

[43] Conseil de l'Emploi des Revenus et de la Cohésion Sociale, 2008.

per employee) or company tax (33 per cent). In addition, the employer has been able to claim a tax credit of 25 per cent – raised to 50 per cent as of January 2009 (the *family tax credit* mentioned above). For instance, providing a 100 euro CESU voucher to workers costs the employer just 42 euro, after all fiscal benefits are taken, making prefunded CESU much less expensive than a direct salary increase.[44] Although some administrative complexities remain, the voucher system is gaining acceptance as an efficient tool for encouraging companies to be family-friendly while also creating jobs in the care sector.[45] It is estimated that 635,000 workers from around 12,300 companies benefited from this system in 2008.[46]

In 2008, France devoted 8 billion euro to support personal service job development, including direct allowances, tax deductions and reduced social contributions related to hiring an in-home caregiver or an *assistante maternelle*.[47] However, this has raised concerns about sustainability and quality, as well as the status and level of qualifications of care-related professions, which may negatively affect the quality of the childcare provided. In practice, most jobs are short term and part time, most workers have few or no qualifications and wages are consequently quite low. It has been estimated that 116,000 personal service jobs were created between 2005 and 2006, but they represent the equivalent of just 30,000 full-time jobs.[48] Another criticism relates to the fact that support to hire personal services does not help the large numbers of self-employed, unemployed and informally employed workers who also need childcare.[49]

Workplace measures

Employers have traditionally supported family policies through their contribution to the social security system (CNAF – Family Branch), which, in turn, subsidizes local-level childcare costs at 25 per cent, on average.[50] In addition, employers, along with trade unions, offer cash benefits through the Works Councils (*Comités*

---

[44] ACCOR Services, Ticket CESU. Available at http://www.ticket-cesu.fr/cesu.aspx?CatId=Entreprise_cesu&PageId=Entreprise_cesu_Avantages [22 October 2008].

[45] Klammer and Letablier, 2007.

[46] Conseil Economique, Social et Environnemental, 2008.

[47] Conseil de l'Emploi des Revenus et de la Cohésion Sociale, 2008.

[48] Jany-Catrice, 2008.

[49] J. Gadrey, quoted in Haddad, 2007.

[50] OECD, 2006b.

d'Entreprise).[51] In France, labour law establishes that, in companies with at least 50 employees, Works Councils receive company subsidies of at least 0.2 per cent of the gross wage bill for the council's operating costs, plus any additional voluntary contribution to implement workplace social policies.

Through Works Councils, some large companies operate their own workplace crèches, leisure care centres or holiday residences, and a larger number of companies offer financial support to their employees, such as holiday vouchers or, more exceptionally, childcare vouchers (see the SNPE case study) or allowances. Some offer additional days off for sick children (instead of the three days stipulated by law) or supplement women's pay during maternity leave when it exceeds the social security benefits ceiling. Works Councils may also be active in organizing, for example, activities for children during school holidays or on Wednesdays.[52] According to a CNAF survey, almost a quarter of employees working in companies with a Works Council say they receive childcare help from it. This is more likely for those working in public services (35 per cent), than those in the private sector (17 per cent).[53]

By stimulating collective bargaining on the structural causes of gender inequality at the workplace, with a focus on work–life balance measures, the Law on Equal Pay for Men and Women (Law No. 2006-340) seeks to eliminate the gender pay gap by the end of 2010. Enterprises are required to set and report on indicators and targets for promoting work–family balance. Enterprises are also required to negotiate the working and employment conditions of part-time employees.[54] The Law also provides for financial assistance or relief for enterprises that take measures in favour of workers with family responsibilities, and consolidates employees' entitlements to parental leave and right to training.[55]

---

[51] Created in 1945, the Works Council is made up of: 1) the senior manager in the company, who acts as President of the Works Council; 2) the Works Council delegates, elected by workers for a period of 2 years; 3) a delegate of each trade union represented in the company. The Works Council is a legal entity in its own right and has to be advised and consulted on nearly every aspect of the management of the company. The *Code du travail* (Article L431-4) states that the Works Council "elaborates, on its own initiative, and examines at the request of the Head of the Company, all proposals which could improve working conditions, improve training and employment among employees and their life in the company".

[52] Silvera, 2005.

[53] Fagnani and Letablier, 2003.

[54] ILO, 2007b.

[55] In particular, the Law extends the scope of eligible expenditure for family tax credit to enterprises' expenditure on training for employees hired following their resignation from or termination of service during parental education leave. It also provides that periods of absence taken for parental education leave shall be counted in calculating entitlements in respect of the individual's right to training.

Employment of women and childcare

France's long-established and generous provisions for childcare, which help women combine maternity and employment, have been used to explain the so-called "fertility paradox":[56] the fertility rate in France was the second highest in Europe (2.00 children per woman) in 2006,[57] while the female employment rate has also remained high. Of women aged 25–49 with children, 65.9 per cent are employed: 3.5 points higher than the EU-27 average.[58]

Nevertheless, family responsibilities – still considered to be women's work for the most part[59] – continue to affect women's labour force participation and the quality of the jobs they accept. The maternal employment rate is 7.7 points lower than the employment rate of childless women of the same age (73.7 per cent)[60] and it decreases according to the number and age of children.[61] Women also tend to be over-represented among temporary, atypical and part-time workers, employment categories that expanded considerably during the 1990s. In 2007, 36 per cent of married or cohabiting women with children worked part time versus 3 per cent of fathers.[62] While part-time work may offer mothers more opportunity to balance their paid and unpaid work, part-time work is often associated with unskilled, unstable and low-wage labour. Many women are working part time involuntarily: 42 per cent of women working part time report that they would prefer to work longer hours if jobs and affordable childcare solutions were available.[63]

A high number of low-income mothers do not return to the labour force after maternity leave, particularly if their former job was precarious, low paid and at atypical hours – characteristics that make it difficult to find affordable quality childcare.[64] On average, 47 per cent of mothers with at least one child under 6 are employed, but the figure is just 20 per cent for those in the lowest income quintile compared to 70 per cent of those in the wealthiest.[65] One out of two of those inactive women declared that they would have continued working if their work

---

[56] Letablier, 2002.
[57] EUROSTAT, 2008.
[58] European Commission, 2008.
[59] Le Feuvre and Lemarchant, 2007; Bauer, 2007.
[60] European Commission, 2008.
[61] Chardon and Daguet, 2008.
[62] INSEE, 2007.
[63] Letablier, 2002.
[64] Marical et al., 2007.
[65] Bressé and Galtier, 2006.

arrangements were more family-friendly, or if suitable and affordable childcare arrangements were available.[66]

Atypical working hours, which make finding childcare more difficult, have increased in France over the last decade and are particularly common in the retail, transport and health-care sectors.[67] In particular, night work increased from 4.6 to 7.1 per cent and working on Sundays soared from 9.2 to 14 per cent between 2001 and 2005.[68] Many parents of young children are working atypical hours. Of all children younger than 7.5 years living in families with two working parents, 80 per cent have at least one parent working atypical or irregular hours. Of them, 29 per cent are in non-parental childcare at least once in the early morning (6.00 a.m. to 8.00 a.m.), 17 per cent in the evening (7.00 p.m. to 10.00 p.m.), 7 per cent at night (10.00 p.m. to 6.00 a.m.) and 17 per cent during the weekend.[69] Although this trend has created pressure for the development of childcare solutions that are more responsive to the needs of workers with atypical hours (see the Rennes Atalante Science and Technology Park case study), few families have yet to benefit, with family networks still playing the main role in ensuring non-parental childcare during atypical hours.[70]

Conditions of work of childcare workers

Preschool teachers

Écoles maternelles are staffed by preschool teachers, who, like primary school teachers, are required to have five years of university education – the highest requirement for preschool teachers among OECD countries.[71] Preschool teachers are public employees and are paid on a national salary scale. They are also entitled to 36 weeks of in-service training during their careers.

Childcare workers

As in other EU countries, most childcare workers in France are women (95 per cent). The childcare sector consists of two job categories: centre-based professionals and home-based carers.

---

[66] Méda et al., 2003.
[67] Le Bihan and Martin, 2005.
[68] Bressé et al., 2007.
[69] Ibid.
[70] Ibid.
[71] Kaga, 2007.

Centre-based professionals, such as child nurses, early childhood educators and assistant child nurses, hold a state diploma and have undergone practical training. Working for local authorities or private non-profit associations, they are usually entitled to regular professional development, a statutory 35-hour working week, and wages above the minimum, according to qualifications.[72] While their working conditions are generally good, some concerns have been raised about the lack of coherence and continuity between the training of crèche staff and preschool teachers, and also about status and salary,[73] which has been related to the increasing shortages of childcare staff in France.

Home-based caregivers include mainly licensed childminders and in-home caregivers who require no certificate and limited training.[74] Almost all licensed childminders are self-employed in their own home, with 2.6 employers on average. In general, these workers are low-paid, low-qualified women over the age of 40, who choose this profession for lack of alternatives:[75] in 2005, 49 per cent had no more than the minimum compulsory education (usually to age 16: Brevet d'Etudes du Premier Cycle – BEPC), although the trend is now moving towards increasing qualification levels. Half of licensed childminders reported working more than 45 hours per week; two-thirds report regular working hours every day. In 2005, their monthly net wage was 700 euro on average and 815 euro for those working full time. Even at 815 euro per month, childminders are earning just 80 per cent of the monthly net minimum wage.[76] The status, working conditions and career prospects of licensed childminders are less and less attractive to new generations of workers, with replacement rates progressively decreasing over the last years, and anticipated staff shortages of up to 18 per cent by 2015.[77]

Similarly, in-home caregivers are predominantly women (98 per cent), hired directly by parents, with no licensing, training or public monitoring requirements. They are usually younger than licensed childminders (37 years on average). One-third work in the sector for a lack of alternatives. In-home caregivers usually have a single employer, and earn less than childminders (a median of 2,322 euro per year compared to 6,554 for a licensed childminder). Although the net hourly salary is higher than the minimum wage, annual working hours are very low at a median

---

[72] OECD, 2006b.
[73] Kaga, 2007.
[74] OECD, 2004a.
[75] David-Alberola and Momic, 2008.
[76] Blanpain and Momic, 2007.
[77] Tabarot and Lépine, 2008.

of 349 hours,[78] which explains the income disparities and the high turnover in these jobs. In-home caregivers comprise roughly 5 per cent of all personal service workers, while licensed childminders are approximately 16 per cent.[79]

The issue of working conditions and professionalization of personal service jobs, as a way to attract and retain more workers in the sector, is on the agenda of the major national stakeholders. In particular, education institutions, employers' organizations and associations have taken steps to set up and promote specialization courses and training opportunities in personal service professions.[80]

Conclusions

France's family policies, backed by substantial financing, have facilitated the reconciliation between work and family life and provided choices in caring for children. This has been made possible by the legitimacy given to the State, in partnership with social partners and major societal stakeholders, to intervene in family matters, hence making childcare a public policy issue. As a result, French families have relatively good access to quality childcare. However, for children under 3, parents still have difficulty finding childcare which is affordable, and expanding crèche places has been a policy priority.

Incentives for employers to support workers' childcare costs, and the development of public–private partnerships promoted by the 2000s reforms, bring potential for increasing the supply and use of crèches. It is still early to assess the impact of the new policies; however, public institutions are key actors in the French childcare system and will need to retain their leadership and monitoring role to guarantee sustainability, to ensure high-quality standards of both childcare services and jobs, and to respond to the needs of low-income working parents.

In April 2008, the new government proclaimed that childcare will become a legally enforceable right by 2012.[81] This commitment requires the creation of 300,000–400,000 new childcare places (both centre- and home-based) for children under 3.[82] The challenges for achieving this goal are many: from defining the authority ultimately responsible for providing parents with a childcare arrange-

---

[78] A full-time position in France accounts for a statutory annual duration of 1,600 hours.

[79] Estimates depend on whether the reference period is a week, a month or a year because of high turnover in this sector. It is estimated that there are between 51,325 and 96,535 in-home caregivers hired to provide care to children under the age of 6: Marbot et al., 2008.

[80] Conseil Economique, Social et Environnemental, 2008.

[81] Chemin, 2008.

[82] Caisse Nationale des Allocations Familiales, 2007.

ment, to filling the unmet demand for childcare in the face of political pressure to keep public spending down – without jeopardizing the quality of services and the working conditions of caregivers.[83]

Rennes Atalante Science and Technology Park (Beaulieu)

Type of business. The Rennes Atalante Park (270 ha) in Beaulieu houses 111 companies in the electronics and information and communication technology sectors, employing more than 7,000 staff. Sévigné, a private polyclinic, and Kéolis, the transport company of Rennes Metropolis, are located in the park.

Workplace. Beaulieu is one of the five company sites of the Rennes Atalante Science and Technology Park and lies in the west of France, in the heart of Rennes (population: 380,500), the capital of Brittany.

Workers. Eighty per cent of the 350 employees of the Sévigné Polyclinic are women, mostly doctors and nurses. Kéolis Urban Transport employs around 800 workers, of whom 550 are drivers. Twenty per cent of the drivers are women.

Working hours. Most health and transport workers work irregular and atypical working hours: early morning, night and weekend work schedules.
- Sévigné Polyclinic work shifts are 6.30 a.m. to 2.30 p.m., 2.30 p.m. to 10.30 p.m. and 10.30 p.m. to 6.30 a.m.
- Kéolis Urban Transport: the drivers' morning work shift starts at 5.00 a.m.; the night shift ends at 1.00 a.m. A line-maintenance team of 50 workers operates from 1.00 a.m. to 5.00 a.m. In both companies, part-time work is voluntary.

Childcare solution. Inter-enterprise and inter-municipality multi-care centre for workers on atypical hours. Regular, occasional and part-time care for children from 2.5 months to 4 years.

Partners. National institutions: Ministry of Labour, Social Relations, Family and Solidarity, through the Regional Delegation for Women's Rights – Brittany. **Local institutions:** The Ille-et-Vilaine CAF; Municipality and Metropolis of Rennes; General Council of Ille-et-Vilaine Department; Municipality of Thorigné Fouillard. **Companies:** Sévigné Polyclinic, subsidiary company of Générale de Santé (private hospital services and patient care); Kéolis, urban transport company of Rennes Metropolis; Equant-Orange (telephony), France Telecom Transpac (telephony) and their Works Councils. **Trade unions:** CFDT, CGT. **NGOs:** ParenBouge Association; OIS, Rennes's Inter-Works Councils Association; PRESOL, a non-profit association supporting the creation of local micro-enterprises; CIDF, the regional information centre for women's rights; and the French Foundation.

---

[83] La Documentation Française, 2008.

The Calaïs Crèche project started in 2001 when a group of working mothers and their Works Councils launched a participatory initiative involving a number of private and public partners. The project aimed to respond to a strong childcare need of working parents and of post-maternity leave job seekers. In general, the area had a high rate of parental employment, but few childcare services addressed the specific needs of employees working irregular and atypical hours.

At the end of 2002, the project gained support from a group of companies (Equant, Transpac, Sévigné Polyclinic, Thomson multimedia) and their Works Councils. The CAF of Ille-et-Vilaine and Rennes's Inter-Works Councils Association, which groups 13,000 employees in 110 Works Councils around Brittany, provided technical assistance for project formulation. The non-profit organization ParenBouge led local consultations and a needs-assessment study and ultimately came to manage Calaïs Crèche.

Preparatory work placed a strong focus on determining the best way to combine quality childcare with the needs of working parents, particularly in the context of non-standard working hours, workplace flexibility and the unequal share of care work between women and men. From the outset, emphasis was placed on the need for support from public local institutions in order to guarantee sustainability and coherence with existing childcare services. The result of this multi-stakeholder participatory process is quality childcare with work–family balance, social inclusion and the needs of the partners among its top-most priorities.

Childcare programme

The facility opened in 2004 at Rennes Atalante Beaulieu, on the ground floor of the Equant-Orange building, in front of Sévigné Polyclinic and next to the park's inter-company restaurant. The facility belongs to Rennes Metropolis and extends over 285 m², including a garden. It was renovated from office space to fit the needs of a non-standard-hour, multi-care centre with activity rooms, bedrooms, breast-feeding space and transition spaces.

Calaïs Crèche is open from 6.00 a.m. to 9.30 p.m., Monday to Friday. It is closed during French public holidays (11 days per year), but runs during school holidays. It operates as a multi-care centre and has a total of 25 childcare places with 24 "allocated" places serving up to 28 registered children per day, for both regular and occasional care. One "open" place is reserved for emergency childcare for non-registered children.

Regular childcare can be provided on a full-time basis (five days per week) or part-time basis (one to four days or half-days per week). The planning can change according to parents' work schedules, as defined in the registration contract. Regular places are allotted to partner companies and institutions (around five places each) according to the terms of the CAF childhood-company contract. Part-time arrangements, along with the extended-hours scheme, allow for a variable number of places for occasional back-up care, which are directly managed by ParenBouge. The emergency place can also be allocated on a full- or part-time basis for up to a maximum of three weeks depending on the parents' specific situation.

Eligibility and use

All categories of workers within the partner companies and institutions are eligible. Places are allocated by a commission of one social worker, one representative from the company's Works Council, and one member of ParenBouge. Priority is given to single parents and to families where both parents work atypical hours. The commission pays particular attention to the applications of low-income families and parents with difficult work–family reconciliation problems.

The service admits children aged 2.5 months (end of maternity leave) to 4 years. Children with disabilities can be admitted from 2 months old to 6 years. The crèche accommodated 92 children during 2007, providing a total of 62,457 hours of childcare per year, including full-time, part-time and back-up care. Kéolis Urban Transport's workers are the main beneficiaries, followed by those at the Municipality of Rennes, Equant, Sévigné Polyclinic, France Telecom and the Municipality of Thorigné Fouillard. In 2007, 31 per cent of Calaïs's children were cared for at irregular or non-standard hours. Ten per cent of the crèche's children lived in single-parent families.[84]

Organization and management

Calaïs Crèche is managed by the non-profit association ParenBouge, which is in charge of crèche staff, budget and accreditation and reports to the CAF. The association is responsible for ensuring that the crèche is 70 per cent full throughout the year, which is a condition for eligibility for the CAF's PSU subsidy. This new target requires a time-consuming place-management system in order to optimize the hourly use of every crèche place.

---

[84] ParenBouge, Rapport d'activité, Assemblée générale du 2 avril 2008, p. 13.

Parents of registered children become members of the association and participate in the organization of activities, such as the pedagogical programme, internal regulations and external activities. They may also assist the staff with volunteer tasks according to their availability and skills; and they may participate in early child development workshops. Parent representatives sit on ParenBouge's governing board and participate in decisions about the crèche and the association. ParenBouge reports a membership of 250 parents.

Childcare staff

Calaïs Crèche has a multidisciplinary team of 13 professionals: three men and ten women. In line with the legal requirements for staff qualifications for childcare centres, the crèche employs:

- three full-time early childhood educators with a 27-month post-baccalaureate specialized training. This includes the director, who has five years of early childhood education experience, and is also in charge of crèche administration;

- one part-time paediatric nurse, responsible for children's daily medical follow-up and care;

- two full-time assistant paediatric nurses, who hold a professional diploma and have undertaken one year of training;

- five part-time caregivers holding a CAP Petite Enfance, an under-baccalaureate professional certificate in early childhood. They work between 20 and 30 hours at Calaïs and also provide home-based childcare for another ParenBouge programme;[85] and

- one cook and one cleaner.

ParenBouge also employs a psychologist who provides support to Calaïs's children and parents as well as to its staff. In addition, an external doctor serves the centre and is in charge of admission medical visits and vaccination updates.

Crèche caregivers are employees of ParenBouge. All staff have a permanent contract, nine on a full-time basis (35 hours per week), from Monday to Friday. Staff share cleaning tasks and each takes one opening- and one closing-hour shift

---

[85] Information on this programme (Parendom) can be found at http://parenbouge.free.fr/experiences/parendom.html [11 June 2009].

per week. In order to respond to employees' own work–life balance needs, the work schedule for the entire year is fixed in September. The child-to-teacher ratio is 6:1 on average; national regulations establish 5:1 for infants and 8:1 for toddlers and up.

Crèche workers earn 105 to 170 per cent of minimum wage (8.50 euro per hour) according to their qualifications and responsibilities. Among other entitlements, ParenBouge provides ten days' paid emergency leave in the case of sickness of a family dependant (the statutory minimum being three days' unpaid leave) and also supplements women's pay during maternity leave when it exceeds the social security benefits ceiling or duration. Finally, ParenBouge provides short periodic training sessions for all staff members and a number of employees are entitled to longer training opportunities.

Costs and funding mechanisms

The initial investment fund of 245,000 euro was cost-shared by the CNAF childcare investment funds FIPE (80 per cent), the French Foundation and companies' Works Councils (20 per cent). Running costs are shared among the CAF of the Ille-et-Vilaine Department (under the single service allowance – PSU), families, partner companies and local authorities in the framework of a childhood-youth contract. The first childhood-youth contract was signed by Calaïs partners in 2004 and renewed in 2006 for four years.

Calaïs Crèche is one of the four inter-company, inter-municipality crèches that the CAF supports in the Department of Ille-et-Vilaine. Ninety-four of the 125 places created by those crèches have been reserved by private companies. CAF research shows that, in 2007, the real average cost of one childcare place in an inter-company crèche of Ille-et-Vilaine was almost 16,000 euro per year, which is shared between partner companies and departmental institutions. Partners' contributions are paid directly to the crèche managing institution, ParenBouge, for "Calaïs Crèche". While families contribute 18.9 per cent of global costs on average, childcare fees are means tested and vary according to family composition, in line with CNAF national scales. The average cost to parents of one hour of childcare in "Calaïs Crèche" was 1.70 euro in 2007.

The CAF, local authorities and the municipality contribute nearly 48 per cent of the cost, while Calaïs partner companies pay a gross contribution of 5,000 euro per year for a reserved place, or around 31 per cent of global costs. But through tax credits and a direct subsidy from the CAF, the final expenditure for a Calaïs partner company is around 2,200 euro per crèche place per year, which is about 14 per cent of global real costs (about 16,000 euro).

Employer perspective

The 2004 needs assessment indicated a clear need for childcare outside normal working hours, especially among health and transport workers, who often work shifts. The managements of Sévigné and Kéolis, in particular, supported the initiative from the outset as a solution for their workers with young children.

Management at Sévigné and Kéolis highly appreciate the location, hours and partnership mechanism of the crèche. The employers noted that the childcare reforms introducing tax breaks and direct subsidies to companies have been a determining factor in their participation in the project. These views coincide with results of a 2007 survey by the CAF of Ille-et-Vilaine, in which partner employers of their four childhood-company contracts expressed satisfaction with the creation and functioning of inter-company crèches. In particular, employers recognized that "developing partnerships with other companies and local authorities is a good solution in order to reduce costs and make the service sustainable".[86]

The companies see the provision of childcare as very beneficial to public image, improved employee commitment and morale (a key issue for workers with atypical hours), and attraction and retention of skilled workers, especially in the health sector where there are shortages of nurses:

> Although the childcare places Sévigné Polyclinic has reserved are limited, this service is an important element that we highlight during the recruiting process. It is part of the "plus" that an employer can set to attract and retain staff. So although the costs per childcare place increased in 2006, we renewed the "childhood contract" without hesitation. (HRD, Sévigné Polyclinic)

Employee/trade union perspective

Working parents also expressed appreciation for the service, especially its location near the workplace, its independence and its flexibility and suitability for workers with atypical hours, which is unique in the area. In fact, a large share of workers in the health and transportation sector cannot afford home-based care and the working hours of licensed childminders do not fit with atypical schedules.

Some two-earner families manage childcare during unusual hours by taking turns providing care or resorting to relatives or friends. Problems emerge mainly when both parents work at atypical hours, and no informal support is available.

---

[86] Kervella, 2008.

For lone parents working atypical hours, finding care is very difficult. Interviewed workers and their representatives highlighted the importance of Calaïs Crèche for these parents:

> It was the difficulty of working parents in finding a childcare arrangement that pushed our trade union to support this project. When a worker starts at 5.00 a.m. or finishes at 10.00 p.m. nobody will agree to take care of his/her baby. So a lot of women, in particular, were in trouble and often the only solution was to take sick leave, which had an impact on absenteeism. (CFDT delegate at Kéolis)

Nevertheless, since the service only covers children up to 4, parents still face difficulties finding childcare for older children during atypical hours.

While working time measures are not explicitly incorporated in a collective agreement at the company level, the employers and workers at Sévigné and Kéolis usually work out schedule arrangements, such as reduced weekend and night shifts that accommodate the needs of workers with family responsibilities.

Lessons learned

This project is based on a partnership mechanism in which social security systems play a unique and central role. The CAF-led four-year contract, the involvement of a diverse range of public and private stakeholders and the spreading of costs and risks across many partners provide medium-term stability for all, so that even if a partner must withdraw (for example, because of changing management priorities, ageing of employees, or other reasons), the initiative as a whole can remain stable.

The initiative takes utmost advantage of the multi-centre system to optimize the use of available childcare places by providing part-time, emergency and occasional childcare, in addition to regular care. ParenBouge plays a key role in scheduling the different childcare services it manages to suit care providers, with predictable working hours, training opportunities, above-average salaries and reduced involuntary part-time work.

One major difficulty is that the occupancy requirements of the PSU take enormous time and energy to coordinate the schedules of all crèche clients, and providers feel this time could be put to better use. Nevertheless, staff members of both the CAF and public institutions are very supportive and cooperate in the administrative management of the programme.

One potential risk raised by stakeholders is that flexible and non-standard-hour childcare at the workplace could result in pressure on employees to work longer hours. Workers expressed discomfort that on-site childcare might mean their employer could use knowledge about their childcare arrangements to schedule work as management saw fit. These concerns seem to have been minimized at Calaïs, since the crèche is managed by a third party and places are allocated by an independent system, leaving employers unaware of which workers actually use the crèche.

Finally, the case of Calaïs demonstrates the power of political will (backed by financial incentives), since neither local authorities nor companies are required by national regulations to support collective crèches. When a generous social security system is available, the establishment and sustainability of a childcare facility requires only the vision and commitment of workers, local authorities and employers to put together a project.

SNPE Le Bouchet Research Centre

Type of business. Research, development and application of energetic materials for the defence, aerospace and automotive industries.

Workplace. Le Bouchet Research Centre (Centre de Recherche Le Bouchet) of the SNPE Group, located in the rural area of Vert-le-Petit town (around 2,550 inhabitants) in the region of Île-de-France (around 40 km south of Paris).

Workers. 225 workers; around one-third are women. Two-thirds of employees are managers, engineers and researchers.

Working hours. 35 hours. Most workers work full time, except a small group of employees on voluntary part time (four-fifths).

Childcare solution:
- Back-up care centre (*halte garderie*), temporary and occasional childcare for children between 3 months and 3 years;
- Pre-primary school leisure-time centre (Centre de Loisir sans Hébergement – CLSH), children between 3 and 5 years;
- Primary school leisure-time centre (CLSH), for children from 6 to 14 years.

Partners. CRB Works Council (CFDT, CGT and CFE-CGC, FO trade unions and SNPE-CRB Management); Municipalities of Vert-le-Petit, Vert-le-Grand, Echarcon and Itteville; the CAF of Essonne Department (local family allowance fund); Centre d'Etudes Le Bouchet – CEB (pharmaceutical research); Eurest-Services (catering); and Quad-Lab Laboratory (air analysis and monitoring).

SNPE (Société Nationale des Poudres et Explosifs) is a state-owned company with a private status, employing nearly 4,300 workers at 34 sites worldwide: two in America, five in Asia and 27 in Europe (18 in France). SNPE Group is divided into three specialized subsidiaries: 1) SNPE Energetic Materials (SNPE Matériaux Energétiques): design and production of chemicals for energetic materials; 2) ISOCHEM: fabrication of pharmaceutical and agrochemical products; 3) Bergerac NC: manufacture and sale of industrial nitrocellulose. This case study focuses on the childcare programme of Le Bouchet Research Centre (CRB; Centre de Recherche Le Bouchet) of the subsidiary SNPE Energetic Materials.

In 1981, the delegates of the CFDT trade union at the CRB Works Council (Comité d'entreprise) started raising concerns about the lack of childcare solutions in the rural area of Essonne and the lack of places in the municipal crèches of neighbouring towns. The trade union started negotiations and obtained support from management through the Works Council to help SNPE working parents better balance family and professional responsibilities by providing workplace childcare.

In 1985, a workplace leisure-time centre was inaugurated, welcoming 50 children between 6 and 14 years – although only on Wednesdays. It was open to SNPE workers and parents from Vert-le-Petit. A non-profit association, Charlie Chaplin, was created to manage the facility. Nevertheless, more efforts were needed to respond to working parents' childcare demands, especially during school holidays.

In 1991, the CRB Works Council, led by the CFDT trade union with the support of the CGT trade union, started exploratory activities with the CAF of Essonne Department for a larger-scale childcare programme. In December 1994 a childhood contract (*contrat enfance*) was signed which established a partnership scheme for co-funding childcare, bringing together the CRB Works Council, the CAF of Essonne and initially three neighbouring rural municipalities. The contract set out cost-sharing modalities for the start-up investment and operating costs, as well as the share of childcare places among partners.

The SNPE-CRB provided its own facilities for the leisure-time centre with a 99-year rental contract with the Charlie Chaplin Association, and covered the cost of roof repairs. The facilities and refitting met accreditation criteria and eligibility for CAF childcare subsidies.

Childcare services

Opened in 1995, the childcare programme is located a few metres from Le Bouchet Research Centre, in a house and garden owned by SNPE. The building was renovated according to national childcare standards. Within three years, the following facilities were set up:

- A back-up care centre (*halte garderie*) for temporary and occasional care, with 15 places that serve a total of 35 children aged 3 months to 3 years. The centre is open on Mondays, Tuesdays and Thursdays from 8.45 a.m. to 4.45 p.m. and on Fridays from 8.45 a.m. to 12.15 p.m. It is closed during both public and school holidays.

- A pre-primary school leisure-time centre (Centre de Loisir sans Hébergement – CLSH), with 25 places for children aged from 3 to 5 years.

- A primary school leisure-time centre (CLSH), with 30 places for children aged 6 to 14 years.

The leisure-time centres are open on Wednesdays and school holidays from 7.30 a.m. to 7.00 p.m. and closed for one week in August and December.

The leisure-time centres provide a full set of recreation, sports and artistic activities, including excursions. In addition, the childcare services include two snacks and a lunch, which are served at the SNPE restaurant, where children can meet with their parents during lunch breaks. A licensed childminder (*assistante maternelle*) as well as a licensed childminder network (*relais assistantes maternelles*) have also been set up in Itteville town (around 5,500 inhabitants) and are available to crèche partners. Every year, more than 300 children benefit from all components of the childcare programme, accounting for a total of more than 8,000 days of service.[87] The CRB Works Council is currently working to create a leisure-time programme for adolescents from 14 to 17 years.

Eligibility and use

According to the terms of the childcare contract, the facilities are open, at CAF-subsidized fees, to all SNPE parents, to the inhabitants of Vert-le-Petit, Vert-le-Grand, Echarcon and Itteville, and to the workers of three partner enterprises in the surrounding employment area (CEB, Eurest and Quad-Lab), who contribute to the budget of the CRB Works Council. The facility is open to any parent outside of these groups at full price.

---

[87] Viganego, 2008.

Organization and management

The childcare programme is managed by a non-profit association called Charlie Chaplin, whose governing board is composed of five representatives of the CRB Works Council, one from each of the four partner municipalities, and one parent. The association's total membership is around 150 families. The programme is accredited and monitored by the Ministry of Youth and Sports and the National Agency on Maternal and Child Protection (Protection Maternelle et Infantile), under the auspices of the General Council of the Essonne Department, and the Departmental Commission on Hygiene and Security.

Childcare staff

The staff includes eight experienced caregivers, all women: a director, three caregivers (back-up care centre) and four educators (leisure-time centre). Additional fixed-term educators are hired during school holidays, the most highly attended period of the leisure-time centres.

- **The director** holds a qualification as a director of out-of-school activities (*BAFD*) and a National Certificate of Activity Leader-Technician in Popular and Youth Education (*BEATEP*), which is an official diploma at the baccalaureate level in the planning, leading and assisting of social and cultural activities. She has been director of Charlie Chaplin for six years.

- **Back-up care centre:** three staff: one early childhood educator (*éducatrice de jeunes enfants*), and two caregivers holding an under-baccalaureate certificate in early childhood (*CAP petite enfance*).

- **Leisure-time centres:** four staff members: one leisure-time centre educator holds a BEATEP while the remaining three have a non-professional qualification related to out-of-school activities, known as Patent for Youth Leadership (*BAFA*).

The CRB Works Council provides financial support and allocates working time for staff to attend a broad variety of training opportunities, including the experience validation process, a training modality open to both the director and caregivers to upgrade their qualifications. This is a new training process started in France in 2002 and open to all individuals working for the same employer for at least three years. The objective is to support workers to obtain a diploma or certificate validating their acquired professional experience. In this framework, and through the support of the CRB Works Council, one caregiver was certified as an early childhood educator, while the director obtained her *BAFD*, which enabled her to fill her current position. In addition, support to earn the *BAFA* certificate is offered to all leisure-time centre educators.

Every summer, the association receives a number of both high-school and university trainees, who help permanent educators at the leisure centre. These interns receive notional compensation (140 euro) from the association and earn a *BAFA* certificate.

All staff members have the status of private non-profit organization employees, which follows the provisions of the collective bargaining agreement on workers in non-profit organizations.[88] All are on permanent contracts; the director works full time and the other staff members work voluntary part time (four-fifths). A full working week is 35 hours and staff members are paid at 115 per cent of minimum wage (8.50 euro per hour in France). Pro-rata salary and benefits are applied to part-time workers. The child-to-teacher ratio is 5:1 at the back-up care centre and 8:1 and 12:1 at the preschool and primary school leisure-time centres respectively.

Caregivers are satisfied with their working conditions and the worker sensitivity of their workplace, which they credit to the Works Council and its policy. They appreciate the training opportunities and working time arrangements, in particular the part-time scheme, which is useful for their own work–family reconciliation.

Costs and funding mechanisms

The childcare programme started with the childhood contract between the Essonne CAF, the CRB Works Council and three municipalities, with the key contribution of SNPE-CRB in terms of the building. The Works Councils of the neighbouring three small enterprises also remit their contribution to the CRB Works Council.

Charlie Chaplin runs the programme, sets up the fees for each service and sells childcare vouchers to the contract partners for either full- or half-day childcare. The vouchers are priced after CAF subsidies, which account for almost half of real costs, as follows:

- Back-up care centre, half day: 16 euro; full day: 34 euro.

- Pre-primary leisure-care centre, half day: 18 euro; full day: 29 euro.

- Primary leisure-care centre, half day: 12.50 euro; full day: 19.50 euro.

---

[88] Convention collective nationale de l'animation, 1989.

Partner companies and local authorities resell the vouchers to their workers/ inhabitants at a more-or-less subsidized price, according to internal social policies and in line with CNAF parameters, as indicated in the childhood contract. For instance, the CRB Works Council covers between 20 and 80 per cent of voucher costs in line with its family quotient, which depends upon family composition and income. In addition, according to national regulations, families benefit from a tax credit of 50 per cent on annual childcare expenses.

Employer perspective

After initial scepticism, the management of SNPE-CRB has supported this trade union initiative in the framework of company-based social dialogue mechanisms by its annual Works Council contribution of up to 2.6 per cent of the gross wage bill and by regularly covering the operating costs of Charlie Chaplin out of its annual investment budget. The childcare programme is part of other work–life balance measures, including working time arrangements for modified working hours, flexible work schedules and voluntary part-time work for childcare and training. In addition, with a view to achieving gender pay equality within SNPE, the company has allocated funds for a pay equity review post. Also, in the frame-work of the last salary agreement with trade union representatives, SNPE-CRB is financing both employer and worker shares of social security contributions to ensure that four-fifths part-time workers, usually women with family responsi-bilities, will receive the equivalent of a full-time-worker pension.

Employee perspective

This innovative trade union initiative arose to respond to the pressing need of working parents for childcare in a rural area, where childcare services were almost non-existent. Indeed, the joint efforts of a large company, its Works Council and its partners has supported a large number of parents beyond just SNPE-CRB workers, ranging from night workers in the health sector to mothers on parental leave. SNPE-CRB workers find that the centre entirely responds to their childcare needs, especially in terms of location and working hours. The lei-sure centre for children on Wednesdays and during school holidays provides an important relief for working parents, whose annual leave days do not cover all the school holidays. However, the back-up care centre, which parents can use for only up to two days per week, seems to be less suitable for solving the regular childcare needs of working parents. For those parents not covered by the CAF or Works Councils' subsidies, the cost of the programme may be too expensive, limiting access.

Lessons learned

The SNPE Le Bouchet Research Centre was the first Works Council in France to be part of a public–private partnership for childcare in the framework of a childcare contract with the CAF and local governments. Established at a time when companies' participation in workplace childcare programmes was at an embryonic stage, this pioneering example has paved the way for further developments of public–private partnerships for childcare in France. Since the creation of Charlie Chaplin, the CRB Works Council has won awards for its innovation and dynamism from the French Ministry of Labour and other national and international institutions.

The employer and trade unions were initially resistant to taking on a workplace social project, not only because childcare was seen as the exclusive responsibility of the State, but also because of the financial risk of such a project. The continued success of Charlie Chaplin 15 years later has proved both the stability of the partnership modality and the relevance of the service, despite the various difficulties related to human resources and financial management, the limited budget allocation of the CRB Works Council, compliance with national childcare regulations and the requirements for optimum occupancy.

> A key lesson learned is that difficulties should not discourage action, especially if the project is solid. It is important to accurately identify the actual needs and put together all partners' competences and strengths in order to provide high-quality services to both children and parents. (Representative of the CFDT trade union, Secretary of the CRB Works Council and President of the Charlie Chaplin Association)

Over the years, this experience and its public–private partnership approach has served as a model to be copied, with attention from both national authorities and peer enterprises. So far, the programme has proven to be an effective and sustainable answer to the lack of childcare services in a rural area.

Aix-la-Duranne Employment Site (Aix-en-Provence)

Type of business. The employment site of Aix-la-Duranne (320 ha) includes 211 companies in the industry, construction, trade and service sectors, employing more than 3,250 workers.

Workplace. Aix-la-Duranne is one of the five company sites of the Aix-en-Provence Activity Pole (1,373 companies, with more than 25,000 workers). Aix-en-Provence (population: 140,200) is in the south of France, in the region Provence-Alpes-Côte d'Azur (PACA).

Workers. Many categories of workers of the 17 partner companies and public institutions, including full- and part-time workers, employees and managers.

Working hours. 35–39 hours.

Childcare solution. Inter-company, inter-local-authority crèche, providing regular, occasional and part-time care for children from 2.5 months to 4 years; out-of-school childcare for children aged 6 years.

Partners. Bouches-du-Rhône CAF; private crèche company: places taken by 13 companies and 4 public administrations.

Opened in September 2006, the Aix-les-Milles crèche is the first inter-company, inter-local authority crèche of the PACA Region. It was created by the crèche company Les Petits Chaperons Rouges (LPCR) following a proposal by Areva TA with the support of Eurocopter who were concerned about the lack of regular crèche places for their employees and actively sought a solution. While these two companies use the largest share of crèche places, their initiative and support for the project has allowed the participation of one medium-size and 11 small enterprises and four public administrations with places as shown in box 8.1.

Les Petits Chaperons Rouges, created in 2000, is one of the major crèche companies in France, providing technical assistance to companies and local authorities seeking to offer childcare services to their workers. The Aix-les-Milles crèche is one of the 40 inter-partner crèches opened by LPCR in France since 2005. LPCR was responsible for the needs-assessment and feasibility study for the crèche, its creation and its management.

Childcare programme

The facility is located in the employment site of Aix-la-Duranne, within 15 minutes by car from all partners' sites. It is 600 m² and includes a large garden.

The crèche, for children of 2.5 months to 4 years old, is open from 7.30 a.m. to 7.30 p.m., Monday to Friday, with closures in August (two weeks) and December (one week). The service includes one meal, snacks and milk, as well as baby hygiene products, towels, sheets, bibs and feeding bottles.

Like all LPCR crèches, the Aix-les-Milles crèche has 60 places and operates as a multi-care centre, providing regular, occasional and emergency childcare (around 10 per cent of all places). The service also includes out-of-school childcare for children aged 6 years, which allows full use of crèche places and takes into account the different needs of working parents. A place for a child with disabilities has also been established along with a specialized childcare programme. As of September 2008, a total of 130 families working or living in the surrounding area of Aix-la-Duranne used the service.

Following the success of this project and the increasing demand of working parents in Aix-la-Duranne, crèche capacity was expanded by 26 places in October 2008. This has helped create ten more jobs and now supports an additional 50 families in balancing their work and family responsibilities.

Eligibility and use

The facility is open to all categories of workers from partner companies and public institutions which have reserved one or more places in the Aix-les-Milles crèche. Places are allocated by a commission according to criteria established by the crèche partners. The commission meets several times a year to manage the waiting list in line with the available places.

Organization and management

Les Petits Chaperons Rouges carried out environment and needs-assessment studies, which identified Aix-la-Duranne among the priority areas of the local CAF in terms of childcare provision. It then undertook a feasibility study and prepared the preliminary architectural plans. LPCR worked with public authorities to identify and mobilize the available childcare subsidies, identified potential company and public institution partners, prepared and presented the childcare project, and took care of the programme start-up. The resulting childcare programme is entirely managed by the crèche company.

Box 8.1 Participating organizations, Aix-la-Duranne Employment Site

Two large companies (more than 250 employees):

- Areva TA: engineering and development of nuclear technology – 1,156 workers; 12 crèche places.
- Eurocopter: conception and production of helicopters – 6,663 workers; 45 crèche places.

One medium-size company (between 50 and 250 employees):

- Polysius: engineering and construction – 155 workers; three crèche places.

11 small companies (less than 50 employees):

- Axilya: nuclear security and industrial environment – 45 workers; two crèche places.
- BO Concept: wholesale trade – one crèche place.
- Clearsy: software development and trade – 18 workers; one crèche place.
- CWI: insurance – one crèche place.
- Easydentic: conception and distribution of biometric products – 35 workers; three crèche places.
- Euro Controle Project: control of petrochemical projects and systems – 17 workers; one crèche place.
- FRP Service Europe: production and trade of glass fibres and polymers – 12 workers; one crèche place.
- Reactis: engineering and ICT – 20 workers; one crèche place.
- Sphinx Informatique: software conception and ICT material trade – 10 workers; one crèche place.
- Supersonic imagine: production of electro-medical materials – 35 workers; three crèche places.
- Tholia: electrical materials installation – three crèche places.

Four public administrations:

- CETE Méditerranée (Technical Studies Centre of the Ministry of Infrastructure – Centre d'Etudes Techniques du Ministère de l'Equipement): public research centre – 570 workers; seven crèche places.
- Joint Association of Arbois: local administration – 20 workers; one crèche place.
- Préfecture of Bouches-du-Rhône: public administration – six crèche places.
- Local branch of the Ministry of Justice: public administration – three crèche places.

Childcare staff

Crèche staff members are employees of LPCR. On average, they are 32 years old and have eight years of childcare experience. At the Aix-les-Milles crèche, there are 30 professionals (increased from 20 in 2008): one director, one deputy director, one nurse, four assistant child nurses, 15 early childhood educators and caregivers, and other support staff.[89] Staff ratios meet existing regulations of one professional caregiver for five infants or eight older children. The crèche hires external services from a paediatrician and a psychologist.

Most staff work full time and hold a permanent contract. The working week is 36 hours over four days. Directors work five days per week. The 36th hour is paid as overtime and workers receive a 13th-month salary benefit, in addition to their regular wage, which ranges from 1 to 2.5 times the minimum wage (8.50 euro per hour). This salary policy allows staff to benefit from an additional weekly day off, while permitting greater flexibility in crèche scheduling. Training opportunities include a workshop on security issues upon recruitment, a staff-development programme for those seeking career advancement, and an annual staff retreat.

Costs and funding mechanisms

The initial costs of the programme were covered by LPCR and the Bouches-du-Rhône CAF, with support from the CNAF childcare investment programme. In addition, the programme benefits from social security subsidies in the framework of the PSU and the company childhood-youth contract, which together cover around 60 per cent of operating costs. The net childcare costs to partner companies are 11 per cent of the total, while the State subsidizes 16 per cent as part of the family tax credit. Parents' contribution (around 15 per cent) is in line with the CNAF national scale and is based on family composition and income.

Employer perspective

LPCR partner companies recognize that the crèche, offering reliable childcare close to the workplace, is a benefit to both their workers and their company. Employers note improvements in productivity and workers' performance, better

---

[89] Across France as a whole, LPCR employs around 1,000 people, among whom 36 are men. Fifty-two are based at the enterprise headquarters (Clichy, Hauts-de-Seine) and 948 in LPCR crèches.

attraction and retention of qualified workers, and reduced absenteeism. "Happy children make happy parents and so happy and motivated workers. This can only benefit the company, in terms of curbing absenteeism, work delays and long parental leaves" (Management of Schneider Electric, a partner company of two LPCR crèches at Rueil Malmaison and Grenoble).[90] Employers highlight the key role of a workplace crèche for promoting workers' return after maternity or parental leave, and more broadly, in enhancing gender equality in their companies.

Employee perspective

Working parents appreciate the Aix-les-Milles crèche for its flexibility, its proximity to the workplace and its suitability for their working hours. They value the ability to visit their children during lunch breaks, allowing them to spend time with their children and feel reassured about their conditions. Parents also appreciate having high-quality services at the same cost as a neighbourhood crèche, while benefiting from tax credits for childcare.

Lessons learned

The example of the Aix-les-Milles crèche shows how the participation of private partners in childcare provision has helped respond to the need for crèche places in France. After initial resistance, this childcare initiative has become popular among working parents and crèche partners. Public subsidies and the expertise of a crèche company in managing the service help encourage employers' participation, and across France more employers are reserving places in inter-company crèches for their workers. Employers feel they are supporting high-quality, low-cost services, without investing a lot of time in administrative work. Indeed, with the support from social security, offering workplace childcare costs employers just 1 to 2 euro per hour while the recognized benefits to both workers and companies are multiple.[91]

Finally, the leading role of large companies in this initiative has allowed many SMEs, which could not have otherwise afforded to start a crèche, to participate. This has also been the case in other regions: once larger companies take

---

[90] *Le Monde*, 2007. "Crèches privées : une solution plébiscitée !" Supplement: *Les Cahiers de la Competitivité*, 29 March.

[91] Ibid.

the lead, smaller companies join in. Among the 250 partners of LPCR crèches, approximately 40 per cent are SMEs, 30 per cent are large companies and 30 per cent are local authorities or public institutions.[92] This innovative form of public–private partnership offers great potential for involving new and diverse local actors in the creation of crèche facilities.

---

[92] LPCR, (2008). "Partenariats sur le lieu de travail pour la garde d'enfants: Profil du cas d'étude." (Les Petits Chaperons Rouges in-house pamphlet.)

Hungary

9

Katalin Tardos[1]

National overview

In 1990, at the beginning of the Transition period, Hungary had a relatively well-developed traditional system for childcare solutions:

- daycare centres were provided for children of 0–3 years old;
- kindergartens for preschool-age children of 3–7 years old; and
- after-school daycare services for primary school students aged 6–14 years old.

The basic structure of childcare provision has stayed the same to date, but there has been a significant decline in access to daycare centres for children under age 3,

[1] Katalin Tardos is the Programme Director of the BA in Business Studies at the International Business School, Budapest, and Research Fellow at the Institute of Sociology of the Hungarian Academy of Sciences. She specializes in Human Resource Management, Business Ethics and Diversity Management. She would like to thank Noémi Ferenczi of IBM Hungary, Lívia Lessi, Szigetvári Istvánné and Piroska Boromisza of the Hungarian Academy of Sciences, Lamoli Tünde and Konczné Hegedűs Éva of Hungarian Post, Tölősi Krisztina and Szőcs Gábor of Magyar Telekom, and finally Tóth Ferencné and Csilla Balogh of Gedeon Richter Plc for their kind collaboration in the project.

while participation rates slightly increased in kindergartens and after-school-care services. The present lack of sufficient childcare services for children under 3 years represents the biggest challenge for childcare provision and a major obstacle for mothers who want to re-enter employment.

Women's employment and childcare

A rather generous maternity and parental leave system of 3 years and childcare allowance is in place in Hungary; this dates from the late 1960s, when politicians wanted to respond to low fertility rates and population decline. Several amendments to the system have been made in the past ten years, but basic financial coverage for leave is provided to both insured and non-insured women.[2] These leave policies have had several effects. On the one hand, they relieved pressures for day-care centres for children aged 0–3 years. On the other hand, they became a major trap for women interrupting their employment, as changing labour market conditions and increased unemployment rates after the Transition period made it more difficult for women with young children to re-enter the labour market.

Women's employment has clearly declined in the last decade in Hungary and is very low among women with young children compared to other developed countries. Overall, women's employment rate decreased in Hungary from 57.3 per cent in 1990 to 51 per cent in 2007 (compared to 64 per cent for men).[3] The employment rate of women with children under 3 is quite low in Hungary at 11 per cent compared to the OECD average of 57.5 per cent.[4] For mothers with children aged 3 to 5 years, the employment rate is 46 per cent in Hungary compared to 61.8 per cent across the OECD, a smaller, but still significant, gap, despite a 90 per cent access rate to kindergarten for children of this age cohort. Finally, the employment gap between the OECD average and Hungary shrinks but does not disappear after children enter primary school (67 per cent versus 60 per cent in Hungary).

A survey by the Hungarian Central Statistical Office[5] in 2005 revealed that, among those inactive and taking care of children under 15 years of age, 39 per cent

---

[2] Maternity leave lasts 24 weeks with 70 per cent of previous earnings. Afterwards, for the non-insured, GYES pays a flat-rate equal to the minimum wage until the child's third birthday. For the insured, GYED pays 70 per cent of earnings, up to a cap of 70 per cent of double the minimum wage in 2008. GYED is paid until the child's second birthday. After that, the insured also receive GYES for the third year. In theory either mothers or fathers can take the allowances, but in practice over 90 per cent are mothers.

[3] Supplied by the Hungarian Central Statistical Office.

[4] OECD, 2005b.

[5] Hungarian Central Statistical Office, 2006.

had a problem in relation to childcare provision. This means that they would like to work but cannot because they lack access or cannot afford the personally needed childcare service. The situation is most critical for mothers living in villages. Very often the only solution is to stay inactive and rely on the childcare allowance system until the child is 3. As noted above, this is a major trap for women as their employability declines and re-entering work becomes more difficult.

Existing facilities for childcare of preschool children

Two ministries in Hungary are responsible for preschool childcare and education. The Ministry of Health is responsible for daycare services for children under 3. The Ministry of Education is responsible for the kindergarten education for children 3–7 years. Kindergarten education is considered the first stage of the public education system.

Daycare centres (nurseries)

In 2006, 543 daycare centres operated in Hungary – roughly half as many as in 1990. In fact, the number of daycare centres has been rapidly decreasing since 1980 as declining birth rates led to low use of existing facilities even before the Transition. Also, the percentage of children under age 3 in daycare centres declined from 13.7 per cent in 1990 to only 6.5 per cent in 2006.[6]

Of the 543 daycare centres in 2006, 511 were financed by local municipalities. This means that 94 per cent of daycare centres were managed by a municipality despite the fact that legally both for-profit and non-profit organizations could set up such institutions.[7]

Before the Transition, about 10 per cent of daycare centres were operated by workplaces. However, between 1990 and 1995 the number of both municipal and workplace daycare institutions dropped by half. For the local municipalities, the major argument put forward was the low utilization rate for demographic reasons. In the case of workplaces, it was the easiest way to cut costs in areas not related to the core profile of the company. In this period many companies were privatizing and workplace welfare institutions were seen as outdated relics from the socialist era. As a result, by 2006 only nine company-run daycare services remained.

---

[6] Hungarian Central Statistical Office, 2007.
[7] Hungarian Central Statistical Office, 2007.

The regional distribution of daycare centres is very unequal. Budapest's rate is above the average of other regions of the country. According to the 1997 law on the provision of daycare centres, local municipalities above 10,000 inhabitants are obliged to set up and operate such institutions, but several towns do not comply with the law due to financial hardship, especially in high unemployment regions, which aggravates women's employment prospects. Of Hungary's 2,856 villages, only 50 had daycare centres in 2005.[8]

The cost of childcare is funded by the state, local governments and parents. The state budget allocates a subsidy based on number of children served per day (547,000 HUF per year in 2007 or about 2,100 euro), but the majority of operating costs need to be covered by the municipality as the state subsidy covers only 25–30 per cent. Parents pay 10–15 per cent of operating costs in the form of payment for meals for the child. From January 2004, daycare centres have provided free meals to children from low-income families.[9]

A temporary demographic boom, starting in 2000, significantly increased the demand for daycare centres. Parents register on waiting lists for daycare centres almost immediately after the birth of the child. While demand has increased, the available places have not. Only the utilization rate has increased, meaning that more children are enrolled in the facilities than the available places, counting on the regular sicknesses of infants. In 2006 the utilization rate of available places was 114 per cent, but the access rate was only 6.5 per cent.

At present, the lack of sufficient childcare services for children under 3 represents the biggest challenge for childcare provision and a major obstacle for mothers who want to re-enter employment. Fortunately the issue has recently been gaining greater media coverage. As an alternative solution, the government has introduced the possibility of setting up family daycare services since 2003. At the same time, private kindergartens, sensing the market demand for childcare for infants, started accepting 2-year-olds.

Kindergartens

Hungary has a strong historical pedagogical tradition in early education. The first kindergarten of Central Europe was set up in 1828 in Hungary. The general trends in implementing early care and education for children under 6 parallel developments in the rest of Europe.[10] In 1993, the Public Education Act officially

---

[8] Koltai and Vucskó, 2007.

[9] OECD, 2004b, p. 15.

[10] OECD, 2004b, p. 16.

recognized kindergarten as part of the public education system. Children can start kindergarten from age 3 and are obliged to attend the last year in preparation for primary school education, which starts at age 6. Most kindergartens are maintained by local municipalities (88 per cent), but church, private and non-profit institutions have a greater share than is the case with daycare centres.[11] Regional disparities are less significant than in the case of daycare centres.

The Transition has had less impact for kindergartens than for daycare centres. The number of kindergartens was fairly stable throughout the past decade. In the 2006/07 school year, there were 4,524 kindergartens in Hungary – just 4 per cent less than in 1990. In the same period, the attendance rate of the age cohort reached 91 per cent and more places were available than were actually needed. This means parents could probably find kindergarten services near their place of living and did not need to be put on waiting lists.

Kindergartens typically have a summer break of four weeks. This period raises difficulties for the parents, and solutions have to be found on an individual basis for families. The daily opening hours of 7.30 a.m. to 5.30 p.m. are conducive to typical working schedules. Nevertheless, more flexible opening hours to match the work schedule of parents is an issue to be resolved.

Kindergartens are financed by a combination of central state budget and local funds. State subsidies cover 50–60 per cent of operating costs. The local government complements these funds from their own resources (coming from local taxes), and parents pay for the meals of the child which amounts to 5,000–10,000 HUF/month (20–40 euro). Low-income families with children who receive supplemental child protection allowances do not pay meal fees.

Family daycare services

Family daycare is a relatively new type of early childcare service. It can be provided either in the home of the childcare worker or somewhere else, and can enrol a maximum of seven children. According to the law, family daycare can offer services to children from 20 weeks to 14 years old. However, most provide care for children under 3 years of age.

This form of service has received a state subsidy since 2003. In 2007, 106 such family daycare services were registered with the local governments. The state subsidy equalled 250,000 HUF per year per child (approximately 1,000 euro), which

---

[11] Hungarian Central Statistical Office, table 5. "Az oktatási intézmények főbb adatai fenntartók szerint, 2007/2008." Found at http://portal.ksh.hu/pls/ksh/docs/hun/xtabla/kozokt/tablkozokt05.html [2 June 2009].

meant that the level of funding was half that of daycare centres. The family daycare provider may sign an agreement for further local funding, but this is not obligatory for the municipality. Since 2006, parents have paid an hourly fee covering food and caring expenses. Typically the hourly cost price for a child amounts to 350 HUF (1.5 euro). The state subsidy covers one-third of the expenses, but if no extra funding is available from the local government, the family daycare service could require a monthly fee of 47,000 HUF (180 euro), two-thirds of the present minimum wage.[12]

Facilities for the care of schoolchildren

After-school daycare is a traditional public school childcare service in Hungary. The service is provided in the same school that the child attends, typically with classmates. In smaller locations, children aged 1–4 and 5–8 are grouped together. A special pedagogue organizes learning sessions for the children to prepare their homework. Free-time activities are scheduled as well. After-school daycare is open from the end of the teaching hours to 5.30 p.m. Thus working parents can fetch their children after regular working hours.

The participation rate of children in after-school daycare services has increased slightly from 37 per cent of the primary school population in 1990 to 42 per cent in 2006. In practice, the participation rate is higher for younger children in grades 1–4, and lower in grades 5–8. Using the catering services offered by the school is common, and in 2006 almost two-thirds of primary school students used them, up from 54 per cent in 1990.[13] For the after-school care and catering services, parents pay only for the meals: breakfast, lunch and snacks in the afternoon. This costs 7,000–8,000 HUF per month (approximately 30 euro).

Summer day camps for primary school pupils are often offered by public schools and local municipalities. These camps are cheap compared to private summer camps. Public camps cost approximately 5,000 HUF per week compared to 10–15,000 HUF (40–60 euro) for private schemes.

Efforts for work–life balance

In recent years, there has been growing awareness among employers of the need to tackle work–life balance and to provide equal opportunities at work for women. In this respect, the Family-Friendly Employer Award launched in 2000 by the

---

[12] Koltai and Vucskó, 2007.
[13] Hungarian Central Statistical Office, 2007.

Ministry of Labour has helped raise awareness. Each year, award-winning companies are identified in small, medium and large company categories. The awards ceremony is well covered by the media to encourage shifts in employers' attitudes.

The Act on Equal Treatment and Promotion of Equal Opportunities (2004) has also played an important role in raising awareness in the country. Equal opportunity plans have been compulsory for public sector employers since 2005 and women are a typical target group for initiatives.

According to a European survey, Hungary has one of the lowest levels of atypical work in the European Union.[14] Some 24.9 per cent of Hungarians are in atypical work forms (part-time work, self-employment and fixed-term contracts), half the EU average (48.5 per cent). In particular, the rate of part-time work, a major source of female employment, is extremely low (4.1 per cent in Hungary versus 18.4 per cent in Europe).

Flexible working hours are more widely spread among employers. The Hungarian Central Statistical Office reported that in 2005 around one-third of employers offered flexible working patterns to help the work–life balance of employees.[15] Nevertheless, the share of flexible working hours is relatively low compared to other European countries.[16]

Compared to employers, work–life balance and equality at work issues are lower on the agenda for trade unions in Hungary.

Government policies and programmes

The policy of government is to provide financial support directly to nurseries and kindergartens. Local authorities are also expected to contribute and to manage many of the facilities. Expenditure on kindergartens for children aged 3–6 years is 0.79 per cent of GDP. Almost 91.7 per cent of this expenditure comes from public sources, and 6.2 per cent from households.[17] Thus, parents' contributions are a very small proportion of the actual cost.

The New National Development Plan proposed the establishment of day-care centres for children under 3 in every settlement of more than 10,000 inhabitants. Long parental leaves have tended to reduce the demand for care for children under age 3 but there is evidence that facilities are insufficient, as discussed

---

[14] European Commission, 2006a.
[15] Hungarian Central Statistical Office, 2006.
[16] Riedmann et al., 2006.
[17] OECD, 2005b.

above. Within the framework of the New National Development Plan, 50 billion HUF (192,000 euro) have been allocated to the seven Hungarian regions to develop childcare services, including daycare centres and family daycare centres, between 2007 and 2013. Estimates suggest that this sum will cover the construction or reconstruction of 70 childcare facilities in the given period.[18] The OECD Economic Survey of Hungary 2007[19] suggests that government review the long parental leave and related cash benefits, noting that savings could help fund the expansion of childcare for children under 3 years. The report also suggests that introducing a system of childcare vouchers for parents would be one way of increasing efficiency in the provision of services.

The government is concerned about the difficulties women face in re-entering employment after a childcare break. The Start Plusz programme was introduced in 2007 to provide employers who employ women after a childcare break with a subsidy for social security contributions. To date, 4,735 women have applied for the programme. Incentives for women to study throughout the duration of the childcare allowance have also been introduced.

Conclusion

To sum up, the major problem related to childcare provision in Hungary is the lack of daycare facilities for parents with children under 3. Despite state subsidies for nurseries, most small municipalities are not in the position to finance such institutions. The family daycare services could offer an alternative and more flexible form of childcare compared to nurseries. However, the relatively low state subsidy and the reluctance of local governments to financially support them limit their attractiveness to both potential service providers and clients.

In the last ten years, a few employers have introduced family-friendly initiatives in order to retain female talent at the company, but only the most innovative ones have invested in childcare provision. The examples which follow show a diversity of cases from companies which have modernized facilities inherited from the socialist era (Gedeon Richter, the Hungarian Post Office and the Hungarian Academy of Sciences) to those taking new initiatives (IBM Hungary and Magyar Telekom). It is interesting that four of the five companies are providing help in accessing summer camp for the schoolchildren of employees, thus meeting a need which is often overlooked in efforts to help with childcare.

---

[18] Found at the web site of the National Development Agency, http://www.nfu.hu/content/1190 [11 June 2009].

[19] OECD, 2007b.

IBM Hungary

Type of business. Information technology (IT).

Workplace. Four independent IBM units are operating in Hungary: two in Budapest (IBM Hungary Ltd plus IBM ISC Hungária as IBM Hungary's subsidiary, and IBM ISSC), one in Székesfehérvár (IBM IDC) and one in Vác (IBM DSS Ltd).

Workers. Mostly IT professionals, sales representatives, business consultants and financial, logistics and human resources personnel.

Working hours. Sales representatives and business consultants have flexitime; 80 per cent of employees have Internet access from their homes, so they can rely on distance working; administrative staff have regular full-time working hours.

Childcare solution. Back-up care (babysitter services), summer camp for children.

Partners. Childcare provider organizations, IBM Global WorkLife Fund.

IBM celebrated the 70th anniversary of its first Hungarian legal entity in 2006. In recent decades, the hardware company has been transformed into a services and solutions provider which has many operations in Hungary, employing thousands of skilled and talented workers.

- **IBM Hungary** is the solution provider and sales organization of IBM, while the two other Budapest-based entities provide shared services to IBM and non-IBM clients.

- The **IBM Shared Services Center** (IBM ISSC) provides financial, human resources, customer relationship management and other services to primarily European and Hungarian clients.

- The Székesfehérvár-based **Integrated Delivery Center** of IBM and the IBM ISC Hungary in Budapest provide system-monitoring services for European clients (such as enterprise resource planning, mainframe, printing services) on different platforms.

- The Vác-based **IBM Data Storage Systems** is a manufacturing and assembly operation of IBM: the DS8000 mainframe subsystem is made here and shipped worldwide.[20]

Globally, IBM launched the first national corporate childcare initiative more than two decades ago; this evolved into a five-year, $25 million IBM Fund for

---

[20] http://www-05.ibm.com/employment/hu/index.html [10 June 2008].

Dependent Care Initiative to help employees balance work and personal needs. As childcare and eldercare became increasingly important to IBMers, the company responded by creating the Global WorkLife Fund with a five-year, $50 million commitment. It was the first fund of its type to address employee issues on a global basis. It emphasizes a complete range of dependent care services, with the specific intent of increasing the number of women in the workforce and the use of IBM technology by providing IBM computers with age-appropriate educational software to childcare centres.[21] In 2005 IBM announced further funding of the multi-year Global WorkLife Fund for an additional $50 million, with a continued focus on increasing the supply and improving the quality of dependent care where IBMers work and live.[22]

Hungary became one of the targeted countries of the Global WorkLife Fund for 2005. As part of the needs assessment process, a group of international consultants were hired in 2004 to conduct interviews and focus group discussions with employees, the Hungarian management team and external dependent-care provider organizations. The consultants prepared a report and action plan identifying two major areas in which employees wanted support: back-up care for children (babysitter services) and summer camps during school vacations.

In addition to the childcare provisions, IBM has a maternity leave and return programme. Women going on maternity leave can keep their Thinkpad and user ID for up to one year. The company also provides various e-learning opportunities to women on maternity leave. A "maternity buddy system" matches mothers-to-be with a mother who has already gone through maternity leave and returned to IBM. Temporary replacements are hired for women returning shortly after maternity leave.

As a result of the needs assessment, IBM has implemented two types of childcare provision: summer camps and back-up care for the children of employees.

Summer camps

IBM offers both international/regional and local summer camps. The international summer camp for children of IBM employees was launched in 2005 in Slovakia. Each year, ten school-age children from Hungary used to participate in the international summer camp together with other IBM children from Central Europe and the United States of America. The international camp was very

---

[21] http://www.ibm.com/ibm/responsibility/s4_4.shtml [19 June 2009].

[22] http://www.ibm.com/ibm/responsibility/s4_4.shtml [19 June 2009].

attractive to employees and applications always exceeded the quota for Hungary. For this reason, IBM enlarged the choice of international summer camps in 2008, offering camps in Bulgaria, Croatia, Poland and Slovakia. The international camps offer English courses and activities like adventure games, music and dance studios, camp radio, night games, a journalist centre, sports activities and others. As of 2008, 40 children from Hungary can now participate in the international programme.

A local summer day camp was first organized by IBM Hungary in 2007 in Budapest. The camp is held at the Petneházy Country Club in the suburbs of Budapest, near a national park area. IBM reserved places in the summer day camp for the children of IBM employees. The duration of the camp was basically one week, but it was also possible for a child to enrol for several rounds during the five-week period. A bus service drives children from IBM to the camp and back in the afternoon. The summer day camp targets children from 6 to 14 years old.

The summer day camp at the Petneházy Country Club, first offered to four of the IBM companies in Hungary, was extended to all Hungarian IBMers in 2008. In 2007 there was no waiting list, and a total of 25 children attended the camp. In 2008, places were reserved over four consecutive weeks, and up to 80 children were able to enjoy the camp.

Back-up childcare

In 2007, IBM piloted a back-up care project to help employees find a babysitter to come to their home while subsidizing the cost. With the help of an external consultant, IBM Hungary chose a babysitter and elder care provider agency whose services were available to IBMers for two-month periods. Positive feedback led to a two-year agreement with the agency (Dédy-sitter & Baby-sitter).[23] The full-range programme started in April 2008.

The agency also has a contract with seven play houses in Budapest, where IBM employees can get a 30 per cent discount off regular prices. IBM employees access the back-up care web site through the internal WorkLife Essentials (WLE) portal.

Back-up childcare services are available only to IBM Hungary employees. Both female and male employees can use the services without limit. Estimates and plans show that roughly 112 days of care will be used during the two-year

---

[23] http://www.dediszitter.hu [11 June 2009].

programme. The agency sends a monthly report to IBM on the exact number of hours used so IBM can monitor and plan resources.

Costs and financing

Overall, 60 per cent of the childcare initiatives is funded by the Global WorkLife Balance Fund and 40 per cent by IBM Hungary. Discount rates differ for each service. For the international summer camp in Slovakia, IBM parents' discount price for the ten camp days is 75 euro (instead of 195 euro); the rest is financed by the Global WorkLife Fund and IBM Hungary. For the daycare summer camp, employees pay 18–20,000 HUF (70–75 euro), depending on the number of weeks and children at the camp.

For the back-up care service, IBM's agreement with Dédy-sitter & Baby-sitter is to provide the service for 1,000 HUF an hour (4 euro). Employees pay 70 per cent of the price, and IBM, through the support of the Global WorkLife Fund, pays the remaining 30 per cent.

The staff

IBM outsources all its childcare programmes to local providers. The summer camps offered by IBM in Hungary are provided by an organization called NIHOA Ltd, a rapidly developing company with the philosophy of holistic approaches. The enterprise organizes events and programmes for families and especially for children, and it provides recreational and natural healing services. All NIHOA activities are based on the belief that children grow best when they are intrinsically involved in their own learning.

Dédy-sitter & Baby-sitter is an agency offering back-up child and elder care services in Hungary, including care for healthy and mildly ill individuals, and those with special needs. Services include overnight or extended hours care for employees to meet business purposes. Childcare providers at the agency have completed a certified babysitter training course, or are qualified teachers. In addition to offering in-home care, Dédy-sitter will build a database of at least 21 childcare centres and childminders (seven per location) that offer back-up care for those employees who prefer out-of-home care.

Management perspective

IBM Hungary's management is aware of the fact that employees with children often have a hard time finding care when they are travelling for business or when regular caregivers are ill or otherwise unavailable. Employees may be forced to miss work in some of these situations. Many employees are not aware of the services available in the community, and researching these options may take a significant amount of their time. The Initiative of the Global WorkLife Fund helps with these problems and was welcomed by the IBM Hungary management team.

Employee perspective

Employees who have used the childcare services are generally quite pleased with the quality, as witnessed by the two examples below. As one mother of two children aged 10 and 14 said:

> Last year my children participated at the NIHOA camp at the Petneházy Country Club. The children really liked the programme. ... For me this was a great help, as I was sure that the children were in the right place, and the price/quality ratio was good. It was not cheap, but the children were getting a high-end programme for this price. I really hope that this initiative will continue because it is extremely difficult to organize a quality programme at an affordable price for the ten weeks of summer holiday.

A father of two children, aged 2 and 4, explained:

> While my wife was on childcare allowance and took care of my daughter we did not really have childcare problems. But after her return to work, life became more complicated. We have a babysitter who has been caring for our children for a long time but on one occasion we were in real trouble. I had read about the new back-up care service on the IBM Intranet page. I contacted the HR department and asked about the service. What I really liked was that the babysitter company was ready to respond to urgent needs, as I telephoned in the evening and the babysitter was there in the morning on time. We were a bit afraid about how the children would respond and behave, but actually there was no problem. The price was favourable, not more expensive than the usual price. I am really happy about the fact that IBM provides such services. It gives a feeling of security for the employees that IBM has selected the babysitter company and has surely made a responsible choice.

Lessons learned

Careful research, assessment and planning were key for designing successful programmes that respond to workers' needs. Providing back-up care for employees is a very rare and innovative practice in Hungary. Many business people in Hungary would think that an employer has nothing to do with childcare provision. At IBM, on the contrary, investing in the work–life balance of employees is a strategic issue and not an act of charity. The goals of work–life balance initiatives are to reduce absenteeism, to increase productivity and to help IBM attract, motivate and retain employees.[24]

Gedeon Richter Plc

Type of business. Pharmaceuticals.

Workplace. Two production sites in Hungary: one in Budapest, the other in Dorog.

Workers. Nearly 5,000, of whom about half are women. More than 800 are in the Research and Development team. Others are production workers, sales representatives, administrative workers, and financial and managerial staff.

Working hours. Depend on type of job and range from continuous shifts to one, two and three shifts, and even flexible working hours for administrative staff.

Childcare solution. Two company kindergartens, summer camp.

Partners. Government, trade union.

Gedeon Richter Plc is a Hungarian-controlled Central-Eastern European multinational pharmaceutical company and the largest pharmaceutical factory in Hungary.[25] Its market network covers nearly 100 countries in five continents. The company is present in 30 countries, with production sites in Hungary, India, Poland, Romania and the Russian Federation, 30 representative offices and 14 commercial subsidiaries and wholesale joint ventures.

Gedeon Richter Plc has been a socially sensitive and responsible firm from its very beginning, originating from the philosophy and personal values of the founder, Gedeon Richter. Its first childcare institution was set up in Budapest in

---

[24] http://www.worldforumfoundation.org/wf/global_leaders/ibm_fund.php [11 June 2009].

[25] Background information has been taken from the company's web site, http://www.richter.hu/en/Pages/our_company.aspx [11 June 2009].

1952 because production workers had difficulties placing their children in locally managed childcare institutions. The socialist regime of this "baby boom" era put strong political pressure on nationalized state-owned companies to provide childcare facilities for their employees. The first facility included both a nursery for children under 3 and a kindergarten. Later, in the 1980s, as fertility rates declined, the nursery was closed but the kindergarten in Budapest remained. A second kindergarten opened in Dorog in 1976 when a new production site was built there.

Today the company owns two kindergartens, two sports grounds, a swimming pool with fitness facilities and a community house. Some of its social services include family sports events for employees every second year and support to employee initiatives for social events.

Although the focus of this case study is on the company kindergartens, it should be noted that Gedeon Richter Plc provides two other benefits for parents: a summer camp and a voucher subsidy at the start of the school year.

- **Summer camp:** The summer camp for children aged 6–12 years old is organized every year in a two-week structure, where the first week is a daycare summer camp in the company's community house and the second is held in the countryside. In 2007, 160 children attended the summer camp. It is sponsored by the company and a trade union-related foundation, which makes it possible to offer the camp at a below-market price to employees.

- **School bonus:** To cover expenses at the beginning of the school year, Hungarian taxation law allows companies to provide a tax-free financial allowance for parents with children aged 6–18. Many companies have adopted such practices, either as part of the compensation package and the cafeteria benefit system, or as a social support. Gedeon Richter Plc offers 20,700 HUF per year per child (80 euro) to employees with school-age children.

Company kindergartens

The two company kindergartens are located in Budapest and Dorog near the production sites. The kindergarten is approximately a 5–10-minute walk from the company headquarters in Budapest. The kindergarten in Dorog is about 1.5 kilometres from the production site.

The kindergartens are open from Monday to Friday all year. The summer break is synchronized with production stops to avoid childcare problems for workers in the summer. Daily opening hours follow the schedule of shift workers and are from 6.00 a.m. to 5.30 p.m. Meals are provided three times a day.

The kindergartens have different pedagogical programmes. In Budapest, the focus is on providing education on a healthy lifestyle; in Dorog, the aim is to nurture traditional Hungarian popular practices. The kindergarten offers gymnastic activities, swimming lessons, excursions, German lessons, horse riding, Ayres therapy and cultural activities. In Budapest, there are four groups organized by age; in Dorog, three groups have children of mixed ages. In 2007, 97 children attended the kindergarten in Budapest and 60 in Dorog.

The Budapest facility is a large two-storey building with a garden and playground. The company's swimming pool and fitness centre are on the same street, so children can walk there to take swimming lessons. The building was built in 1973 and reconstructed in 1981, with smaller repairs done on a yearly basis. The rooms are nicely furnished; toys are regularly bought for the children. Each group has a separate bathroom, including toilets, basins and a shower. There is also a kitchen available. The Dorog kindergarten has similar features.

Eligibility and use

Children of all Richter employees are eligible for the kindergarten, as are grandchildren of Richter pensioners. Nobody else is accepted, even though enrolment is below capacity.

At present the kindergarten is open to children aged 3–6 years old. As there is an apparent demand to accept children from the age of 2, the company accepts applications under the age of 3 if the child is sufficiently mature for admission.

In Budapest the capacity is 120 places, but just 97 children were enrolled in 2007, for a utilization rate of 80 per cent. The utilization rate in Dorog is also 80 per cent.

Parents from the many different occupations at Richter use the crèche. However, employees living in the countryside and commuting to Budapest would rather use local kindergartens despite the fact that monthly fees are approximately 30 per cent higher.

Costs and financing

Gedeon Richter Plc applies for the state funding available for kindergartens in Hungary. As a private company, it is entitled to 30 per cent of the state subsidy paid according to the number of children. The state subsidy represents approximately 5 per cent of the kindergartens' yearly costs. The remaining 95 per cent is financed by the company. Overall costs are increasing yearly, partly because national regulations on kindergarten equipment and standards are becoming more demanding.

Employees using the kindergarten pay a daily fee of 314 HUF for the meals, or about 6,500 HUF per month (25 euro), which is very cheap – equivalent to 10 per cent of the national minimum wage. For grandchildren of Richter pensioners the price is 30 per cent higher.

The staff

The staff consists of experienced educators and other support personnel. Educators have a higher-education diploma in Hungary. Turnover is very low and most of the staff have worked at the kindergarten for more than 15 years. They are officially employed by Humanco Ltd, an independent company to which the kindergarten staff were outsourced by Richter in 1998, together with other social service-related job holders. Humanco Ltd finances 100 per cent of their salaries and social security coverage, which is equivalent to the industry average.

The head of the kindergarten has worked there for 25 years. She is satisfied with the functioning of the organization and feels that outsourcing the personnel did not impact the level and quality of the service provided. Every year management and kindergarten staff discuss the developmental areas and the key issues of financing. On a yearly basis, the heads of the kindergartens are required to prepare a report on their activities and operations.

Management perspective

Gedeon Richter Plc has long offered kindergarten facilities to employees even as other companies closed such facilities when political pressure for them waned in the 1990s. They did so for three reasons. First, the founder, Gedeon Richter, was a socially committed person, and his spirit is considered important in the present company culture. Second, the enlightened self-interest of the company is to support the work performance of employees by providing high-quality childcare for employees during their working hours. Third, the company was able to outsource the maintenance of the kindergarten together with other social services in 1998, to lower the costs for financing the childcare services, while keeping control over the quality of services provided.

Gedeon Richter Plc is devoted to maintaining its childcare institutions. Nevertheless, the largest challenge is to maintain the financial sustainability of the two kindergartens. Despite the difficulties, each year there are investments made by the company.

Every year the company organizes a satisfaction survey among parents. Generally parents ask for new equipment and toys to be purchased. Employees can also discuss their concerns and ideas on the company's Intranet forum page.

Gedeon Richter Plc considers providing kindergarten services to employees a good means to support performance during working hours as employees do not need to be disturbed by childcare problems. It also sees it as a benefit for attracting and retaining employees.

Employee perspective

Employees who have used the kindergartens are generally quite pleased with the service. In the words of one mother:

> My daughter has been attending the kindergarten since last year. The educators are very friendly, the activities are good. Related to the main philosophy, "education for a healthy lifestyle", the kindergarten organizes a lot of excursions to the open air, for example to farms. In the playground, there are many types of equipment that help develop their physical capacities. Another positive factor is its proximity to the company.

Another mother said of the kindergarten:

> It is very good that the parents know each other from work ... it gives a sense of security. Also at the primary school, they are always very happy to have the children from the Richter kindergarten because they are considered well prepared for school.

Lessons learned

The case of Gedeon Richter Plc is a good example of a company which, driven by enlightened self-interest, invests in maintaining and developing the company's childcare institutions even at a time when most Hungarian firms shed such facilities. Outsourcing the personnel at the end of the 1990s provided a more economical form of financing, but did not decrease the level of services. Higher performance, employee retention and attracting jobseekers to the company are the most important benefits Gedeon Richter Plc gains from its childcare provision.

Hungarian Academy of Sciences

Type of business. Academic.

Workplace. Central administrative building plus 48 research institutes.

Workers. The number of employees in research institutes amounted to 4,300 in 2007, of which most were highly qualified researchers, 30 per cent were under 35 years old,[1] and about 25 per cent were women.

Working hours. Full-time researchers work two days a week at the research institute and three days distance working; full-time administrative staff work 8.00 a.m. to 4.30 p.m.

Childcare solution. Nursery and kindergarten taking children from 18 months to 7 years.

Partners. National Methodological Centre for Nurseries (a state organization).

[1] See http://www.mta.hu/index.php?id=634&no_cache=1&backPid=390&tt_news=8419&cHash=6defa8343d [11 June 2009].

The Hungarian Academy of Sciences (HAS) was founded in 1825. Today the Academy is a scholarly public body whose main task is the study of science, the publicizing of scientific achievements, and the aid and promotion of research. The Academy maintains 48 research institutes and other institutions (libraries, archives, information systems and so on) assisting their work, and extends aid to university research centres. The Academy is financed by the state budget, income derived from its assets, and by foundations and donations.[26] The majority of employees are highly qualified researchers in all areas of human and natural sciences. Most of them are employed on a full-time basis.

The Hungarian Academy of Sciences has run a nursery daycare institution in a rented building near its central building in Budapest since the 1950s. In the mid-1970s, when the children of Hungarian baby boomers from the 1950s started to reach kindergarten age, the idea of setting up a kindergarten was raised. Six large institutions affiliated to the Academy decided to raise funds, buy a building plot and build a new kindergarten. The kindergarten opened in 1980 under the control of the investing institutions until 1986, when the central administrative body of the Academy took responsibility for financing the kindergarten.

In 1995, the nursery was merged with the kindergarten to deal with declining enrolment numbers and to save costs. In the new set-up, the kindergarten groups were reduced from four to three and one nursery group was added.

---

[26] http://www.mta.hu/index.php?id=687 [11 June 2009].

The nursery and kindergarten

With the merging of the nursery and the kindergarten, quite an innovative pedagogical approach was adopted: the kindergarten educators were reorganized in such a way as to lead the same group of children throughout their entire preschool education. The new approach has proved to be successful, leading to a state award for the head of the kindergarten.

The pedagogical programme focuses on maintaining traditional Hungarian popular practices. From the outset, great emphasis has been put on providing a high-level educational programme corresponding to the profile of the mother institution. Educators have above-average qualifications, with highly valuable specializations such as dance therapy, zoo-pedagogy and art pedagogy, among others. The kindergarten offers special gymnastic activities, swimming lessons, excursions, dance therapy, logo pedagogy classes and cultural activities, like museum visits and invited music and theatre performances, over and above the standard curriculum.

The kindergarten is open from Monday to Friday from 7.00 a.m. to 5.30 p.m., with a summer break from around the beginning of July to mid-August. Meals are provided three times a day. Full capacity is 90 places: 15 places in the nursery and 75 places in the kindergarten. At present the institution is run at full capacity.

The kindergarten is located in one of the elite, residential parts of Budapest. It is not particularly near either the central administrative building of the Academy or the research institutions, but not too far away either. A great strength of the facility is the big garden with a well-equipped playground and the quality of the air.

The facility consists of a large two-storey building with a separate area for gymnastics. The rooms are nicely furnished; toys are regularly bought for the children. Each group has a separate bathroom, including toilets, basins and a shower. There is also a kitchen available.

Eligibility and use

The nursery accepts children from 18 months to 3 years, the kindergarten from 3–7 years. The children of all Academy employees are eligible for the nursery and kindergarten. Parents pay only for meals – approximately 13,000 HUF per month (50 euro), equivalent to about 10 per cent of net earnings on average. Grandchildren of academicians or Academy pensioners are accepted at a special price of 50 per cent of the cost. Non-academy-affiliated children are accepted for the remaining places on a market-based price. At present there is a waiting list for nursery places, with ten non-Academy applications rejected in 2007.

Currently, 50 per cent are children of Academy employees, 25 per cent of the children are the grandchildren of Academy-affiliated people and 25 per cent are non-Academy, private enrolments.

Finance and management

The yearly budget of the Academy Kindergarten and Nursery comes from three sources:

- payments from the Hungarian Academy of Sciences' central budget;
- payments of non-Academy parents who are obliged to pay a market-based cost price (350,000 HUF per year (1300 euro) in 2007);[27] and
- fees paid for the meals by all the parents.

Approximately 80 per cent of the budget comes from the Academy central budget.[28] The central administration of the Academy conducts an annual internal audit. In addition, every two years a thorough financial investigation is carried out.

Official inspection of the kindergarten is carried out by the Ministry of Education, while the National Methodological Centre for Nurseries inspects the operation of the nursery.

The staff

The staff of 20 employees includes eight educators, six nurses, four cleaning personnel, an accountant and the head of the institution. According to the head of the kindergarten, from the staff's perspective, the most important problem is the low salaries. Until 2000, their salaries were somewhat higher than of those working at institutions financed by the municipalities, but now the salaries have lost a great deal of their value.

---

[27] The parents of children whose grandparents were affiliated with HAS have to pay 50 per cent of the yearly cost price (175,000 HUF (650 euro) in 2007).

[28] http://ovoda.office.mta.hu/uvegzseb.html [11 June 2009].

Nevertheless, the staff seem to appreciate the atmosphere and pedagogical approach as described by one of the educators, who has worked at the kindergarten for 19 years:

> Management is in favour of our self-development, this is why practically all of the educators have some kind of specialization, above-average qualification. ... Continuous learning also helps us to keep good relations with parents, as the generations have changed extremely in terms of expectations. ... Overall, I think that the technical equipments available at the institution are much higher than at an average local kindergarten. The head of the kindergarten has always put an extra effort to maintain standards, and create an environment that matches the high standards of the Academy both physically and intellectually.

Management perspective

The most important issue for the administration is maintaining the financial sustainability of the nursery and kindergarten. Still management believes that providing childcare for the research community is important and also a means to support the younger generation of researchers.

Employee perspective

Parents expressed satisfaction with the services. As one mother said:

> This is the second year that my son has been attending the kindergarten. I visited some local institutions, too, and then I decided to look here. I talked with the head of the kindergarten, and decided that this can be a good choice for us. ... I am completely satisfied with the institution from a professional point of view. The only thing I would be happy to have is more flexibility regarding opening hours. Being a researcher, many times there are conferences or meetings that start in the afternoon, and it can be difficult sometimes to get here by 5 o'clock. It would be ideal if – even for extra cost – a babysitter service could be provided after regular closing hours. It would be much simpler for everybody.

And according to another mother:

> Before deciding on this kindergarten I visited another local kindergarten, but I found the head of the kindergarten too rigid there, and the garden was very

small. Afterwards I came here with my older daughter to visit the nursery. I liked the educators, the environment and the garden. So I decided to apply here despite the 50 per cent cost price we had to pay as not direct employees of the Academy. In the case of our younger daughter, the decision was automatic. Overall the kindergarten is very friendly, its pedagogy is really child centred.

Lessons learned

The Academy Kindergarten and Nursery is an interesting initiative from the Communist era as six independent research institutions cooperated to collectively finance the creation of a joint kindergarten. The institution has gone through several reorganizations, including the merger with the nursery, becoming a part of the central budget of the Academy, and the financial regrouping of all welfare institutions recently. From a professional point of view the institution has maintained its high level of pedagogical services, including integrating nursery and kindergarten education, and thus provides an attractive childcare solution not only for Academy employees, but also for clients paying the market price for the services. Charging outsiders for use of surplus capacity has helped the financial sustainability of the facility.

Hungarian Post Office Ltd

Type of business. Postal services.

Workplace. State-owned company with 35,600 employees, of whom two-thirds are women; 57 per cent are over 40 years old.

Workers. Customer service personnel in post offices, postmen/post women, administrative and managerial staff.

Working hours. 85 per cent of staff work full time, 15 per cent are part time.

Childcare solution. Summer camp for children.

Partners. Hotel for facility; primary school for staff; Hungarian National Recreation Foundation.

The Hungarian Post Office Ltd (Hungarian Post hereafter) is the largest employer in Hungary. Established as a public institution in 1867, Hungarian Post has gone through several reorganizations during its history, but is still 100 per cent state owned. With the upcoming liberalization of postal services in the European Union in 2011, Hungarian Post is in the process of modernizing products, organizational structure and culture. As part of the modernization process, the company's welfare services have been reorganized, and in 2004 were centralized into a national office. The Welfare Services Office is responsible for the maintenance and operation of Hungarian Post's summer resorts, workers' hostels, sports facilities, catering services and company apartments.

Besides offering summer camps for children, Hungarian Post invests in organizing and subsidizing family holidays, as well as paying a subsidy for parents with school-age children at the start of the school year. It is important to note that Hungarian Post has a well-developed equal opportunities policy, which includes initiatives for women and for employees with more than three children.

The summer camp

The summer camp initiative at Hungarian Post has existed for more than 20 years, although the company's new market-driven business strategy has affected how summer camps are organized for children. Previously the summer camp took place in one of the summer resorts of the company at Lake Balaton in Siófok. The infrastructure, however, became outdated and the costs of renovation would have been extremely high. So in 2006, management decided to sell the former summer resort and find a new place for the summer camp on a market basis which would provide a much higher-quality environment and service for the children. Providing high-quality services (accommodation, food, sports facilities) for the children was a major objective in the implementation of the new initiative.

Hungarian Post issued a call for applications in several national and local newspapers for hotels located on the banks of Lake Balaton which would volunteer to provide the accommodation, catering and sports facilities for children from 1 July to 20 August. Approximately ten hotels applied. The representatives of the Central Workers Council and those of management investigated all the offers and chose the Vadkacsa Panzió[29] in Balatonlelle as the new premises for the summer camp. The hotel is located on the banks of the lake, with a two-storey building including rooms with bathrooms for two to three persons, a balcony for each room, a garden, playground, tennis court, table tennis and a media room.

---

[29] http://www.vandvtravels.hu/szalloda/szallodah.htm [11 June 2009].

The camp is organized in ten-day sessions. The programme is planned ahead for each day, but the activities are offered mostly on an optional basis for the children. Activities include swimming, sports activities (tennis, football, table tennis, chess, basketball, volleyball, handball, athletics), disco, group games, beauty contest, "Who knows what?" competition, visits to museums, movies, boat-excursion, drawing, painting and other artistic activities.

Eligibility and use

In 2007, five ten-day camps were held. Each camp offers 60 places, allowing for 300 children in total. For the 300 places, there were more than 700 applications, which meant that Hungarian Post needed to implement a selection policy. The criteria were as follows: children who had received less holiday subsidy previously had priority; for those with equal amounts of previous subsidy, children whose parents had longer years of company service had priority. From an income point of view, 80 per cent of the children participating in the camp had parents who fell into the lowest income category.

As a response to the high application rate among employees, Hungarian Post decided to add one more camp session in the second half of June, thus increasing the available places from 300 to 360 in 2008.

A new regulation was introduced in 2006 to reduce the maximum age of eligible children from 14 to 12 years of age. Thus eligible children must be between 7 and 12 years old. Some parents were dissatisfied with the new regulation but the rationale was to avoid behavioural problems within the group related to the relatively large age gap.

Finance and management

Traditionally, parents had to pay for the children's summer camp at a relatively low discounted price (5,000 HUF – 20 euro in 2006). Since 2007, as part of the new initiative, Hungarian Post has introduced the employee-friendly measure of providing the summer camp completely free, including the costs of transporting children from all over the country to the camp site.

The costs of the summer camp per child for ten days amounted to 65,000 HUF (250 euro) in 2007. The total cost for Hungarian Post reached approximately 20 million HUF (75,000 euro). The method chosen to finance the costs of the summer camp is innovative. Hungarian Post buys recreation vouchers from the Hungarian National Recreation Foundation which can be offered to the children of employees as a benefit on a tax-free basis.[30]

The staff

Hungarian Post has had a long-term partnership with a primary school in Budapest (ETALONSPORT Általános és Sportiskola Pestszentlőrinc),[31] from which the educators have been recruited and selected. Thus educators are professional teachers who work as camp educators during the summer. For each camp session, six educators assist and care for the children, for a ratio of one educator to ten children.

Selection criteria for educators working in the camp consist of being dynamic and extroverted with good communication and problem-solving skills. In addition, being sportive and able to facilitate group activities is a must.

Management perspective

Providing recreation services for employees and their children is not new at Hungarian Post. Nevertheless, seeking alternative ways to provide the same services, if possible at higher quality, is a new aspect of Hungarian Post's welfare strategy. It is important to stress that maintaining the existing services is a strategic decision by Hungarian Post's management. There has been an agreement to reinvest the revenue from the sales of summer resorts into the renovation of existing ones or into other holiday opportunities for staff. Offering a free summer camp opportunity to staff is also a tool to increase employee satisfaction among relatively low-income earners. Since a large proportion of employees are women with relatively low incomes, support for childcare during the summer is of great help.

---

[30] The Hungarian National Recreation Foundation, founded in 1992 by the government and six trade-union federations, supports the recreation opportunities of disadvantaged groups. Employers can offer recreation vouchers to employees on a tax-free basis up to the level of the minimum wage. Since 2005, Hungarian Post has been awarded each year for being among the top ten employers buying the largest amount of recreation vouchers.

[31] http://www.c3.hu/~benedek [11 June 2009].

Employee perspective

According to the satisfaction questionnaires sent out to parents in 2007, the initiative to search for a new and better equipped site for the children's summer camp was well received by employees. Satisfaction rates equalled 4.8 on a five-point scale, up from the previous year. One mother said:

> In 2007, my daughter who is 11 years old volunteered to participate in the summer camp. This was the first time my daughter attended a summer camp. Fortunately she was very happy, and not at all disappointed, about her decision. Every day when I called her she was so enthusiastic, always busy with some kind of activity. I was completely calm. The camp was completely free for us, including the transportation. It is really amazing that an employer provides such welfare services for their employees nowadays.

Another mother of two sons, aged 10 and 11, said:

> This was a rare opportunity and I was really in favour of the camp. They provided full service and transportation. The boys were very enthusiastic. This camp was really a present for me. I have to admit that I am not satisfied with my wages, but the camp is a great help. Otherwise the children would have gone to some daycare camp for an entrance fee which would have been difficult to finance. I was very satisfied with camp. Fortunately, my sons were given access this year, too.

Lessons learned

Many state-owned or privatized companies in Hungary have inherited summer resorts, kindergartens and other facilities from the socialist era. The maintenance and operation of these buildings is a huge cost for these organizations. A major dilemma companies have faced is whether to sell or maintain the facilities. The most typical business decision has been to sell the facilities and discontinue those welfare activities. Hungarian Post is a good example of a different approach. The company decided to keep the welfare services while searching for more economical ways to finance them without decreasing (and even increasing) the level of the service. The children's summer camp seems to be highly appreciated because of its quality and its responsiveness to workers' needs to find summer care for their children. Moreover, the programme reaches many lower-paid workers, providing them access to what would otherwise be expensive holiday activity programmes and increasing their job satisfaction, as noted by both workers and management.

Magyar Telekom Plc

Type of business. Telecommunications.

Workplace. 6,500 employees, of whom 65 per cent are men and 35 per cent are women.

Workers. Mostly technical professions, operations, sales, call centres, administrative and managerial jobs.

Working hours. 85 per cent of staff work on a full-time basis, 15 per cent in atypical work forms (teleworking, part-time jobs and flexible working hours).

Childcare solution. Kindergarten and nursery services for preschool children aged 2–7, summer camp for school-age children aged 7–18.

Partners. Childcare provider organizations (summer camps and kindergartens), Dimenzió Insurance and Self-Supporting Association.

Magyar Telekom Plc is a leading info-communication service provider in Central Europe. The Magyar Telekom Group members offer the full range of telecommunications for residential, SME and large corporate customers.[32] The majority shareholder is Deutsche Telekom. Magyar Telekom is renowned for its high social and environmental performance and has won several awards as a result of its corporate social responsibility (CSR) practices, including first prize in the large company category of the Inclusive Workplace Award in 2006; first place in the Accountability Rating Hungary in 2006 and 2007 and the Diversity Award among member companies of the Deutsche Telekom Group in 2007. Sponsorship, donations, sustainability and diversity issues form important pillars of the company's CSR practices.

As part of its diversity policy, Magyar Telekom has set up several initiatives to support the employment of women:

- A cross-company survey investigated how atypical work forms could be used to a greater extent. Information was gathered on jobs in which it would be possible to introduce atypical work practices in order to increase the number of women and other vulnerable group members.

- A conference and HR roundtable discussion was organized on the topic of life after maternity leave. This initiative aimed at changing attitudes of upper management toward women with small children.

---

[32] http://www.telekom.hu/about_magyar_telekom/company_history [11 June 2009].

- A series of lectures and consultations to inform employees about the most recent research results on balancing work and family life and provide opportunities for professional consultations about typical problems.

- As part of the reorientation programme for women on maternity leave, women receive company news via the email system, including invitations to various company events. After maternity leave, a one-day training programme is offered to women. Flexible working hours are available upon request.

Magyar Telekom was one of the first companies in Hungary to apply the Global Reporting Initiative (GRI) criteria in its sustainability reporting system. As one of the standard questions of the indicator is related to how the company supports the work–life balance of employees with children, using the GRI indicators was a key factor in starting to focus on employees with children. Providing a subsidy at the start of the school year for employees with school-age children, and offering a children's camp for school-age children in the countryside[33] as part of the Telekom's recreation services, were the only supports provided above the legal minimum until 2007.

Childcare services

The company's first new childcare initiative targeted the provision of temporary solutions for parents during summer closures of regular kindergartens and childcare centres. It was visible at the workplace that, during these periods, many employees were accompanied by their children during working hours. Initially, in spring 2007, Magyar Telekom planned to contract a kindergarten to provide summer care for children. However, a needs assessment survey showed that relatively few people responded positively to this option as they had already searched for other solutions. Instead, employees signalled that they would prefer summer activities for their school-age children. This gave rise to the idea of organizing camp opportunities for school-age children.

Summer camps

As the time was too short to organize a camp only for Telekom children, the company looked for good-quality existing camps on the market. As a company,

---

[33] The recreation site is in Gyöngyöstarján, a small village in the hilly area of the Matra. Each year, two one-week sessions of children's camp were organized for a total of 80 participants.

Telekom could negotiate discount prices for these camps. It signed general contracts with provider organizations on the level of discount and then advertised internally the list of camps available for employees.

There was a deliberate decision to select camps that varied in terms of length, location and content. In 2007, 15 camps were chosen, including summer day camps, one- or two-week summer camps in Budapest and in the countryside, and camps with thematic focuses (such as language, sports). The average discount was 10–15 per cent. Approximately 35–40 children participated in four or five of the listed camps during the summer of 2007. In this scheme, Magyar Telekom was not in any legal relationship with the employees. Employees were simply offered camp services for children at discount prices as a result of the contracts signed by Magyar Telekom and the camp providers. Parents decided on the camp and made their payments directly. In 2008, Magyar Telekom planned to continue a similar scheme to offer summer camp opportunities for employees, but reduced the list of camps to seven or eight and further developed the subsidy system (see the section *Costs and finance* below).

Childcare for preschool-age children: Kindergartens and nurseries

From the needs assessment, it became clear that employees were not really interested in a temporary kindergarten during summer holidays, but would be very much in favour of a permanent company facility.

Typically, the two options available for companies in the field of childcare are to either maintain their own facility, as was typical in the socialist period of the company, or to lease places in external kindergartens. Magyar Telekom decided to use a combination of these two solutions, given the geographical dispersion of its employees. The company conducted a second needs assessment in the spring of 2008 to gain information on how much employees would be ready to pay for this service. Approximately 300 employees responded positively to the possibility of having company kindergarten services through the Dimenzió Insurance and Self-Supporting Association.[34] (See Option 2 in the section *Costs and finance* below.)

Telekom started to search for childcare providers near the largest Telekom locations. To date, it has signed agreements with four private kindergartens to reserve places for Telekom children, and has bought a kindergarten in Budapest.

---

[34] Dimenzió Insurance and Self-Supporting Association is a member organization of the Dimenzió Insurance Group, a non-profit organization open to both individuals and employers. It provides different life, health and pension insurance schemes, as well as company-tailored cafeteria systems, of which Magyar Telekom represents a good example.

At present 90 places are ensured for Telekom employees in these five institutions, of which 40 are in the newly bought kindergarten. In five large cities of Hungary, additional partnerships will be sought if at least five applications are handed in (employees had to officially apply for the childcare service by 25 April 2008). The age group of children accepted in private kindergartens is more flexible than in those in local municipalities and, in most, children are accepted from 2 years old. For 25 of the places, children less than 2 years old can also be enrolled. Thus the childcare solution offered by Magyar Telekom covers both traditional nursery and kindergarten services.

Costs and finance

In 2008 a new subsidy system was developed by Magyar Telekom for both the summer camps and the kindergarten services:

- **Option 1:** For summer camp, all employees are entitled to the 10–15 per cent discount.

- **Option 2:** In addition to Option 1, Magyar Telekom offers a family package at the Dimenzió Insurance and Self-Supporting Association, which includes the summer camps and kindergarten services in the Portfolio of benefits. Sixty per cent of Telekom employees are members of this Association, to which they pay 1 per cent of their monthly salary. Telekom also contributes 2.2 per cent of the employee's salary. As a result, the employee who is a member only has to pay one-third of the service price for the camp or the kindergarten, while the Dimenzió Insurance and Self-Supporting Association pays for the remaining two-thirds. This system is part of the company's cafeteria benefit system.

- **Option 3:** Those who are not members of the Dimenzió Insurance and Self-Supporting Association can receive subsidies for the camp or kinder-garten services through the Matching Fund programme. This is a programme to stimulate individual charity donations by employees. If an employee donates to any foundation or NGO and brings a certificate, Magyar Telekom will contribute to the same organization an equal or double amount of money depending on the amount. If the donation is to a camp or a kindergarten operated by a foundation or NGO, the company will contribute double the amount. Thus the company contribution will be two-thirds as in the case of the family package of the Dimenzió Insurance and Self-Supporting Association, as described in Option 2.

Management perspective

Magyar Telekom strives to have the most professional human resource management system in Hungary.[35] In addition, the company aims to become a best-practice case in diversity management on an international level. According to its human resource vision, "Committed professionals with independent initiatives are the key factor for the Magyar Telekom Group's business success." Magyar Telekom considers employees as strategic resources and focuses on employee satisfaction as a strategic issue. Thus investing in childcare provision for employees is a business-driven practice at Magyar Telekom.

Lessons learned

Magyar Telekom represents a case where corporate social responsibility practice and diversity management initiatives raised awareness of the need for new welfare provisions for employees. Childcare solutions for employees are treated as part of the total compensation and benefit system, and needs assessment has played a key role in shaping and re-orienting the company's strategies for childcare support. While part of the benefits system, the company also promotes individual responsibility for these services, designing innovative ways for combining individual and company contributions. Employees must contribute financially through the Self-Supporting Association and via individual payments. Magyar Telekom represents an interesting example of how human resource management, corporate social responsibility and diversity management practice can be implemented in an integrated manner.

---

[35] Magyar Telekom, Sustainability Report 2006. http://www.telekom.hu/static/sw/download/sustainability_report_2006.pdf [11 June 2009].

India

10

N. Hamsa[1]

National overview

Childcare facilities for working parents are still relatively scarce in India. The Government, through its Integrated Child Development Service, has made a major effort to provide half-day preschool education for disadvantaged children aged 3–6 and this programme is estimated to reach about 33 million children, perhaps about 30 per cent of the age group. For younger children, there are few publicly supported facilities. In some sectors, legislation has long existed requiring employers of a certain number of women to provide a crèche, but implementation

[1] N. Hamsa has a doctorate in political sociology, with a long experience of working for the Federation of Indian Chambers of Commerce and Industry and the Council of Indian Employers. She is currently the Executive Director of WomenPowerConnect, a women's network organization, with membership across India. She would like to thank Parikrama Gupta, Kavya Boppanna and H. Ratna for their help in desk and field research. She would also like to express her appreciation to B.C. Prabhakar, President of the Employers' Federation of Karnataka, and his team, for their inputs and help in arranging the meetings in the selected companies. She would like to thank the Indian National Trade Union Congress (INTUC) for facilitating interaction with trade union representatives. She gratefully acknowledges the time and cooperation given by the organizations studied.

has been weak. Few figures are available on the extent of childcare provision, whether by employers, NGOs or commercial organizations. Nevertheless, it is clear that with the increase in nuclear families and the increasing employment of women, more facilities are required. These are especially needed by poor parents working in the unorganized sector, who constitute the majority of workers.

Work and childcare

Indian women are less likely to be employed than those in many other countries, although the economy has witnessed an increase in the proportion who are working for pay.[2] The work participation rate for women was 25.6 per cent in 2001, up from 22.3 per cent in 1991. It is higher in the rural areas, 30.8 per cent, while in the urban areas it was 11.9 per cent.

A household survey in 2006 in Delhi suggests that the key factors that may push up women's workforce participation rates are higher education, reduction in time spent on housework (domestic technology, water and electricity, childcare arrangements) and safety in public spaces (transport, lighting). Working and non-working women alike felt that children are neglected when women work, suggesting the absence of acceptable alternatives for childcare.[3] The lack of crèche facilities hinders the economic participation of women and affects their employment choices since, in the absence of alternatives, women are usually expected to give up their other pursuits to rear children.

Until recently, the custom of the joint family was still strong, thus ensuring that children with two working parents were tended by a family member. However, this is no longer the case. The idea of the nuclear family has become increasingly common, with more and more couples opting to live on their own. Those in the higher-income brackets can afford to hire full-time maids or nannies, or enrol their children in private childcare facilities. But those from lower socio-economic communities are forced to find other means, such as removing an older child from school to look after the younger children. For the majority of working women who are in the unorganized sector (about 94 per cent), their children are often themselves absorbed into the informal economy due to lack of education or are deployed as child helpers so that adults earn more (for example, as home-based workers, vendors or self-employed).

---

[2] India, Ministry of Labour and Employment, 2008.
[3] Sudarshan and Bhattacharya, 2008, p. 23.

Labour legislation

The many informal workers who make up 92 per cent of India's total workforce do not benefit from the protection of labour legislation. And even for the minority in the organized sector, legislative provisions exist mostly on paper and not in practice. For example, the Factories Act (1948) covers working conditions, health and safety, basic amenities such as toilets, working hours and crèches, but does not apply to workplaces with fewer than ten workers using power-driven machinery or to those with less than 20 workers without power. The Contract Labour Act (1971) has made it easier for employers to deny benefits to workers since subcontracting production into small units allows employers to evade existing laws.

Two types of labour legislation relate to childcare. The first is the Maternity Benefits Act (1961), which provides 12 weeks of maternity leave, paid by the employer at the average daily wage, and entitles women to two breastfeeding breaks per day after leave until her child is 15 months old. However, given that few women work in factories, mines, plantations, performance establishments and shops with more than ten employees and that most are in informal employment, few women would benefit from this legislation.

The second type of legislation is labour acts in specific sectors which mandate the provision of childcare facilities depending on the number of women employed and the size of the plantations/factories. Specific acts that provide for crèches are listed in box 10.1.

Although crèches for working women are mandated by law in these different sectors, no figures are available on the implementation of this legislation. It would seem that, in practice, very few crèches exist. A recent report notes that employers either refrain from employing women if it is mandatory for them to provide daycare for their children or they avoid the obligation by failing to show the employment of women in their official records.[4] The report also notes underutilization of the existing crèches because fathers cannot use them. The childcare needs of a father are not recognized.

It is recognized that crèche facilities need to expand and that some expansion could occur if the obligatory legal stipulation for provision of crèches at the place or site of work were strictly enforced. A recent government report notes that, "learning from the past experiences, it is amply clear that placing the entire liability on employers is a nonstarter and thus, under the Eleventh Five Year Plan, some form of shared liability is required to be designed".[5]

---

[4] India, National Planning Commission, 2007, p. 64.
[5] India, Ministry of Women and Child Development, 2007, p. 129.

Box 10.1   Legislation on childcare facilities
for working women in India

The Factories Act (1948). Provision of crèches in every factory in which more than 30 women workers are employed.

The Mines Act (1950). Provision of suitable rooms to be reserved for the use of children under the age of 6 belonging to women working in the mines.

The Plantations Labour Act (1951). Provision of crèches in every plantation in which 50 or more women workers (including those employed by contractors) are hired or where the number of children of women workers is 20 or more. In addition, women workers are provided time off for feeding children.

The Beedi and Cigar Workers Act (1966). Provision of crèches for the benefit of women workers in industrial premises in which more than 50 female employees are ordinarily working.

The Contract Labour Act (1970). Provision of crèches where 20 or more women are ordinarily employed as contract labour.

The Inter-State Migrant Workers Act (1980). Provision of crèches for the benefit of women workers in establishments in which 20 or more women are ordinarily employed as migrant workers and in which the employment of migrant workers is likely to continue for three months or more.

The Building and Other Construction Workers Act (Regulation of Employment and Conditions of Service) (1996). Provision of a suitable room or rooms for the use of children under the age of 6 in which 50 or more women are ordinarily employed as building workers.

Government programmes for childcare

The 86th amendment to the Constitution of India made education for children aged 6–14 a fundamental right. For children under age 6, it states that the "State shall endeavour to provide early childhood care and education to all children until they complete the age of six years";[6] recognizing this goal is still a national challenge. While the concept of early childhood care and education (ECCE) is not new, it is only now slowly coming more into focus. Government initiatives in the field of ECCE for children below the age of 6 began with the National Policy for Children (1974).[7] This was strengthened by the National Education Policy (1986),

---

[6] Article 45 under the Directive Principles of State Policy.

[7] This policy clearly recognized the need to provide for the full physical, mental and social development of a child before and after birth as a distinct goal.

the adoption of the World Fit for Children Declaration and Plan of Action, and ratification of the UN Convention on the Rights of the Child in 1992. Very recently, the total responsibility for ECCE has been shifted from the Department of Education to the newly created Ministry of Women and Child Development.

The Government has taken a number of childcare initiatives for children up to age 6, the most important being preschool education for disadvantaged children aged 3 to 6 as part of the Integrated Child Development Service (ICDS).

The Integrated Child Development Service (ICDS)

Begun in 1974, the ICDS, implemented by the Ministry of Women and Child Development (MWCD), concentrates on urban slums, tribal areas and more remote and backward rural regions of the country. It is the only major national programme that addresses the needs of children under 6, and aims at providing an integrated package of services relating to nutrition, health and preschool education. The programme also covers pregnant women, nursing mothers and adolescent girls. The services are provided through a vast network of ICDS centres (*anganwadis* – AWCs),[8] with each centre meant to cover approximately 1,000 people (about 200 families) or 700 people in the case of tribal areas.

The *anganwadi* preschool education component is for children aged 3 to 6 and seeks to promote growth and development, and the necessary preparation for primary schooling, while also freeing siblings, especially girls, to attend school. In 2008, there were almost 1 million AWCs providing preschool education, reaching an estimated 33 million children from disadvantaged groups. Expansion has been rapid since 2004, when the number of children being reached was much less at about 20.4 million.[9] In 2005, it was estimated that almost 21 per cent of the 3 to 5 age group were attending AWC preschool.[10] Given the rapid increase in enrolments, the proportion is probably closer to 30 per cent in 2008.

There have been various concerns regarding the effectiveness of the AWCs. A 2005 study[11] on ICDS infrastructure revealed that, on average, an AWC functions for approximately only four hours a day, for 24 days out of a 30-day month.

---

[8] The *anganwadi*, literally a courtyard play centre, is a childcare centre located within the village itself.

[9] Ministry of Women and Child Development, http://www.wcd.nic.in (select Child Development, then Data Tables of ICDS and then the table Statewise number of beneficiaries (children 6 months–6 years and pregnant & lactating mothers)) [19 June 2009].

[10] India, National Institute of Public Cooperation and Child Development, 2006, figure 11.

[11] National Council of Applied Economic Research (NCAER). The NCAER conducted a Rapid Facility Survey on the ICDS infrastructure in 2004. The main findings of the report can be found on the web site of the Ministry of Women and Child Development, http://wcd.nic.in/icds.htm [19 June 2009].

It also found that, on average, only 66 per cent of eligible children (and 75 per cent of eligible women) were registered at AWCs, indicating that AWC workers were not identifying and registering all eligible women and children. *Anganwadi* workers and helpers are "honorary workers" from the local community who come forward to render their services on a part-time basis and are paid a monthly honoraria. These workers face increased workloads, inadequate facilities and very low wages. Despite inflation and constant requests to the Government, *anganwadi* workers earn just Rs1,000 ($23.20) a month, and helpers, Rs500 ($11.60).[12]

The Rajiv Gandhi National Crèche Scheme

In January 2006, the MWCD launched the Rajiv Gandhi National Crèche Scheme for the Children of Working Mothers, by merging the National Crèche Fund[13] with the Scheme of Assistance to Voluntary Organisations for Crèches for Working and Ailing Women's Children.[14] The new scheme is implemented mainly through the Central Social Welfare Board as well as two national-level voluntary organizations – the Indian Council for Child Welfare and Bharatiya Adimjati Sevak Sangh.

The scheme provides crèche services for children under 6, including supplementary nutrition, preschool education, emergency medicines and contingency. Those eligible to use the services under this scheme are families with a monthly income of less than Rs12,000 ($283).[15] A user charge of Rs20 ($0.47) per child per month is collected from Below Poverty Line families, while other families pay Rs60 ($1.41) per child per month. The guidelines for running crèches under this scheme clearly state that 50 per cent of children in a crèche must be from families below the poverty line.

Every crèche serves about 25 babies for eight hours from 9.00 a.m. to 5.00 p.m. About 28,000 crèches are functioning under the scheme, benefiting around 700,000 children.[16] Catering to the childcare needs of the approximately 220 million

---

[12] Integrated Child Development Service (ICDS) Scheme: found at http://wcd.nic.in/icds.htm [2 June 2009].

[13] To meet the growing need for more crèches, the National Crèche Fund, set up in 1993–94, made assistance available to voluntary organizations/*mahila mandals* (women's groups) through interest earned from the corpus fund to convert existing AWCs (preschool centres) into AWC-cum-crèche centres.

[14] In support of the commitments made in the National Children's Policy (1974), a scheme called Assistance to Voluntary Organisations for Crèches for Working and Ailing Women's Children was introduced to provide a safe environment for the children of working mothers, through health care, sanitation, nutrition, play materials, cradles, beds and the provision of a supervisor in every crèche.

[15] Prior to this scheme, only families with a monthly income of Rs1800 ($44) were eligible to receive benefits.

[16] India Ministry of Finance, *Economic Survey 2007–2008*, p. 261, http://indiabudget.nic.in/es2007-08/chapt2008/chap108.pdf [2 June 2009].

women in the informal economy would require an estimated 800,000 crèches.[17] Thus the scheme still requires substantial expansion if it is to serve its purpose.

State governments/Union Territory administrations do not play a role in the existing crèche and daycare schemes run by the MWCD. As a result, there is no possibility of involving local community-based organizations and self-help groups, other large national NGOs, trade unions or workers' boards such as the Building Workers' Association.

Hostel Buildings for Working Women with a Day Care Centre

In order to promote greater mobility for working women, the MWCD launched in 1973 a scheme entitled Construction/Expansion of Hostel Buildings for Working Women with a Day Care Centre, which provides accommodation for a period of five years to single working women who are either unmarried, widowed, divorced, separated or married with husbands working out of town. Working women with children below the age of 8 are eligible to live in a separate hostel where daycare facilities are provided. To date, these facilities have been provided to 5,907 children in 229 hostels across the country.

To conclude, with respect to government measures, although there has been a major effort to provide some preschool education to 3–5-year-olds from poor backgrounds, care facilities for younger children are seriously lacking and the limited hours of preschool also do not cover the needs of working parents. After-school care has received little attention although a recent working group report recommends that it be provided by all schools within the school premises for children whose mothers are working women.[18] It is encouraging that the budget allocation for the Ministry of Women and Child Development was increased in the 2008–09 Union budget by 24 per cent from the previous year. Also approximately 70,000 more crèches are being considered for establishment under the Rajiv Gandhi National Crèche Scheme in the Eleventh Five Year Plan.

Private commercial providers

Private for-profit initiatives for childcare tend to focus on the children of families that are socio-economically better off and include daycare centres, nurseries, kindergartens and preliminary classes. Many of the working women in the middle

---

[17] Committee for Legal Aid to Poor (CLAP), 2004.
[18] India, National Planning Commission, 2007, p. 151.

and upper middle classes use the services provided by neighbourhood childcare centres, often called "play homes". They provide good services with homely atmospheres. In the absence of any registration system, no figures are available on the number of children attending private centres. A report in 2006[19] quoted a 1998 estimate that about 10 million children were enrolled in private facilities, and the number is likely to have been much greater by 2008.

According to the same report, this type of preschooling tends to be oversubscribed, with intense competition for space (sometimes as many as 300 children vying for a single place). More low-income families in urban areas are also seeking private preschools for their children from the age of 4. The quality of the programmes offered is highly variable, and probably related to the fees that are paid.

As in other countries, commercial childcare companies are increasingly present. One example is Kidzee, a franchise chain of preschools, with more than 600 schools across India and abroad, for children 2 to 6 years old.[20] Kidzee is the pre-primary segment of Zee Interactive Learning Systems. The CEO of Zee Interactive notes:

> Professional childcare has become a dire need in today's commercialized society, with increasing nuclear families, more working women and non-availability of reliable nannies. A mature industry in developed economies, it is gaining greater prominence in India now. Our Kidzcare initiative is well-poised to handle this untapped potential.[21]

Non-governmental initiatives

Apart from profit-making ventures, there are many national and local non-government organizations (NGOs) which are active in early childhood care and education either through direct service delivery or through supportive activities such as training. NGO initiatives operate on government and/or non-government funding sources, and may charge nominal fees to the parents.

There are no figures available on the number of children covered by the NGO sector, but estimates place it between 3 million and 20 million children.[22]

---

[19] India, National Institute of Public Cooperation and Child Development, 2006, p. 35.

[20] Information found at the Kidzee web site, http://www.kidzee.com/about_kidzee.php [11 June 2009].

[21] Televisionpoint.com, 2007. "Zee Kidzcare bullish on childcare business", 25 May. Available at http://www.televisionpoint.com/news2007/newsfullstory.php?id=1180112947 [11 June 2009].

[22] India, National Institute of Public Cooperation and Child Development, 2006, table 6.

The spread and nature of the services provided by the NGO sector vary, but include some of the most innovative and high-quality programmes in the country. In the enterprise examples that follow (Gokaldas Images, BHEL), NGOs have been used to help with the training of crèche staff and, in the case of the Peenya Industries Association, the NGO actually runs the daycare centre. A well-known example of an NGO which has been providing care and education for the children of construction workers is "Mobile Creches", which is described in box 10.2.

Another voluntary initiative is the Forum for Crèche and Child Care Services (FORCES), created in 1989 in response to the inadequacy of child services. As a national advocacy network, it is dedicated to securing the rights of

Box 10.2 Mobile Creches at construction sites

Mobile Creches is an NGO founded in 1969 to help the millions of children who live on construction sites. The construction industry employs about 30 million workers, of which over 30 per cent are women. Construction workers are migrants, often young couples who come to the city with their children to escape extreme rural poverty. With their children, they move from one construction site to the next, often living in makeshift shanties on construction sites. Usually both parents work so the children are left to play in dangerous and unhealthy circumstances and often primary-age children do not attend school.

Initially the centres were intended for infants. But it was realized that older children on the construction sites also suffer from lack of access to care and education so the centres now also include preschool and non-formal education for children up to age 12 as well as support for school admission. Health is integrated into the programme through nutrition, hygiene, immunization and regular visits by doctors. To date, Mobile Creches has reached out to 650,000 children, trained 5,500 childcare workers and runs 550 daycare centres.

To start a centre, Mobile Creches negotiates with the builder for support in terms of salary for personnel and provision of infrastructure (water, electricity, a safe enclosure, kitchen and toilet). Negotiations can take 2–4 months, but support from the builders has been increasing since the early days: one out of two now covers at least 50 per cent of the costs and most provide a part-time helper.

In setting up Mobile Creches, many sources of funding were tapped. Fundraising continues to be a major activity for ensuring the operation of its activities. An impressive list of funding partners including corporations, institutional donors and trusts, both in India and elsewhere, is given on its web site.

Sources: Information comes from the web site of Mobile Creches, http://www.mobilecreches.org/about.htm [16 June 2009]; Anandalakshmy and Balagopal (1999) also provide interesting detail on the operation of the crèches.

underprivileged children from age 0 to 6 and focusing attention on the basic need for child support for millions of women in the unorganized sector. The network comprises 50 member organizations (trade unions, women's organizations, NGOs, academic institutes), individual members and regional networks in 11 states.

Case studies

The enterprises in the examples which follow are all found in the state of Karnataka, which is one of the most progressive and industrialized states in India. Although 56 per cent of the workforce is still in agriculture, proactive government policies and cordial labour relations have helped Karnataka emerge as a favoured destination for domestic and overseas businesses that have set up manufacturing facilities in automobiles, machine tools, electronic components, pharmaceuticals and garments. In the organized sector, the proportion of women is relatively high for India, as women constitute almost one-third of employees.[23]

The case studies were selected in consultation with the leading trade union and employers' associations in the country, the Indian National Trade Union Congress (INTUC), and the Karnataka Employers' Association (KEA). KEA has been particularly proactive in its programmes to ensure gender parity in people management practices, as highlighted in box 10.3.

Box 10.3 The Karnataka Employers' Association (KEA)

KEA is committed to upholding strong ethics in human resource practices. Many member organizations have been deemed best employers for the past several years in areas such as corporate social responsibility, corporate governance, business leadership and business ethics.

KEA has constituted a committee to produce studies on gender issues, organize programmes and disseminate information among member organizations. In 2006, a workshop on gender sensitivity in the workplace was conducted with technical support from ILO, New Delhi. Over 50 delegates from 27 organizations attended and a research book entitled *Gender Sensitivity at the Workplace* was published.

KEA has formulated a model policy and procedure framework to prevent sexual harassment at the workplace. Many member organizations have now adopted the policy.

---

[23] Government of Karnataka, Planning and Statistics Department, 2005.

The first two cases (Gokaldas Images and Bharat Heavy Electricals Ltd) are examples of organizations where employers are statutorily required to provide crèche facilities and are going beyond legal requirements, in particular by offering the service to male employees. The other four organizations (Infosys, Wipro, the National Centre for Biological Sciences and Peenya Industries Association) provide childcare facilities even in the absence of a legal requirement because they realize the potential benefit for employees and themselves. The case studies include different types of industries with employees from very different economic levels, from IT professionals and academics to factory workers.

Gokaldas Images Private Ltd

Type of business. Garment manufacturing.

Workplace. Factory in Bangalore.

Workers. Approximately 13,500 employees in India; roughly 85 per cent are women. Of these, 900 work at the Bangalore factory.

Working hours. The factory is open from 9.00 a.m. to 7.00 p.m. daily; employees are free to complete eight hours of work at a stretch during the day, within these hours.

Childcare solution. Crèche for employees' children from 6 months onwards.

Partners. The Indian Council for Child Welfare (ICCW) and the Karnataka State Council for Child Welfare (KSCCW).

Gokaldas Images Private Ltd is one of India's largest integrated clothing corporations. Established in 1979, the company is based in Bangalore and competes with some of the world's largest fashion houses in fashion wear, outerwear, denim, knitwear, lingerie, and women's and men's formal wear. It has 50 exclusive shops and 500 franchises all over India. Its 16 automated factories employ approximately 13,500 people.

At Gokaldas Images, there were basically two reasons for deciding to provide crèche facilities at its factories. First, the company's management realized there was a need when it observed that several employees – the majority of them being women – were bringing their young children to the workplace due to the absence of other childcare options. Second, the Factories Act (1948) mandates that any factory employing more than 30 women is to provide such services. The management solicited the KSCCW and the ICCW to train *balsevikas*[24] in

---

[24] Trained personnel in institutions that implement welfare programmes for children.

taking care of the children. In this instance, therefore, the initiative to provide crèche services was management's, while the training for crèche staff was provided by external agencies. All 18 factories provide a crèche and this case concerns the factory in Bangalore.

Childcare programme

The crèche is open from 8.45 a.m. to 7.00 p.m. on working days. It is located on the ground floor and has three rooms, with a kitchen and counselling centre-cum-clinic. The rooms are well ventilated and good hygienic conditions are maintained. The crèche can take 30 children and at present there are 19 (five are infants and the rest are between the ages of 2 and 4).

Uniforms are supplied to the children, and snacks are provided (such as bananas, bread, biscuits, milk). Additionally, meals are provided by the child's family. For lactating mothers, privacy is provided in the crèche for breastfeeding. Parents are kept informed about nutrition, healthy, low-cost foods, balanced diets, health, hygiene and the importance of education.

Apart from ensuring that the children are kept busy with toys and crafts, they are also toilet-trained at the crèche. Non-formal educational activities are organized for the older children, including painting, learning nursery rhymes and songs, the basic concepts of colours and numbers. Health checks are conducted regularly and growth charts and medical charts are maintained for each child.

Eligibility and use

The service is available to all employees, both men and women, across the organizational hierarchy. However, most users are young mothers who earn about Rs3,094 ($71) a month as tailors, shop-floor assistants and so on. There is no waiting list. The number of children at present remains low because most employees are young, unmarried women, or married women who have not yet had children. Moreover, there are many women who have children who are much older and are capable of looking after themselves during the day. No men use the service at present, either because they too have no children or do not require the service. However, there are some married couples (where both the husband and wife work in the factory) who make use of the crèche.

Organization and management

The operation of the crèche is the responsibility of the counsellor manager, who reports to the human resources department, the caregivers, and a nurse who is permanently stationed there. There is also a clinic nearby with a visiting doctor who attends to any health problems or injuries.

Employees using the crèche are charged a token amount of Rs10 ($0.23) per month, and this fee is used to meet the expenses of the children's birthday celebrations at the crèche. Thus, virtually all of the cost of the crèche is paid by the company.

Assessments of the crèche have been made by external and internal authorities. The Inspector of Factories has conducted several inspections. Internal assessments are made by Gokaldas Images' Department of Human Resources, and also by the ICCW. A parents' meeting is held monthly, where the welfare officer and a human resources executive are present to listen to the parents' concerns/suggestions. There is a suggestion box in the vicinity so people can submit their comments in written form at any time and there is a grievance committee, all making it possible for the parents to play a role in ensuring the best childcare for their children.

Childcare staff

The staff members at the crèche say that they feel a distinct sense of pride in looking after the children of the employees at Gokaldas Images. They feel the management is extremely supportive, and they have a very good rapport with the parents. The main problems they encounter are usually the illnesses of children or their late collection from the crèche due to the erratic working time of the parents.

Management perspective

The crèche of Gokaldas Images is known in the area for providing good childcare services. There have been instances of mothers with 4-month-old infants who have joined the factory because of its good crèche facility. In some families, two to three generations of women have availed of this service (grandmother to granddaughter). The management has therefore benefited from an increase in company loyalty among its employees and attracted new employees.

The management also reports that due to employee satisfaction with the service, fewer employees worry about their children while at work, which translates into better productivity and greater regularity at work. This is reflected in the fact that employees using the service are taking fewer days off.

Employee perspective

Employees are very happy with the services provided, as their children are under proper care and supervision. Since most of these women live in nuclear families, the absence of alternatives for childcare would have forced many to quit their jobs. The crèche at Gokaldas Images, therefore, makes it possible for a young mother to resume her work shortly after giving birth, and relieves her concerns for the safety, security and well-being of her child during her work shift. Moreover, and very significant, the service is extremely affordable and convenient to all employees.

Lessons learned

The management at Gokaldas Images plans to further improve the crèche in terms of space, with separate play area and services. The demographic profile of the workforce changes every 5–6 years, which affects the number of children requiring crèche admission. The management therefore seeks to keep pace with these changes to accommodate as many children as would require their services and aims at ensuring optimum childcare and child development. Key lessons from their experience are:

- Providing services such as a crèche can be decisive in terms of securing the loyalty of employees, especially female employees.

- Specialized training of staff has helped in running the crèche professionally and efficiently.

- Making the service more innovative, and encouraging the involvement of parents in the process, increases its acceptability among employees.

Bharat Heavy Electricals Ltd (BHEL)

Type of business. Electricals and electronic manufacturing (public sector).

Workplace. Manufacturing unit in Bangalore.

Workers. About 1,900 workers, of which approximately 350 are women.

Working hours. 7.30 p.m. to 4.30 p.m.

Childcare solution. Crèche for children aged 1 year onwards; holiday sports for school-age children.

Partners. Indian Council for Child Welfare (ICCW); the Church of South India (CSI); Sports Authority of India.

BHEL is a public sector company that is one of the largest engineering and manufacturing enterprises in India. It works in the sectors of power generation and transmission, industry, transportation, telecommunication and renewable energy.

As BHEL employs approximately 350 women at its manufacturing unit in Bangalore, the management provides crèche services for its employees with young children, as mandated by the Factories Act (1948) and the Karnataka Factories Rules (1969). The crèche adheres to all legal stipulations. ICCW and CSI assisted in engaging competent staff and providing training in childcare, nutrition and other activities.

Childcare programme

The crèche is open from 7.30 a.m. to 4.30 p.m. (sometimes extended to 5.30 p.m.). It can take about 30 children, but only 12 are currently enrolled. Five are less than 1.5 years old, and the remainder are 1.5 to 5. The crèche is located in the vicinity of the factory. It is spacious and hygienic, is equipped with a kitchen and toilets and has privacy for breastfeeding. Parents are not charged anything to use the crèche. Meals and milk are routinely provided from the company canteen. Regular health check-ups and immunization camps are conducted and referrals can be made for medical treatment.

In addition to the crèche, older children can access swimming and other sports activities during their vacations, as a result of a collaboration between BHEL and the Sports Authority of India. Free company transport for the children is provided.

Eligibility and use

The crèche is available to all male and female employees, including daily-wage workers, contract workers, trainees, diploma trainees and regular factory employees. There is no waiting list. It is used mainly by younger staff with young children. Both men and women use the service. Most workers using the crèche are artisan-level employees (employees in lower-paid jobs). Higher-level employees usually do not use the service because they are well paid and prefer to hire a domestic worker for their children. The crèche is below capacity partly because very few company employees are of childbearing age any more.

Organization and management

BHEL handles the organization and financing of the programme. The Human Resources Department allocates funds for welfare measures carried out by the factory, which includes the crèche. Parents are encouraged to give feedback and suggestions on the crèche to those managing it. If no action is taken, parents are advised to contact an official from the Women in Public Sector organization (WIPS), their respective floor supervisors, or even the HR department directly.

The crèche is managed by two permanent staff, two assistants, two helpers and a trained nurse. There is also a clinic within the premises with a doctor stationed there. Employees also have health schemes at reputed hospitals, which cover their families in the case of illness.

Assessments by the Department of Factories have found the crèche to be fully satisfactory. Apart from this, the company's HR manager visits the crèche once a week.

Childcare staff

Crèche staff say they derive much satisfaction from their work at the crèche. They also appreciate the able guidance of the management and HR department. They report cordial relationships with the management as well as with the parents.

Management perspective

The management finds that its employees are very satisfied with the crèche and reports that it has a positive impact on the attrition rate (which is almost zero).

The management sees the provision of crèche services as essential wherever women are employed in large numbers, and believes this should be done regardless of whether it is mandated by law or not. Improved services including flexitime have helped increase productivity, especially of women, and absenteeism has reduced.

Employee perspective

Employees report satisfaction with the supportive management, and feel greater loyalty to the company. They also believe that their children are very well taken care of, and that this is the next best option to the mothers caring for their children themselves. They also appreciate the opportunities for sports activities for the older children.

Lessons learned

The increasing numbers of nuclear families and working women necessitates the provision of support structures for proper childcare. The crèche is appreciated and used by both men and women workers. Being a public sector company, BHEL was guided by government norms and it was able to access professional help to set up the crèche and appoint trained personnel. In the future, BHEL plans to relocate the crèche to a new building and expand the services.

Infosys

Type of business. Software engineering (private sector).
Workplace. Office (Infosys Technologies Limited), Bangalore.
Workers. 21,000 workers; 35 per cent at this office are women.
Working hours. 8.00 a.m. to 5.15 p.m.
Childcare solution. Crèche for employees' children aged 2.5 months to 5 years.
Partners. Childcare consultant.

Infosys is a private sector corporation which provides comprehensive software engineering solutions to maximize business opportunities. Infosys has over 40 offices and development centres in Australia, Canada, China, the Czech Republic, India, Japan, Poland and the United Kingdom. Infosys has over 91,000 employees.

Infosys has a strong diversity programme to attract more women and encourage them to stay in the workforce and attain leadership positions. In 2007, it won an award from Nasscom and India Today: Woman Corporate Award for Excellence in Gender Inclusivity.[25] The backbone of its programme is the Infosys Women's Inclusivity Network (IWIN), which was set up in 2003 to promote a gender-sensitive work environment recognizing the aspirations and needs of women. There is also a new Family Matters Network providing support to employees on parenting matters. Since 2003, the proportion of women employees has grown from 17 to over 30 per cent (box 10.4 provides more information on the strategy).

This case study covers the Bangalore office, which employs workers in software engineering, supervision, accountancy and housekeeping. Lower-end jobs have been outsourced.

Although Infosys is not required by law to provide a crèche, in the early 1990s, with nearly one-quarter of the staff being women, management decided to provide one for its workers. This decision was arrived at through discussions between the management, parent employees and a childcare consultant. Both parents and the management found each other to be willing and encouraging partners.

Childcare programme

The crèche is located in a rented 3,000 square foot building. The building is well ventilated, extremely hygienic, centrally located and easily accessible from all sides. It is located opposite the Infosys bus stand. The crèche is open daily, from 8.00 a.m. to 7.00 p.m. and is equipped with child-sized lavatory facilities, 17 cots, a wide variety of toys and a clean kitchen with a gas range and refrigerator.

Eligibility and use

The crèche is available for children aged 2.5 months to 5 years; at the time of the study, it catered to 70 children between the ages of 6 months and 3 years. The service is open to all office members and is usually used by young, entry-level employees who have young children and live in a nuclear family. Some male employees who have working wives also make use of the facility. The incomes

---

[25] Infosys Annual Report 2007–08, p. 9. Found at http://www.infosys.com/investors/reports-filings/annual-report/annual/Infosys-AR-08.pdf [11 June 2009].

Box 10.4 The Infosys Women's Inclusivity Network (IWIN)

The vision and strategy of IWIN can be summed up as "AIR":

ATTRACT: Enable thought leaders to share gender-specific concerns in key forums; provide platforms where women can network and share best practices; participate in key forums that attract women laterals to identify Infosys as an employer of choice.

INCREASE: Invest in high-potential individuals through a strong mentoring system; provide new opportunities to exhibit leadership skills.

RETAIN: Furnish options for keeping women in careers while they balance marriage and young children (alternative work models and schedules such as teleworking).

Source: Information provided by Infosys.

of the employees using the service vary; however, the service is more-or-less affordable to almost all staff from the lower management level upwards.

Management and finance

The fees collected from parents are used to meet the costs of the services provided (apart from rent). The employees are charged for this facility according to the age of the children, ranging from Rs4,274 ($98) per month for infants to Rs3,663 ($84) for older children.

The crèche employs a staff of 38 people (a director, a centre manager, 16 caregivers, 15 maids, four cleaning staff and a driver). Staff members are screened for tuberculosis and HIV, and are trained in childcare, feeding, toilet training and Montessori methods. A child development consultant monitors the facility.

A committee of management, parents and the crèche director meets every Friday to discuss the operation of the crèche. Children's feedback is also taken into account. All complaints must be issued in writing. The child development consultant reviews any complaints, takes appropriate action and monitors follow-up weekly. In addition, Parent–Teacher Association (PTA) meetings are held once every four months, to discuss child health and parenting topics.

The crèche has been assessed by the US company SISCO,[26] but not by the Government since the company was not obliged by law to establish it.

---

[26] Systems Integration Specialists Company, Inc. (SISCO) is a private company that applies standards to address practical problems in the electric utility, manufacturing and automation industries.

Childcare staff

The staff report a high level of satisfaction and report little problem with parents. However, they feel a need for more space, and for keeping specialists such as paediatricians on call to deal with problems that may suddenly emerge.

Management perspective

The management feels that employees with young children greatly value the childcare service. They believe this is the reason why, despite completing their technical training on the job and accumulating enough work experience to move to other jobs, many decide not to leave. They identify the success of the crèche service therefore as one of the major contributors to the company's relatively low attrition rate.

Employee perspective

Company employees feel the crèche has taken a huge burden off their shoulders, as now they do not have to worry about their children's well-being during their own working hours. Otherwise, they would have to employ a full-time caregiver, find another crèche or quit work and stay at home until the children are old enough to be left alone. Most of these options are not feasible, affordable or convenient for the employees. In addition to the convenience of the Infosys crèche, employees feel that their children benefit greatly from the holistic design of the crèche's teaching programme. However, they, too, highlight the need for more space.

Lessons learned

Workplace initiatives for childcare services are very much appreciated given the problems of parents with young children. Although fees are relatively high, with employees paying a major proportion of the cost, the crèche is still in great demand and employees are willing to pay this cost given its convenience and quality.

The company plans to add more rooms and personnel, and hopes to establish an accrediting agency that would be a pioneer in providing good and safe child daycare services.

Wipro Technologies

Type of business. Information technology (IT) and software.

Workplace. Offices in Bangalore.

Workers. Approximately 21,000 persons, of whom women make up 27 per cent.

Working hours. 8.30 a.m. to 6.00 p.m.

Childcare solution. Crèche for children aged 1–4 years; also after-school care and emergency care (under special circumstances).

Partners. Outsourced to organization specializing in childcare.

Wipro Technologies is a private global services provider which delivers technology-driven business solutions to meet its clients' strategic objectives. It is one of India's major IT companies, is based in Bangalore and has 20 offices in that city alone.

Wipro's crèche services for young children began in 1993, following worker pressure and seeing that almost 30 per cent of Wipro employees were female. The IT industry is not covered under legislation requiring the provision of a crèche, so Wipro's efforts in this field have been voluntary, for its employees' welfare and in the context of an industry seeking to attract the best talent.

Employees' exposure to crèche schemes abroad played a key role in deciding the type of childcare offered by the company. The management, employees, human resources personnel, administration and security department staff were collectively responsible for deciding the services provided. An organization specializing in childcare called Nirale helped design the programme and now operates the services. Employees found management extremely cooperative and were very appreciative of its efforts.

The crèche is located in an area with a high concentration of Wipro offices (nearly eight offices are in the surrounding area). The crèche can be used by employees at any of the 20 Wipro offices in Bangalore; however, it is used mainly by employees working in offices close to the crèche. Wipro is willing to offer similar facilities to employees in other offices if there is sufficient demand.

Childcare programme

The crèche is in a 4,000 square foot bungalow and is open from 8.00 a.m. to 7.30 p.m. on working days. At present, it has 45 children aged 1 to 4. Parents placing children younger than 1 in the crèche must bring their own personal caregiver for the child.

Children are provided with toys, snacks and milk, but parents are responsible for sending proper meals for their children. A trained nurse provides regular health check-ups. Educational activities, special activities for child development and summer training programmes are organized, and birthdays and festivals of different cultures and religions are celebrated. In addition, the crèche has special spaces for children who are unwell, thus allowing parents to bring their children even if they are slightly ill.

There is a separate scheme for employees whose children attend school and need after-school care (that is, for the second half of the day). These employees are required to make their own arrangements for delivering their children to the crèche after school and must pick them up after work hours. This service is extremely popular, as many parents find it difficult to find reliable care for their children at home. Even if they can find such care, many find the Wipro service a better option.

Parents are also able to leave their children in the crèche for up to a fortnight under special circumstances such as urgent work, going out of town on business, or a family emergency. Employees need to make arrangements for the drop-off and pick-up of their children at the crèche each day. For this scheme, the crèche accepts children aged 1 to 7. This special service of the crèche was created when the need arose and is used from time to time when employees have an emergency.

Eligibility and use

The crèche facilities are available to all employees, irrespective of sex or staff rank. It is used by employees from contract-level staff to fresh recruits and top management. Several male employees with working wives also put their children in the crèche.

Organization and management

The crèche is staffed and operated by Nirale under a contract with Wipro. Crèche programmes are organized with the prior consent of the parents, Nirale, the management and security.

The company covers expenses through a combination of fees collected from those using the service and a planned outlay usually budgeted by management at the beginning of the year, with about Rs254,276 ($5,824) being earmarked annually for overall expenses (rent, water, electricity, security and maintenance).

Fees charged to employees for full-time use of the crèche are approximately Rs4,100 ($94) a month. These charges are quite affordable for most Wipro employees.

Programme feedback is collected via an Internet portal, where the parents' association, Nirale and Wipro's HR department can contact each other and discuss problems and suggestions. The HR department collects the feedback and, depending upon the issue, takes policy decisions or gives suggestions for improvement to Nirale. In addition, company management, parents and Nirale representatives meet to discuss problems, suggestions and plans for the crèche.

Assessments have only been conducted by the management at Wipro and the parents' association, comprising employees who use the facility. There has been no external assessment to date.

Childcare staff

The staff of about 12 are employees of Nirale and appear to be satisfied with the working conditions. They do not report any space or financial constraints and attribute this to proper planning, budgeting and organization by the management, although they mentioned the need for more workers.

Sometimes they face the problem of parents coming late to pick up their children, but this has been curbed by the introduction of a fine. Both management and crèche staff say the fine is necessary because crèche hours completely cover office hours and repeated adjustments cannot be made for those employees who need to work overtime.

Management perspective

The management attributes a higher rate of employee retention to the fact that the crèche services have been very well received by employees with young children.

Employee perspective

All employees using the crèche services, particularly the women, report that this facility has made it possible for them to have a stress-free work environment. Were this service unavailable, most employees say they would have had to depend on other family members, hire caregivers for their children or find a suitable crèche in their neighbourhood – all of these being infinitely more tedious options. Employees also felt that, in addition to being looked after, the children benefit from all-round development due to the educational activities at the crèche.

Lessons learned

Wipro has been able to voluntarily offer crèche services to its employees while using a professional organization, Nirale, to operate and staff the crèche which reduces its own day-to-day responsibilities. The crèche is valued by both management and employees. Introducing after-school services has also been highly popular, as finding after-school care is otherwise very difficult for parents.

The National Centre for Biological Sciences (NCBS)

Type of business. Academic and research institute.
Workplace. Office.
Workers. 75 employees (including faculty), of which 35 per cent are female.
Working hours. 9.00 a.m. to 5.30 p.m.
Childcare solution. Crèche for children aged 6 months to 7 years old; summer holiday activities.
Partners. None.

The National Centre for Biological Sciences is a constituent unit of the Tata Institute of Fundamental Research (TIFR), working under the aegis of the Indian Government's Department of Atomic Energy. It is one of the premier research institutes in the field of biology.

The crèche started in 2004 as an initiative of a few faculty members and women associated with NCBS, who hired domestic workers to care for children in a guest house provided by the management. In 2005, the crèche was handed over to NCBS to manage as the number of children rose with the growth of the faculty and staff. To run the crèche professionally, NCBS nominated a committee to manage the crèche, and later, teachers were appointed to ensure that the children could engage in both educational and recreational activities.

Childcare programme

The crèche facility is located on campus. The age of the children using the facility ranges from 6 months to 7 years. Currently, there are 23 children in the crèche, which is open from 8.30 a.m. to 6.30 p.m., six days a week. The attendant–child ratio is 1:4. The building is spacious and clean, and has a kitchen. The children are provided with toys, activity games, recreation items and so on. There are two teachers and three attendants, all with formal training in childcare and human development.

Monthly medical check-ups are conducted and a growth chart is maintained for each child. In the case of emergencies, there is a doctor on call from 10.30 a.m. to 4.30 p.m. There are monthly parents' meetings, where parents are informed about their child's progress.

The crèche also provides summer holiday activities (such as field trips, swimming classes, music, painting, karate). Children attending such classes are accompanied by one of the crèche attendants, although some classes are provided in the crèche itself. The management has also provided computers for the school-going children.

Eligibility and use

The facility is available to all institute employees at all levels (faculty to administrative) and is used by both male and female staff, and by permanent as well as temporary and contract employees and students. The summer holiday programmes are very popular.

Organization and management

A six-to-seven member committee of parents and management oversees the management of the crèche. Provision is made in the institute's annual budget for expenses towards crèche maintenance.

NCBS provides the space, snacks, milk, toys, other facilities and all infrastructure for the crèche. Operating expenses are paid mainly from the fees paid by parents, which range from Rs1,500 ($34) for toddlers to Rs600 ($13.70) for children above the age of 4, who stay at the crèche only part time as most also go to pre-primary school. These fees cover the crèche's daily expenditures and part of the staff's salaries. The crèche fees are relatively low compared to those of other crèches in major organizations due to the subsidy provided by the institute.

Childcare staff

Staff members work eight-hour shifts per day. Employed by the crèche committee, the staff are professionally trained and receive wages on par with the market.

Overall, crèche staff members are satisfied with their conditions of work. A couple of staff members have been working there since the inception of the crèche.

Management perspective

The institute's management is committed to effectively responding to its employees' needs. For the institute, the crèche is a part of welfare measures: if the children are happy, the parents will be happy and parents can devote more time to their work.

Employee perspective

Employees were involved in the conception and implementation of this programme. They find management receptive to suggestions and improvements, and are satisfied with the services. Since the crèche is located on campus, parents can visit their children during their breaks. The crèche has greatly facilitated staff members' capacity to balance their work and family responsibilities, particularly given the reasonable cost.

Lessons learned

This study is an interesting example of a crèche that started as an informal initiative by employees and was later taken over and subsidized by management. The staff continue to be involved in the management of the crèche through the crèche committee. The institute plans to provide more space for the crèche and to improve its services, thus bringing it to international standards.

Peenya Industries Association

Type of business. Association of small and medium industries.

Workplace. Factories in Peenya Industrial Area, a suburb of Bangalore.

Workers. About 500,000 people, of whom around 40 per cent are women.

Working hours. Eight hours a day for most industries but three shifts for manufacturing industries (typically 6 a.m. to 2 p.m., 2 p.m. to 10 p.m. and 10 p.m. to 6 a.m.).

Childcare solution. Crèche.

Partners. Peenya Infrastructure Corridor Upgradation Project (financed by the Government of India, the Government of Karnataka, local industries); the Karnataka State Council for Child Welfare (KSCCW); Bangalore Metropolitan Transport Company; security company.

The Peenya Industrial Complex, established in the early 1970s with a few industries, is now spread over an area of about 40 km^2 with about 5,000 small-scale industries and 30 of medium scale.[27] A wide variety of industries is found in the area, including electronics, automobile parts, packaging, garments, lubricants, pharmaceuticals and machine tools, many producing for export. About 40 per cent of the employees are women, many of whom work in the garment factories, mostly as tailors, stitching assistants and other associated roles. A small minority of the women are highly qualified professionals (engineers, scientists) or work in administrative or commercial positions. Most of the male workers are employed in more technical jobs (such as turners, millers, electricians, welders, fitters) while a sizeable minority are professional engineers, scientists, diploma holders and commercial graduates.

The Peenya Industries Association (PIA) is more than 25 years old and has a membership of nearly 3,000 micro, small and medium industries. Over the years, the Association has transformed from a welfare organization into a facilitator for the promotion and growth of small-scale industries. Some of the major large industries in the zone are PIA patrons.

A crèche facility has been included in a major government-supported project, the Peenya Infrastructure Corridor Upgradation Project (PICUP), which PIA is supporting and facilitating. The project has included the construction of a building for the crèche with all necessary facilities, which was expected to be inaugurated by September 2008. PICUP is Karnataka's foremost public–private partnership initiative, with major funding from the Government of India and contributions by the state government as well as the industries. Under this project, the industrial estate Peenya Industries Association has, in partnership with the state government, taken up the task of improving the working area and providing various infrastructural facilities including the crèche. PIA notes that the crèche has been established "to meet a long term need of both industries as well as employees".[28] This is a voluntary initiative as there is no legal requirement.

---

[27] Information available at http://www.peenyaindustries.com/Profile.aspx [11 June 2009].

[28] PIA, PICUP Progress communiqué at http://www.peenyaindustries.com/Uploads/003_big.jpg [11 June 2009].

Childcare programme

The crèche is nearly 1,800 square feet in extent and has capacity for 100 children. It is open from 8.30 a.m. to 5.30 p.m. All facilities are available at subsidized rates for working women in the Peenya Industrial Area.

The crèche is close to the local bus terminus, providing easy access for workers. The PIA management has agreed with the Bangalore Metropolitan Transport Company for shuttle services to be provided at a nominal fee.

Organization and management

While PICUP has provided all the required physical facilities, some employers in the zone garnered administrative and maintenance support from the Karnataka State Council for Child Welfare, a voluntary NGO that already provides and maintains crèches and childcare teachers throughout Karnataka. The Council has given its in-principle consent for this project. Crèche staff will be provided by KSCCW, with working conditions and facilities on par with other good working models.

The facilities will be funded through the pooled resources of member companies who use the crèche, corpus creations (a fund created through contributions by member companies for the purpose) and costs picked up by sponsors (large companies in the industrial cluster). PIA will collect the money from employers to pay the council. A nominal fee for workers of Rs250 has been proposed.

Daytime security of the building and facilities was a problem addressed by the voluntary services of a security agency. At night, the building will be locked up.

Management perspective

For the many workers with young children in the complex, this facility would enhance productivity and improve attendance. Most industries in the Peenya Industrial Area are likely to benefit, as no such facilities are currently available.

Lessons learned

The crèche of the Peenya Industries Association provides an example of how an employers' organization in an industrial zone has partnered with government to build a crèche and with an NGO to run it. As micro and small businesses could not provide such facilities on their own, this example represents how such facilities can be provided by pooling resources through a "cluster approach". The broad partnership for this initiative brings together complementary financial, human and material resources, and holds great promise for stability and sustainability.

Photo © Laura Addati

Kenya

11

Laura Addati[1]

National overview

The childcare needs of working parents receive little attention in this mainly agricultural country where the enormous problems of employment creation and poverty predominate. Since most women work in traditional agriculture or the informal economy, the prevailing assumption is that childcare is compatible with work, and if not, a family member can help out. However, as seen below, the lack of childcare facilities does affect the work opportunities and productivity of women, and can lead to bringing children to work, withdrawing older children from school to help care for younger children, hiring child domestic workers or

[1] Laura Addati is a Technical Officer in the Conditions of Work and Employment Programme, ILO, Geneva. She would like to thank the following for their time and collaboration: Mr Etienne Delbar, General Manager of SOCFINAF Co. Ltd, Ms Isabelle Henin Spindler, General Managing Director of Red Lands Roses Ltd, and their staff teams and workers, including Gitothua, Mchana, Maendeleo and Tatu crèche staff and teachers. In particular, she would also like to express her gratitude to Mr Hassan Ndisho, SOCFINAF Human Resources Manager, for his invaluable support during the ILO field visit carried out in Ruiru (Kenya) in July 2007, the quantitative data collection and the preparation of the case studies of this country chapter.

leaving children on their own. Parents are concerned and stressed when children accompany them to unhealthy or dangerous work environments or are left in the unreliable care of others.

Employment of women and childcare

Despite its important role in some export markets and a significant tourist industry, the employment situation in Kenya has deteriorated in the last 15 years: the creation of productive jobs with decent wages has not kept pace with the growth of the labour force. Figures for 1998–99 indicate that more than half the population (52 per cent) lives in poverty. About 42 per cent of the employed work in traditional agriculture and 32 per cent work in informal employment, often as own-account workers or as owners of small unregistered businesses or their employees. Only 26 per cent of the employed are paid employees in the modern sector (public and private).[2]

Most women work and their labour force participation rate is high, estimated at 76 per cent of those aged 15 to 64 years.[3] Nevertheless, their share of the scarce wage employment in the modern sector is low: only about 28 per cent of wage employees are women and only 15 per cent of employed women are in the modern sector.[4] Thus few women workers are regular employees who would be able to benefit from labour legislation and provisions such as annual, sick and maternity leave.[5]

Women are much more likely than men to be subsistence farmers, partly because of the greater migration of men to urban areas: 54 per cent of employed women are in traditional farming compared to 30 per cent of the men. Finally the informal economy has been an important source of employment for both men and women with almost one-third in this type of employment.

Family responsibilities broadly affect the scope and quality of women's economic activities. The total fertility rate in Kenya, despite recent declines, remains high at 4.6 children per woman in 2005.[6] Consequently, Kenyan parents have considerable family responsibilities associated with large families. This affects women's paid economic activities in particular; these decline with the number

---

[2] Figures are from Kenya's Integrated Labour Force Survey 1998–99, in Zepeda, 2007, table 3.
[3] ILO, 2008.
[4] Zepeda, 2007, table 3.
[5] ILO, 2004.
[6] United Nations Development Programme, 2006.

of small children in the household. Only 29.4 per cent of young mothers (aged 18–25) with a child under 6 are working for pay. In households with four or more children, only about 25 per cent of mothers work for pay.[7] Of course, almost all women are still engaged in economic activity, for example working in subsistence agriculture or as family workers, for which they do not receive pay. Having children often necessitates staying closer to home, which appears to decrease the extent to which women can accept paid work, thus lowering their income.[8]

National policies and measures for childcare

Among African countries, Kenya enjoys one of the longest traditions of collective approaches to caring for children. Nursery schools for children under 5 were first set up in the 1940s in semi-urban areas where parents worked in tea, coffee and sugar plantations during the colonial period.[9] With independence (1963), Kenya developed and expanded preschool education throughout the country in response to socio-economic changes and the culture of *Harambee* or "self-help" in nation-building.[10] By 1972, there were 8,000 preschools established and managed by the communities, with an enrolment of about 300,000 children under 6.[11]

In 1980, preschool education was transferred to the Ministry of Education, Science and Technology (MOEST). At the same time, a decentralized system was developed based on an amendment to the Local Government Act (1982), which facilitated service delivery by local government authorities. MOEST remains responsible for developing and overseeing the country's early childhood development and education (ECDE) programmes. It sets policy guidelines for early childhood programmes; registers preschools and guarantees quality and standards; coordinates government grants and funds from external donors; and trains and supplies early childhood personnel at all levels.[12]

MOEST has adopted "partnership" as the founding principle with a view to promoting the involvement of various stakeholders in the ECDE sector. The major partners of MOEST in ECDE services provision and funding include various government ministries, parents, local communities and the private sector

---

[7] Lokshin et al., 2004.

[8] ILO, 2004.

[9] Haddad, 2002.

[10] The call for *Harambee* by President Jomo Kenyatta encouraged communities to create programmes to address their needs.

[11] Kenya, MOEST, UNESCO, OECD, 2005.

[12] Kenya, MOEST, 2005.

(individuals, private companies, NGOs, faith- and community-based organizations) as well as bilateral and multilateral partners.[13]

Kenya's level of investment in education is relatively high. In 2004, public expenditure on education as a percentage of GNP was 7.1 per cent, higher than the average of developed countries (5.4 per cent), and represented 29.2 per cent of total government expenditure. In particular, current public expenditure on pre-primary education has increased over the last decade and made up 0.1 per cent of GNP in 2004.[14]

In 2005, the Government adopted the 2005–2010 Kenya Education Sector Support Programme (KESSP), the country's key educational policy implementation document. The overall goal of the ECDE component is to expand access to and enhance the quality of ECDE services for children aged 4–5,[15] especially those living in Arid and Semi-Arid Lands (ASAL) and urban slums. An innovative aspect of the ECDE component is community support grants (CSG) which account for most of the component's budget. The grants aim at providing financial support to 5,000 ECDE centres in 35 priority districts with low preschool access and high poverty levels. However, the launch of the scheme has been postponed and remains uncertain.[16]

Service provision, use and costs

Childcare provision for children aged 2 or 3 to 5 in Kenya is very diverse, including nursery schools, day schools, religious Madrassa schools and kindergartens, all of which are under the supervision of MOEST. In 2007 there were around 30,000 ECDE centres in the country, reaching around 1.5 million children. ECDE services cover about 35 per cent of all children aged 3–6, which is relatively high compared to other sub-Saharan countries. There are services for children from 0 to 3 years in slums and ASALs, usually informal home-based care centres, but programmes for this age group are not part of public childcare provision in Kenya.[17]

Most ECDE services are community-run programmes managed by parent–teacher associations (PTAs). It is estimated that parents and local communities

---

[13] Kenya, MOEST, 2005.

[14] UNESCO, 2006, p. 320.

[15] The emphasis on this age group seems to reflect less priority on the needs of working parents for younger children, which gave rise to earlier, more spontaneous initiatives.

[16] Kenya, MOEST, 2007.

[17] Kenya, MOEST, 2007.

started and manage more than 75 per cent of ECDE centres in the country.[18] The Service Standard Guidelines for Kenya formalize this practice and establish that all ECDE centres shall be managed by a committee of representatives elected by parents. ECDE committees are responsible for identifying ECDE needs and strategies for their communities, mobilizing parents and other partners for support, managing programmes and ensuring staffing, resourcing and quality.[19]

Except for local government-run centres, all ECDE services rely heavily on parents' fees for operating costs, especially teachers' salaries. Fees are set by the village or PTA, and can vary significantly. Centres with more qualified teachers, smaller classes, food and learning materials charge higher fees. Land, facilities, furniture and material are often donated by parents and by churches and NGOs, which are a key source of support.[20] Fees vary depending on the childcare service quality, duration and location, and range from a monthly 4.5 USD for regular nursery schools to 225 USD for private kindergartens in rich urban areas. Research carried out by an ILO field visit in two nursery schools in Nairobi in July 2007 indicated that the overall annual costs per child for full-time services including meals stood at 210 USD for a public nursery school located in a central wealthy area of Nairobi and 84 USD for the same service in a suburban area, around 10 km from the city centre.

While the gross enrolment ratio (GER) in ECDE education had been on the rise, reaching 40.4 per cent in 2001,[21] MOEST reported a decline in enrolments to 35 per cent following the introduction in 2003 of free primary education (FPE).[22] These trends seem to be confirmed by UNESCO reports, which observed that the free primary education policy had a negative impact on ECDE centres serving poor children because parents no longer want to pay for services for younger children that are free for older children.[23]

In sum, there have been significant government efforts and investments in early childcare and education. However, facilities are far from meeting the demands of working parents, especially for children under 3 and in urban slums and rural areas. For many families, existing facilities are too expensive; in other cases, the focus on children's education means the hours are not compatible with working hours.

---

[18] Haddad, 2002, p. 16.
[19] Kenya, MOEST, 2006a, p. 19.
[20] Lokshin et al., 2004.
[21] Kenya, MOEST, UNESCO, OECD, 2005.
[22] Kenya, MOEST, 2006b.
[23] Kaga, 2006.

Conditions of work of childcare workers

There is very little information on the training or qualifications of those pro-viding most of the childcare in Kenya as they are family members, informal con-tacts and domestic workers. More than 1 million domestic workers are estimated in Nairobi alone, where one in two households employs a domestic worker, many of whom provide childcare. Most of these are female, and many under the age of 18. In general, they have few qualifications or training; a UNICEF/government report indicates that 84 per cent of domestic workers in Nairobi either had no edu-cation at all or had dropped out of school before completing primary education.[24]

Although entitled to a minimum wage of 5,195 KShs (around 77 USD)[25] per month and a working week of 52 hours maximum,[26] domestic workers in Nairobi earn on average between 2,000 and 5,000 KShs and work between 9 and 18 hours a day. These workers are often illiterate, underage, underpaid, over-worked and not unionized.[27] Many are exposed to physical abuse and/or sexual exploitation by the employer or his/her relatives. Most of the time, if the domestic worker becomes pregnant, she is kicked out of the house even if the male head of the household is responsible for the pregnancy.[28]

Those working in formal ECDE programmes are part of the basic education system. However, ECDE teachers remain isolated from their primary-education counterparts and their status, working conditions and training are inferior in comparison. Although most of Kenya's ECDE centres are public and usually attached to primary schools, they are mainly funded and managed by parents and local communities through the PTAs or ECDE committees. Teachers' salaries are mostly, if not entirely, covered by parental fees, unlike primary teachers, who are paid by the Government according to an official salary scale. Thus, the level of ECDE teachers' remuneration depends on the total number of children enrolled as well as parents' contributory capacity.

In general, the monthly salaries of ECDE teachers have changed little in the last ten years and are below the basic minimum wage recommended by the Ministry of Labour, although large variations exist between rural and urban areas.

---

[24] GOK/UNICEF, 1992, "Children and women in Kenya: A situation analysis", quoted in Karega, 2002, p. 39.

[25] The exchange rate used is 1 USD = 67 KShs (July 2007).

[26] Regulation of Wages (General) Order, 1982, and Regulation of Wages (General) (Amendment) Order, 2006.

[27] Otieno, M.A., 1998. "Social investment in human capital among housemaids and its implication for public education policy", quoted in Karega, 2002.

[28] Otieno, 1998.

In addition, salary payment is irregular and fluctuates each month depending on the level of parents' contribution. In some cases, teachers work beyond official working time to provide paid care for children of working parents while others provide paid home-based childcare.[29]

The introduction of free primary education in 2003 increased pressure on teachers' already low and unstable salaries as reduced ECDE enrolments resulted in lower salaries for teachers and greater job insecurity.[30] The teacher/child ratio in pre-primary schools remains high, sometimes at 1:30 per class. The ratio of trained teachers to pupils is even worse, at 1:41 in 2002. While teachers recognize the pedagogical benefits of a low ratio, they tend to accept high numbers of children because their earnings increase with each additional child.[31]

The educational requirements for ECDE teachers include a certificate of secondary education plus the completion of a two-year in-service training programme. Recently a new five-week course has been introduced as a bridging programme for ECDE teachers who do not meet the secondary education requirement. However, with no monitoring mechanism in place, the number of untrained teachers is still high, accounting for 56 per cent of staff in public ECDE centres. In addition, due to poor working conditions, turnover is very high, with an annual rate of 40 per cent.[32]

The Kenya Education Sector Support Programme (KESSP) includes a component on ECDE curriculum review and teacher training. A training programme to upgrade ECDE teachers' skills has been established. It aims at training 120 teacher-trainers over five years and in-servicing 8,000 ECDE teachers: 6,000 will be trained under the two-year in-service training course and 2,000 through the five-week short course.[33]

Workplace initiatives and their impact: the role of employers and trade unions

A 2002 ILO report on the status of work and family reconciliation in Kenya highlights that the existing social security and working condition laws show a very low level of responsiveness to the needs of workers with family responsibilities,

---

[29] UNESCO, 2005.
[30] Kaga, 2006.
[31] UNESCO, 2005.
[32] Kenya, MOEST, 2005.
[33] Ibid.

and few effective measures exist to facilitate work and family balance in Kenya.[34] However, a group of trade unions and employers have supported the inclusion of some family-friendly measures in a number of sectoral collective bargaining agreements (CBAs), with a view to providing childcare facilities to workers and to improve maternity protection.

Building on the tradition of the *Mama Uji* (women from the community who looked after small children while parents were at work), some employers in the agricultural sector have maintained and developed childcare facilities in coffee or sugar plantations. The case studies below present two employer-supported childcare schemes for agricultural workers, one in coffee plantations and the second on a rose farm.

The Kenya Plantation and Agricultural Workers' Union (KPAWU), recognizing the crucial role that childcare plays for workers' welfare and performance, succeeded in negotiating and introducing a reference to childcare in the CBA governing the working conditions of coffee workers. In particular, section 24 of the CBA states: "It is agreed between the [Kenya Coffee Growers' and Employers'] Association and the Union that where possible, employers should be encouraged to provide a nursery school and a teacher."[35]

However, low, declining and gender-biased trade union membership and low priority placed on work and family issues, combined with low CBA coverage, have generally resulted in slow advances on the improvement of working conditions legislation and its enforcement. Family-friendly measures at the workplace, in particular childcare provision, remain isolated initiatives, often by foreign large companies. Yet the two examples which follow indicate that, for both workers and employers, valuable benefits can result from childcare programmes for low-income workers given the many difficulties they are experiencing in combining work with their childcare responsibilities.

Conclusions

The Government has made major efforts to extend and improve early childhood development and education facilities, which are long established in Kenya. It has emphasized the strong role traditionally played by parents and communities in childcare provision, in partnership with public and private institutions. While

---

[34] Karega, 2002.

[35] Memorandum of Agreement between the Kenya Coffee Growers' and Employers' Association and the Kenya Plantation and Agricultural Workers' Union, 2007–2008.

Photo © Laura Addati

this modality has allowed the creation and functioning of a number of child-care facilities, meeting in part the needs of working parents, access to preschools remains inequitable in Kenya. Many poor families cannot afford the fees so children cannot attend or, in some cases, quality is sacrificed in order to be able to lower fees. Also, coverage of children between 0 and 3 years is still very limited.

In reality, however, neither parents nor the Government have the level of resources necessary to significantly expand or improve the facilities and their quality. Yet investment in childcare can result in multiple benefits for the country: releasing parents' time for productive work and training, thus increasing poor families' income, improving children's, and in particular, girls' school enrolment, and promoting children's early development and health.[36] Childcare and early education is an investment which merits greater donor support and better integration into strategies for poverty reduction. In addition, there is scope for increased workplace initiatives, given the benefits found by both workers and some employers.

---

[36] Amuyunzu-Nyamongo and Ezeh, 2005.

SOCFINAF Co. Ltd – Ruiru Coffee Plantations

Type of business. Coffee industry for export.

Workplace. Nine coffee plantations in Ruiru (around 54,000 inhabitants), 35 km north-east of Nairobi.

Workers. 1,450 permanent agricultural workers, of which around 45 per cent are women. During the peak harvest season, workers can total up to 10,000 people, including casual workers.

Working hours. From 7.00 a.m. to 3.00 p.m., 46 hours per week, over a period of 6 days.

Childcare solution. Childcare centre on each plantation, including a crèche for children between 3 months and 3 years; nursery school for children between 4 and 6.5 years.

Partners. Kenya Plantation and Agricultural Workers' Union (KPAWU); Ministry of Education, District Centres for Early Childhood Education (DICECEs); National Occupational Safety and Health Environment Programme (OSHEP).

Since the creation of the crop production sector for export in Kenya (such as coffee, tea, sugar) during the colonial era, both men and women have been actively involved, as paid workers, in the entire process of coffee harvesting and processing. Large coffee-growing areas, such as Ruiru, are major employment hubs attracting migrant workers from the farthest and most economically depressed areas of the country. During harvest periods, thousands of workers, mostly young women and men, gather at recruiting points as early as 6.30 a.m. in hope of casual work.[37]

Because around two-thirds of agricultural workers in Ruiru are migrants, leaving behind their extended families, most working parents cannot rely on traditional kin networks for help with daily childcare. Moreover, like most agricultural workers in Kenya, they do not have access to formal childcare services. Public ECDE centres are only available in distant urban Ruiru. Moreover, no affordable assistance is available for children under 3.

Nevertheless, a share of Ruiru agricultural workers benefit from one of the most extensive workplace childcare programmes in the country: that of SOCFINAF Co. Ltd, one of Kenya's oldest coffee-growing companies and leading coffee exporters, with nine coffee estates and two engineering and milling departments in the Ruiru area and a childcare centre on each estate.

---

[37] The Kenyan Employment Act (Cap. 226) Section (2) defines a "casual employee" as any individual who is not engaged for a longer period than 24 hours at a time. Casual workers are not unionizable and so not covered by the Coffee Industry CBA. Casual workers are remunerated at a picking rate of 0.52 USD per tin of 20 litres and do not benefit from housing and social protection coverage.

The group has developed a strong corporate social responsibility (CSR) programme on environmental issues as well as labour standards for its workers, including childcare facilities at the workplace. Crèches in SOCFINAF are as old as the company itself, being established in the early 1950s in the tradition of the *Mama Uji* (the community caregiver). The crèches started as feeding and play facilities and gradually added an educational component.

Childcare programme

In line with the national structure of Early Childhood Development and Education, the SOCFINAF childcare programme is divided into crèche services (for children between 3 months and 3 years) and nursery schools (4–6.5 years). In July 2007, a total of 566 pre-primary schoolchildren were enrolled: 340 children (160 girls and 180 boys) in the crèches and 226 children (118 girls and 108 boys) in the nursery school system.

The facilities are located on each coffee plantation, very close to both the workplace and workers' houses. Parents, usually the mothers, either permanent workers, spouses/partners of permanent workers or community beneficiaries, drop their children before going to work or searching for casual work.

The programmes run all year, six days per week, from 6.45 a.m. to 5.00 p.m. The caregivers wait until all children are collected, often staying well beyond official closing hours. The facilities are basic, situated in one-room buildings, with wood heating and a bed, a kitchen and external latrines. Children are usually fed and play in the surrounding area outside the building. Equipment includes cooking and cleaning tools, plastic dishes and cups, blankets and sheets.

The service includes two meals per day, such as porridge, rice, beans, potatoes, milk and fruits; regular health care is provided by a professional nurse and her assistant, who are located in a dispensary on each plantation. Children in the nursery school attend an educational programme aimed at enhancing social skills and basic knowledge. Teaching is provided until 1.00 p.m., then children have a meal and follow the regular crèche programme.

Eligibility and use

SOCFINAF childcare services are designed for permanent SOCFINAF employees and are offered free of charge. In July 2007, a total of 414 parents benefited from the service: 384 SOCFINAF permanent workers and 30 poor parents from the surrounding community of Tatu Estate. Around 45 per cent of the beneficiaries are women; many are single mothers. The only enrolment requirement is the child's updated vaccination card.

Organization and management

Each crèche and nursery is managed by a SOCFINAF plantation manager, located in a management office on each plantation. This manager oversees childcare operations and maintenance, the work of the nurses and caregivers and the remuneration and working conditions of the staff. All plantation managers report to the SOCFINAF human resources manager, who is in charge of the programme as a whole. All crèche and ECDE staff report to the plantation nurse, who is assisted by an assistant nurse. Each plantation has a dispensary with these staff members.

Childcare staff

The SOCFINAF crèche programme employs 52 caregivers: 11 ECDE teachers, 21 regular caregivers and 20 support staff, of whom 14 are casual workers, recruited when extra help is required. On average, each crèche is staffed with three caregivers selected from agricultural workers in the surrounding communities. The main requirement for recruitment is having completed secondary education. Caregivers participate in training supported by SOCFINAF, such as the National Occupational Safety and Health Environment Programme (OSHEP), or internal training organized by Human Resources on nursing care, ECDE programmes, first aid, health and safety at the workplace, social equality and HIV/AIDS at work.

An early childhood development and education (ECDE) teacher is allocated to nursery schools to provide basic teaching to preschoolers. In addition to internal training, ECDE teachers receive support to attend short courses (five weeks) at the District Centres for Early Childhood Education (DICECEs), decentralized institutions created by the Ministry of Education to develop ECDE training programmes at the local level.

Childcare staff members can join the trade union, and as such, their working conditions are regulated by the collective bargaining agreement (CBA) between the Kenya Coffee Growers' and Employers' Association (KCGEA) and the Kenya Plantation and Agricultural Workers' Union (KPAWU). The monthly basic wage of a caregiver or support staff equals that of a plantation employee:

4,774 KShs (71 USD).[38] ECDE teachers earn between 71 and 95 USD based on qualifications and experience, while a nurse and an assistant nurse earn respectively 330 USD and 98 USD. In addition to their salary, childcare staff receive benefits including health insurance, the pension fund, a housing allowance, transport and subsistence allowances on annual leave, severance pay, maternity leave and breastfeeding breaks.

Costs and funding mechanisms

SOCFINAF funds its crèche programme as part of its CSR policy, under which it allocates an annual labour and welfare budget. Aside from all crèche- and nursery-related costs, this budget covers all welfare programmes targeting workers and their families, including health-care staff, dispensaries, all medical treatment and transportation costs, but also training programmes. On average, SOCFINAF expends an annual budget of around 20,000 USD to fully cover the costs of the crèches and nursery programme. This annual budget represents 0.15 per cent of SOCFINAF annual turnover and 1.6 per cent of its profits.[39] Since about 550 children participate in SOCFINAF crèches and nursery programmes, the cost to SOCFINAF is around 3 USD per month per child.

Employer perspective

The SOCFINAF management finds that this programme is relatively inexpensive, while the returns are great in terms of company image, worker commitment, productivity, worker welfare, good industrial relations with workers' organizations, and ability to attract and retain quality workers.

Indeed, because workers can better concentrate on their work, the company has reduced costs related to workplace injuries and to women's absenteeism:

> Unplanned annual leaves, and especially absenteeism, have a cost for SOCFINAF in terms of loss of productivity. Thanks to the crèches and the related health-care service that SOCFINAF provides free of charge, family-related absences or leaves are virtually non-existent in our company. (SOCFINAF human resources manager)

---

[38] According to the Employment Act, the minimum wage for agricultural work is fixed at 1.8 USD a day, the CBA providing better conditions of remuneration (2.4 USD a day). The exchange rate used is 1 USD = 67 KShs (July 2007).

[39] http://www.socfinal.be/Public (select Economy) [19 June 2009].

It has also been pointed out that caring for children while working seriously affects workers' performance:

> Women carrying babies on their back have a lower picking rate than other workers, experience work interruptions and are very likely to miss the required daily tasks. This definitely restrains their earning capabilities. (Plantation manager)

> Childcare introduces efficiency in the workplace, as parents can work in a peaceful state of mind. They know that their children are well fed, in security and protection in the case of sickness. They feel at ease and comfortable and they can concentrate much better. Mental comfort is key to workers' safety at work, but also to employers, enabling them to reduce costs resulting from workplace injuries and health claims. Childcare has an obvious impact on the company's productivity. (Plantation manager)

> [Thanks to childcare] the workplaces are pacified. In addition, employees' turnover is low. We have more applicants on a daily basis and this is due not only to our concern for workers' conditions of service, but also to our overall policy on corporate social responsibility. (Human resources manager)

Employee and trade union perspective

Trade union

The representative of the Kenya Plantation and Agricultural Workers' Union (KPAWU) in Ruiru recognizes the crucial role of the crèches and nursery schools for workers' welfare and work performance. It is for this reason that the new CBA includes a specific clause on nursery schools.[40] Another important advantage of this policy is the creation of good industrial relations between the employers and employees:

> When workers see what the management is doing for them, they feel more committed to the enterprise and devoted to their work. Childcare, and in general the enterprise's welfare policies, strengthen workers' feeling of belonging to SOCFINAF as they know that they can dialogue with the management through the committees and participate in the solution of their problems.

---

[40] Section 24 of the Coffee Workers CBA, titled *Welfare*, states: "It is agreed between the Association and the Union that where possible, employers should be encouraged to provide a nursery school and a teacher."

Parents

All interviewed parents expressed great satisfaction with the service, its location and its relevance in relation to their working hours as well as the quality of care. In particular, they appreciated the nutrition and health services, which provided relief and a guarantee of children's welfare.

Workers indicated that the service has helped increase their earnings and access to paid work. First, since workers, both permanent and casual, are less stressed and can work without interruption, they are more likely to pick their daily goal of three derbies of coffee, and they are more likely to earn productivity-based picking rate bonuses of 0.60 USD per derby.[41] With more time available for work, women reach the same picking rate as men. For instance, a coffee picker who used to bring her baby to work reports that:

> Picking coffee with a baby on the back is exhausting, especially on an empty stomach. A baby requires constant care and does not allow you to work properly. When I had to leave my kid unwatched in the fields, while I was working, I was constantly worried that she could get hurt, bitten by an animal or even carried off. So I had to repeatedly interrupt my work to go and check that she was fine.

Second, spouses of permanent workers (and the handful of community members with access) benefit from the childcare because it frees them to look for and accept paid work. For these spouses and community beneficiaries, most job opportunities are in casual work, whose unpredictable nature makes it difficult to plan for childcare. Plus, savings from additional earnings and reduced care expenses allow families to participate in community-based borrowing schemes, where parents can take out loans, usually for supporting children's education (especially secondary school fees or equipment) and for improving the family's housing or living conditions.

Lessons learned

Childcare is an urgent priority for poor families in Kenya. Without childcare, the families of SOCFINAF workers would be decisively worse-off, paying considerably more for poor-quality and unreliable childcare by domestic workers or relying on their older children to care for younger siblings.

---

[41] In addition to their basic salary, workers can also gain a production bonus for each extra tin or derby of coffee they manage to pick beyond the daily requirement of three tins. A derby is a 20-litre measuring tin and can contain 15 kilogrammes of coffee cherries (red ripe coffee).

The childcare at SOCFINAF benefits both the workers and the employer: workers enjoy better working conditions, reduced stress at work, better concentration and higher earnings, while management sees improved efficiency and productivity, less absenteeism and turnover and harmonious industrial relations. In management's view, the programme has been relatively inexpensive, particularly in comparison to the benefits that it provides.

Red Lands Roses Ltd – Ruiru Rose Farm

Type of business. Rose exporting.

Workplace. Rose greenhouses and factory in the Ruiru area.

Workers. Around 360 permanent workers, of which 60 per cent are women, and 80 seasonal workers during peak seasons.

Working hours. Usually from 7.00 a.m. to 4.30 p.m., 46 hours per week, over 6 days. The distribution of the 46 weekly hours is flexible and established by the employer according to production needs, in particular during peak production periods (around three times per year), when rose purchases are high in Europe. Overtime is frequent.

Childcare solution. Daycare centre for children between 2 months and 4 years.

Partners. Companies. Red Lands Roses Ltd and Pollen Ltd.
International donors. German Development Bank (DEG) and Max Havelaar Foundation.

Established in May 1996, Red Lands Roses Ltd grows roses for export. The company has a 10-hectare farm, producing several varieties of cut roses. During peak production periods, workers can be required to work overtime, sometimes until very late in the evenings.[42] These conditions are difficult for workers with families, particularly single parents.

Sixty per cent of women working in Red Lands Roses are single parents; most lack any form of childcare support and bear a heavy load of household work. Lack of access to clean drinking water near the housing settlement requires long walks to fetch water. Also, care needs are high given the number of people infected by HIV and AIDS in the area.[43]

---

[42] The terms and conditions of employment for employees of flower grower companies are regulated by the "Memorandum of Agreement between the Agricultural Employers' Association (AEA) and the Kenya Plantation and Agricultural Workers' Union (KPAWU) in the matters of minimum wages and terms and conditions of employment for employees of Flower Grower Members of AEA".

[43] Red Lands Roses, Gitothua Children and Community Centre, *Day Care Centre Profile*, p. 20 (internal unpublished document).

To address these work–family conflicts and to promote the welfare of workers and their families, Red Lands Roses, together with Pollen Ltd (a subsidiary of Syngenta Seeds), another company in the area, mobilized funds from the German Development Bank (DEG) and the Max Havelaar Foundation to create a workplace daycare centre for their employees. The project was conceived in 2003, when the annual performance appraisal of Red Lands Roses highlighted the need for childcare as a priority for workers. Thus the companies invested efforts in creating a workplace childcare centre and successfully applied for a DEG Public–Private Partnership (PPP) grant.

Childcare programme

The Gitothua Children and Community Centre is situated on a 2.25-acre piece of farm with a concrete building of 12 rooms used for various purposes, including an office, a clinic, counselling facilities, a bed area, a kitchen, a laundry and a changing room, a classroom, and playing and dining rooms.

The centre is open all year, 6 days per week, from 6.45 a.m. to 5.45 p.m. The caregivers wait until all children are collected, even beyond the official opening hours, and during peak production periods, including late hours. Gitothua Day Care has capacity for 100 children aged 2 months to 4 years; as of June 2008, it enrolled 60 children.[44]

The service includes full nutrition and health-care services. In addition to the on-site nurse, the local family physician conducts regular visits together with a paediatrician to advise on the adequacy of the facilities and to carry out medical check-ups. The centre also has its own water well and grows its own vegetables and fruits.

Eligibility and use

Gitothua Day Care Centre is mainly for employees of Red Lands Roses and Pollen Ltd, although five infants from the poorest families of Gitothua settlement are also enrolled free of charge. The facility is a 30–40-minute walk from Red Lands Roses. Parents drop their children off at the crèche before walking or riding to work. The management of Red Lands Roses has cost-shared bikes for its employees, to facilitate the commute to work and for breastfeeding breaks.

---

[44] http://www.redlandsroses.com/En/News.asp (now no longer available – last seen 2008).

Organization and management

Gitothua Centre is managed by a director with assistance from a nurse. The director reports to the Red Lands Roses human resources manager. As shown in the following sections, the project has a strong participatory component. Representatives from the community are part of the project steering committee and play a key role in decision-making related to both childcare issues and resources allocation.

Childcare staff

The centre is staffed by 15 employees: a director, a nurse, ten caregivers and three support staff (two cooks and one gardener). All have permanent worker status, although they are classified as non-unionizable staff; as such the CBA for flower growers, including the provisions on overtime compensation, does not apply to them. Red Lands Roses Ltd and Pollen Ltd also support periodic visits to the family physician and paediatrician and provide full coverage for all health-related expenditures and related transportation costs. Monthly salaries range from 90 USD for caregivers and support staff to 343 USD for the nurse. In addition, childcare staff are covered by health insurance, the pension fund, a housing allowance and a transport allowance on annual leave. Internal training is provided periodically.

Costs and funding mechanisms

The project was carried out in the framework of the Public–Private Partnership (PPP) grant from the German Development Bank (DEG) and the Max Havelaar Foundation, which awards a fair trade label to socially responsible companies. Through the partnership, the DEG provided an initial investment grant (150,000 euro in this case) to build a community-run project while the private outfits, Red Lands Roses and Pollen Ltd, committed to a corresponding amount to run the project. Parents pay a monthly nominal fee of 500 KShs (about 7 USD)[45] per child. This amount represents around 10 per cent of the real cost, and 7 per cent of an average income at Red Lands Roses.

The project is managed by a steering committee of representatives from the community, Red Lands Roses, Pollen Ltd and the Max Havelaar Foundation.

---

[45] The exchange rate used is 1 USD = 67 KShs (July 2007).

According to the Max Havelaar labelling mechanism, the price of roses sold in Europe is 12 per cent higher. This difference reverts to the workers of Red Lands Roses, who can use it for community-welfare projects. Funds are entirely managed by workers through the steering committee. Part of the Max Havelaar bonus has been used to support the Gitothua Children and Community Centre. The community identified a key group of people, who have been trained to manage and monitor the childcare facility.

Employer perspective

The management of Red Lands Roses reports that the creation of Gitothua Day Care has reduced women's absenteeism (unpaid leave for urgent matters) and unplanned annual leave to care for their sick children. These absences reduced both their earnings and productivity and, therefore, the company's output delivery. After the Gitothua crèche opened, unplanned leave for caring for sick children decreased by 25 per cent in 2006. The same lower rate was expected in 2007, according to the trends registered during the first six months of the year.

Aside from absenteeism, the management sees several broad benefits to childcare.

> It is important for a company to have healthy and concentrated workers. Often workers are undernourished and sleep only four hours. For women, childcare is a main source of stress. All these factors affect productivity. That's why our company believes in the importance of childcare. It helps workers concentrate more and produce better. It also has an impact on their loyalty and commitment. If they feel that we take care of them and their children, they would not leave the company after investment in their training. (Red Lands Roses director)

Employee perspective

Parents value the high quality of the facilities and the services provided, in particular the professionalism of caregivers. In particular, parents appreciate that their children receive much better-quality care, compared to the services they would otherwise secure from domestic workers. They noted that private childcare would be double the cost, but of much poorer quality.

A number of mothers had relied on domestic workers to help with childcare, and experienced considerable stress at work as a result, which affected their concentration and productivity. They worried about the harmful effects on their kids, some of whom were sick quite often or showed signs of ill treatment. A rose grader at Red Lands Roses who used to hire a child domestic worker said:

> My former maid was 14 years old and I paid her 1,200 KES per month [around 18 USD]. When I was at work I could not concentrate. I was not sure my child would be well fed and looked after adequately. Once she left him alone and did not show up any more.

Since Gitothua opened, parents have been able to work more peacefully and efficiently. They can more easily achieve their daily quotas and even earn bonuses for extra production. They see a definite improvement in their families' living standards and their children's health and social skills. Indeed the improvement in children's health has meant that they are sick less often.

Moreover, the service seems to have particularly benefited single mothers, who experience great economic and social hardship because, on their own, they must guarantee food security, care and education for their children. For example, when asked how her life had changed since the crèche was created, one single mother reported that she could now afford both a lunch and transportation to work, instead of walking for almost an hour per day. Before Gitothua was open, the costs of hiring a domestic worker (about 20 USD per month) and feeding her child left no money for lunch or transportation. She would skip lunch, subsisting through the work day on just a cup of tea and a piece of bread at breakfast, a practice that was not good for her health and was likely to undermine her performance at work.

Lessons learned

Childcare has been key to improving parents' working conditions and earnings at Red Lands Roses and has reduced absenteeism related to family responsibilities. When childcare is not available, workers, especially women, are more likely to be absent (taking unpaid leave, annual days or sick days off) to care for a sick child or to replace an unreliable maid. Absenteeism and unplanned annual leave due to a sick child carries heavy costs for workers' earnings or rest time and for employers' output.

Childcare improves educational outcomes not only for those who attend but also for older siblings who might otherwise be kept at home to look after younger siblings. As the nurse at the Gitothua facility noted, "Lack of childcare obliges children as young as 5 years old to be charged of the care of their young siblings." When adequate childcare is not available, those who cannot afford a domestic worker may have no choice other than deploying an older sibling.

Finally, it is important to highlight the benefit of the international partnership which helped start the initiative. It represents a good example for other companies in industrialized countries that are buying from producers in developing countries.

South Africa   **12**

Jill Cawse[1]

National overview

As a developing country, South Africa has recognized childcare as a national priority yet progress has been hampered by many challenges. A number of historical and social factors have contributed to the many problems facing the current government on issues relating to children and families. Characterized by widespread poverty, HIV/AIDS and the erosion of traditional family support structures, investment in the education, health and development of children is considered an essential part of South Africa's socio-economic development. However, the related problems of working parents have received much less attention. Government policy is to support early childhood development facilities in disadvantaged communities. Workplace support for childcare is rare.

[1] Jill Cawse is a freelance consultant on human resources and HIV and AIDS in the workplace and is based in Port Elizabeth. She would like to thank the staff of the companies involved and of the childcare facilities for their collaboration on this project.

Family responsibility for children

Family members such as grandparents, cousins, sisters and aunts traditionally play a key role in providing childcare support for working families. In the African culture, the concept of *Ubuntu* is strong, resulting in extended family arrangements which encourage childcare support.[2] With the HIV and AIDS epidemic, South Africa had an estimated 1.2 million AIDS orphans in 2005 and so the burden of childcare on the surviving women in the family is increasing.

Another factor which contributes to the disruption of traditional family structures and impacts on childcare is the old apartheid system, which saw African people based in homelands or pockets of land within the country. This policy of separateness has resulted in many families maintaining a rural homestead where the grandparents retire, the unemployed stay and young children remain while parents live in the urban areas to earn money to send to the family in the rural area.

This often results in a worker having two homes – one in the city and one in the rural area, with a partner and possibly children in each area. This has been a direct result of the migrant labour system that was set up to ensure a supply of labour for the mines and is one of the legacies of apartheid. This also leads to the increased spread of HIV and AIDS due to long-term concurrent multi-partner relationships. In terms of childcare, the young children are either cared for in the urban areas by carers at home or in community childcare facilities, or grow up in the rural areas with very little access to resources.

Women's participation rates in the workforce have steadily increased and parents often have little option but to leave increasing numbers of children to fend for themselves at home, especially after school. Many social problems can be related to this lack of supervision, ranging from substance abuse to the onset of early sexual encounters and associated issues of teenage pregnancy, and the transmission of HIV and sexually transmitted infections.

Working conditions and family responsibilities

Women's participation rates are high and, in 2007, women comprised almost half (47.6 per cent) of the economically active population. The overall structure of employment is:

---

[2] Former President Nelson Mandela has spoken of *Ubuntu*, calling upon South Africa's people to unite in support of one another.

- 64 per cent in the non-agricultural formal economy;

- 16 per cent in the informal economy;

- 8 per cent in domestic work (nearly all women); and

- 9 per cent in agriculture.[3]

Women in the informal economy often take their children to work with them as they cannot afford to pay for childcare and may not have family to call upon. For a domestic worker, it is not uncommon to leave her children with family in the rural area or closer to home with urban-based family members, especially when she lives at the employer's place. In these circumstances, the domestic worker may not see her children for months at a time as distance and lack of time prevent her from travelling back to her home very often.

Parents in the formal economy typically work full time (40–45 hours per week) with three weeks' annual leave, much less than the approximately 15 weeks of school holidays. Part-time and flexible work arrangements occur rarely in formal settings but, in domestic employment, many work part time. Contract employment, which increases or decreases depending on production needs, as well as shift work, are predominant in sectors such as manufacturing and health.

In the case of emergencies, workers (including fathers on the birth of a child) can take up to three days of family responsibility leave to attend to a sick child or for a family member. This does provide some assistance to workers as this is paid leave provided by employers. For other circumstances, parents have to utilize family members or make ad hoc arrangements for emergencies. Strikes in the schools during 2007 left many parents helpless and without childcare facilities. Many children stay at home in these circumstances without adult supervision. Pregnant workers are entitled to at least four consecutive months of unpaid maternity leave to be taken one month before their due date, or earlier or later as agreed or required for health reasons.

National policies on childcare

Since 1994, the ANC-led government has acted to address the needs of children and the inequities of the past. Welfare and social security spending, including subsidies for early childhood development facilities (ECDs), was set to increase by over 14 per cent in 2008 and to account for nearly 15 per cent of total government

---

[3] Statistics South Africa, 2007a.

spending (almost 5 per cent of GDP). Recent reforms acknowledge that "the care and development of young children must be the foundation of social relations and the starting point of human resources development strategies from community to national levels".[4]

In 1996, the National Programme of Action for Children (2000 and Beyond) was established for better coordination between government departments, NGOs and related parties for improved services to children. Great emphasis has been placed on early childhood development (ECD), bringing sectors together for the full development of the child – primary health care, nutrition, sanitation and clean water, birth registration, protection from abuse and violence, psychosocial support and early childhood care and education.

The two key departments involved with childcare facilities are:

- The **Department of Social Development** (DSD), which is responsible for providing social grants and subsidies to registered ECD sites and the provision of psychosocial programmes where needed.

- The **Department of Education** (DOE), which has prioritized ECD within the education sector and is responsible for phasing in Grade R as a Reception year prior to Grade 1, for accreditation of early childhood development providers and for inter-sectoral programmes for children aged 0–4 years.

The Department of Local Government and Local Authorities, including municipalities, also has a mandate for early childhood development facilities. The local municipality is required to approve ECD services as part of the registration process, and many have by-laws that regulate and monitor daycare facilities and childminding (up to six children cared for by a private person).

Government policy is to use childcare subsidies for community facilities that cater for the disadvantaged. There has been a move to withdraw subsidies previously provided to workplace facilities (as they are private facilities) in favour of NGO community-based facilities for the poor. There are no legislative requirements or incentives for employers to provide childcare facilities.

Childcare facilities

The compulsory education age in South Africa is 7 years. When children are not in school, options for childcare for working parents include:

---

[4] UNESCO, IBE, 2006b.

- ECD centres/crèches (private or community based, some school based, rare at workplaces);
- playgroups (home-based centres);
- after-school centres (mainly attached to schools but with limited facilities);
- home-based caring in the child's or other home (nanny/childminders);
- family member or friends; or
- a combination of the above.

The under-7s

The percentage of children under 7 years attending ECD sites increases with age. Just 5 per cent of under-3s are enrolled in ECD sites, compared to 15 per cent of children between 3 and 5 and 21 per cent of children between 5 and 7.[5]

Thus, few children receive any preschool education before starting Grade 1. Most are in childcare arrangements at home with informal caregivers, and often lack adult attention, access to educational toys and equipment, or learning experiences outside their immediate environment. Furthermore, in formal childcare centres in poor communities, most caregivers lack resources and training, and few children go through a formal reception year programme at age 5–6 before starting Grade 1. African children are somewhat underrepresented in ECD; 73 per cent of enrolled children are African, although Africans constitute 80 per cent of the population.[6]

About half of ECD sites are community-based facilities: of a total of 21,892 sites in 2000, 49 per cent were community based, 34 per cent home based and 17 per cent school based. Twelve per cent of these open for less than five hours per day, 68 per cent operate between five and ten hours a day and 20 per cent operate for more than ten hours a day. Most home-based sites stay open for longer than ten hours to cater for after-school childminding.[7]

Minimum standards must be in place before a facility will be registered, but where a facility meets most of these standards, it can be conditionally registered and eligible for subsidies to help it to meet the minimum standards. There is currently a drive by the DSD for registration of ECD sites, as about one-third are currently not registered. At least 1,500 additional centres were registered from April 2006 to March 2007, with even more expected in 2008.

---

[5] Williams and Samuels, 2001.

[6] Statistics South Africa, 2007b. Figures for the other groups are as follows (% of the population: % of the age group enrolled): coloured 8.9:10; Indian/Asian 2.5:2; white 9.1:13.

[7] Williams and Samuels, 2001.

On the educational side, the pre-primary programme provided at most ECD centres has two components, namely:

- Grade R (Reception year) preceding Grade 1, which prepares 6-year-olds; and

- Pre-Grade R programmes, which cater for children between 0 and 4 years.

It is the DOE's aim for 100 per cent of Grade 1 children to have participated in an accredited Grade R programme by 2010. Enrolment went from 280,000 in 2002 to 500,000 in 2004. Public expenditure has increased from 12 million rand (R) in 1995 to R538 million in 2005. A total of 54,503 teachers are employed in the pre-primary sector, but only 12 per cent are trained.[8]

Most pre-primary schools operate Monday to Friday during school term time. The hours are usually 7.30 a.m. to 12.30 p.m. and some offer after-school care. The after-school facilities usually operate from 12.30 p.m. to 3.00 p.m. or up to 5.00 p.m.

Cost to parents

Fees are the principal source of income in the ECD sector and more than a quarter report that they have no other source of income.[9] Monthly fees vary enormously by community, ranging from less than R25 per month (33 per cent) to over R75 per month (33 per cent).[10] In half of the sites charging fees of less than R25 per month, parental fees are not paid. Many sites are financially crippled.

Childminders (either in a small group at the childminder's home or at the home of the child) are sometimes preferred for children under 3 and costs range from R800 to R2,500 per month. Due to costs, this option is mainly limited to the high-income earners while low-income earners rely on family and social networks.

ECDs in poorer communities are targeted for subsidies and support. Public pre-primary schools as well as NGO facilities receive funding from the DSD. ECD sites, once registered, qualify for grants based on a range of requirements. A "place of care" grant may be paid to a registered site for children older than 1 month. In the next financial year, subsidies of at least R9 per child per day will be provided countrywide. A total of 314,000 children from poor households

---

[8] UNESCO, IBE, 2006b, table 1.3.3.
[9] Williams and Samuels, 2001.
[10] In July 2008. 1 US$ = 7.6 R.

received subsidies in 2007. An additional 435,000 children were targeted for subsidies in 2008.

The parents still need to pay the difference to cover the fee. However, many parents cannot afford even this additional amount. In 2000, more than 50 per cent of sites recovered less than half their fees. But they continue to take the children as they receive government subsidies. The quality in such facilities is very poor and is reflected in the low salaries of childcare workers: 44 per cent earn less than R500 per month.[11]

School-age children

Full-time working parents must arrange before- and after-school childcare as both primary and secondary schools end at 2.30 p.m. Recent government interventions include extending extracurricular services at schools to increase the use of these facilities and to provide care for children without adult supervision in the afternoons. However, extracurricular activities are still provided mainly at private or parent-funded schools.

School holidays are quite difficult as parents have to resort to a mix of childcare from formal providers, family members and holiday clubs (these are run by churches, youth groups and sports clubs). These clubs can be expensive for parents and not affordable for many.

The workplace and childcare support

Work-based initiatives for childcare are few and far between and very little private–public partnering appears to be occurring. Employer and union efforts to help workers with childcare have been somewhat limited in South Africa.

Childcare benefits are on the agenda for unions, and Cosatu, one of the main trade union federations, addressed this issue in the Women's Day 2007 Resolution. But competing priorities such as basic wages tend to result in issues of gender and children taking a back seat. There are a few cases where the union has been instrumental in bringing in a childcare facility at a workplace, an example being NUMSA at BMW (see the case study below).

In our research, we found very few examples of organizations that provide childcare benefits for employees, although indications are that more businesses

---

[11] Biersteker, 2001.

are implementing family-friendly initiatives. Often this extends to paid maternity leave and even paternity leave, but very few have gone so far as to provide childcare support. A childcare facility on-site is seen by most managers as the only form of childcare support and thus business has been slow to respond to childcare needs, given the costs of such a facility.

There is not much evidence of government or business engaging in any dialogue concerning work–family issues. Nor do businesses seem to partner with community organizations or childcare facilities to improve workers' access to childcare.

Recently, more companies are considering the provision of ECD at the workplace, particularly in the financial sector. Two of the cases that follow come from the financial sector – Old Mutual in Cape Town and First National Bank Head Office in Johannesburg. A key motivating factor in the financial sector is the retention and attraction of skilled professional employees. Senior leaders in the organizations were key drivers of these initiatives, often due to their personal experiences as fathers of young children.

Examples of childcare facilities were also found in the health-care sector where, as in other countries, shift work and high numbers of female employees make childcare a problem for many workers. A final example is of a wine farm, which shows how childcare facilities in an isolated rural area can be of considerable help to both the employees and the employer.

Conclusion

South Africa provides an example of a developing country experience where the country is facing competing priorities and many social and economic challenges with limited means. Early childhood development has been recognized as a key issue but the problems of working parents much less so. Yet the two are inextricably linked. Government has implemented far-reaching reforms to deal with the crisis of children in the country, but it is going to take many years to make the improvements that are so desperately needed. There might be scope for greater engagement of the business sector in public–private partnerships for childcare support, given the implications for the labour market and the well-being of working parents and the next generation.

BMW South Africa

Type of business. Car manufacturing.

Workplace. Two worksites: the Rosslyn factory with 3,000 employees, mostly manufacturing workers and technical experts, and the Midrand office with 400 employees, mostly professional and sales employees.

Working hours. A three-shift manufacturing operation: a 40-hour week from 8 a.m. to 4.30 p.m. on average in the administrative offices.

Childcare solution. Two early learning centres for children aged 3–6 years. Both provide some emergency back-up care and care during school holidays.

Partners. Trade union (NUMSA); childcare consultant.

In South Africa, BMW, the well-known German car manufacturer, has two main sites: the Rosslyn factory just outside Pretoria and a marketing and services division based in Midrand in Johannesburg.

The early learning centres at BMW were established in 1989 at the Rosslyn factory and in 1992 at the Midrand office, in direct response to a union demand on behalf of employees. According to a company representative, when BMW started to employ more women, the National Union of Metalworkers of South Africa (NUMSA) approached the company regarding on-site childcare facilities. Consultations followed and the company agreed to provide the facility.

The main company objectives of setting up the childcare centres seem to have been to socially invest in family-friendly benefits for their employees, which includes flexible working hours and family emergency leave as well. The company acknowledges other business gains such as reduced absenteeism, but these were not the main reasons they introduced the facilities. Good-quality education is provided for children of employees, who often come from disadvantaged communities. The facilities offer an excellent curriculum with well-qualified teachers and support staff.

Early learning centres

Both facilities are on company premises in walking distance of the factory and offices. The schools are open Monday to Friday, 7.00 a.m. to 5.00 p.m. All meals are provided. The facilities are closed weekends, public holidays and during the December/January shutdown. The schools are well equipped with toilets, washbasins, classrooms, covered verandas and outdoor play areas.

The schools only cater to children of 3–6 years. The facility management considers children younger than 3 to be vulnerable to illness and better off in home care. Back-up arrangements can be made in the case of emergency. A limited care programme is offered during school holidays for school-age children.

Health services are provided by the on-site medical centre at the factory and at the Midrand site medical centre. All children have medical records kept at the medical centre and immunization is provided by the local clinic.

Eligibility and use

The facility is open to all employees and used by parents from all levels of the organization. Midrand is currently full to capacity with 45 children. The Rosslyn facility can cater for 80 children and currently has 66 enrolled. The principal reports that employees are having fewer children, hence less demand. Only children who attended the centre can utilize the facilities for holiday care.

Finance and management

Start-up costs were covered by BMW and donations, mostly from parents. The company owns the buildings and oversaw construction in the mid-1980s. The school principal sourced all educational equipment and school furniture and interviewed the teachers and other support staff with the help of the human resources department.

Fees paid by employees are extremely reasonable at R380 per month for salaried staff and R340 per month for hourly paid workers (approximately 6 per cent of their salaries). The costs are heavily subsidized by BMW. BMW pays teachers' salaries and benefits as well as cleaning and security contracts. Parental fees cover the food and day-to-day running of the schools.

The facility is managed and run by the general manager of the learning and development division and the school principal. The governing body is made up of the principal, the general manager and the human resources director.

The parents and the union can visit the school and attend meetings held twice a year. Parents are encouraged to ask questions and/or offer suggestions on the running of the schools. The union is consulted on any changes or problems at the facility.

The schools are registered pre-primary schools and regularly inspected by the DSD and the DOE and by the Independent Schools Association of Southern Africa (ISASA).

The staff

One principal oversees the running of both facilities. Each school has three qualified teachers and an assistant teacher. The number of children per worker is approximately 20:1. The teachers are well qualified; three have a four-year degree in pre-primary education and four have teaching diplomas. All staff can study further through the Education Scheme at BMW, and can take e-learning courses, attend workshops and conferences or further their studies through a university.

Teachers' and teaching assistants' salaries range from about R5,000 to R11,000 per month, plus bonuses (13th cheque, performance bonus and profit share bonus), pension and medical aid. Hours of work are flexible between 7.00 a.m. and 5.00 p.m. Staff seem to have excellent working conditions and appear happy in their environment.

Management perspective

It does not appear that any assessment of benefits to the company has been conducted. Although the company reports less absenteeism among employees due to child commitments, this is not measured and no direct link has been made between the two. The company believes that it has a corporate responsibility to educate and create better opportunities for the children of employees. The company also benefits from a more committed workforce as workers know their children are being looked after in a caring environment at the workplace.

Employee/union perspective

The union supports the initiative and is well informed and consulted, and the facilities are well appreciated and well used by parents. They are offered very reasonable fees, excellent facilities, qualified teachers and balanced meals for their children. Their children are provided with a strong start in life, which many would not have been able to afford if working for another company.

Lessons learned

In South Africa, this facility is considered the best practice by which others are measured. This is undoubtedly a huge success but does require massive input from the company. The principal reports receiving visits from many large companies, from mining houses to banks and manufacturers. Some have gone on to set up great facilities while others have not – perhaps intimidated by the costs and perceived legal implications.

BMW believes that the following lessons can be learnt from their experience:

- A consultative approach must be used when establishing and running the childcare facility.

- It is critical to enlist the services of an experienced and qualified professional to guide the set-up process to avoid unnecessary mistakes.

- All equipment purchased should be of a very good quality as inferior equipment will only cost more in the long run as it does not last.

- The principal should be able to select all the staff as he/she would have the knowledge needed for this task. Other employees of the company must also be available during the selection process to serve on the selection panel.

First National Bank (FNB) Head Office, Johannesburg

Type of business. Financial services, banking.

Workplace. Head office, downtown Johannesburg.

Workers. Over 8,000 employees at head office, mostly financial and related professionals, business consultants, administrators, clerical and all associated logistics and human resources personnel.

Working hours. Predominantly a 40-hour working week although some work much longer hours as part of the corporate culture.

Childcare solution. Childcare centre for children aged 3 months to 6 years.

Partners. Childcare consultant; trade union (SASBO).

First National Bank (FNB) is one of the four largest commercial banks in South Africa. It is a major player in commercial, corporate and personal banking, with 700 branches throughout the country and 26,000 employees.

FNB opened its childcare facility in 2008 after four years of research, planning and construction. The key motivator is to attract and retain employees in this competitive sector where skills are becoming paramount. The bank reports that it needs to attract not only local skilled personnel but also personnel from overseas who expect benefits on par with elsewhere. Providing a childcare facility for employees is thus part of its human resources strategy and was identified in an employee survey as a need.

One of the key challenges was finding space to house the facility. After much investigation, the bank decided to renovate two floors of an existing downtown building situated close to Bank City. FNB, through its Bank City management team, appointed a project manager and a specialized architect to convert the space into a school. Research into preschool childcare was undertaken by a team in FNB in consultation with various experts. Representatives on the in-house team included specialists in industrial relations, human resources, finance, legal affairs, occupational health and maintenance.

A consultative approach has been used throughout the project with all stakeholders, including the finance sector trade union (SASBO). The in-house management team handling this project did comprehensive research and prepared thorough analysis based on information available. Checklists supplied by the relevant authorities were reviewed and risk analysis conducted.

The childcare centre

The facility caters for up to 240 children from 3 months to 6 years old on a full-time basis from Monday to Friday. The school is split into two areas, namely the nursery and the preschool. The nursery takes babies aged 3 months to 2 years, and toddlers from 2–3 years. From 3 years to 6 years, a pre-primary school curriculum is followed, meeting Gauteng Education Department (GDE) requirements.

Opening hours are 7.30 a.m. to 5.30 p.m., Monday to Friday, closed on weekends and public holidays. It will however remain open for the school holidays with the exception of three weeks at Christmas holidays in December.

Children are provided with meals and snacks prepared in the school kitchen under the supervision of the bank's canteen in the building. In line with the daycare guidelines, a separate sick room is provided. In the event that children fall ill, they can be isolated in this sick bay until the parents can collect them and take them home. For medical support, there is a primary care clinic on the FNB Precinct.

The facility meets all health and hygiene regulations and is registered with the Department of Social Development and the ISASA. As a private school, the facility does not get any government subsidies or grants.

Eligibility and use

The facility is open to all permanent and contract employees of FNB. Both mothers and fathers who are employees are eligible. Although the facility has been open less than a year, 70 children are enrolled, and enrolments for children under 3 are already at full capacity.

Finance and management

The facility is run on a cost-recovery non-profit basis. Childcare staff are employed by FNB and receive the same benefits as other bank employees.

The bank will run the unit as any other division in the organization, where management will be held accountable for the successful running of the facility. A highly qualified and experienced principal has been recruited to run the facility and an "owner/manager" culture will apply. Teachers are all qualified with the necessary experience in preschool teaching.

Employees pay R1,400 per month per child, which compares favourably with other childcare facilities provided in the finance sector (FNB advised that their research showed that other financial institutions charge approximately R1,700 to R1,900).

Management perspective

Management is heavily committed to this initiative, as witnessed by the significant investments made. Once the decision was made, the process forward was relatively smooth, with ownership resting with senior management. Apart from attracting and retaining staff, management sees the value in contributing to corporate social investment through providing access to education and care for the children of employees.

Employee/union perspective

SASBO confirmed that it has participated in the consultative team formed by the bank. SASBO has over the years lobbied for improvements in working conditions, including the issue of childcare facilities; however, past efforts had been without much success, economic costs being prohibitive.

The union would like more workers to be able to benefit from such facilities, particularly in high concentration work areas. It is generally accepted that this type of facility can only be provided where sufficient numbers justify a centre. The bank has indicated that one other site may be considered but that the newly opened centrally based facility will need to be assessed before making further expansion commitments.

Lessons learned

Based on its experience so far, FNB feels its success results from:

- careful planning and assessment;
- getting "buy in" from all relevant internal and external stakeholders;
- using professionals to do the work to ensure quality; and
- ensuring senior management ownership.

Old Mutual Head Office, Cape Town

Type of business. Financial services, insurance.

Workplace. Head office – Old Mutual Park, Cape Town.

Workers. Over 8,000 workers, mostly financial and insurance professionals, sales representatives, business consultants, and all associated logistics and human resources personnel.

Working hours. Predominantly a 40-hour working week for all employees with senior executives and management and professional levels working much longer hours as part of the corporate culture. Sales representatives and business consultants have flexitime; many employees have Internet access from their homes, so they can rely on distance working; administrative staff work regular full-time hours.

Childcare solution. On-site childcare facility which can cater for up to 375 children from ages 3 months to 6 years.

Partners. Childcare consultant.

Old Mutual is the largest and most established financial service provider in southern Africa. Historically, Old Mutual had planned to have a childcare facility at its Cape Town head office for the past 20 years but it never got off the ground until recently. This was largely due to the financial implications as well as lack of interest from a male-dominated workforce.

The company reports that there was considerable pressure from women in the organization for childcare benefits. In addition, the newly appointed MD has young children himself and is sympathetic to the needs of working women and families. The company surveyed employees and conducted a needs analysis. Of 8,000 employees at Old Mutual Park, 1,700 responses were in favour of providing childcare at work.

A consultant oversaw the design and construction of the childcare centre which opened in April 2008. The team worked closely with the Departments of Education, Social Development and Health to ensure that the facility would be in line with government standards.

Childcare programme

The new early learning centre, Greens'cool, has been built next to the main building so is easily accessible by employees.[12] In every respect the facility meets requirements relating to space, ventilation and hygiene, as well as toilet facilities, kitchen and educational resources. This is a fully accredited site with the Department of Social Development and is registered as a private facility.

The centre is open from Monday to Friday from 7.00 a.m. to 6.00 p.m. throughout the year, staying open during school holidays. It is large and can take up to 375 children. There are 13 classrooms and a nursery. The nursery takes children from ages 3 months to 17 months. There are classes for children aged 18–23 months, 2–3 years, 3–4 years, 4–5 years and Grade R.

An extensive security system has been installed to ensure the safety of children and others at the facility. The latest fingerprint technology is used to control access to the centre.

Eligibility and use

The facility is only open to permanent and contract employees of Old Mutual. Both mothers and fathers who are employees are eligible. As the Mutual Park building is zoned "business" the childcare facility cannot be extended to anyone other than an employee of the company (this seems to be a limitation placed by the municipality).

---

[12] For more details see http://www.omgreenscool.co.za [11 June 2009].

Demand for the facility has been high; it opened in April 2008 with 97 children and by May 2009, 273 were enrolled. Services for children under 3 are full to capacity. Services for older children still have space but are expected to reach capacity as younger children progress through the programme.

Finance and management

The cost of setting up the facility to date has been approximately R25 million and has been totally funded by the company. Employees pay school fees of R1,100 per child per month. This is a very reasonable cost compared to other private facilities. Parental fees and fundraising or donations if needed are expected to cover operational costs. Although still early, the project is on track to be a successful facility which is self-funded and provides a high standard of quality care.

The staff employed at the childcare centre are mainly employees of Old Mutual, with an independent consultant contracted to oversee the day-to-day running of the facility. A parent board is being established to assist in fundraising and running the facility.

A unique arrangement exists where Old Mutual is exploring options with the South African Revenue Services (SARS) to allow this to be a pre-tax benefit for Old Mutual employees utilizing this service. This is a remarkable initiative between the private sector and government to assist employees with childcare benefits which results in real savings for the employee. However, this is yet to be finalized and confirmed.

The staff

There are 62 staff, including teachers and caregivers, two nurses, administrative staff and cleaners. All teachers are qualified and get regular updated training through the Parent Council, which runs courses for the teachers as well as the parents.

Management perspective

The company is committed to providing childcare facilities at its head office in Cape Town to provide social support for employees and their children and to attract and retain quality staff. It is very pleased with the facility and is considering facilities at offices in other cities.

Employee perspective

Parents are very happy with the crèche and demand has been good and steadily increasing. The convenience of having children close to working parents is well established.

Lessons learned

Lessons learned include:

- the importance of using expertise in childcare when establishing a site to ensure that all aspects are considered; and

- the importance of conducting analysis on the cost–benefit ratio of providing childcare.

The benefits include attracting and retaining skilled employees and reducing absenteeism; and the corporate responsibility investment of facilitating access to quality care and education through on-site facilities for children of employees.

Melsetter Agricultural Farm

Type of business. Agriculture, wine-producing farm.

Workplace. Vineyards, orchards.

Workers. Approximately 100 men and 100 women.

Working hours. 7.30 a.m. to 5.30 p.m. in winter, 7.00 a.m. to 5.00 p.m. in summer (45 minutes for lunch).

Childcare solution. On-site childcare facility for children aged 0–6 years; holiday and after-school care.

Partners. None.

Melsetter is a privately owned 360-hectare farm producing fruit and wine and is part of a larger group. It is located near Somerset East in the Western Cape, approximately 150 km from Cape Town.

Most of the workers live in the approximately 50 houses on the farm. Originally from Ladismit, a town close to the farm, most of these families have lived on the farm for over 20 years. The community includes extended families as well as single parents.

The Graymead Daycare Centre was started by management in 1987 as the nearest childcare facilities are situated 20 kilometres away. The management felt that they had a responsibility to provide safe care for the children on the farm as well as education in preparation for formal schooling. Prior to the creation of the centre, children of farm workers would stay at home and be cared for by older family members or siblings and supervision was not good. Thus the initiative was seen as both a social investment as well as a business decision to reduce work time lost for childcare. It was also seen as job creation since two ladies from the farm were hired to work at the facility.

The childcare centre

The childcare centre is on the farm, within walking distance of the homes of the farm workers. It is a brick building with a surrounding playground, and has a kitchen, a baby room and two educational rooms. Equipment includes a TV, mattresses, tables, chairs, toys and equipment. While in need of a bit of attention, the facility appears to be of a good standard.

The centre is open from 7.00 a.m. to 5.00 p.m., Monday to Friday, and it is closed on weekends and public holidays. It is open during school holidays except for about three weeks during the December school holidays. The children are provided with breakfast, tea-time snacks and a nutritious cooked lunch. A registered primary health-care nurse is always available for any emergencies as the centre is located next to the farm clinic.

The centre seeks not only to provide good care for the children but also basic educational learning to prepare them for formal schooling. While no formal curriculum is followed, educational exercises are in line with current teaching protocols for children in pre-primary school.

Eligibility and use

All employees who live on the farm can enrol their children between the ages of 6 months and 5 years. In line with the company's policy of supporting social development in the local community, the school will accept children from outside the farm. However, no applications have been received, probably because of the distance to the farm.

The facility can take up to 40 children, but currently only 14 children are enrolled. At one stage, 30 children were using the facility. One reason numbers are down is that employees are not having as many children as in the past.[13] Another reason cited is what the employer refers to as the "granny syndrome": some children stay with grandmothers at home (in the farm community) until Grade R. There seems to be a belief that children are better off at home and a lack of understanding of how critical the crèche is for children's development and school preparedness. Also, despite very low fees, cost savings are another reason why children are left with granny.

Occasionally schoolchildren will utilize the facility but there is not a big demand for this. Currently five children use the centre after school and during holidays. The school offers a limited holiday programme of supervised play.

Finance and management

Although once registered with the Department of Social Development as a pre-primary crèche receiving government subsidies, the facility no longer draws a subsidy although it remains registered for administrative purposes and is regularly inspected by local authorities. This is due to the numbers of children, which have declined over the past three years, resulting in the subsidy being so minimal that the administrative cost of maintaining the system did not warrant drawing the subsidy. Thus management decided to take on the full cost at this point.

The facility is now registered as a daycare facility (which falls within the scope of an ECD but does not require a formal curriculum or qualified teachers); Grade R has been dropped and is now provided at the local school, approximately 5 kilometres away. The farm provides transport for children attending Grade R.

The centre is still inspected annually by government agencies so an ongoing relationship has continued with government. Possibilities for obtaining government subsidies are being investigated at the moment as well as other possible funding.

The farm's human resources practitioner liaises with centre staff and is responsible for the management of the facility. A qualified teacher who resides on the farm is retained by the company to visit the facility once a week and to provide

---

[13] Nationally, over the last ten years, the fertility rate has declined rapidly from 5.7 children per mother to 2.77.

guidance and training for the unqualified teachers. She acts as a consultant to ensure quality in teaching methods and equipment.

Currently, the facility is financed by the farm and the parents. The farm provides the building, furniture, appliances and so on. Teaching staff are paid by the farm and are entitled to a range of benefits. The total cost per child is estimated at R24 per day, of which the employees pay R5.50 per child per day. The R24 excludes the cost of the HR practitioner and consultant. Management in general is very supportive of the childcare facility and supports fundraising initiatives and other needs.

There is a parent board made up of parents and management members. They meet monthly to give direction to the school and deal with financial issues. The board was a new initiative in 2008 and a lot of support was given by management, but in the long run management would like the board to run itself.

Parents have been more involved with the school since 2008, when the first fundraising event was held. Parents are encouraged to participate and make decisions regarding their children and the facility. The company is striving for an ownership culture whereby parents feel empowered to be involved with the school.

The staff

Two women employees work at the centre: a childcare supervisor and a childcare assistant/cook/cleaner. Thus the ratio of about seven children per staff member is good. The two employees have a Standard 8 education. While they are not qualified teachers they are trained in basic childcare, health and safety and childcare education. They regularly attend training or are being trained by the consultant who visits the facility weekly and is very involved with the day-to-day decisions and training and support for the childcare workers.

The childcare workers work 43.25 hours a week (lunch excluded). They earn R2,570 per month which is more than double the minimum wage for the agriculture sector (which is R1,150 per month). Their benefits further include free housing, subsidized electricity, free water, free transport to town, a provident fund and an annual bonus.

Employee perspective

Parents report that the service is of great benefit to them. In the case of emergency, parents can be at the facility quickly. The local schools have also commented that the facility provides a good basis for schooling and children are well prepared for Grade R compared to other children, progressing much faster in school.

Management perspective

The employer reports that the benefits of having the childcare facility in place include reduced absenteeism and improved productivity of employees. Management is very supportive of the facility but acknowledge that it is due for an upgrade.

Lessons learned

The childcare centre is a good example of what can be achieved by a private company to support low-wage employees with the care and education of their children. The facility functions well with very few problems. This example shows that, for a reasonable cost, employers can provide childcare facilities which are at least as good as, if not better than, many community facilities.

The current challenge is that the cost per child is increasing as the number of children decreases. However, the employer still feels it is important to keep the centre running as it reduces absenteeism and improves productivity while providing a very useful service for the care and education of employees' children, and the company is very committed to social investment within the community.

Lessons from the Melsetter example include:

- the importance of parental involvement as a means of empowering parents and workers to play a role in taking responsibility for their children's future;

- despite educational limitations in resource-limited settings, childcare workers should be carefully selected to ensure that they are genuinely passionate about children and hence their jobs; and

- childcare facilities have both social as well as business benefits and the company reaps the benefits of a happier workforce and community.

Zuid-Afrikaans Hospital, Pretoria

Type of business. Independent private hospital (registered as a section 21 company – incorporated association not for gain).

Workplace. Private hospital (not for profit) based in Pretoria.

Workers. Approximately 275 employees, mostly (90 per cent) female employees who are nurses and some administrative staff.

Working hours. Two shifts are worked by nursing staff – 7.00 a.m. to 7.00 p.m. Some nurses and administrative staff work day shifts from 8.00 a.m. to 5.00 p.m.

Childcare solution. On-site childcare facility (ECD) catering for children from 4 months to 6 years old, providing care during normal working hours (this includes extended hours for shift workers).

Partners. None.

The Zuid-Afrikaans Hospital was founded as a result of the Anglo-Boer War (1899–1902).[14] In 1904, the Boers (Afrikaans speaking) were refused admission to the strictly British military hospital in Pretoria. They wanted their own facility and to be treated in their own language. This led to the establishment of the hospital, which started out as a six-bed nursing facility. It has always been a private general, non-profit, independent hospital funded by various donor agencies. Today, 182 beds and a wide range of medical services are available.

The idea of an on-site crèche for the children of employees was first raised with the Board of Management in 1970, largely through the efforts of a matron employed in the hospital who championed for the facility on behalf of the mostly female workforce in a shift work environment. The crèche was seen as an added benefit for employees and the idea was adopted by the Board, which was supportive from the start and financed the establishment of the crèche as well as making available a former nurse's home to be converted to a school to look after the children of the hospital's working mothers.

Childcare facility

The Kleuterland Childcare Facility caters for children aged 4 months to 6 years. It can accommodate 35 children – 20 in the 3–6 age group and 15 babies from 4 months to 2 and a half years of age. The school is open Monday to Friday from

---

[14] Information found at http://www.zah.co.za/about_history.asp [11 June 2009].

6.00 a.m. to 7.00 p.m. It is closed on weekends, public holidays and three weeks over December during the Christmas holidays.

The facility is not open to school-going children during holidays; only enrolled children may utilize this. At one stage older children were accepted during school holidays, but parents complained that the bigger children were too rough with the smaller children and this practice was stopped.

The school provides a formal Grade R and preschool curriculum in line with Department of Education requirements. Children progress to Grade 1 with a sound Grade R basis. Children are provided with healthy balanced meals, planned and prepared by the in-house hospital food services department.

All physical conditions including size, space and hygiene, as well as toilets, toys and resources, meet DED requirements. Clearly with the hospital at their disposal, medical issues are not of concern. In addition, a qualified nurse is employed as a childcare assistant, so on-site medical care is available.

Eligibility and use

The facility is open to children of hospital employees (nurses, doctors and other employees). In the past the facility accepted children from the surrounding community; however, employee demand has steadily increased so preference has been given to the children of employees. Employees from all levels in the hospital use the facility.

Currently 14 pre-primary children and 13 babies are enrolled. Although slightly under capacity, management and school staff are satisfied with current trends that show an increasing demand from staff.

The staff

The staff consists of a qualified teacher (principal), a crèche assistant (who is a qualified nurse), a supervisor for afternoons and three general workers. All employees are full time except for one half-day post. Salaries and conditions of employment are considered good, and are at least equal to those in other private facilities.

The principal reports that ongoing development and training of staff is a priority. Teachers belong to the Nursery School Association and attend up to two courses a year to stay abreast of developments.

Finance and management

The facility is run and owned by the hospital, which covers the cost of maintenance on the school building, the salaries of the childcare staff, and other expenses such as playground equipment and educational toys. A parents' committee assists with fundraising for the school. Funds raised are used to upgrade equipment and facilities.

Parents pay minimal monthly fees of approximately R650 per month for a half-day service and R850 per month for a full-day service. These fees cover the cost of food for the children.

The crèche is registered as a private facility with the Department of Social Development and with the Department of Education. It is regularly inspected and a close relationship exists between the crèche management and the authorities. The facility once attracted government subsidies but, due to a policy review, these were withdrawn several years back.

Employee/union perspective

The union HOSPERS was not a party to the original initiative, but in principle supports the initiative as a benefit for members. Employees clearly find the facility a great benefit and appreciate having their children close to them at work in the event of emergency or just being able to visit their child at lunchtime, which they regularly do. The standard of education is high, and thus they can enjoy peace of mind that preparation for school is made easier for their children.

Management perspective

Good-quality nursing staff are in short supply in South Africa, thus the crèche is seen as a very important benefit in attracting and retaining staff. The crèche is highlighted as part of the attraction of working at the hospital and is promoted on the web site to attract quality employees.

Lessons learned

After 40 years, Kleuterland Childcare Facility is possibly the first facility of its kind provided by an employer in South Africa, and the fact that it is still operating so successfully is a testimony to the dedication of the management of the hospital and the staff at the school.

The following lessons are highlighted in the hospital example:

- The success of such a facility lies in employing qualified, experienced but most importantly passionate employees to take care of children. It is important that those taking care of children love what they do and do not just see it as a job.

- Strong leadership at the facility (that is, the principal) ensures good management in terms of the quality of the service and financial management.

Thailand

13

Supawadee Petrat[1]

National overview

In Thailand, for the many urban workers on low salaries, the most convenient childcare solution is often to send young children to their grandparents or relatives in rural areas. The distress caused by this practice was a major reason for the childcare initiatives of trade unions in the late 1980s. The case of Thailand is quite unique because the unions have actually set up some childcare centres in industrial areas (two examples are included in this chapter). Although partnerships have been important in the sustainability of these efforts, there is clearly a need for greater support from government and employers to improve the sustainability,

[1] Supawadee Petrat is an activist who works with local and regional NGOs on women, women workers, and youth and human rights issues both within and outside Thailand. She would like to express her sincere gratitude to leaders of the workers' unions, staff, employers, and employees from Phra Pradaeng Industrial Zone (Metal and Steel Workers Union of Thailand), Network of Nawanakhon Labour Unions, Aeronautical Radio of Thailand (AEROTHAI), Business Trade Organization of the Office of the Welfare Promotion Commission for Teachers and Educational Personnel (BOWT) and Nong Nooch Tropical Botanical Garden for their collaboration. She would like to express her appreciation to Arunee Srito and Wilaiwan Saetia of Women Workers' Unity Group (WWUG) for their important cooperation.

quality and quantity of childcare available for working parents, particularly those on low salaries.

Work and childcare

In Thailand, the participation of women in the labour force has always been high and married women continue to be economically active throughout their lives. In March 2008, 45.3 per cent of currently employed workers were women. Of the total female population above 15 years old, about 64 per cent were economically active in 2008 (compared to about 80 per cent for men).[2]

When extended families were living together in villages, the work of mothers posed little problem as grandmothers could look after the children. Indeed, Thai culture expects grandmothers to look after grandchildren. In the past, there were always other people like aunts and uncles and grown-up cousins who could support grandmothers in their role in childcare.

Nowadays, children are still often left with grandparents as parents migrate outside the village or even outside the country for jobs. Grandchildren are left with grandparents in rural areas, and they often have little support either in terms of finance or other people to help. A significant percentage of households in rural areas is composed of persons aged 60 or more living with at least one grandchild but no child or child-in-law. About 10.3 per cent of rural households were these "skip generation households" in 2002, up from 8.9 per cent in 1994.[3]

If the grandparents are poor and the money sent by parents is irregular, it is a burden for them to support young children and this can create hardship for both. Parents typically live far away and have long working hours, little leave and low wages. It is therefore difficult for them to visit their children often or long enough to build bonds with them. Some of the childcare centres described in this chapter were initiatives resulting from the distress of working parents whose children didn't know them when they visited.

Leaders of the Women Workers' Unity Group (WWUG)[4] indicated that workers often have to leave their babies with grandparents or some other relatives in up-country provinces once the 90-day maternity leave is over. They become depressed with little motivation to perform their jobs. They may go back

---

[2] Thailand National Statistics Office, Labor force survey, summary tables. Found at http://web.nso.go.th/eng/en/stat/lfs_e/table8_q408.xls [2 June 2009].

[3] Knodel and Saengtienchai, 2005.

[4] WWUG is a group of women leaders from different workers' unions which was founded in 1992 to protect women's rights.

up-country when their children are ill or because they miss their children, and so are frequently absent. As a result, they lose income and may not receive annual rises or other benefits for which they might be eligible. In some cases, frequent absenteeism can put their jobs in jeopardy.

Childcare facilities

In Thailand, there has been a considerable effort by the Government to provide early childhood education services. The 1997 Constitution states that government must provide basic services, including care and development for young children and families. The National Education Act of 1999 provides that:

- Parents or guardians shall be entitled to state support in bringing up and providing education for their children (section 13(1)).

- Individuals, families, communities, community organizations, private organizations, professional bodies, enterprises and other social institutions, which support or provide basic education, shall be entitled to state support for knowledge and competencies in bringing up those under their care (section 14(1)).[5]

In Thailand, facilities for young children include:

- private and public childcare for under-3s for employed parents;

- kindergarten (for children aged 2 and 3 years);

- preschool classes (in normal primary school, just one year prior to grade 1); and

- child development centres receiving children aged 2–5 years.

The kindergarten and preschool classes are mostly run by government, especially the Ministry of Education, as well as other public and private organizations. The Office of Basic Education Commission (OBEC) under the Ministry of Education has concentrated on expanding access to kindergartens in rural areas, where access and participation rates are lower compared to urban centres. By 2001, OBEC had established a total of 67,200 preschool classes in 29,410 rural primary schools.[6]

At present, most child development centres are managed by local governments. Thus the Department of Local Administration, Ministry of the

---

[5] http://www.edthai.com/act/index.htm [19 June 2009].
[6] UNESCO, IBE, 2006c.

Interior, supervises about 19,000 childcare development centres.[7] The Bangkok Metropolitan Administration itself has 663 centres.

In addition to the Ministry of the Interior, a number of other government ministries have functions concerning childcare:

- The **Ministry of Social Development and Human Security** grants licences to establish private childcare centres, makes monitoring visits and organizes meetings, workshops and training to ensure that centres meet set standards.

- The **Ministry of Education** develops policy and curriculum for early childhood education, develops and promotes technical standards, provides technical assistance, monitors and evaluates the quality of children's development and provides training for teachers and caregivers.

- The **Ministry of Public Health** provides support for promoting children's health, organizing training for caregivers and providing advice on meeting health and sanitation standards.

In 2002, about 2,682,835 children were enrolled in preschool classes, kindergarten and child development centres, of which about 80 per cent were in the public sector.[8]

The National Statistical Office reported that 48 per cent of 3-year-olds and 74 per cent of 4-year-olds were attending early education in 2006, with higher attendance in urban areas (64 per cent compared to 59 per cent in rural areas) and among children in better-off families (78 per cent of children in families in the richest quintile compared to about 55 per cent in poor families).[9]

All types of facilities usually run for the whole day, starting at about 7.30 a.m. or 8.00 a.m. and finishing around 4.00 p.m. or 4.30 p.m. However, for many workers, this is insufficient to cover their working hours. Also, few nurseries operate for 24 hours to accommodate the needs of workers on night shifts. A major problem is the lack of affordable facilities for children under age 2.

For school-going children, school starts at 8.30 a.m. and finishes at 3.30 p.m. and childcare after school is needed. There are some NGOs and religious groups that provide extra-curricular activities, for example the Forward Foundation provides after-school activities for children of low-income families. In general, however, there are few facilities for the care of schoolchildren before or after school and private arrangements must be made. Similarly for school holidays, most children stay at home or are sent back to rural areas.

---

[7] UNESCO, IBE, 2006c.

[8] Thailand, Ministry of Education, Office of the Education Council, 2004.

[9] Thailand, National Statistical Office/UNICEF, 2006.

Initiatives for working parents

A number of government services have their own childcare centres. For example, the Border Patrol Police Bureau of the Royal Thai Police has 15 centres and the Directorate of Education and Training, Royal Thai Airforce, Ministry of Defence, has three centres.[10]

Administrative information available from the Department of Labour Protection and Welfare indicates that there are 67 childcare centres in enterprises: nine belong to government enterprises and the rest to private companies. This is very few given that there are more than 300,000 workplaces throughout the nation.

Given the problems of workers with the hours of community childcare centres, the Ministry of Labour set up a model childcare centre in 1993 and another in 1999 using its regular budget. However, the Bureau of the Budget determined that running childcare centres was not the function of the Ministry, so the Ministry is now trying to keep the two centres from being abolished and to hand them over to another organization.

The Department of Labour Protection and Social Welfare conducted a survey about two years ago to explore the possibility of establishing childcare centres on ten industrial estates. Officials reported that some employers would like to establish childcare centres, but the costs deterred them from doing so. For the most part, however, managers do not pay attention to the issue of childcare.

In 2004, five ministries (Labour, Education, the Interior, Public Health, Social Development and Human Security) signed a Memorandum of Understanding (MOU) to coordinate in implementing a Childcare Centre Project for Workers in the Workplace and Community. They agreed to coordinate in providing the financial support, promotion, enhancement and maximization of the project. The Department of Labour Protection and Welfare provides the secretariat and facilitates coordination among involved agencies.

The Department has organized workshops on the issue of work and childcare. It has also included having a childcare centre among the criteria for the prizes given to enterprises for providing good working conditions.

Labour organizations have been advocating for childcare centres since 1987, when the International Confederation of Free Trade Unions (ICFTU), in collaboration with the Labour Congress of Thailand and the Thai Trade Union Congress, worked to support the roles of women workers. The need for childcare centres was one of the issues that encouraged women workers to participate in

---

[10] Thailand, Ministry of Education, Office of the Education Council, 2004.

the unions and take higher level functions. Some study trips to Singapore and Japan were organized. After that, some unions actually established preschool childcare centres, such as the Siam Textile Labour Union (currently run by the Metal and Steel Workers Union of Thailand – see the case study below), the Labour Union of the Thai Blanket Industry and Textiles, the Labour Union of Lucky 3 Textile and the Network of Nawanakhon Labour Unions (see the case study below).

The Women Workers' Unity Group has been advocating for the provision of childcare. Each year, since 1993, this issue has been included on the agenda for the International Women's Day, demanding that government set up childcare centres in industrial communities.[11] Advocacy by the WWUG was instrumental in bringing about the 2004 Memorandum of Understanding on coordination between the five ministries for the Childcare Centre Project for Workers in the Workplace and Community.

Senior members of the WWUG feel that, since signing the MOU, no significant progress has been made, except for a couple of meetings organized with the workers. They note that the existing childcare centres do not sufficiently take into account the needs and the lifestyle of workers. They advocate for government action in ensuring a clear policy and implementation regarding the establishment of childcare centres.

Conclusions

For working parents, having an affordable, reliable childcare centre can make the difference between being able to keep their young children with them and sending them back to their grandparents. As noted by some parents, their children's development is noticeably better when they are at the childcare centre rather than sent to the grandparents.

Employer initiatives for childcare remain rare. Yet, initiatives such as Nong Nooch Botanical Garden below suggest that organizations gain significant benefits from their support for childcare. Setting up a childcare centre may not be feasible for many employers, but other forms of assistance (allowances, subsidized places) and partnerships with the community or trade union initiatives can also be highly valuable.

---

[11] Baker and Wanaboribun, 2004.

Government could consider how it might effectively provide incentives to support the establishment of new daycare centres and strengthen existing centres in communities and workplaces. Priority should be given to ensuring that low-income workers can access childcare that meets their needs in terms of costs and hours. Attention is also needed with regard to the quality of childcare, with more efforts required to strengthen national and local government efforts to train staff, monitor quality and help more centres reach the standards required for registration.

As in many other countries, a number of ministries are involved in childcare, and coordination and coherence is a problem. In addition, the needs of working parents tend to be overlooked. A coordinating body to develop measures for making suitable childcare more available to working parents might be established, consisting of key stakeholders such as government, employers, employees, workers' unions, community representatives and parents as well as experts.

Phra Pradaeng Industrial Zone

Type of business. Manufacturing zone: factories in textiles and garments, metal and steel production, bicycle production, food processing.

Workplace. Phra Pradaeng industrial area, Samut Prakan province (29 kilometres from Bangkok). There are about 2,594 factories.

Workers. Almost 100,000; many are migrants from rural areas.

Working hours. Most work from 8.00 a.m. to 5.00 p.m. although some work in shifts.

Childcare solution. Early childhood centre, holiday and vacation care for school-age children, currently managed by the Metal and Steel Workers Union of Thailand.

Partners. Siam Textile Workers Union, Metal and Steel Workers Union of Thailand, AFL-CIO, Terre des Hommes, local temple, Community Savings Group, Triump Company, Ministry of Social Development and Human Security, Ministry of Public Health, Department of Local Administration (Ministry of Interior) through the municipality (milk and food subsidy).

Phra Pradaeng is one of the most important industrial hubs in Thailand. It houses medium and large industries employing mostly workers who come from the provinces. The Early Childhood Centre was founded in 1989 by workers who were members of the Siam Textile Workers Union. Siam Textile was a spinning mill which employed about 400 workers, 90 per cent of whom were women.

How it started

The story goes that, in 1987, a worker at the Siam Textile factory went home to the countryside to visit her children for the Thai New Year. Upon returning, she cried and told her colleagues that her children treated her as if she was a stranger and refused to hug her. As a common problem among workers, it was brought forward to a meeting of the union committee (six women and two men at that time), which agreed that a preschool centre should be set up for the children of the union's workers and for other workers in the area.

The union began with a survey of workers in the zone, which confirmed their need for childcare. To raise funds, various activities were organized, such as robes ceremonies in different temples and lucky draws.

In 1989, the Early Childhood Centre of the Siam Textile Workers Union opened with one caregiver in a small rented room on the ground floor of an apartment building, and welcomed about 17 preschool children. Later, the centre moved to another building, with funds for rent and utilities donated by Terre des Hommes for one year. The union then purchased the building, contributing 300,000 baht and borrowing the remaining 450,000 baht through an interest-free loan from AFL-CIO.

In 1991, the Siam Textile factory closed and all workers were laid off. The daycare centre was subsequently handed over to the care of the Metal and Steel Workers Union of Thailand, whose workers are employed by the Japanese-owned Aoyoma Thailand Company. A former committee member of the Siam Textile Workers Union volunteered to manage the centre, surviving on a small salary provided by AFL-CIO for the first year.

Childcare programme

Today, 60–70 children from 18 months to 4 years old attend the centre. It is open from Monday to Saturday, 6.00 a.m. to 6.00 p.m. Some days, it stays open until 9.00 p.m. as parents have to work overtime. In such cases, parents pay 10 baht per hour extra. Children sometimes stay overnight with staff living at the centre because their parents fail to turn up after drinking too much. The centre also provides holiday services for school-age children, although most stay with older siblings at home on the holidays.

Located in a two-storey building in the community, the centre is 35 m² with two classrooms, a kitchen and bathrooms. Equipment includes TV, VCD player, toys, glasses, toothbrushes and bedding.

Daily schedule

6.00 a.m.	Children arrive, and are fed with food prepared by parents. Some parents stay to give their children breakfast.
8.30 a.m.–9.30 a.m.	Playtime, wash hands and feet.
9.30 a.m.–10.00 a.m.	Physical exercise, hygiene inspection (fingernails, hair, clothing). Each child is then given one milk pack.
10.00 a.m.–11.30 a.m.	Self-help skills such as toilet use, getting dressed, along with activities such as bead stringing, painting, paper cutting and educational games.
11.30 a.m.–12.30 p.m.	Lunch of soup and rice plus fruit.
12.30 p.m.–1.30 p.m.	Tooth brushing, prayer.
1.30 p.m.–3.00 p.m.	Siesta.
3.00 p.m.–6.00 p.m.	Bathing and preparing to go home.

The centre is registered with the Ministry of Social Development and Human Security and uses its curriculum. The Ministry conducts unannounced inspections once a year and, as of 2007, requires each child to have an evaluation book recording various development aspects. The Ministry of Public Health provides vaccinations and a yearly health check.

Eligibility and use

Most parents are factory workers; the rest are street vendors and earn about the minimum wage. Few workers from Aoyoma use the centre because it is far from the factory. According to the licence, the centre cannot take more than 45 children; however, financial difficulties mean they have to take more children. They try to cap it at 70 children, and sometimes have to turn children away.

Costs and financing

The centre's director reports to the board of the union on both work progress and finances. The centre's finances are precarious. The only regular income is parental fees, a food subsidy of 10 baht per child per day and a milk subsidy of 600 dozen per year from the Department of Local Administration. Every year, the Community Savings Group, which shares the same building, makes a donation, including blankets. Some years, the Group also donates some money, as in 2007, when they made some profit and set aside 10,000 baht for the centre.

The centre charges 700 baht per child per month and 650 baht for members of any union. About 20 per cent of parents ask to pay in instalments. Holiday childcare is 50 baht per day. Parents' fees total about 24,000 to 42,000 baht per month, while the regular monthly expenses of the centre come to about 38,000 baht. This doesn't include expenses for building maintenance, or replacing equipment and pedagogical materials (such as teaching aids, paper, toys). "Due to limited funding, we have to carefully manage our budget. We can barely survive during certain months. Without the support from the Department of Local Administration, it would be difficult for the centre to survive" (a centre teacher).

Staff

The staff includes a director with a vocational education, a teacher with high school education, a teacher with junior high school education and a housemaid. The personnel are insufficient compared with the number of children, particularly from June to October when there are a lot of children. Each teacher has to look after about 20 children, more than the standard ratio of 1 to 15 (for children aged 3–5 years).

All staff receive accommodation and food at the centre. About 1–3 times per year, each teacher gets the chance to attend training organized by the Ministry of Social Development and Human Security and there is an annual training on nutrition and child development. They can also attend courses on media by Spirit in Education Movement (SEM) and training on nutrition twice a year. Staff appreciate the training. In the words of one teacher, "Getting to train helps to give me skills I can apply with myself and my work."

The work of the staff is tiring and involves many challenges. Parents work long hours and have little time for parenting, many children come from broken homes, and some parents are as young as 14 to 18 years old. Teachers often care for children into the evening and even the night, and often have to play the role of parent. Because the staff is small, the teachers have to play many roles.

Despite the challenges, the teachers are very proud and passionate about their work. One teacher remarks that a daycare centre can survive only by the integrity, sincerity and devotion of the administration (which in this case is the teachers). They value the child development and child-centred approaches of their work as essential to the children and to the nation. One teacher notes:

> Most parents take education for granted, and do not realize how important preschool education is. ... What we are trying to do is to bestow healthy saplings on the nation. I am proud to have a chance to work here.

After working there for 15 years, the director remarks:

> The experiences I had while working with the union urges me to work for common interests, to work for children and to bestow on them good things. But now, it's like I am working alone and lacking support in many ways. Even though this place is for poor children, we also hope the children will get the best development just like children of those living in urban areas.

Management perspective

The centre's director noted that, when the union first set up the daycare centre, the employer refused to provide space for it in the factory. Later the union negotiated with the employer and the company supplied electric equipment and rice for a year, until it closed. At present, the Triump Company, whose workers use the crèche, contributes rice through its Tomson Foundation. In general, however, few employers seem to recognize the importance of the centre or support it.

Worker perspective

Traditionally, workers have had to send their children to their parents in the province since they cannot afford private daycare centres or maids. Parents who were interviewed appreciated the crèche and reported that the centre had helped their children's development and skills, especially compared to children raised by grandparents in the province. Several parents were not sure what they would do without the centre. Some noted that their relatives in the province were not able to help; others cited the high costs of a babysitter or the poor quality of affordable alternatives. Nevertheless, several recognized the need for more staff and space for the children at the centre.

Lessons learned

This case illustrates how workers in an industrial zone, working together through trade union organizations, were able to mobilize the resources for a childcare centre for workers in formal and informal employment. Various partners have been involved in the past but the main source of income currently comes from parents' fees.

Financial sustainability on parents' fees is clearly a problem, especially when workers earn low incomes. The devotion of the staff, who work long hours for pay at low salaries, has kept the centre running. The centre has been obliged to take more children than standards recommend in order to generate the income needed to keep the centre running. The space, the staff and the equipment are all overextended for this number of children.

Nevertheless, the benefits for the parents who are able to work knowing their children are safe and receiving some education are substantial, as seen in the testimony of the parents. Greater support from employers in the zone, who are also benefiting from the centre, as well as from government, would help to ensure that the centre can continue operating under reasonable conditions for both the staff and the children.

Network of Nawanakhon Labour Unions

Types of business. Electronics, toys.

Workplace. The Nawanakhon industrial area is located in Pathum Thani. It houses more than 200 factories, mostly owned by foreigners.

Workers. Over 100,000 workers; 70 per cent come from rural areas, the rest are local.

Working hours. 8.00 a.m. to 5.00 p.m.

Childcare solution. Early childhood centre for ages 2.5 to 4.5 years, including holiday care for schoolchildren who are former pupils.

Partners. Network of Nawanakhon Labour Unions, Department of Local Administration (Ministry of Interior) through Thaklong Municipality (milk subsidy), Ministry of Social Development and Human Security, Ministry of Public Health, AFL-CIO, Nawanakhon Personnel Managers Group, Kawazumi Company.

The Nawanakhon industrial area includes factories and a huge residential area housing local people as well as the many workers who have come from the provinces, often with their families. In this industrial complex, the unions formed the Network of Nawanakhon Labour Unions[12] from about 30 labour unions, to provide mutual help for settling labour disputes between employees and employers, negotiating with employers, and building good relations between employers, employees and government.

---

[12] Now called the Council of Independent Labour in Thailand.

How it started

The Network raised the idea of setting up daycare centres to address the problems of the approximately 40 per cent of workers in the area who sent their children to be raised by grandparents in the countryside. Workers saw their children rarely, sometimes just once a year, and their worry about their children affected their well-being and work performance. A survey by the Network found support for the idea, and the Network consulted with experts in early childhood centres.

In 1992, the daycare centre opened with one caregiver in the office of the Network. After a couple of years, the number of children rose to 20–30. A new building was needed. An officer at the Ministry of Labour offered to draw the building blueprint free of charge. The construction budget was raised from different sources such as workers, unions and factories through the Nawanakhon Personnel Managers Group, fundraising activities and an interest-free loan from the AFL-CIO. During construction, the Kawazumi Company provided a temporary space free of charge for the daycare centre to continue operating.

Childcare programme

The centre is open from Monday to Saturday, 6.30 a.m. to 6.00 p.m. and provides breakfast, lunch and one snack. There is no playground but there is a plan to build a playground on the rooftop. It has a kitchen, bathrooms and a staff room, and also houses the office of the union. Facilities include three TV sets and DVD players, and two refrigerators. Most of these electrical appliances have been donated by employers.

Daily schedule

6.30 a.m.	Open.
7.30 a.m.–8.00 a.m.	Breakfast.
8.00 a.m.–8.30 a.m.	Group activity: greeting friends, singing, storytelling.
8.30 a.m.–9.00 a.m.	National anthem, prayer, physical exercise, aerobic dance.
9.00 a.m.–11.00 a.m.	Small children have activities such as drawing along the dotted lines, painting, Lego, watching DVDs on certain days, singing.
9.00 a.m.–11.30 a.m.	Older children have preschool courses including mathematics, Thai, English, social science, life skills, behavioural improvement.
11.00 a.m.	Small children's lunch.

11.30 a.m.	Medium and older children's lunch.
12.00 p.m.–2.30 p.m.	Drink milk provided by parents, followed by siesta.
3.30 p.m.	Drink milk provided by the Municipality. Prepare children for pick up. Assign homework for older children.
6.00 p.m.	Close.

In 1993, the centre was the first daycare centre in Pathum Thani to be registered. No government agency has inspected it.

Eligibility and use

There are currently about 100 regular children. Children aged 2.5 to 4.5 years are eligible to enrol. Services are also available for school holidays for those school-age children who used to be at the centre, but only 3–4 such children are enrolled.

About 80 per cent of the children in the centre are children of workers who earn the minimum wage of 194 baht per day. Often both parents work in a factory. The remaining 20 per cent are children of vendors in the community. The centre is located close to where they live in the Nawanakhon industrial complex. There is a high turnover of small children as their parents move or send them back to rural areas.

Finances and management

The Committee of Nawanakhon Labour Unions Network is responsible for the centre. It assigned a chairperson (who is also the Vice-Chairperson of the Council of Independent Workers in Thailand) as the manager. The full-time staff of the Network can help the manager in daily management.

The fee is 900 baht per month for children aged 2–3 years, and 750 baht for children 3 and older and for schoolchildren in holiday care. Parents pay for uniforms and stationery for medium and older children, each for 200 baht, and provide bed sheets for their own children.

Currently, the centre relies mainly on parents' fees, which cover the teachers' and housemaid's salaries, utilities and other basic expenses. In the past, the Department of Social Welfare under the Ministry of Labour[13] provided the

---

[13] The new name is the Department of Social Development and Welfare, Ministry of Social Development and Human Security.

allowance of one teacher, but this was discontinued due to lack of budget. Thaklong Municipality provides a milk subsidy of 10 baht/child per month. The Ministry of Social Development and Human Security provides some teaching equipment.

According to the Chairperson of the Network of Nawanakhon Labour Unions, if the centre needs anything, it can request support from the Nawanakhon Personnel Managers Group.

Staff

There are five staff members: three teachers, a housemaid and an officer of the Network who collects fees, shops for food and purchases books and stationery. Of the three teachers, one completed junior high school, one completed vocational college and one completed a diploma. Teachers' salaries range from 5,800 to 7,100 baht per month. The centre provides lunches for the staff and a one-month annual bonus.

During their first two years, the caregivers received one training session each on child rearing at the Thammasat Hospital. Since then, they have had no other opportunities for training, although they all want to improve their knowledge of child development. Most of them acquire knowledge through reading and asking teachers in other schools, and apply the knowledge in their teaching. At present, they are simply concerned with how to improve the centre in many ways.

Perspective of employers

The Chairperson of the Nawanakhon Labour Unions Network mentioned that the Network had meetings with the Nawanakhon Personnel Managers Group to consult with them about the daycare centre. Most factories have a positive attitude toward the centre and when they ask for support they are never ignored.

Perspective of parents

Interviewed parents find the centre very useful as they have little time to look after their children. If not for the centre, some would have to send their children to the countryside while others would turn to private centres whose fees and location are less suitable. Parents appreciate the services; for example, their children can help themselves, learn quickly, develop reading skills, are courageous to express themselves and so on. As one parent noted:

Compared with children raised by our parents in the countryside, we find children raised at the centre can attain much higher development. Our parents simply teach what they want to, but at the centre the children are assisted to develop their skills fast, learn to read English, learn to answer phone calls.

According to the parents, the centre is overcrowded and should be expanded. They would also like to see courses in English and more toys.

Lessons learned

This example shows concrete results achieved by trade unions working together as a network in an industrial zone. The childcare centre is clearly responding to an important need of workers. On the employers' side, the Group of Personnel Managers in the zone was a partner for dialogue with the unions.

Partnerships are key in this initiative. The Network was able to make the centre a reality by various fundraising strategies and by mobilizing partnerships to help. Partners from the local municipality, employers, the employers' Personnel Managers Network, national government and the American trade unions (AFL-CIO) have contributed a diverse array of material and financial resources to support the centre.

Nevertheless, the centre is overcrowded. In order to increase its income, it admits too many children for the space available and the number of staff. Financing childcare facilities on the basis of fees paid by low-income parents alone is difficult to balance with providing quality services with reasonable numbers of children per teacher. In addition, caregivers lack opportunities to attend training and build their capacities. Increased support from government and local employers would seem to be called for – particularly as the amounts of money involved are not great.

Aeronautical Radio of Thailand (AEROTHAI)

Type of business. Non-profit state enterprise for air traffic control and aeronautical telecommunication services.

Workplace. Office in Bangkok.

Workers. 2,800 employees. Most highly skilled.

Working hours. 8.00 a.m. to 5.00 p.m.

Childcare solution. Early childhood centre (newborn to 4 years); back-up care, holiday care for school-age children.

Partners. Welfare Management Committee, Ministry of Social Development and Human Security, Ministry of Public Health, Council of Daycare Centres, Aeronautical Radio of Thailand Union.

Aeronautical Radio of Thailand Limited (AEROTHAI) is a state enterprise under the Ministry of Transport and Communications. Under the contract with the Government, AEROTHAI operates on a cost-recovery basis in providing air traffic control and aeronautical telecommunication services within the Bangkok Flight Information Region and at all provincial airports and assumes certain other areas of responsibility entrusted by the International Civil Aviation Organization (ICAO).[14]

The previous CEO of AEROTHAI recognized that if employees have an opportunity to raise or look after their children closely and warmly, they can work efficiently. A feasibility study revealed that most employees wanted a daycare centre. Consultations were held with the Department of Social Welfare (Ministry of Labour)[15] to set one up.

In 1998, the daycare centre was founded and registered with the Department of Social Development and Welfare, Ministry of Social Development and Human Security. At the beginning, the ground floor of a two-storey building was used, but in 2005, the CEO proposed a new building for the daycare centre.

Childcare programme

The centre is one of 20 daycare centres recognized as an outstanding daycare centre by the Ministry of Social Development and Human Security and the Ministry of Education's National Education Commission in 2001. Located on company premises, it is open from 6.30 a.m. to 6.30 p.m., Monday to Friday. It has an anteroom, reception room for parents picking up children, dining room, breastfeeding room, classrooms and bathrooms. The centre provides breakfast, lunch and snacks. At present, there are 32 children, although the centre can take up to 45 children.

---

[14] AEROTHAI. Retrieved from http://www.aerothai.co.th [29 April 2008].

[15] The new name is the Department of Social Development and Welfare, Ministry of Social Development and Human Security.

A few mothers come during the day to breastfeed their children. Some prepare milk in bottles and ask caregivers to feed their babies. For older children, parents sometimes call to ask caregivers about their children.

Parents who pick up children after 6.30 p.m. have to pay an extra 70 baht per hour; this service is only available for workers in the company. If parents pick up their children after 10.30 p.m., they pay double and must drive the caregiver home.

The Ministry of Public Health provides vaccinations once or twice a year. The Ministry of Social Development and Human Security requires that each child has a book to record development.

Eligibility and use

The services are available for normal children from newborn to 4 years. The centre is also open to non-members of the company. Currently 70 per cent are children of company employees. There are 11 children under 1 year, ten between 1 and 2 years and 11 over age 2.

The centre offers a daily service for employees of AEROTHAI, although they have to inform the centre beforehand. For example, if a child's school class is cancelled or the nanny is sick, their parents can bring them to the centre on the daily service basis. The centre also receives children during school holidays.

Finance and management

The daycare centre is managed by the Welfare Management Committee, which has about ten members from three types of groups: high-ranking executive officers, those nominated by the Aeronautical Radio of Thailand Union and those elected by all employees. The committee approves and manages all centre expenses. An annual meeting is held with parents for evaluation, discussion of child development and self-help. About 80 per cent of parents attend the meeting.

The committee has recently increased the fees because they were far from covering the approximately 2 million baht cost of the centre in 2008. The fee for workers' children is 4,200 baht per month per child, for non-workers' children 5,500 baht per month per child, and for daycare on a daily basis, 340 baht per day. Parents can afford the fee increases because they are relatively well-paid workers.

Photo © Supawadee Petrat

Staff

There are 13 caregivers and five staff members, meeting the standard of one caregiver to three children under 2 years and one to six older children. Caregivers earn between 7,700 and 10,000 baht per month, including overtime work, and their employment is based on yearly contracts. The caregivers include men and women; all have completed at least junior high school education, and a number also have vocational or university educations. Five of the staff work for the company but help in the daycare centre, including teaching.

Some staff participated in training on preschool education with the Department of Social Welfare, but there have not been many chances recently for staff to attend training. For the AEROTHAI staff, there was some training on healthy childrearing organized by the Council of Daycare Centres.

Employer perspective

The centre was set up in order to allow employees to be close to their children. It still depends on budget from the company's employees' welfare fund, which is already strained to cover various welfare benefits for employees. The costs to the company for staffing the centre are high, particularly when the centre is underutilized. Therefore the company is now considering outsourcing to an out-side specialist organization which could run the centre more efficiently, although the company would retain oversight. In addition, it wants the daycare centre to develop into a place where university students in childcare could intern.

Employee perspective

In interviews with two fathers and two mothers, all agreed that the daycare is very important, making it possible for working parents to work fully and effectively. It saves time in travelling and parents do not need to hurry to drop off or pick up their children. For some parents who start work at 6.30 a.m. or do not finish until 6.30 p.m., it is particularly helpful. If not for the centre, they would have to place their children at other daycare centres, or divide the care between babysit-ters and a centre.

The parents appreciate that caregivers have been carefully selected and often have certificates to guarantee their skills. Also, some company employees super-vise the caregivers. The parents find this reassuring, and they appreciate that the centre does not operate for profit but for the welfare of the employees.

The parents have witnessed how their children have learned to help them-selves. One father of two children explained:

> I have two children. The older one was raised by my parents until he could start school while the younger child is at the centre. I can compare the difference in development between my two children. My older child who had been raised by my parents tends to be pampered. It takes him a while to learn to help himself since, in the past, his grandparents always did many things for him. ... My younger child can help himself better – also better than children of the same age.

Some parents feel the centre should improve its management. They would like opportunities to see their children at lunch, which is currently not allowed (except for breastfeeding mothers) for health reasons (especially the spread of foot and mouth disease). Also, the frequent rotation of caregivers means the children have no regular caregivers and the parents find it difficult to talk to the right caregiver. This can lead to miscommunication, for example if a parent asks one caregiver to give medicine to a child, but the rotation leaves a different caregiver in charge.

Lessons learned

This case provides an example of an employer who recognized the benefits that childcare would have for the workplace and partnered with workers and government agencies to establish an on-site daycare service that has received widespread recognition. Parents appreciate the fact that the company daycare is on-site so they can easily monitor what their children are doing. They also appreciate that caregivers have been carefully selected and that the centre is a non-profit undertaking. Despite its success, financial costs are a continuing challenge, and management has considered outsourcing the operation of the centre as a way of reducing costs. In an effort to meet shortfalls, the Welfare Management Committee has recently increased parental fees. Meeting costs will probably continue as a key concern for the initiative.

Business Trade Organization of the Office of the Welfare Promotion Commission for Teachers and Educational Personnel: BOWT

Type of business. Educational equipment, study and teaching materials (BOWT has a printing production house).

Workplace. Office in Bangkok.

Workers. 2,051, of which 1,091 are women.

Working hours. 8.00 a.m. to 4.00 p.m.

Childcare solution. Early childhood centre for children 3 months to 4 years; holiday care for schoolchildren and daily care.

Partners. Kurusapa Workers Union, Health Department of Bangkok Metropolitan Administration, Ministry of Social Development and Human Security, UNICEF, Department of Public Welfare (Ministry of Labour) and Suan Dusit Teachers' College.

Business Trade Organization of the Office of the Welfare Promotion Commission for Teachers and Educational Personnel (BOWT) produces teaching and learning materials, equipment and books for schools. The main functions of BOWT are providing welfare as well as ensuring the security of teachers and educational personnel, promoting and supporting education management in terms of studying and teaching, supporting research relating to welfare and developing the educational management system.

The Kurusapa Workers Union, with 1,771 members, initiated the idea of setting up a childcare centre because it wanted to help low-income employees who could not afford private childcare. It also wanted to keep mothers and children together according to the policy of the Ministry of Labour at that time. The Union organized a workshop with the Ministry of Labour and went abroad to learn about childcare services in Scandinavian countries like Denmark and Sweden.

The Union worked with management to move forward on the issue and in 1989 the childcare centre was established; in 1990 it was registered with the Department of Public Welfare (Ministry of Labour).[16]

The childcare centre

The on-site childcare centre is in a one-storey building. It accepts children aged 3 months to 4 years and provides a school holiday and daily care service. The centre is open Monday to Friday from 7.30 a.m. to 4.30 p.m. and provides lunch and two snacks.

Currently there are 19 children (seven newborns and 12 children), of which 80 per cent are children of employees, 10 per cent are nephews or nieces, and another 10 per cent are the children of non-employees. The centre has capacity for about 50–60 children. The number of children has been decreasing because more private childcare centres are available near the workplace, which appear to offer better-quality services. There are about three or four children during school holidays and a few children for daily care.

Funding and management

The childcare centre is a part of the welfare benefits for employees. It is steered by the Welfare Committee, comprised of management and union representatives. The management has appointed a company official to oversee the centre, in addition to his/her regular company duties.

The centre is funded by the user fees and BOWT, which provides caregivers' salaries and 10,000 baht per month for other expenses like meals and educational equipment. For preschool children, workers' fees are 1,500 baht per month for their children and 2,000 baht per month for their nephews and nieces. Outsiders pay 2,500 baht/month. Holiday care and daily services cost 100 baht per day for employees' children, 120 baht per day for nieces and nephews, and 150 baht per day for outsiders.

---

[16] The new name is the Department of Social Development and Welfare, Ministry of Social Development and Human Security.

Various agencies supported the centre with financial assistance and training at its inception; UNICEF provided assistance for one year and the Department of Public Welfare and Suan Dusit Teachers' College provided help. At present, the Ministry of Social Development and Human Security supplies 36 boxes of milk formula once a year and some teaching materials once every two years. The Health Department of Bangkok Metropolitan Administration (BMA) annually assesses children's health status and body weight, and gives vaccinations.

Staff

There are five caregivers at present, most of whom started working there when the centre was opened. All are members of the Workers Union. Their educational background ranges from elementary level to lower secondary level and they earn 7,000–8,000 baht per month on average. In the past, caregivers were hired on a daily basis, but the Workers Union advocated extending the status of an employee of BOWT to them. The caregivers are satisfied with their income, status and benefits.

When the centre opened, personnel undertook training for a period of 70 days. Since then, only one caregiver and one supervisor have attended training twice a year provided by the Ministry of Social Development and Human Security. Other caregivers did not wish to attend the training. The level of training and motivation of the staff is an issue raised by parents. Staff have no background in child psychology or development, and have no specific training in this area. Also, childcare service is not their job of preference.

Management perspective

Management indicated that BOWT will continue supporting the centre because it allows parents to be close to their children. It is part of the social welfare package which BOWT provides for staff.

Perspective of parents

Interviews with a father and a mother indicated that the centre is convenient because it is located in the same compound as their workplace. They feel that they can trust and rely on the caregivers, who work for the same employer as them. Parents find the centre spacious and clean. One of the parents suggested that the centre enhance the capacity of its caregivers in terms of their knowledge in childcare and child development.

Lessons learned

This case provides an example of a trade union successfully demonstrating to management the benefits of a childcare centre, resulting in a strong and positive partnership between workers and management in establishing and running the centre through a Welfare Committee.

There is a declining number of children in the childcare centre, which seems to be the result of other alternatives opening in the area. Parents may prefer these other centres, even if they are more expensive, because staff are better qualified. The number is also declining because fewer staff have young children. To ensure the continued usefulness of the childcare centre, the Welfare Committee may need to look into the childcare needs and concerns of employees at BOWT and review the policies concerning staff, curriculum and fees.

Nong Nooch Tropical Botanical Garden

Type of business. Botanical garden (agriculture and tourism).

Workplace. The botanical garden is located in Sataheep district, Chonburi province, which is 25 kilometres from Pattaya and 150 kilometres from Bangkok.

Workers. 1,500 workers; about half are women. Fifty per cent work in the garden and the rest work in service sectors like the restaurant, the resort and the performance business (cultural performance, animal show). Most workers are housed on-site.

Working hours. Workers in the service section (resort, restaurants) work in two shifts: 4.00 a.m. to 2.00 p.m. and 11.00 a.m. to 10.00 p.m. The workers in other sections (such as garden, business performance) work from 8.00 a.m. to 5.30 p.m. but may work as late as 10.00 p.m. on overtime.

Childcare solution. On-site centre provides daycare for children aged 18 months to 5 years and after-school and holiday care for school-age children.

Partners. Ministry of Public Health.

Started in 1980, the Nong Nooch Tropical Botanical Garden, initially established for botanical conservation, is today a tourist attraction with Thai-style buildings, seminar and banquet halls, swimming pool and restaurants, as well as other facilities constructed for tourists. It is one of the biggest botanical gardens in South-East Asia and more than 2,000 visitors visit daily.

The garden employs 1,500 workers; 300 are foreign, coming from Cambodia, the Lao People's Democratic Republic and Myanmar. Most workers earn the minimum wage of 5,000 baht per month. Benefits include housing, food and coverage under the social security system. Most workers stay in the on-site housing.

The childcare centre was established in 1981 because the workers with children had no one to look after them, with families living far away, both parents working and private nurseries too expensive. This problem prevented workers from working at full capacity.

Later, the owner decided to found the Nong Nooch Tropical Botanical Garden Foundation to fund botanical research and activities. The Foundation also supports activities for public benefit and runs an educational institution for preschool children. Therefore, the centre is now known as the "Nong Nooch Tropical Botanical Garden Foundation School". The Foundation School has the following objectives:

- to ensure responsiveness to the policy of the company;
- to improve discipline among employees, including reducing absenteeism and tardiness;
- to nurture, look after and train schoolchildren with love and motivation; and
- to promote the teaching and learning process as well as skill training appropriate for children in each age group.

The childcare centre

The centre is a one-storey building in the Nong Nooch Garden compound with bathrooms, a kitchen, a storeroom, a bedroom and a big hall with a television and VCD player. The centre also has a playground for children.

Open every day from 7.00 a.m. to 6.30 p.m., the centre provides lunch and an afternoon snack. It accepts children aged 18 months to 5 years. Currently there are 55 children, of whom 20 are the children of foreigners, mainly Cambodians. Only the children of employees/workers (both Thais and foreigners) are eligible. For most of the children, both parents work in the Garden.

The centre also provides after-school care for primary schoolchildren when parents are still working. About ten children stay after school and during school holidays.

Funding and management

The human resource section manages the childcare centre. Most of the operating budget comes from the company, including caregiver salaries, lunches and some snacks, electricity and water supply. The centre does not receive any support from the Government or any agencies other than the Ministry of Public Health.

Parents pay 400 baht per month for children aged 18 months to 2 years, 200 baht for children 2 to 5 and 200 baht for after-school and holiday care. Parental fees do not cover operating expenses, and additional funds come from the company's employee welfare fund and the Foundation (donated by the owner).

Staff

Currently there are five caregivers, who take care of the children, prepare food and clean. One is Cambodian, and helps with communication with the Cambodian children, although most of them can speak Thai. Staff are paid the minimum wage and work in two different shifts: from 7.00 a.m. to 4.30 p.m. and from 8.30 a.m. to 6.30 p.m. Most have previously worked in other sections of Nong Nooch Garden. Most are satisfied with their job at the centre.

The caregivers have elementary education, and have not received any training in childcare. However, they have tried to teach the children through various activities such as reading the alphabet and vowels, and telling tales they read from a book or heard during their own childhood. The head of the company's training section hopes to have future training by organizing a study tour to other child-care centres.

The centre has not been assessed by any public sector agency. However, a recent effort has been made to coordinate with the Ministry of Public Health for health checks for the children and information for parents on the need for vaccinations.

Perspective of management

The human resource section mentioned that, before the daycare centre, employees were often absent from work because they had nobody to take care of their children. Some left their children at home alone and, because they were worried, they could not concentrate on their work. With the daycare centre, there is less absenteeism and tardiness and both fathers and mothers can better concentrate on their work.

Management is aware of the shortcomings of the centre, including the fact that the centre has not focused much on teaching and learning but rather on care for children. The lack of qualifications of the caregivers is recognized as a factor hindering the effectiveness of the teaching and learning process. The centre does not follow any curriculum for early child development and there could be more toys and teaching materials. Their plan is to increase the number of caregivers and train them to work more effectively.

Perspective of workers

In interviews with two parents, they reported that the centre is useful, helps lessen the burdens on parents, and is not very expensive. A father said he has seen the progress in the development of his child, such as speaking and reading skills. For example, the child can now read the alphabet. If such a centre was not available, he might have asked his wife to quit her job to take care of the child.

Lessons learned

The Garden has found that the daycare centre brings considerable benefits because employees can concentrate on their work and do not need to be absent or late because of childcare problems. It is a fairly inexpensive facility that costs the employer relatively little.

However, the staff at the centre have no qualifications in early childhood development and are doing their best with the limited equipment available. Increasing partnerships with organizations specializing in early childhood development that could provide training and advice would be useful for improving the quality of the centre.

United Kingdom (England) **14**

Catherine Hein[1]

National overview

The United Kingdom provides an example of an industrialized country where childcare has only recently (since 1997) become a major issue on the government agenda. A driving concern has been to reduce child poverty and disadvantage. Thus some measures are targeted at poor families in order that disadvantaged children can profit from early childhood education and that their parents are able to work. Other more general measures include provision of 12.5 weekly hours of free early education for all 3- and 4-year-olds. Workplace incentives have also been put in place to reduce childcare costs for both employers and employees. Nevertheless, the cost of formal childcare, even after public subsidies, remains high for many parents. Many women work short hours and the use of informal family care is high.

[1] Catherine Hein is a researcher on work and family issues and a former staff member of the Conditions of Work and Employment Programme of the ILO. She would like to thank the management of the Royal Marsden NHS Foundation Trust and in particular the Care Coordinator, Barbara Harrington, for their collaboration.

National policies

Since 1998, when the Government launched the National Childcare Strategy, there has been increasing public financial support for childcare. Support has been in two main forms: funding to local authorities to increase the supply and quality of available childcare and tax credits for working parents to reduce the cost of childcare. Public spending on childcare in the United Kingdom rapidly increased from 0.2 per cent of GDP in 1998–99 to 0.4 per cent of GDP in 2003–04.[2] This review focuses on England as policies vary somewhat within the United Kingdom.

Apart from promoting the availability of childcare, in order to widen choice for parents, government has also provided more possibilities for working fathers and mothers to take time from work to look after their children. Paid maternity leave was increased to six, then nine, months. Since 2003, fathers also have a right to two weeks of paid paternity leave. A proposal is being discussed to give fathers the right to up to six months' additional paternity leave, some of which could be paid, if the mother returns to work. There is also a right to unpaid parental leave of 13 weeks (in total, not per year) for each child, up to their fifth birthday.[3] Parents of young children have the right to request flexible or reduced working hours.

A major objective of the National Childcare Strategy is to alleviate child poverty based on the premises that childcare measures can reduce the gap between disadvantaged children and others as well as encourage parents to obtain work as the main way out of poverty and social exclusion. The government targets are to get 70 per cent of lone parents into work by 2010, and to end child poverty by 2020. Two of the main measures include Sure Start and the Working Tax Credit.

Sure Start

Sure Start covers a wide range of programmes within England, some universal (in particular, the provision of free early education – see below) and others targeted on particular local areas or disadvantaged groups. In targeted programmes, the Government has been providing start-up funds, mainly through the local authorities, for setting up children's centres in disadvantaged areas. The Sure Start children's centres programme is based on the concept that providing high-quality

---

[2] OECD, 2005a, p. 203.
[3] Details on leave entitlements can be found at http://www.direct.gov.uk/en/Parents/Moneyandworkentitlements/workandfamilies/index.htm [12 June 2009].

integrated services (health, education, family support and care), particularly in disadvantaged areas, leads to positive effects for children, families and their communities. The children's centres are thus multi-purpose, bringing together childcare, early education, health, employment and family support services.

Children's centres provide early learning integrated with full daycare (a minimum of ten hours a day, five days a week, 48 weeks a year). Governance arrangements vary between centres, but all are managed through partnerships that reflect local needs and represent all agencies involved in delivery as well as the users of services themselves. Primary health-care trusts, local authorities, Jobcentre Plus, education and childcare providers, social services and community and voluntary agencies are all expected to work together to deliver holistic services, although collaboration has not always been easy to establish. Since 1999, the network has expanded to include about 2,900 centres across the country in 2009.[4]

In children's centres, most services or classes are virtually free of charge except for childcare, for which the average price was about £133 per week according to a study in 2006.[5] The study found that some centres had empty places, and focus groups with parents indicated that some families could not afford to pay for childcare beyond the 12.5 free hours guaranteed for children aged 3 and 4. Many centre managers were uncertain whether they could generate sufficient new income and savings to break even when start-up funding ended. To help low-wage parents pay for childcare, the Government has put in place a childcare element of the Working Tax Credit.

Childcare element of the Working Tax Credit

This is an allowance (not a tax deduction) for people in employment but on a low wage. For low-income parents in employment (at least 16 hours per week), this credit pays 80 per cent of the costs of registered or approved childcare for children under 15 years (increased from 70 per cent in 2006). The maximum the parent can receive for one child is £175 per week and £300 for two or more.[6] The amount actually paid depends on the number of hours worked, the level of earnings received, how many children are in the family and the amount of eligible childcare costs.

---

[4] Information found at http://www.everychildmatters.gov.uk/earlyyears/surestart/centres [12 June 2009].

[5] United Kingdom, National Audit Office, 2006.

[6] United Kingdom, HM Revenue and Customs, 2007a.

The number of government payments towards childcare costs has risen from a maximum of 45,400 claims under Family Credit in 1999 (average claim worth £22.08 per week) to more than six times that number in January 2004 (worth an average £49.57 per week).[7] Nevertheless, available data for the 2005–06 year suggest that take-up of the childcare element of the Working Tax Credit is low, with only 16 per cent of eligible families benefiting.[8] Because working parents eligible for the Working Tax Credit still have to pay 20 per cent of the cost of childcare, many prefer informal unpaid care by family or friends, when available. Other reasons for low take-up may include lack of awareness of its existence as well as problems identified with the administration of the tax credits.[9]

Organization

Local authorities have a major role in childcare provision. Government provides various types of grants to help local authorities increase the number of childcare places available and improve the qualifications of the staff. As part of the Government's National Childcare Strategy, every local authority has a Children's Information Service which can provide parents with details of local providers of registered childcare, including day nurseries, childminders, play schemes and after-school provision. The role of local authorities has been further increased by the Childcare Act in 2006 which places on them a legal duty to ensure that there is sufficient childcare in their area to meet the needs of working families and families with disabled children.

At the national level, as part of an integrated approach to the education and care of children, the Government created in 2007 the Department for Children, Schools and Families, which is responsible for all issues affecting people up to the age of 19, including education.

Inspection of all registered childcare providers, including workplace nurseries and childminders, is the responsibility of the Office for Standards in Education (Ofsted).[10] Every childcare provider must meet 14 national standards, which have been developed to ensure baseline quality.[11]

---

[7] Masters and Pilkauskas, 2004, p. 18.

[8] Archer, 2007.

[9] Kazimirski et al., 2008.

[10] Details on standards and guidance notes can be found at http://www.standards.dcsf.gov.uk/eyfs/site/requirements/index.htm [12 June 2009].

[11] For more details see Sure Start, 2003.

Service provision and use

The system of childcare is a mixture of public and private provision and thus a variety of services is available. In addition to various types of centres which provide care for children, there are childminders who provide care in their own homes as well as nannies who look after children in the child's home. By late 2007, the number of registered childcare places had almost doubled since 1997, reaching 1.2 million.[12] Nevertheless, in a survey in 2008, more than two-thirds of Children's Information Services in England responded that parents have reported a lack of affordable childcare in their area.[13]

Use of informal care by relatives and friends and particularly by grandparents is common for children of all ages. A 2007 study of families with children under age 15 found that 39 per cent had used relatives, friends or neighbours for childcare during the previous week, including one-quarter that used grandparents. Use of multiple carers was common: 42 per cent of children were looked after by more than one provider in the last week. Forty per cent of the families had used some formal care, the type varying with the age of the child.[14]

Under age 3 years

Full daycare services are largely commercial and private, while playgroups (of rather short duration) are often organized by NGOs and churches. The 2008 Childcare Costs Survey of the Daycare Trust indicates that childcare costs have been rising faster than inflation. A typical full-time nursery place for a child under 2 is £159 a week which amounts to over one-third of average weekly earnings (£457 a week in 2007).[15] At about £8,000 a year, the cost of care for a child under age 2 costs well over twice the cost of universities, which charge up to £3,145 a year for their courses.[16]

Childminders are slightly less expensive than nursery places. According to the Childcare Cost Survey, the typical cost of a full-time place with a childminder is £144 a week. Nannies who work in the child's home are an even more expensive solution.

---

[12] Information found at http://www.surestart.gov.uk/aboutsurestart [15 March 2008].

[13] Daycare Trust, 2008.

[14] Kazimirski et al., 2008, table 2.5.

[15] Daycare Trust, 2008.

[16] http://www.ucas.com/students/studentfinance/cost_of_study/studying_in_england [12 June 2008].

A 2007 study indicates that 32 per cent of under-3s had attended some form of centre care or playgroup in the previous week while another 5 per cent had been with a childminder and 3 per cent with a nanny or babysitter.[17] Use of formal care is highly linked to income: 63 per cent of under-3s in the highest income groups had received formal care but only 25 per cent in the lowest income group.[18]

Age 3–4 years

All 4-year-olds have been entitled to a free early education place for 12.5 hours per week for 33 weeks since 1998. From April 2004, this entitlement was extended to all 3-year-olds and the duration has been extended to 38 weeks. In January 2007, virtually all 4-year-olds and 96 per cent of 3-year-olds were benefiting from some free early education.[19] Providers of early education in schools, and in private and voluntary settings, receive funding from their local authority to offer the free places. However, providers may charge for additional services outside the free entitlement.

A major problem for working parents is the short duration which means that they must often resort to a patchwork of arrangements, both formal and family, for care of children outside the school hours.

School-age children (5+)

School typically finishes at 3.30 p.m. – well before typical working hours end. Out-of-school care is likely to be organized by either NGOs or local authorities. Some nurseries also provide out-of-school care for primary schoolchildren. In 2008, an after-school club typically cost £43 for 15 hours a week, an increase of more than six times the inflation rate.[20] For children aged 5 to 11 years, the use of out-of-school clubs is fairly limited, at 18–19 per cent in 2007.[21]

Finding affordable care for children during school holidays remains a difficult problem for working parents. Holiday clubs are not as widespread as other kinds of care provision. For instance, many after-school programmes are located in schools which cannot be used during holidays. Therefore, in many places, holiday clubs are run in sports centres, youth clubs and churches. Some can be quite expensive and not very affordable for parents.[22]

---

[17] Kazimirski et al., 2008, table 2.8.
[18] Kazimirski et al., 2008, p. 42.
[19] United Kingdom, Department for Education and Skills, 2007.
[20] Daycare Trust, 2008.
[21] Bryson et al., 2006, table 2.18; Kazimirski et al., 2008, table 2.8.
[22] European Foundation for the Improvement of Living and Working Conditions, 2006.

Children whose parents have atypical working hours

Atypical working hours (working evenings, early morning or weekends) are associated with higher than average use of informal care.[23] This may reflect the absence of formal care outside typical working hours. A study in 2003[24] found that around half of childminders provided care in the early morning, but few did so before 7 a.m., and hardly any offered care after 7 p.m. or on weekends. Indeed, many childcare workers are reluctant to work atypical hours, primarily because of the impact on their own families. Other types of childcare service were even less likely to offer care at such times. Development of such services is difficult since demand may be limited and costs higher than care during typical hours. Services for parents with atypical hours seem more likely to be developed when there is significant backing from employers, as has occurred with some National Health Service hospitals.

Employment of women and childcare

In the United Kingdom, many women workers are part-timers. Labour force surveys indicate that about 43–44 per cent of women workers continued to work 30 hours per week or less throughout the 2000–06 period.[25] This corresponds with the fact that increases in the use of the types of childcare used mainly by working parents (that is, provision for under-3s, care to wrap around early years education and out-of-school services) have been modest. Although there is some evidence that more mothers were working longer part-time hours, many seemed to be covering these hours by using "free education" (i.e. the free early education entitlement and school for older children), combined with informal arrangements.[26]

It is difficult to know the extent to which the cost and availability of formal childcare prevent parents from working. Some mothers retain a preference for parental care and a mistrust of formal provision, which may limit the extent to which the childcare strategy can be effective in increasing maternal employment.[27] Nevertheless, the 2007 study of parents with children under 15 years found that, for a significant minority, a lack of affordable childcare was cited as a reason for not working (17 per cent said they could not find childcare that would

---

[23] Kazimirski et al., 2008.

[24] Statham and Mooney, 2003.

[25] Labour Force Survey data taken from Grimshaw et al., 2008, table 9.

[26] Daycare Trust and National Centre for Social Research, 2007.

[27] Daycare Trust and National Centre for Social Research, 2007.

make working worthwhile). When asked whether they would work if they could arrange "good quality childcare which was convenient, reliable and affordable", 51 per cent of non-working parents said that they would, the proportion being much higher in low-income families (65 per cent).[28]

Conditions of work of childcare workers

Despite the high cost of childcare, the profession of childcare worker is one of the lowest paid in the country. There are thus recruitment problems with little financial incentive to enter the profession.[29] Turnover is also high (reaching 40 per cent annually in some instances) and is a threat to both quality and the attachment needs of young children.

One of the reasons for low earnings is the lack of professional qualifications. The number of graduate-level leaders in early years settings, outside schools, is very low. Around two-fifths of the workforce have only a basic qualification, particularly in the private and voluntary sectors. Government is currently working on programmes to standardize and improve the qualifications of early years providers and establish career paths to make the profession more attractive.[30]

Workplace incentives

Since 2005, three types of childcare provision are exempt from tax and national insurance contributions (NICs) for the employee and the employer:[31]

1) **Childcare vouchers:** A maximum of £55 per week (£243 per month) per parent is covered by the exemption. Within an organization where a voucher scheme operates, access to the scheme must be generally available to all employees. To be eligible, the child must be under 15 years old.

2) **Direct payments to a childcare provider:** Again a maximum of £55 per week per parent is exempt from tax and NICs on employer payments to a registered childcare provider. The provider could be a nursery, crèche, registered childminder, after-school club or other approved child carer.

---

[28] Kazimirski et al., 2008, p. 13.
[29] Fagan and Hebson, 2006, p. 10.
[30] United Kingdom, Department for Education and Skills, 2006b.
[31] This section is based on United Kingdom, HM Revenue and Customs, 2007b.

3) **Workplace childcare provision:** If the employer provides childcare in a nursery or play scheme at the workplace, the full amount of the cost of the childcare place, including the subsidy provided by the employer, is exempt from tax and NICs. The same applies if the premises are provided jointly with other employers.

A direct cash payment for childcare by the employer to employees would be considered part of their salary and be taxable. The system thus ensures that payment is only to registered or approved childcare providers but, in the first two systems, allows parents to decide on the provider.

In the case of the first two options, the employer payment can be made:

- **in addition** to the salary; or

- **instead** of the salary. This is known as salary sacrifice since the official salary of the employee is reduced by the amount paid for childcare.

The salary sacrifice option is obviously most beneficial to employers since there is no additional expenditure and they save on the NICs because of salary reduction. If employers choose to provide childcare vouchers through the salary sacrifice scheme, they can either contract a specialist childcare voucher organization to run the scheme (of which there are a number) or they can administer it themselves. Apparently savings on NICs can more than cover the administrative costs.

The savings of employees who opt for salary sacrifice for childcare expenses depend on various factors. The amount employees save on tax and NIC exemptions on the £55 per week would seem to be about £1,000 per year. But because of the reduction of their official salary and the effects on their childcare costs, salary sacrifice may reduce the amounts of their Working Tax Credit so the scheme may not be in their interest. The calculations for individual cases can be quite complex.[32]

When the childcare payment is made in addition to salary, some employers offer a flat rate to all qualifying employees; others have a sliding scale so that those on lower salaries receive a greater allowance than those with higher incomes. A few employers impose a time limit on the allowance (payable only for one year) while others limit payment to preschool childcare only. Some employers continue to pay the allowance for primary school-age children (albeit at a lower rate).[33]

---

[32] The web site of HM Revenue and Customs provides guidance and examples for workers about the interaction of tax credits with vouchers. It is really quite complicated: http://www.hmrc.gov.uk/childcare/interaction-tc-cv.htm [12 June 2009].

[33] Working Families, 2006.

For the option of a workplace nursery, employers can claim tax relief on the day-to-day costs of running a workplace nursery as well as a play scheme (rent, wages, food, rates). As noted above, neither the employer nor the employee pays tax or national insurance on the amount that they pay for childcare in a workplace nursery. There are government grants available for employers to help with the start-up costs of equipping a workplace nursery (such as furniture, durable play equipment and equipment for heating, washing and cooking). On the whole, parents using a workplace nursery would pay less per place than they would for a place in a conventional nursery. Nevertheless, this is still the most expensive possibility for the employer.

Results of workplace incentives

Data from workplace surveys in 1998 and 2004 indicate that, although the proportion of workplaces offering childcare support remains low, there has been a significant increase. About 7 per cent of British workplaces had a workplace crèche in 2004, up from 4 per cent in 1998.[34] Financial assistance for childcare is slightly more common according to this survey (8 per cent in 2004, up from 5 per cent in 1998) but has probably increased further with the new fiscal incentives in 2005.

Employer support of childcare is more likely in large organizations, organizations in London and those with a higher proportion of women staff according to a 2005 survey by the Government's HM Revenue and Customs department. Indeed only around half of medium-sized employers and a minority of smaller employers even knew about the new exemption rules.[35]

Childcare vouchers were by far the most popular form of support provided by employers, being twice as common as either workplace nurseries or direct payments to the provider. Childcare vouchers were primarily offered to employees through salary sacrifice rather than in addition to salary. However, direct provision of childcare was offered in addition to salary by almost half of organizations offering it.

The interviews with employers suggested that the exemptions have had an important impact on the take-up of childcare vouchers. The majority of organizations had found that the scheme was cost neutral while 13 per cent of those offering childcare vouchers were making a profit from the scheme!

Surveys of parents in 2004 and 2007 indicate that, of those paying for childcare, the percentage receiving help from their employer had more than tripled

---

[34] Whitehouse et al., 2007, table 1, based on Workplace Employment Relations Surveys 1998 and 2004.

[35] Kazimirski et al., 2006.

over the period, from about 1 per cent to 3.4 per cent.[36] This probably reflects the 2005 reforms of the tax and National Insurance exemptions for employer-supported childcare. For the majority of those receiving help (77 per cent) in 2007, the benefit involved salary sacrificing. Higher-income families were more likely to have received help from an employer than lower-income families.

Similarly the employer survey[37] indicated that employees taking up childcare support were more likely to be in professional occupations, managers and senior officials, while take-up was less among plant and machine operatives and workers in skilled trades and unskilled occupations. In the latter case, the employees may not want vouchers because of the effects on other childcare support benefits or they may not be able to afford formal care since the benefit covers only a small proportion of the costs (for example, if using vouchers on a salary sacrifice scheme means the worker saves about £1,000 per year, this is only a small proportion of the total cost of about £7,000 a year for a full-time childminder).

Role of trade unions

The trade unions have been active in providing information to their affiliates and members on how to improve workers' access to childcare. Both the TUC and UNISON have published detailed comprehensive guides on negotiating for childcare explaining the new possibilities resulting from government measures.[38]

The complex nature of the government-funding possibilities means that it is difficult to know the interests of individual workers. The TUC brochure notes: "It would also be worth advising members to discuss the financial implications with a financial adviser or expert to ensure that they are clear of the long and short-term consequences of accessing a salary sacrifice scheme." Similarly, UNISON advises that "Parents need to be careful how they combine different types of help in paying for childcare. This needs to be worked out in individual cases." The complex calculations necessary for parents may mean that it is difficult for them to know which option is more favourable. Nevertheless, the TUC is very supportive of the system of tax credits for low-paid workers with children as it feels this is having important redistribution effects, reducing poverty and inequality.[39]

---

[36] Calculated from Kazimirski et al., 2008, pp. 78–79.

[37] Kazimirski et al., 2006.

[38] TUC, 2006; UNISON, 2004.

[39] *Why the TUC supports the tax credits*, http://www.tuc.org.uk/welfare/tuc-14334-f0.pdf [19 June 2009].

Conclusion

The ongoing and relatively recent experience of the United Kingdom shows the importance of government leadership and increased funding in order to move ahead with a childcare agenda. The system of providing targeted support for childcare expenses to low-income workers leaves them considerable choice concerning the type of childcare used and has allowed more parents to join or re-enter the workforce. There has been a significant decrease in the number of children living in workless households, from 19 per cent in 1997 to 15.7 per cent in 2005.[40] Nevertheless, many low-income families are not using the tax credit available for childcare. The cost of childcare still remains a barrier to working for many parents in both low- and middle-income groups.

The UK example also indicates the usefulness of government incentives as a way of increasing the participation of employers in childcare provision. To expand the number of workers benefiting, there would seem to be a need to create greater awareness of incentives among employers and employees as well as to simplify the calculations involved.

The Royal Marsden NHS Foundation Trust

Type of business. National Health Service – specialist acute hospital.

Workplace. The Royal Marsden NHS Trust is based on two sites, one in Chelsea (Fulham Road, London) and the other in Sutton, Surrey.

Workers. The Trust has 2,376 employees, of whom 1,810 (or about three-quarters) are women. The staff includes nurses, radiotherapy technicians, doctors and researchers, administrative personnel, catering staff, porters and managers.

Working hours. Staff work on rotating shifts to cover 24/7 and also standard hours; that is, 9.00 a.m. to 5.15 p.m.

Childcare solution. Carer Co-ordinator, on-site workplace day nursery, discounts with local nurseries and holiday camps, holiday play schemes, emergency childcare service, childcare vouchers on salary sacrifice and as subsidies to certain employees.

Partners. Employer; Royal Brompton Nursery for staff in Chelsea; Kensington and Chelsea Community Play; a voucher provider; a nanny agency; Family Information Services of the local Boroughs; Sutton Early Years for training nursery staff; government for tax exemptions and early education grants.

---

[40] United Kingdom, Department for Education and Skills, 2006b.

The Royal Marsden Trust is a Foundation Trust within the National Health Service (NHS), the publicly funded health-care system which provides the majority of health-care in the United Kingdom. It was the first hospital in the world dedicated to cancer treatment and research into the causes of cancer. Today the hospital with its academic partner, the Institute of Cancer Research, forms the largest comprehensive cancer centre in Europe with over 40,000 patients from the United Kingdom and abroad seen each year. The Trust provides inpatient, daycare and outpatient services for all areas of cancer treatment. The Trust pioneers and innovates in all areas of cancer treatment.

In 2000, the NHS launched its own childcare strategy to complement the Government's national strategy and as part of an overall strategy for improving the working lives of staff and attracting returnees, particularly from maternity leave. A major element of the NHS strategy was that all staff should have access to a childcare coordinator, a post that was created at the Royal Marsden in 2003. The Royal Marsden has a number of policies to facilitate the work–life balance of its staff and is committed to giving staff greater flexibility and control over their own time and improving access to childcare. The Royal Marsden is proud to have been awarded "practice plus" status in the Improving Working Lives Standard for NHS organizations.

In order to provide flexible working opportunities, there are flexible working advisers throughout the organization who are able to advise on the options available and how best to proceed with a request for flexible working. When women return from maternity leave, they often prefer to work on some sort of part-time basis and are looking for flexible options. For the organization, it is important to operate the expensive machinery for as long as possible and so various shift patterns are offered. All staff have the right to request flexible working (not just those with children under age 6 as required legally) and a number of staff work part time, job share or compress their hours.

For childcare, given the very diverse needs of its staff and the rather different contexts of its two sites, a variety of options has been developed by the Carer Co-ordinator, a post which is itself an integral part of the programme.

Childcare programmes

Carer Co-ordinator

The Carer Co-ordinator has, since the beginning, covered all types of dependant care, not only childcare. She is responsible for providing information and signposting employees so they can access different types of care. She can also give more general advice on possible arrangements for reconciling work and care responsibilities, including advice on how to apply for tax credits and the Trust's policies concerning leave. When the post was created, considerable initial work was required to assess the needs of staff and a number of surveys were carried out.

In order to be able to offer a palette of possibilities for children of different ages, the Co-ordinator networks with various kinds of childcare providers (as can be seen in the various programmes which follow). The local boroughs are key partners as they have Family Information Services with listings of childcare available and also run their own programmes.

The Co-ordinator receives around 50 calls per month from staff, both men and women. Discussions with the Co-ordinator are treated as confidential and the human resources department is not informed unless the employee requests.

In the case of pregnancy, particularly for a first child, parents typically do not know their childcare alternatives in terms of Trust policies and childcare facilities. The Co-ordinator encourages expectant mothers to consider carefully their options and plan well ahead in terms of work schedules, childcare arrangements and how they will pay for whatever childcare they need. Maternity "drop-ins" are organized for staff on maternity leave to encourage them to stay in touch and discuss the arrangements they need to make for coming back to work. Planning ahead not only helps ensure that employees can exercise their preferred options but also helps the Trust to plan for its human resource needs.

Initially, the Co-ordinator post was funded by the Strategic Health Authority. However, since 2005, the Trust has had to cover the costs from its own budget. Unlike some other trusts, the Marsden has been able to continue the post from its own funding.

On-site day nursery

The Sutton site has a 42-place on-site day nursery for employees. The nursery can take children from age 6 months to 5 years and is open from 7.45 a.m. until 5.45 p.m. on weekdays. Places are generally offered on a full-day basis but it is possible to have a half-day place either with or without lunch.

The Sutton nursery is popular with staff and currently is full. Waiting times to get a place can be as long as 12 to 18 months. Places are allotted on a first-come first-served basis without distinction related to occupation within the Trust.

The nursery is run by the Royal Marsden and has 16 staff including the Manager and Deputy Manager. The Manager reports to the Assistant Director of Human Resources. As well as early years training, the Manager also has training in management, which has proven to be a valuable asset. Nursery workers are all qualified with either a two-year diploma or a National Vocational Qualification in Early Years Care and Education at varying levels. Three staff are currently studying for the Early Years Foundation Degree. As educational standards for nursery workers are increasing, it is important for staff to be able to improve their qualifications. The Trust provides regular training from organizations such as Sutton Early Years run by the local borough and also pays fees for other training courses followed. Staff turnover is very low.

Currently fees for the nursery are £32.00 per day for a baby place and £29.00 for a child place. Fees do not cover all the running costs and thus the Trust is subsidizing the facility. Employees can save money on the fees by joining the Workplace Nursery Salary Sacrifice scheme or the Childcare Voucher scheme (see below for vouchers).

The Workplace Nursery Salary Sacrifice scheme is possible since the nursery is provided by the employer, in which case, the full amount of the cost of the childcare can be exempt from tax and NICs. It is possible for the employee whose child is at the nursery to sacrifice salary up to the total amount of the fee – a much larger amount than for vouchers. However, the resulting official reduction in their salary would affect, even more than vouchers, their pension, life insurance and pay during a future maternity leave. Calculating the repercussions of salary sacrifice can be difficult as implications are sometimes not entirely clear and subject to interpretation.

The nursery delivers the official early education programme and applies for the Nursery Education Grant provided by government for eligible children. The funding commences the term following the child's third birthday and, once the grant is received, this is deducted from the monthly fee bill of the employee.

The staff at the Chelsea site in London do not have an on-site nursery but can access places at the Royal Brompton Nursery. Also, since there is no on-site nursery at the Chelsea site, staff based there who have children of 5 years or under in a nursery and who earn less than £25,000 basic full-time salary can apply for a direct voucher subsidy of up to £10 per day.

On-site facilities seem to be more popular in the more suburban context of Sutton than in London where fewer employees live nearby and many often have long rides on public transport to get to work.

Discounts with local providers

For workers who cannot use the on-site nurseries, the Carer Co-ordinator has negotiated discounts with a number of nursery providers. These are often only valid for a certain period and usually amount to about 10 per cent of the standard rate. For some providers, discounts apply for NHS staff generally, not just the

Marsden staff, and are negotiated by a number of childcare coordinators. The provider involved may have a number of nurseries in different areas.

Similarly for summer camps, discounts have been negotiated with a number of providers. One camp organization offers to NHS staff free use of the extended care option, which means their children can stay beyond the usual closing time at no extra cost.

Staff can learn about the organizations offering discounts by consulting the Carer Co-ordinator. A discounts Intranet page is currently being set up. It is difficult to know how much these discounts are actually used. The list needs to be updated regularly as new possibilities arise and previous ones may no longer be valid.

Emergency childcare

At the Marsden, the absence of a key staff member (for example, a surgeon to operate or run a clinic) could affect services to patients, with appointments delayed or cancelled. In order to prevent unpredictable absences because of a sick child, an emergency childcare service has been set up. Although emergency childcare is expensive, it was felt to be an important service.

All members of staff are able to access the service, which is provided by Tinies Childcare, a nanny agency, which sends a nanny to their house. Staff can use the service on up to three occasions in a 12-month period. A period can be for up to two consecutive days. The entire cost is covered by the Trust. It is up to staff members to decide whether they want to use this option in any particular emergency and not for managers to insist that they use the service.

This service is funded from funds bid for from the Charity budget of the Trust. Use is highly variable from month to month but remains within the budget allocated. The scheme has proved to be very popular.

Childcare vouchers

The Carer Co-ordinator has set up a childcare voucher scheme on the basis of salary sacrifice (see above for details on salary sacrifice). All employees with children under age 15 are able to apply to join the scheme. The vouchers can be used to pay for registered or approved childcare at nurseries, childminders, nannies, breakfast and after-school clubs and holiday clubs.

The scheme is managed by the Carer Co-ordinator and Accor Services. Each month the coordinator must place a voucher order with Accor which places the funds in the online accounts of the employees concerned. This is apparently well organized and does not take too much time. Employees can then pay providers from these accounts, in some cases setting up regular payments to their registered provider. A management fee of 5.5 per cent of the value of the voucher order is charged by Accor.

In the period April–December 2008, about 136 workers were taking vouchers, of which almost one-third were men. Most employees take the maximum possible and their savings on tax and national insurance amount to up to £1,195 per annum.

With almost 5 per cent of staff taking vouchers, it is difficult to know whether there are many workers who would be eligible that do not apply. The scheme is publicized on the Intranet and also roadshows have been organized. Every month there are three to six additional employees who join the scheme. The savings which the Royal Marsden makes on the salary sacrifice scheme are returned to the childcare budget and thus help cover other childcare expenses.

Holiday play schemes

For employees with children who need care during the school holidays, the Trust has set up a play scheme at a local school in Sutton; in Chelsea, it works in partnership with another trust and Kensington and Chelsea Community Play.

The Sutton scheme is run every holiday period for children aged from 4 to 14. The scheme is currently run at a school by a private provider that is a charitable foundation. The Marsden Trust provides a subsidy and is allocated 24 of the 40 places at the reduced daily rate of £16. The scheme is open to the public at a rate of £22 per day. Places are filled on a daily basis so a child could go, for example, three days per week. This flexibility can make it difficult for the provider to maximize daily use of the places available. Also the provider has the problem of finding appropriate staff available to work only during the holidays (often students or schoolteachers).

It has proved to be difficult to find a service that, while ensuring quality, charges a reasonable rate that results in an acceptable fee for parents even after the subsidy from the Trust. Previously some schemes were only for NHS staff but, given the difficulties in predicting demand, schemes are now open to other users.

For the Chelsea scheme, the Marsden Trust, in collaboration with another NHS trust in the region, takes places at a scheme run at a local school near the hospital by Kensington and Chelsea Community Play, a service of the Borough. Few places are actually reserved given the unpredictability of demand from staff. The Trust can organize the registration of staff's children without them having to waste time queuing. The daily rate is £10.50. Activities include arts and crafts, IT and the Internet, sports, cookery, music and trips.

A play scheme subsidy is available as a childcare voucher for employees who wish to use a private holiday play scheme. The amount of the subsidy can be up to £10 per day.

The play schemes have proved to be popular with staff and are particularly used by those with primary school-age children. Although parents are concerned about supervision of the 12–14 age group, children of this age are less attracted to play schemes and may not want to go. An effort is being made to try to develop more interesting activities for this age group within the play scheme at Sutton. Holiday solutions for teenagers can be difficult to find and may lie more in specialized camps than in play schemes.

Costs and benefits to the organization

The performance of the hospital is dependent on its high-quality, dedicated, skilled workforce. Childcare support is an important part of the Trust's recruitment and retention of quality staff as it can be a vital factor in the choices of the younger generation where both men and women are looking for better work–life balance.

It is difficult to measure the effect that help with childcare has on staff turnover and the attraction of skilled personnel, although a high level of staff return from maternity leave. For the Trust, this is seen as a positive outcome of the various family-friendly measures that are in place, including childcare support.

The costs of childcare are more obvious than the benefits and, despite clear evidence, not all managers are convinced about the value of childcare.

Lessons learned

The example of the Royal Marsden Hospital illustrates the advantages of having an internal person who can advise staff on work–family issues. Staff are often stressed when they have childcare problems and need someone they know and trust who can work through the problem with them, taking into account their legal rights, the policies of the organization and their family situation. This is a great help to managers, who would have to support the individuals otherwise. A childcare information service, for example, would be much more limited in the type of help that could be offered and not be able to provide as comprehensive a service as a person inside the organization. In addition, employees coming from other trusts that do not have a carer coordinator find there are many more care options that have been developed.

By managing the nursery itself, the Trust feels that it can have more control over the quality of the childcare provided for its staff and keep fees lower than would be the case if the management were outsourced to a for-profit provider. Opting for this alternative requires careful selection of the nursery manager as the quality of the care and the efficiency of the management depends greatly on his/her competence.

As can be seen at the beginning of this case study, the list of partners for the Royal Marsden childcare programmes is long. These partnerships have been very important for finding cost-effective and appropriate solutions for the various programmes run by the Trust. Partnerships also help staff access other programmes, run by municipalities or private providers, under good conditions.

Another type of partnership is the network of childcare coordinators which was initially established by the NHS within specific regions and which continues to operate informally. The Marsden Co-ordinator continues to network with colleagues in South-West and North-West London and finds that having a network of colleagues can be helpful for finding joint solutions for common problems.

Parents appreciate the fact that help with work–family balance, in terms of work schedule options and childcare support possibilities, is not limited to the period before children start school but continues into the teens.

United States

15

Joanne Land-Kazlauskas[1]

National overview

Labour force participation rates for women are high in the United States and the vast majority of mothers work. Childcare services, like many other services in the United States, operate through the market, so parents' ability to pay affects access and can influence both the quality and convenience of care options. As such, relatives provide care for about half of all preschool children while parents work. Governmental support to offset childcare costs is available to some through the tax system. Also, for low-income working parents, support is provided through systems of block grants to the states and through Head Start preschools, designed to prepare children from disadvantaged backgrounds for school. Even with these offerings, many low- and middle-income parents do not seem to benefit. Given the major problems of cost and quality, both employers

---

[1] Joanne Land-Kazlauskas is currently an adjunct faculty member at the University of Connecticut, where she teaches an organizational behaviour course online. She also works as a freelance consultant on issues of gender and work and family balance.

and trade unions have been active in the struggle to help workers access childcare which is affordable and of an assured quality.

Employment of women and childcare

Trends since the 1970s show a steady increase of women in the workforce, and in particular, women with children through the late 1990s. Although these advances have levelled out, participation rates of mothers with children under age 18 in 2008 were estimated at 71.4 per cent (69.5 per cent among those who have a spouse present compared to 76 per cent of those without a spouse present). Participation rates for mothers depend somewhat on the age of their children: 64 per cent of those with a child under age 6 and 56.4 per cent of those with a child under the age of 1.[2] Women with more than one child are also less likely to be in the paid workforce than are women with only one child.[3]

The labour participation rate of university-educated mothers is higher than for those with a high school diploma or less. For mothers with less formal education, and therefore less earning power, the high cost of childcare may mean that it doesn't make financial sense to work. Also, professional women tend to have the greatest control over their work schedules and work in environments that provide more extensive family-friendly policies and paid leave options, yet they make up a relatively small percentage of the workforce.

Working conditions provide many challenges for working mothers. The United States does not provide for paid maternity or paternity leave, or sick, holiday or vacation days. Instead of maternity leave, at the birth of a child, some women workers are eligible for 12 weeks of unpaid leave under the Family Medical Leave Act (FMLA) if their employer has more than 50 employees and if the employee has worked for that employer for at least 1,250 hours during the prior year. The National Partnership for Women and Families estimates that 40 per cent of the current workforce is ineligible for this leave because they work in small enterprises with less than 50 employees. Some states have implemented their own Family Leave programmes.[4] In addition, some employers also provide paid maternity leave.

---

[2] United States Bureau of Labor Statistics, 2008a.

[3] Cohany and Sok, 2007, p. 12.

[4] California, for example, allows working parents covered by the State Disability Insurance System up to six weeks of leave per year, with partial wages, to address care for sick family members and for a child during its first year. See United States Government Accountability Office, 2007, p. 6.

Another challenge relates to working hours. The average workweek (2005) for women over 25 with a bachelor's degree in the United States was 42.2 hours, and 45 hours for women with an advanced university degree. And an estimated 30 per cent of the female workforce works night and/or weekend shifts, times when it is difficult to arrange for formal childcare.[5]

National and state policies

Rather than developing public services, the federal government supports childcare in two major ways: block grants to the states and tax credits to families. The block grants target low- to moderate-income families, with the majority aimed at those families living in poverty or who earn just over the official poverty line.

Block grants to states

The Childcare and Development Fund (CCDF), for example, is a federal block grant, to provide childcare subsidies to low-income parents preparing to enter or in the workforce. In 2006, five billion dollars of CCDF funds were allocated to the states to encourage greater childcare options for eligible families, via vouchers and contracts with providers.[6] States have considerable leeway in determining the specifics of their childcare policies and programmes. Eligibility for CCDF-funded programmes, as well as costs to parents and minimum standards required of providers, vary by state.

Another federal block grant, TANF (Temporary Assistance for Needy Families), also allows funds to be used by states in a variety of ways to help needy families achieve self-sufficiency. One of the eligibility requirements for TANF is that recipients be in the workforce or engaged in qualified work activities.[7] To strengthen access to childcare options for the working poor, a percentage of TANF funding to states can be transferred to CCDF initiatives.

It is estimated that only a fraction of potentially eligible low-income families benefit from the CCDF and other subsidies. About 1.8 million children receive vouchers each month from the federal–state CCDF programme but this is a small proportion of the children in low-income working families that might benefit

---

[5] Labor Project for Working Families, *Quick Facts*. Available at: http://www.working-families.org/familyfriendly/worktime_quickfacts.html [12 June 2009].

[6] United States Department of Health and Human Services, 2008.

[7] Details about TANF are available at the web site of the US Department of Health and Human Services, http://www.acf.hhs.gov/programs/ofa/tanf/about.html [12 June 2009].

from such assistance – according to one estimate, only about 14 per cent of feder-ally eligible children are served by the CCDF.[8] As of 2007, 17 states had waiting lists or stopped intake to individuals that were otherwise qualified for subsidized childcare assistance. California was estimated to have over 207,000 children on waiting lists, Florida, 44,000 children, and the State of Georgia, 24,800.[9]

Additional federal funding is allocated to preschool programmes, such as the Head Start programme to prepare disadvantaged children for the public school system.[10] Not-for-profit agencies can apply for Head Start grant funding, but participating communities must also contribute a percentage towards the total operating costs. Early Head Start serves eligible children under the age of 3, and the federal Head Start programme serves eligible 3- and 4-year-olds.

Tax policy

Both federal and state governments use tax policy to subsidize parents' use of market services. Of working parents who owe federal taxes and have a dependent child under the age of 13, some may be qualified for the Federal Dependent Care Tax Credit, which offsets a proportion of the private costs associated with childcare, or up to 35 per cent of qualifying expenses, depending on parental income.[11] Additional options include the Federal Earned Income Tax Credit and the Federal Child Credit.[12] Tax credits are also issued at the state level, and parents may be eligible for various options depending on their state of residence, earnings and other individual factors.

In order to help working parents with dependant care expenses, govern-ment has also created the possibility of having a Dependent Care Reimbursement Account created at their workplace. These accounts allow eligible employees to allocate up to $5,000 pre-tax towards expenses for caring for the elderly, children under age 13 and dependants with special needs. Parents who are taxpayers can profit from a decrease in taxable income and therefore from the possibility of tax savings. Employers benefit because their payroll becomes less and they save on payroll contributions and taxes. These Dependent Care Reimbursement Accounts are a form of government subsidy but of limited use to families who pay little in income tax.

---

[8] Winston, 2007, p. 5.
[9] Schulman and Blank, 2007, p. 1, and table 2, p. 16.
[10] United States Government Accountability Office, 2005, pp. 7–8.
[11] United States Internal Revenue Service, 2008.
[12] National Women's Law Center, 2007.

Services for children under 5

A survey conducted by the United States Census Bureau on the primary care arrangements for children under 5 whose mothers are working shows the great importance of family members as primary carers for children under 5 (table 15.1): for children with working mothers, about 18 per cent are cared for by the other parent, 20.5 per cent by a grandparent and 7 per cent by other family members, indicating that about 45 per cent of children under 5 whose mothers are working are being looked after mainly by a family member. Care by a relative is not necessarily unpaid and estimates of the childcare workforce suggest that there are many more paid relatives than daycare homes.[13] Indeed, many subsidy schemes include the possibility of payments to relatives, although the subsidy may be less than for other providers. In contrast, systems in France and the United Kingdom exclude payments to relatives unless they are registered care providers.

It is somewhat surprising that about 10 per cent of the children have no regular care arrangement – perhaps because of difficulties in making regular arrangements. The same study found that about one-quarter of children had multiple arrangements in order to cover the parents' working hours.

Among the non-family arrangements, the most frequently used is the daycare centre, which is the primary arrangement for 19 per cent of the children. The next most frequent arrangement (9 per cent) is non-relative care, which includes a variety of arrangements, from someone working in the child's home to neighbours or friends who may look after the child.

Another almost 8 per cent of children with working mothers are in family daycare. This consists of providers who care for two or more children outside the child's residence, typically in the provider's home. A ten-year study of family childcare homes found that, although the majority of homes were deemed adequate, there were some basic health and safety concerns and concerns that less time was spent engaging children in enrichment activities than would occur in organized childcare facilities. Advantages of family daycare were said to be the hours of operation (average of 13 hours daily) and year-round availability (about 50 weeks). Weekend care was also offered, and unlike typical childcare facilities, many providers were willing to accommodate sick children.[14]

Very few care facilities are actually accredited. It is estimated that less than 1 per cent of family day homes are accredited, meaning that the quality of care in

---

[13] National Association of Child Care Resource and Referral Agencies (NACCRRA), 2008, table on childcare workforce.

[14] Layzer and Goodson, 2007, pp. 2–7.

Table 15.1 Primary childcare arrangements of preschoolers under 5 years old living with employed mothers by selected characteristics, United States, Spring 2005

Percentage of children in arrangement

Age of child	Designated parent[1]	Other parent[1]	Grand-parent	Sibling or other relative	Daycare centre	Nursery, preschool	Head Start	Family daycare	Other non-relative	School[2]	No regular arrangement[3]
Less than 1 year	6.3	19.3	25.4	7.1	16.2	0.4		8.5	9.9		14.2
1–2 years	4.3	18.5	20.7	7.0	21.0	2.9	0.1	9.1	9.5		11.1
3–4 years	4.2	17.5	18.4	6.8	18.5	9.5	1.7	6.4	8.1	6.1	8.4
TOTAL	**4.6**	**18.2**	**20.5**	**6.9**	**19.1**	**5.3**	**0.8**	**7.8**	**9.0**	**2.6**	**10.5**

Notes: The primary childcare arrangement is defined as the arrangement used the most hours per week. The numbers for all arrangements may exceed the total number of children because of ties among arrangements in the greatest number of hours per week.   [1] Time in parental care is only shown for women who worked as an employee or were in school.   [2] Attendance in kindergarten/grade school is not considered to be a childcare arrangement and is shown here for informational purposes only.   [3] In a regular childcare arrangement, including those who are only in school or self-care.

Source: US Census Bureau, 2005, table 2B, based on data from the Survey of Income and Program Participation (SIPP), 2004 Panel, Wave 4. For information on sampling and non-sampling error see http://www.sipp.census.gov/sipp/source.html [18 June 2009]. Internet release date: February 2008.

the vast majority of arrangements is unregulated and that only 9 per cent of child-care centres are accredited (accreditation varies by state).[15]

Table 15.1 also shows that another 8 per cent of the children with working mothers are in some kind of preschool or school and 0.8 per cent are in Head Start. The percentage of children in preschool rises with age so that among 3–4-year-olds this reaches 15.6 per cent plus another 1.7 per cent in Head Start. As of 2007, 39 states had preschool programmes, but only three (Florida, Georgia and Oklahoma) opened their doors to all 4-year-olds. Eligibility requirements in other states are based on family income and additional criteria and long waiting lists are the norm in many areas. An estimated 20 per cent of eligible 4-year-olds nationwide participate in state pre-kindergarten programmes. Programmes run an average of 2.5–3.5 hours daily during the school year.[16]

Nationwide, the Head Start programme covers relatively few children. Even among eligible children, in fiscal year 2004, it is estimated that only half of eligible 3- and 4-year-olds were attending. Half-day and full-day programmes are offered, but not all sites operate full daycare,[17] and 2008 budget cuts to the programme are forcing operations to be scaled back nationwide.[18] The half-day programme is at best a partial answer to the childcare needs of poor working parents.

Childcare is expensive. Costs per child fluctuate considerably by location, the age of the child and the type of care used. Full-time infant care in a centre costs between $4,542 and $14,591 annually, while family childcare homes range from $3,900 to $10,787. Costs of infant care in an accredited facility are greater than the average tuition at a public university ($6,185).[19]

School-aged children: 5–14

Mandatory school enrolment in the United States requires that children from 5–7 years of age until age 16–18 be enrolled,[20] with exact ages differing by state. The standard school year is approximately 180 days, with school beginning in late August or early September and ending in June or July. School hours, again with some variance by state and local district, are typically 7.30 a.m. to 3.30 p.m. This

---

[15] NACCRRA, 2008, table on childcare patterns and supply.

[16] Ewen and Matthews, 2007, p. 5.

[17] Ewen and Matthews, 2007, p. 5.

[18] Parrott, 2008, para. 1-5.

[19] NACCRRA, 2008, table on cost of childcare.

[20] Age of required school attendance by state can be found at http://www.dol.gov/esa/whd/state/schoolattend.htm [12 June 2009].

schedule means that many working parents must secure care for their children during non-school hours, as well as care during holidays and professional development days for teachers.

As with other childcare arrangements, before- and after-school care costs can differ greatly depending on the type of care utilized. The annual cost for a childcare centre is approximately $2,500–$8,600 and for a home provider from $2,080 to $7,648.[21]

Public school systems support the majority of America's after-school programmes and activities, as do other crucial contributors, such as the YMCA and the Boys and Girls Club, religious groups and private school programmes. Approximately 6.5 million children are estimated to use after-school programmes each year, for an average of eight hours per week, according to a study in 2003, *America after 3pm*.[22] This study indicates that children in grades 1–5 (aged 6–11) are most likely to attend after-school programmes (15 per cent), dropping to 6 per cent for children in grades 6–8 (aged 12–14). Costs average 22 dollars per week per child, but depend on age.

As children get older, many are left to take care of themselves during non-school hours, but a surprising number of younger children are also unsupervised. The 2003 study estimates that approximately 1 per cent of kindergarten-aged children are in self-care after school, 7 per cent of children in grades 1–5 and 34 per cent of children in grades 6–8. The safety of unsupervised children is a major concern for many of America's communities.

A number of families indicated they would participate if a quality after-school programme were available to them. This participation would add an additional 15 million youth to the 6.5 million currently in programmes. The study concludes that the supply of after-school programmes continues to fall far short of the demand.

Conditions of work of childcare workers

Given the costs of childcare and the overall demand, we might wrongly assume that providers are well paid, with good benefits such as sick leave and paid vacations. In reality, earnings are very low: the 2008 national (median) yearly income

---

[21] NACCRRA, 2008, table on cost of childcare.
[22] Afterschool Alliance, n.d.

of childcare workers was just $18,970[23] and the vast majority received nominal benefits, if any. Variations depend on the hours worked (many work part time), type of care facility, educational levels and geographic location. Preschool teachers are considered as a separate occupational category and on average would be more qualified than childcare workers. Their median annual income in 2008 was somewhat higher at $23,870.[24]

To date, most states require that childcare providers in centres hold at least a high school diploma. This fluctuates based on the type of location, with regulated facilities often requiring additional certification or training requirements. For relatives and family childcare providers, there are likely to be no minimum requirements.

Employment in childcare is expected to grow faster than the average for all occupations between the years of 2006 and 2016 with an 18 per cent employment growth projected. Job prospects are expected to be excellent not only because of the growth in the demand for childcare but also because of the many workers who leave and need to be replaced.[25]

Employer initiatives

To encourage greater childcare and other family-friendly provisions at the workplace, the US Economic Growth and Tax Reconciliation Act of 2001 provides federal tax incentives to promote employer-provided childcare and referral services. Employers can receive a credit of 25 per cent of their spending on the construction or rehabilitation and operation of an on-site childcare facility or on purchasing childcare services. In addition, employers can receive a credit of 10 per cent of their spending on resource and referral services for employees. The total credit cannot exceed $150,000 annually.[26]

To date, 20 states for which data are available offer similar tax incentives to employers. Nevertheless, research indicates that these incentives are ineffective, mainly because most employers have little or no state tax liability. In particular, the study found that, in 16 of the 20 states, fewer than five corporations used the credit, and in five of the 16, no claims were made. The study challenges the

---

[23] Occupational employment statistics are available on the web site of the United States Bureau of Labor Statistics. For childcare workers see: http://www.bls.gov/oes/current/oes399011.htm [12 June 2009].

[24] Occupational employment statistics for preschool teachers found at http://www.bls.gov/oes/current/oes252011.htm [3 June 2009].

[25] United States Bureau of Labor Statistics, 2009, section on childcare workers.

[26] Washington State Child Care Resource and Referral Network, 2008.

assumption that these incentives further childcare initiatives, as the earmarked resources remain unused, and therefore unavailable to support other established programmes.[27]

Dependent Care Assistance Plans, which allow employees to put aside tax-free funds to pay for care (as discussed above in the section on tax incentives), are the most frequent form of childcare benefit provided as there is no cost to the employer, any administrative costs being covered by the savings on payroll taxes. A national study of for-profit and not-for-profit companies with 50 or more employees found that, in 2005, 45 per cent of all companies offered Dependent Care Assistance Plans and 72 per cent of large companies with more than 1,000 employees. A childcare resource and referral service was the next most frequent type of assistance provided (34 per cent). Only 7 per cent offered childcare on- or near-site, although this reached 17 per cent among large companies.[28]

Information on benefits received by full-time workers in private industry is available from a 2007 National Compensation Survey conducted by the US Department of Labor. Again, the most frequent benefit to which workers had access (31 per cent) was to Dependent Care Reimbursement Accounts. Fewer had access to on- or off-site care (5 per cent), funds for childcare (3 per cent) or referral services (11 per cent). Managerial and professional employees were most likely to have access to childcare assistance while employees in construction, maintenance and service-related industries were the least likely to be offered access to employer-provided childcare assistance.

The 2007 survey also found that the higher an employee's earnings, the more likely he or she would be to have access to childcare assistance. More than 20 per cent of employees earning more than $15 an hour had childcare-related benefits available, compared to less than 10 per cent of those earning $15 or less. Moreover, workers in larger firms (over 100 or more workers) had greater access to childcare assistance and other family care benefits, than did their counterparts in smaller organizations. Organized union workers were also more likely to be offered childcare assistance (20 per cent versus 15 per cent) as a result of collective bargaining efforts with employers.[29]

In addition to individual company initiatives related to childcare support, some employers have grouped together to try to influence policies. In the case of Corporate Voices for Working Families, which represents about 50 businesses in the United States, employing over 4 million people, the objective is to

---

[27] Fitzpatrick and Campbell, 2002, pp. 4–5.

[28] Bond et al., 2005, table 9.

[29] United States Bureau of Labor Statistics, 2007, tables 23 and 24.

communicate the corporate viewpoint on public policy issues related to working families. As concerns childcare, Corporate Voices has been pushing for legislation to increase the amount of pre-tax funds which employees can set aside for their care expenses in Dependent Care Reimbursement Accounts.[30]

Role of unions

Unions have been active in various ways, including bargaining for more family-friendly conditions of work, lobbying for more public support for childcare and organizing childcare workers to improve their working conditions.

In response to members' changing needs and the increasing significance of childcare to working parents, unions have been negotiating family-friendly contract terms with employers including childcare support. The United Auto Workers (UAW), for example, has negotiated with the big three American car-makers for various types of childcare support including resource and referral services and on-site childcare at some locations. In 1999, the UAW/General Motors Child Development Center won a Work–Life Innovative Excellence Award from the Alliance for Work–Life Progress.[31]

A number of unions have succeeded in negotiating for childcare funds, such as the 1199 SEIU/Employer Child Care Fund for health workers in New York City (see details in the case study which follows and also section 4.3 for other examples).

Lobbying for improvements in public policy is also a strategy of organized labour. For example, the California Labor Federation, made up of over 1,200 AFL-CIO and Change to Win locals, co-sponsored that state's groundbreaking, paid family leave bill.[32] The New York Union Childcare Coalition (currently made up of over 25 unions, including SEIU, OPEIU, CWA, District 1 and CSEA, TWU, UNITE HERE, United Postal Workers and many others) mobilized to strengthen state-level funding for renovation and childcare construction projects, to subsidize care programmes and to increase accessibility to childcare for working parents.[33]

Unionizing childcare workers, particularly family care workers who work in their homes, is difficult. However, SEIU (Service Employees International Union)

---

[30] Information found at Corporate Voices, Home and Public Policy pages, http://www.cvworkingfamilies.org/our-work/family-economic-stability [19 June 2009].

[31] A list of winners over the years is available at http://www.awlp.org/awlp/about/html/award_winners.html [12 June 2009].

[32] California Labor Federation. Available at http://www.calaborfed.org/issues/paid_leave.html [12 June 2009].

[33] Firestein and Dones, 2005, pp. 14–15.

Kids First, for example, managed to organize family care providers in the states of Illinois, Maryland, Oregon and Washington. These workers were impacted by the low rates of childcare assistance subsidies imposed by the state governments. Unionizing was seen by family care providers as a way of bettering pay and benefit options, as well as obtaining a voice in legislative matters. Although some variations exist among states, the core gains included higher reimbursement rates for infant care, access to professional development funds, incentives to become licensed, health insurance and bonuses for offering extended care hours.

Opponents worried that any increase of benefits for providers would translate into higher childcare costs for parents. Yet in Oregon, for example, the union also negotiated to raise the eligibility thresholds for low-wage parents to receive subsidies (from 150 per cent of the federal poverty level to 185 per cent) and to lower the amount parents must contribute towards subsidized care by 20 per cent.[34] A possible long-term benefit to parents and their children will be reduced turnover rates, and therefore greater consistency and quality of care.

Other unions, such as the American Federation of State, County and Municipal Employees (AFSCME), via Childcare Providers Together and in collaboration with the United Child Care Union, are doing similar work on behalf of childcare providers, and have focused efforts on legislative reform and fighting federal budget cuts of care programmes.[35]

Conclusion

The lack of a comprehensive national policy to address childcare in the United States and the major dependence on a market approach results in very unequal access to childcare and problems of access to quality care. Financial ability to pay for childcare is a major determinant of access and of the quality of the care obtained. The Government's targeted support to working, low-income families has eased the burden for some, but many poor families do not benefit, and the cost of childcare is high for the many families that are not eligible for government subsidies. Tax exemptions tend to favour the better off, so middle-income families tend to be left out of government assistance.[36]

---

[34] Information from the web site of SEIU. Found at http://www.seiu.org/a/publicservices/raising-standards.php [12 June 2009].

[35] Information from the web site of AFSCME at http://www.afscme.org/legislation-politics/13.cfm [12 June 2009].

[36] Folbre, 2001.

In this context, there have been many interesting examples of initiatives by both employers and trade unions to try to help workers access care of quality as can be seen in this chapter and throughout the examples in Chapters 3 and 4 of this book. NGOs promoting childcare quality, as well as academic research, have also been contributing to the policy debate. Thus the experience of the United States provides interesting examples of workplace initiatives for childcare in a context where public facilities are rare and private childcare is expensive for most working families.

1199 SEIU/Employer Child Care Fund [37]

Workplace. Hospitals and nursing homes in New York City.

Type of business. Health care.

Occupations of workers. Wide range, from maintenance workers and clerical workers in hospitals to physicians' assistants.

Working hours. Many workers are on shifts over a 24-hour period, including weekends. The majority are women.

Childcare solution. Childcare fund based on contributions of employers as a result of collective bargaining.

Partners. SEIU 1199, managements of hospitals and homes, childcare providers (for profit and not-for profit), municipal and community organizations, federal government (tax exemptions).

Beginning in 1989, work–family issues became a topic of discussion and great interest at meetings of New York's Health and Human Service Union (Local 1199 of the Service Employees International Union – SEIU). Downsizing and recourse to forced overtime in hospitals, coupled with declining or no childcare supports in the community (for instance, after-school programmes were being cut), led the members to bring their concerns to the union.

At the end of 1989, the yearly contract survey conducted prior to negotiations indicated that 80 per cent of respondents said they thought the union should fight for a childcare benefit. Yet at that time, only 40 per cent of the membership were actually parents. In the beginning, 16 health-care institutions signed

---

[37] Case study information compiled by Catherine Hein from Joyner, 2003, and the web site of 1199 Family of Funds, Child Care and Youth Programs, http://www.1199seiubenefits.org/child_care/default. aspx [12 June 2009].

up to the fund initiative, agreeing to pay 0.3 per cent of their gross yearly payroll into a childcare fund. Getting agreement was not easy and the intervention of the Catholic Archbishop of New York helped persuade the 16 Catholic hospitals in his Archdiocese to accept the union demand.[38]

The number of employers contributing to the fund has grown rapidly since it started operations in 1991, to 450 by 2007. The number of children benefiting each year from the services and programmes of the fund has almost doubled in the last ten years from about 6,500 in 1997 to over 12,000 children in 2007.

Organization and management

The fund was set up as a Taft-Hartley (Union–Employer) Jointly-Trusteed Employee Welfare Benefit Fund. It is administered by a Board of Trustees composed of equal numbers of trade union and management representatives. The Board of Trustees appoints the Executive Director, who is responsible for the day-to-day running of the fund. In 2005, the fund had about 90 employees.[39]

Childcare advisory committees exist at each contributing institution. When the fund began, it was felt that local committees of rank and file members were the key to real parent participation. The parents of the children needed to have a say in the types of programmes that would be offered and how the collective bargaining money would be spent. In the past, each institution had a separate budget, so the local committees were involved in administering funds. However, the growing number of institutions has meant that the funds are now combined.

Currently the childcare advisory committees, composed of 1199 SEIU volunteers from participating institutions, help to shape the fund's programmes in various communities, act as liaison between institutions and the funds, give the funds important feedback on programmes used and help to register members during the registration period.

Childcare services

The fund provides a wide variety of childcare benefits for children up to the age of 17 years including on-site and off-site daycare facilities, childcare referral services,

---

[38] Public Broadcasting Service, n.d.

[39] Career Welfare League of America, 2005, Career Center Job Listing #970, at http://www.cwla.org/jobs/jobsearchdetails.asp?JOBID=970 [12 June 2009].

college preparation, summer camp and holiday and cultural arts programmes, as well as voucher and expense reimbursement and emergency care programmes.

Full-day care

Full-day childcare services are available through the 1199/Employer Child Care Corporation which manages two licensed childcare facilities. Lunch and two snacks are served and the centres are open from 6.45 a.m. to 6.00 p.m. Parents make a co-payment on a sliding scale and the fund covers the balance of the tuition. The fund also has contracted childcare seats at other centres and the tuition fees for parents are similar to those of the Child Care Corporation.

Childcare resource and referral services

The fund administers a referral service that can provide childcare referrals for parents seeking information about daycare centres, family daycare homes, special needs programmes and after-school care. There is no fee for this service.

Summer day camp (5 to 17 years)

The fund contracts with many licensed programmes that provide childcare services during the holidays when schools are closed in February, April and December and during the summer. Parents select the programme of their choice and then make a co-payment to the fund. The fund covers the balance of the cost. It also contracts with camps which cater for children with special needs and subsidizes children at these sites.

Weekend care

Parents who require childcare to work weekends are able to have the partial costs for their child's weekend classes in the arts, education or recreation reimbursed.

Voucher system

The voucher system reimburses parents a portion of their childcare and after-school expenses on a quarterly basis. Parents can use documented care or informal care but the amount provided is less if they use informal care. They can receive reimbursement for their children from birth to 6 years old for daycare and from 6 to 12 years old for after-school care.

Emergency care relief

Parents who are experiencing a personal or family crisis that affects their childcare arrangements, necessary for work, can apply for emergency care relief. Applicants' situation must meet the criteria adopted by the Trustees to qualify as an emergency for reimbursement.

Eligibility and access

To be eligible, workers must be employed on a full-time or part-time basis (two-fifths of a working week) at a participating 1199 institution and have passed the 90-day probation period. Children must be under 18 years old.

There is no guarantee that a worker will be able to access the benefit requested. Each year, the Trustees approve a budget that the fund cannot exceed. If the demand for benefits is greater than the budget (which it often is), applicants are approved for benefits in priority order. Members with no benefit history will be given priority by seniority over those with a previous history. All requests have to be made at the beginning of the school year.

Generous as it is, the fund cannot afford to finance the needs of all the 35,000 eligible children among the union members each year.[40] Since members cannot get the benefit every year, there is a type of rotation system. According to the previous executive director:

> At times, members have even coordinated with one another, to help make sure families with the greatest needs are served. They have said things such as, "I know you need it more than me – I'll decide not to register this year." It has created a community mindedness amongst our members.[41]

Resources

Employers typically pay 0.5 per cent of their gross payroll to the Child Care Fund. Employers' contribution rates are set forth in the applicable collective bargaining agreements. They are estimated in order to meet the anticipated cost of requests

---

[40] Public Broadcasting Service, n.d.
[41] Joyner, 2003, p. 11.

for benefits and for administration. In 2005, the fund received contributions totalling approximately $26.5 million.[42]

Various partners who make contributions in kind or reduce their fees for fund members are also increasing the resources of the fund. Such partners include the New York City Board of Education, New York University Metropolitan Center, the Harlem School of the Arts, the YMCA and other community agencies. Parents also provide resources since they make a co-payment for childcare in most programmes.

Indirectly, the federal government is also providing resources. The childcare benefit is exempt from income tax for parents of children under 13 years up to a maximum of $5,000 per single parent or married couple. If married, to be eligible for the exemption, the spouse must also be employed, looking for work, a full-time student or unable to care for him/herself.

Employee perspective

The local committee members have reported that parents greatly appreciate the fund, and they see it as an integral part of their work. They need these benefits to work.[43]

A medical technician at St Vincent's Hospital is a single dad strapped with college tuition and living expenses for two older children and with daycare expenses for a 4-year-old daughter whom he is raising on his own. He relies on the childcare fund's subsidy to help pay a babysitter to watch his daughter while he works what are often irregular shifts in the hospital operating rooms.

Another couple were pleased that their two school-age boys blossomed last year at a summer camp partly subsidized by the childcare fund. It eased their minds to know where their boys were every day and to know that they were involved in supervised activities, rather than at home watching television.[44]

Lessons learned

Various kinds of partnership have been involved in the success of the 1199/ Employer Child Care Fund:

---

[42] Career Welfare League of America, 2005, Career Center Job Listing #970, at http://www.cwla. org/jobs/jobsearchdetails.asp?JOBID=970 [11 December 2008].

[43] Joyner, 2003, p. 11.

[44] Public Broadcasting Service, n.d.

- partnership and solidarity among union members, including those without young children, to bargain for childcare;

- partnership between employers and the trade union for supervising the fund;

- partnership among employers as contributors to the fund (many of whom might not individually have been able to help with childcare needs);

- partnerships with community organizations that help provide benefits and those that are strengthened by the guaranteed funding, for example for summer camps;[45] and

- partnerships of parents and children with organizations in their community.

The main partner that is missing is government. An executive director has noted the need to pay good salaries for the staff in the childcare centres in order to keep the best teachers.

> The problem that every center in this nation is experiencing is that most parents can not afford to finance the full expense of running a center and centers that care about quality can not afford to balance the expenses on the backs of its workers. ... The piece that is missing is money from the government.[46]

---

[45] Joyner, 2003, p. 8.
[46] Joyner, 2003, p. 12.

Annex
Characteristics and services
of workplace initiatives by company

Country	Workplace	Workplace characteristics		Workers' needs addressed		
		Industry[1]	Size[2]	Preschool age	After school and holiday care[3]	Emergency/ back-up care
Brazil	Oswaldo Cruz	Research	L	● (4m–6yrs)		
	Natura	Manuf.	L	● (4m–4yrs)		
	FURNAS	Electricity	L	● (0–7yrs)	AS, HC	
	Medley	Manuf.	L	● (0–6yrs)		
Chile	Concepción Univ.	Education	L	● (3m–4yrs)		
	Aguas Andinas	Water supply	L	● (3m–5yrs)		
	CAHMT	Agric.	P (L)	● (2–12yrs)		
	Plaza Mall	Retail	L	● (3m–2yrs)		
France	Rennes Atalante Science and Technology Park	Services	P (L)	● (2.5m–4yrs)		● (2.5m– 4yrs)
	SNPE Research Centre	Research	P (L, S)		HC (3–14yrs)	● (3m–3yrs)
	Aix-la-Duranne Employment Site	Multiple	P (L, M, S)	● (2.5m–4yrs)	BS (6yrs)	● (2.5m– 4yrs)
Hungary	IBM	Info. services	L		HC (6–14yrs)	●
	Gedeon Richter	Manuf.	L	● (3–6yrs)	HC (6–12yrs)	
	H. Academy Science	Research	L	● (1.5–7yrs)		
	Hungarian Post Office Ltd	Transport	L		HC (7–12yrs)	
	Magyar Telekom	Comms	L	● (2–7yrs)	HC	

Childcare assistance				Partners						
On-site/ workplace-related care	Link to community facility	Financial support	Advice or referral	Employer	Trade union/ workers	Employers' organizations	National govt.	Local govt.	Service providers, private and non-profit	Internat./ national donors, foundations, etc.
●		●		●	●					
●				●	●				●	
	●	●		●	●	●			●	
●				●				●		
●	●	●		●					●	
	●	●		●	●					
●				●	●		●	●		
	●			●					●	
●				●	●				●	●
●		●		●	●			●	●	
●				●				●	●	
	●	●	●	●					●	
●		●		●	●		●			
●				●			●			
●				●	●					●
●	●			●					●	

Country	Workplace	Workplace characteristics		Workers' needs addressed		
		Industry[1]	Size[2]	Preschool age	After school and holiday care[3]	Emergency/ back-up care
India	Gokaldas Images	Manuf.	L	● (6m–4yrs)		
	BHEL	Manuf.	L	● (1–5 yrs)	HC (6–12yrs)	
	Infosys	Info. services	L	● (2.5m–5yrs)		
	Wipro	Info. services	L	● (1–4yrs)	AS, HC	● (1–7yrs)
	NCBS	Research	M	● (6m–7yrs)		
	Peenya Industrial Area	Manuf.	P (L, M, S)	●		
Kenya	SOCFINAF	Agric.	L	● (3m–6.5yrs)		
	Red Lands Roses	Agric.	P (L)	● (2m–4yrs)		
South Africa	BMW	Manuf.	L	● (3–6yrs)	HC	● (3–6yrs)
	First National Bank	Finance	L	● (3m–6yrs)		
	Old Mutual	Finance	L	● (3m–6yrs)		
	Melsetter	Agric.	M	● (0–6yrs)	AS, HC (6–12yrs)	
	Zuid-A. Hospital	Health services	L	● (4m–6yrs)		

Childcare assistance				Partners						
On-site/ workplace-related care	Link to community facility	Financial support	Advice or referral	Employer	Trade union/ workers	Employers' organizations	National govt.	Local govt.	Service providers, private and non-profit	Internat./ national donors, foundations, etc.
●				●					●	
●	●			●			●		●	
●				●						
●				●					●	
●				●						
●				●		●	●	●	●	
●				●	●		●	●		
●				●						●
●				●	●					
●				●	●					
●				●			●			
●				●						
●				●						

Country	Workplace	Workplace characteristics		Workers' needs addressed		
		Industry[1]	Size[2]	Preschool age	After school and holiday care[3]	Emergency/back-up care
Thailand	Phra Pradaeng Industrial Zone	Manuf.	P (L, M, S)	● (1.5–4yrs)	HC (6–12yrs)	
	Nawanakhon Industrial Area	Manuf.	P (L, M, S)	● (2.5–4.5yrs)	HC (6–12yrs)	
	AEROTHAI	Comms	L	● (2m–4yrs)	HC (6yrs+)	● (2m+)
	BOWT	Education	L	● (3m–4yrs)	HC	
	Nong Nooch Garden	Agric.	L	● (1.5–5yrs)	AS, HC (6–12yrs)	
UK	Royal Marsden	Health services	L	●	AS, HC	●
USA	SEIU Employer Fund	Health services	P	●	AS, HC	●

1. Industry categories are based on the International Standard Industrial Classification (ISIC, Rev. 4).
2. P: Partnership between two or more companies; S: 50 or fewer workers; M: 51–250 workers; L: 250+.
3. BS = Before-school; AS = After-school; HC = Holiday care.

Childcare assistance				Partners						
On-site/ workplace-related care	Link to community facility	Financial support	Advice or referral	Employer	Trade union/ workers	Employers' organizations	National govt.	Local govt.	Service providers, private and non-profit	Internat./ national donors, foundations, etc.
•				•	•		•	•		•
•				•	•	•	•	•		•
•				•	•		•			
•				•	•			•	•	•
•				•			•			
•	•	•	•	•			•	•	•	
•	•	•	•	•	•		•	•	•	

Bibliography

Accor Services. n.d. *Childcare vouchers: What makes for a successful scheme?* Available at http://www.childcarevouchers.co.uk/Pages/DownloadBrochures.aspx [10 June 2009].

Adema, W. 2007. "Babies and bosses: What lessons for governments?", in *The OECD Observer*, No. 264/265, pp. 18–19.

Afterschool Alliance. n.d. *America after 3pm: A household survey on afterschool in America: Executive summary* (Washington, DC).

Amuyunzu-Nyamongo, M.; Ezeh, C.A. 2005. "A qualitative assessment of support mechanisms in informal settlements of Nairobi", in *Journal of Poverty*, Vol. 9, No. 3, pp. 89–107.

Anandalakshmy, S.; Balagopal, I. 1999. *Site visit: Mobile Creches at Delhi, Bombay and Pune, India: ECCD at the construction sites* (Washington, DC, World Bank, The Consultative Group on ECCD).

Ananian, S.; Bauer, D. 2007. "Le temps périscolaire", in *Etudes et Résultats*, DREES, No. 611.

ANDI (Agência de Notícias dos Direitos da Infância). 2003. "500 mil crianças e adolescentes trabalham como domésticos", in *Análise do Clipping*, No. 472, April. Available at http://www.andi.org.br/tid/conteudo/pub/listagem.asp?cat=3 [11 June 2009].

Archer, G. 2007. *Take up of formal childcare by lower income working families* (London, Department for Children, Schools and Families, Childcare Division).

Artiles, A.M. 2006. *Role of immigrant women in the domestic services sector.* Available at http://www.eurofound.europa.eu/eiro/2006/04/articles/es0604029i.htm [17 June 2009].

Australia, House Standing Committee on Family and Human Services. 2006. *Inquiry into balancing work and family* (Canberra, Parliament of Australia).

Bachelet, Michelle. 2008. *Statement of the President of the Republic at the inauguration of the international seminar "Equal pay for work of equal value"* (Santiago, Chile).

Bailleau, G. 2007. "L'accueil collectif et en crèches familiales des enfants de moins de 6 ans en 2006", in *Études et Résultats*, DREES, No. 608.

Baker, C.; Wanaboribun, P. 2004. *For Thailand's women workers: Twelve years of struggle* (Bangkok, Srimuang Printing).

Barbeau, C. 2001. *Work-related child-care centres in Canada, 2001* (Quebec, Human Resources Development Canada, Labour Program).

Bauer, D. 2007. "Entre maison, enfant(s) et travail: Les diverses formes d'arrangement dans les couples", in *Études et Résultats*, DREES, No. 570.

Biersteker, L. 2001. *Early childhood development: A review of public policy and funding* (Cape Town, Institute for Democracy in South Africa (IDASA)).

Blanpain, N.; Momic, M. 2007. "Les assistantes maternelles en 2005", in *Études et Résultats*, DREES, No. 581.

Bond, T.J. et al. 2005. *2005 national study of employers* (New York, Families and Work Institute).

Brazil, Departamento Intersindical de Estatística e Estudos Socioeconômico. 2003. *Equidade de gênero nas negociações coletivas: Cláusulas relativas ao trabalho da mulher 1996–2000* (São Paulo).

Bressé, S.; Galtier, B. 2006. "La conciliation entre vie familiale et vie professionnelle selon le niveau de vie des familles", in *Études et Résultats*, DREES, No. 465.

Bressé, S.; Le Bihan, B.; Martin, C. 2007. "La garde des enfants en dehors des plages horaires standard", in *Études et Résultats*, DREES, No. 551.

Bruschini, M.C.A. 2007. "Trabalho e gênero no Brasil: Nos ultimos dez anos", in *Cadernos de Pesquisa*, Vol. 37, No. 132, Sep/Dec, pp. 537–572. Available at http://www.oei.es/genero/trabalho_genero_brasil.pdf [19 June 2009].

Bryson, C.; Kazimirski, A.; Southwood, H. 2006. *Childcare and early years provision: A study of parents' use, views and experience* (United Kingdom, Department for Education and Skills).

Caisse Nationale des Allocations Familiales (CNAF). 2006. *Le point sur le contrat "Enfance-Jeunesse"* (Paris).

—. 2007. *L'accueil du jeune enfant en 2006: Observatoire national de la petite enfance* (Paris).

—. 2008. *Fonds national d'action sociale (FNAS) 2008: Communiqués de presse* (Paris).

Caizzi, A. 2008. *La politique familiale demain: Quatre scénarios exploratoires* (Paris, Caisse Nationale des Allocations Familiales).

Campanha Nacional pelo Direito à Educação; MIEIB (Movimento Interfóruns de Educação Infantil do Brasil). 2006. *Consulta sobre qualidade da educação infantil.* Available at http://www.concepto.com.br/mieib/i/biblio_qualidade_educ.pdf [11 June 2009].

Caparas, M.V.Q. 2008. *Work–life balance: Best practices from family-responsible employers and executives* (Pasig City, Philippines, Center for Research and Communication Foundation).

Carrion, V. 1997. *Comentários à Consolidação das leis do trabalho*, 22 ed. (São Paulo, Saraiva).

Cassirer, N.; Addati, L. 2007. *Expanding women's employment opportunities*, Interregional Symposium on the Informal Economy: Enabling Transition to Formalization, 27–29 November 2007 (Geneva, ILO).

Centre d'Analyse Stratégique. 2007. *Rapport sur le service public de la petite enfance* (Paris, La Documentation Française).

Chakravorty, B. 2002. "Baby sitting the corporate way", in *Business Today* (India).

Chalfie, D.; Blank, H.; Entmacher, J. 2007. *Getting organized: Unionizing home based childcare providers* (Washington, DC, National Women's Law Center).

Chardon, O.; Daguet, F. 2008. "Enquêtes annuelles de recensement 2004 à 2007: L'activité des femmes est toujours sensible au nombre d'enfants", in *INSEE Première*, No. 1171.

Chemin, A. 2008. "Le gouvernement veut instaurer le droit opposable à la garde d'enfants", in *Le Monde*, 20 April.

Chile, Dirección del Trabajo. 2007a. *Encuesta laboral (ENCLA) 2006* (Chile). Available at http://www.dt.gob.cl/documentacion/1612/article-95152.html [10 June 2009].

—. 2007b. *Inequidades y brechas de género en el empleo: análisis de los resultados de la encuesta nacional (quinta versión)*. Available at http://www.dt.gob.cl/documentacion/1612/article-95445.html [22 June 2009].

Code Blue for Child Care. 2007. *Making space for child care: Getting good child care policy back on the agenda* (Ottawa, Canada, Canadian Union of Public Employees).

Cohany, S.R.; Sok, E. 2007. "Trends in labor force participation of married mothers of infants", in *Monthly Labor Review*, Vol. 130, No. 2, pp. 9–16.

Comisión Económica para América Latina y el Caribe (CEPAL). 2007. *Estadísticas de America Latina y el Caribe 2006–2007* (Santiago).

Committee for Legal Aid to Poor (CLAP). 2004. *Exploring rights of the child in early childhood: A report of the interface for perspective building on legal aspects of early childhood care and development* (Geneva, Day of General Discussion on Implementing Child Rights in Early Childhood (CRIN)).

Conseil de l'Emploi des Revenus et de la Cohésion Sociale (CERC). 2008. *Les services à la personne* (Paris, La Documentation Française).

Conseil Economique, Social et Environnemental (CESE). 2008. *Les services à la personne (avis de suite)*, Avis et Rapports du Conseil Economique, Social et Environnemental, No. 34 (Paris).

Corey, B.; Freeman, R.D. 2003. "Bridging the gap between workplace demands and family obligations: Lessons from the United Auto Workers/Ford Partnership", in S.C. Cass (ed.): *Labor-management partnerships for working families* (Cambridge, United States, Massachusetts Institute of Technology Workplace Center).

Cronin, M. n.d. *Employer childcare options*, speech given at employers' conference Babies and Bosses: Reconciling Work and Family Life.

Da Roit, B.; Sabatinelli, S. 2007. *The cost of childcare in EU countries* (Brussels, European Parliament, Policy Department for Economy and Science).

Daune-Richard, A.M.; Odena, S.; Petrella, F. 2007. *Innovation et diversification des modes d'accueil de la petite enfance: Quelle participation des entreprises pour quelle gouvernance?* (Paris, Caisse Nationale des Allocations Familiales (CNAF), Laboratoire d'Economie et de Sociologie du Travail (LEST)).

Daune-Richard, A.M.; Odena, S.; Petrella, F. 2008. "L'engagement des entreprises dans l'accueil des jeunes enfants: De nombreux enjeux et des partenariats public-privé complexes", in *Recherches et Prévisions*, No. 92, pp. 61–71 (Paris, Caisse Nationale des Allocations Familiales (CNAF)).

David-Alberola, É.; Momic, M. 2008. "Le métier d'assistante maternelle", in *Études et Résultats*, DREES, No. 636.

Daycare Trust. 2002. *Big Employers Childcare Survey* (London).

—. 2008. *Childcare Costs Survey 2008* (London).

—; National Centre for Social Research. 2007. *Childcare nation? Progress on the childcare strategy and priorities for the future* (London, National Centre for Social Research).

De Mello, L.; Menezes Filho, N.; Scorzafave, L.G. 2006. *Improving labour utilisation in Brasil*, Economics Department Working Paper No. 533 (Paris, OECD).

Del Boca, D.; Locatelli, M. 2007. "Motherhood and participation", in D. Del Boca; C. Wetzels (eds): *Social policies, labour markets and motherhood: A comparative analysis of European countries* (Cambridge, UK, Cambridge University Press).

Den Dulk, L.; Van Doorne-Huiskes, A. 2007. "Social policy in Europe: Its impact on families and work", in R. Crompton; S. Lewis; C. Lyonnette (eds): *Women, men, work, and family in Europe* (Houndmills, UK, Palgrave Macmillan).

Denmark, Family and Work Commission. 2007. *Chance for balance*. Available at http://www.familieogarbejdsliv.dk/udgivelser/udgivelser [16 June 2009].

Dones, N. 2001. "ATU Local 192 and AC Transit shift into gear over work and family issues", in *California Public Employee Relations Journal*, No. 147, April. Available at http://www.working-families.org/organize/pdf/atu_actransit.pdf [16 June 2009].

Durham-Vichr, D. 2000. "Emergency childcare an important corporate benefit", in *Washington Business Journal*, No. 20.

Employers' Confederation of the Philippines (ECOP). 2004. *Cases on business initiatives on work-life* (Makati City).

European Commission. 2006a. *Employment in Europe 2005* (Brussels).

—. 2006b. *Making work pay: Debates from a gender perspective* (Brussels, European Communities).

—. 2008. *Report on equality between women and men* (Brussels).

European Foundation for the Improvement of Living and Working Conditions. 2006. *Employment developments in childcare services for school-age children: United Kingdom* (Dublin).

EUROSTAT. 2008. *Total fertility rate, number of children per women: Data for 2006* (Luxembourg). Available at http://epp.eurostat.ec.europa.eu [10 June 2009].

Ewen, D.; Matthews, H. 2007. *Title I and early childhood programs: A look at investments in the NCLB era*, CLASP Child Care and Early Education Series Paper No. 2 (Washington, DC, Center for Law and Social Policy).

Fagan, C.; Hebson, G. 2006. *"Making work pay" debates from a gender perspective: A comparative review of some recent policy reforms in thirty European countries* (Luxembourg, Office for Official Publications of the European Communities).

Fagnani, J. 2007. "Fertility rates and mothers' employment behaviour in comparative perspective: Similarities and differences in six European countries", in *Choice*, Vol. 45, No. 3, pp. 71–72.

—; Letablier, M.T. 2003. "Qui s'occupe des enfants pendant que les parents travaillent?", in *Recherches et Prévisions*, No. 72 (Paris, Caisse Nationale des Allocations Familiales (CNAF)).

Fiocruz. 2008. *Contanto histórias, tecendo redes, construindo saberes: Projeto político-pedagógico: Creche Fiocruz* (Rio de Janeiro).

Firestein, N.; Dones, N. 2005. "Unions fight for work and family policies – Not for women only", in D.S. Cobble (ed.): *The sex of class: Women transforming American labor* (Ithaca, New York, Cornell University Press).

Fitzpatrick, C.S.; Campbell, N.D. 2002. *The little engine that hasn't: The poor performance of employer tax credits for childcare* (Washington, DC, National Women's Law Center).

Folbre, N. 2001. "Accounting for care in the United States", in M. Daly (ed.): *Care work: The quest for security* (Geneva, ILO).

Frew, R. 2004. *NHS childcare strategy impact analysis* (United Kingdom, Daycare Trust, National Health Service (NHS)).

Friedman, D.E. n.d. *Hospital: Pioneers in caring for employees' children* (Watertown, MA, Bright Horizons Family Solutions).

Glick, P. 2002. *Women's employment and its relation to children's health and schooling in developing countries: Conceptual links, empirical evidence, and policies* (Ithaca, New York, Cornell University).

Government of Karnataka, Planning and Statistics Department. 2005. *Karnataka human development report: Investing in human development* (Bangalore).

Gregory, A.; Milner, S. 2008. "Fatherhood regimes and father involvement in France and the UK", in *Community, Work and Family*, Vol. 11, No. 1, pp. 61–84.

Grimshaw, D.; Carroll, M.; Rubery, J. 2008. *UK report on decent work: Trends, linkages and gaps* (Geneva, ILO).

Haddad, L. 2002. *An integrated approach to early childhood education and care*, Early Childhood and Family Policy Series (Paris, UNESCO).

Haddad, P. 2007. "Les services à la personne: Quel modèle pour un développement durable des services à la personne", in E. Heurgon; J. Landrieu (eds): *L'économie des services pour un développement durable* (Paris, L'Harmattan).

Harty, S. 2005. *Backup caregiver services help keep workers on the job in business insurance*. Available at: http://www.workforce.com/archive/article/24/09/75.php [10 June 2009].

Hein, C. 2005. *Reconciling work and family responsibilities* (Geneva, ILO).

Hernandez, H.; Montero, R. 2004. *Cobertura de la protección social para los trabajadores de temporada* (Santiago, ILO Subregional Office for the Southern Cone of Latin America).

Hertz, T. 2004. *Have minimum wages benefited South Africa's domestic service workers?* Paper presented at the Forum on African Development and Poverty Reduction: The Macro-Micro Linkage, Cape Town, 13–15 Oct.

Hetzel, P.; Cahierre, A. 2007. *Temps des familles, temps des enfants: Autour de la scolarité: Conférence de la famille 2007* (Paris, La Documentation Française).

Hope, H. 2008. *Corporate Voices members identify need for comprehensive backup care* (Washington, DC, Corporate Voices for Working Families).

Hungarian Central Statistical Office. 2006. *A munkavégzés és a családi kötöttségek összeegyeztetése, 2005* [Reconciliation between work and family life, 2005] (Budapest).

—. 2007. *Társadalmi ellátórendszer, 2006* (Social services, 2006) (Budapest).

Immervoll, H.; Barber, D. 2005. *Can parents afford to work? Childcare costs, tax-benefit policies and work incentives* (Paris, OECD).

India, Ministry of Labour and Employment. 2008. *Annual Report 2007–2008* (New Delhi).

India, Ministry of Women and Child Development. 2007. *Working group on development of children for the eleventh five year plan (2007–2012): A report* (New Delhi).

India, National Institute of Public Cooperation and Child Development. 2006. *Selected issues concerning ECCE India*, Background paper for the Education for All Global Monitoring Report 2007: Strong Foundations: Early Childhood Care and Education (Paris, UNESCO).

India, National Planning Commission. 2007. *Sub-group report: Child protection in the eleventh five year plan (2007–2012)* (New Delhi).

Institut National de la Statistique et des Etudes Économiques (INSEE). 2007. *Pères et mères travaillant à temps partiel selon la durée du temps partiel* (France).

International Labour Organization (ILO). 1999. *Direct request made by the committee of experts on the application of conventions and recommendations (CEACR) to Guatemala concerning the Workers with Family Responsibilities Convention, 1981 (No. 156)*. See APPLIS database available at http://webfusion.ilo.org/public/db/ standards/normes/appl/index.cfm?lang=EN [10 June 2009].

—. 2000. *Observation made by the CEACR to Chile concerning the Workers with Family Responsibilities Convention, 1981 (No. 156) (2000/71st Session)*. See APPLIS database available at http://webfusion.ilo.org/public/db/standards/normes/appl/ index.cfm?lang=EN [10 June 2009].

—. 2004. *Kenya, Tanzania and Uganda: Gender and employment dimensions of poverty: Policy issues, challenges and responses*, GPE Regional Brief, Policy Integration Department (Geneva).

—. 2007a. *Observation made by the CEACR to Chile concerning the Workers with Family Responsibilities Convention, 1981 (No. 156) (2007/78th Session)*. See APPLIS database available at http://webfusion.ilo.org/public/db/standards/ normes/appl/index.cfm?lang=EN [10 June 2009].

—. 2007b. *Observation made by the CEACR to France concerning the Workers with Family Responsibilities Convention, 1981 (No. 156) (2007/78th Session)*. See

APPLIS database available at http://webfusion.ilo.org/public/db/standards/normes/appl/index.cfm?lang=EN [10 June 2009].

—. 2008. *Key indicators of the labour market*, 5th edition (Geneva, ILO).

International Organisation of Employers (IOE). 2008. *Trends in Workplace Survey, 2008: Enterprises in a globalizing world* (Geneva).

Jany-Catrice, F. 2008. *Les services à la personne: Niveaux et évolutions in l'aide à domicile face aux services à la personne: Mutations, confusions, paradoxes*, Clersé, Crida and Réseau 21 (Lille, Délégation Interministérielle à l'Innovation, l'Expérimentation Sociale et l'Economie Sociale (DIIESES)).

Johnson, S. 2008. "Unions' appeal to women includes caregiving help", in *WeNews*, 13 May. Available at http://www.womensenews.org/article.cfm/dyn/aid/3599 [10 June 2009].

Joia, A. 2008. *Panorama da primeira infância: Avanços e desafios* (São Paulo, Fundação Abrinq).

Joyner, C. 2003. "Meeting the family care needs of the health care workforce: reflections on the 1199 child care fund", in S.C. Cass (ed.): *Labor-management partnerships for working families* (Cambridge, MA, Massachusetts Institute of Technology Workplace Center).

Kaga, Y. 2006. *Impact of free primary education on early childhood development in Kenya*, Policy Brief on Early Education (Paris, UNESCO).

—. 2007. *The training and working conditions of preschool teachers in France* (Paris, UNESCO).

Karega, R.G.M. 2002. *Work and family study in Kenya: Implications of combining work and family responsibilities* (unpublished) (Geneva, ILO).

Kazimirski, A. et al. 2006. *Monitoring of the reform of the income tax and national insurance rules for employer-supported childcare: A study of provision and experiences of employers* (United Kingdom, HM Revenue and Customs; National Centre for Social Research).

Kazimirski, A. et al. 2008. *Childcare and early years survey 2007: Parents' use, views and experiences* (United Kingdom, Department for Children, Schools and Families).

Kelly, E.L. 2003. "The strange history of employer-sponsored child care: Interested actors, uncertainty, and the transformation of law in organizational fields", in *The American Journal of Sociology*, Vol. 109, No. 3, pp. 606–649.

Kenya, Ministry of Education, Science and Technology (MOEST). 2005. *Delivering quality equitable education and training to all Kenyans: Kenya education sector support programme 2005–2010* (Nairobi).

—. 2006a. *Early childhood development service standard guidelines for Kenya* (Nairobi).

—. 2006b. *National Early Childhood Development Policy Framework* (Nairobi).

—. 2007. *Ministerial public expenditure review* (Nairobi).

—; UNESCO; OECD. 2005. *The UNESCO/OECD early childhood policy review project: The background report of Kenya* (Nairobi, Government Document).

Kervella, M.C. 2008. "Les crèche d'entreprises: Leur développement se poursuit", in *CAF 35 Magazine*, July.

Kiger, P. 2004. "A case for child care in workforce management", in *Workforce Management*, April, pp. 34–40.

Kim, T.; Kim, H. 2004. *Reconciling work and family: Issues and policies in the Republic of Korea*, Conditions of Work and Employment Series No. 6 (Geneva, ILO).

Klammer, U.; Letablier, M.T. 2007. "Family policies in Germany and France: The role of enterprises and social partners", in *Social Policy and Administration*, Vol. 41, No. 6, pp. 672–692.

Kleiner, B.; Nolin, M.J.; Chapman, C. 2004. *Before- and after-school care, programs, and activities of children in kindergarten through eighth grade: 2001: Statistical analysis*, Report No. NCES 2004-008 (Washington, DC, National Center for Education Statistics). Available at http://nces.ed.gov/pubs2004/2004008.pdf [10 June 2009].

Knodel, J.; Saengtienchai, C. 2005. *Rural parents with urban children: Social and economic implications of migration on the rural elderly in Thailand* (Ann Arbor, MI, University of Michigan, Institute for Social Research, Population Studies Center).

Koltai, L.; Vucskó, B. 2007. *A munka-magánélet összeegyeztetését segítö és gátló tényezök Magyarországon* [Factors enabling and hindering work–life balance in Hungary] (Hungary, Fövárosi Esélyegyenlöséget Segítö Iroda).

Kusakabe, K. 2006. *Reconciling work and family: Issues and policies in Thailand*, Conditions of Work and Employment Series No. 14 (Geneva, ILO).

La Documentation Française. 2008. *Famille: Un droit opposable à la garde d'enfants dès 2012?* (Paris, Actualités de la Vie Publique).

Layzer, J.I.; Goodson, B.D. 2007. *National study of child care for low-income families: Care in the home: A description of family child care and the experiences of the families and children that use it: Executive summary* (Cambridge, MA, Abt Associates Inc.).

Le Bihan, B.; Martin, C. 2005. "Atypical working hours: Consequences for childcare arrangements", in *Social Policy and Administration*, Vol. 38, No. 6, pp. 565–590.

Le Feuvre, N.; Lemarchant, C. 2007. "Employment, the family and 'work–life balance' in France", in R. Crompton; S. Lewis; C. Lyonette (eds): *Women, men, work and family in Europe* (New York, Palgrave Macmillan), pp. 210–229.

Lefèvre, C.; Solaz, A.; Pailhé, A. 2008. "Les employeurs, un autre acteur de la politique familiale? Un état des lieux de leur participation dans la conciliation vie familiale–vie professionnelle", in *Recherches et Prévisions*, No. 92.

Leprince, F. 2003. *L'accueil des jeunes enfants en France: Etat des lieux et pistes d'amélioration* (Paris, La Documentation Française).

Letablier, M.T. 2002. "Fertility and family policies in France", in *Journal of Population and Social Security (Population)*, Vol. 1, Supp., pp. 245–261.

Liquor Hospitality and Miscellaneous Union (LHMU). 2007. "National childcare crisis: Skills and pay of workers critical", in *LHMU News* (Australia), 16 November.

Litchfield, L.; Swanberg, J.; Sigworth, C. 2004. *Increasing the visibility of the invisible workforce: Model programs and policies for hourly and lower wage employees* (Boston, MA, Boston College Center for Work and Family, Carroll School of Management).

Lokshin, M.; Glinskaya, E.; Garcia, M. 2000. *The effect of early childhood development programs on women's labor force participation and older children's schooling in Kenya* (Washington, DC, The World Bank Development Research Group).

Lokshin, M.; Glinskaya, E.; Garcia, M. 2004. "The effect of early childhood development programs on women's labor force participation and older children's schooling in Kenya", in *Journal of African Economies*, Vol. 13, No. 2, pp. 240–276.

Lowe, E. 2007. *Setting a new industry standard in Canada: CIBC* (Ottawa, The Vanier Institute of the Family).

Marbot, C.; Dejonghe, V.; Bruniaux, V. 2008. "Les salariés des particuliers-employeurs en 2006", in *INSEE Première*, No. 1173.

Marical, F.; Minonzio, J.; Nicolas, M. 2007. "La PAJE améliore-t-elle le choix des parents pour un mode de garde?", in *Recherches et Prévisions*, No. 88, pp. 5–20.

Masters, J.; Pilkauskas, N. 2004. *Access to good quality, affordable childcare: The role of demand subsidies in the United Kingdom* (Boston, MA, Harvard University, John Kennedy School of Government).

Matthews, H. 2006. *Childcare assistance helps families work: A review of the effects of subsidy receipt on employment* (Washington, DC, Center for Law and Social Policy).

Méda, D.; Simon, M.-O.; Wierink, M. 2003. "Pourquoi certaines femmes s'arrêtent-elles de travailler à la naissance d'un enfant?", in *Premières informations premières synthèses* (Direction de l'animation de la recherche des études et des statistiques (DARES)), No. 29.2.

Merritt, J. 2008. "Backup childcare, cubicle doctor visits: keeping workers loyal, happy." Posted at *Wall Street Journal*, 23 March, http://blogs.wsj.com/juggle/2008/05/23 [16 June 2009].

Morel, N. 2007. "From subsidiary to 'free choice': Child- and elder-care policy reforms in France, Belgium, Germany and the Netherlands", in *Social Policy and Administration*, Vol. 41, No. 6, pp. 618–637.

Morgan, J.K.; Zippel, K. 2003. "Paid to care: The origins and effects of care leave policies in Western Europe", in *Social Politics*, Vol. 10, No. 1, pp. 49–85.

National Association of Child Care Resource and Referral Agencies (NACCRRA). 2008. *Child care in America: 2008 state fact sheets* (Washington, DC).

National Women's Law Center. 2007. *You've been working hard – Get the credit you deserve!* (Washington, DC).

Open Society Institute. 2002. *Equal opportunities for women and men in Hungary* (Bucharest).

Organisation for Economic Co-operation and Development (OECD). 2004a. *Early childhood education and care policy in France* (Paris).

—. 2004b. *Early childhood education and care policy: Country note for Hungary* (Paris).

—. 2005a. *Babies and bosses: Reconciling work and family life. Vol. 4: Canada, Finland, Sweden and the United Kingdom* (Paris).

—. 2005b. *Society at a glance 2005* (Paris).

—. 2006a. *Education at a glance: OECD Indicators 2006* (Paris).

—. 2006b. *Starting strong II: Early childhood education and care* (Paris).

—. 2007a. *Babies and bosses: Reconciling work and family: A synthesis of findings for OECD countries* (Paris).

—. 2007b. *Economic survey of Hungary 2007*, Policy Brief (Paris).

Ortiz, L. 2008. "Quand l'employeur découvre l'utilité du baby-sitting", in *Le Monde*, 26 February.

Öun, I.; Trujillo, G.P. 2005. *Maternity at work: A review of national legislation* (Geneva, ILO).

Parrott, S. 2008. *2008 omnibus appropriations bill cuts funding for Head Start: Bipartisan reauthorization bill enacted two weeks before omnibus was completed called for increased investment* (United States, Center on Budget and Policy Priorities).

Party of European Socialists (PES). 2006. *Childcare provision: Contributing to the achievement of social democratic goals* (Brussels).

Platat, S. 2007. "Crèche: la petite enterprise qui monte", 22 January. Available at http://www.liberation.fr/economie/010191657-creche-la-petite-entreprise-qui-monte [16 June 2009].

Plantenga, J.; Remery, C. 2005. *Reconciliation of work and private life: A comparative review of thirty European countries* (Brussels, European Commission).

Platinga, M. 2006. *Employee motivation and employee performance in child care* (Groningen, University of Groningen).

PricewaterhouseCoopers (PWC). 2004. *Universal early education and care in 2020: Costs, benefits, and funding options* (United Kingdom, Daycare Trust; Social Market Foundation).

Promundo. 2007. *Breve panorama sobre a primeira infância no Brasil* (Rio de Janeiro).

Public Broadcasting Service (PBS). n.d. *Juggling work and family: Local 1199 and the New York hospitals: A daring approach from an imaginative union*. Available at http://www.hedricksmith.com/site_workfamily/aboutProgram_story.html [11 October 2008].

Ramirez-Machado, J.M. 2003. *Domestic work, conditions of work and employment: A legal perspective*, Conditions of Work and Employment Series No. 7 (Geneva, ILO).

Reddock, R.; Bobb-Smith, Y. 2008. *Reconciling work and family* (Geneva, ILO).

Reid, P.; White, D. 2007. *Out-of-school care services for children living in disadvantaged areas* (Dublin, European Foundation for the Improvement of Living and Working Conditions).

Riedmann, A. et al. 2006. *Working time and work–life balance in European companies*, Establishment Survey of Working Time 2004–2005 (Dublin, European Foundation for the Improvement of Living and Working Conditions).

Ruault, M.; Daniel, A. 2003. "Les modes d'accueil des enfants de moins de 6 ans: Premiers résultats de l'enquête réalisée en 2002", in *Études et Résultats*, DREES, No. 235.

Schulman, K.; Blank, H. 2007. *State child care assistance policies 2007: Some steps forward, more progress needed* (Washington, DC, National Women's Law Center).

SERNAM; FAO. 2005. *Mujeres rurales en Chile*. Santiago de Chile, Chile.

Services, Industrial, Professional and Technical Union (SIPTU). 2005. *Childcare in Ireland: A trade union view* (Dublin).

Shapiro, A. 2005. *IBM Work/Life Fund*, PowerPoint presentation at Global Leaders (Montreal, World Forum).

Sharif, A. 2007. "Learning vision checks in at Changi Airport", in *Hand in Hand*. Available at http://www.childcarelink.gov.sg/ccls/uploads/HIH.pdf [16 June 2009].

Shore, R. 1998. *Ahead of the curve: Why America's leading employers are addressing the needs of new and expectant parents (executive summary)* (New York, Families and Work Institute).

Silvera, R. 2005. *Reconciliation of work and private life in France* (United Kingdom, European Commission, EWERC, University of Manchester).

Singapore, Ministry of Community Development and Sports. 2004. *New home-based infant care service*, Press Release, 16 Jan. (Singapore). Available at http://app.mcys. gov.sg/web/corp_press_story.asp?szMod=corp&szSubMod=press&qid=272 [11 June 2009].

Singapore, Ministry of Manpower. 2006. *Work–Life Excellence Award 2006: Success stories of award winners* (Singapore).

Sorj, B. 2004. *Reconciling work and family: Issues and policies in Brazil*, Conditions of Work and Employment Series No. 8 (Geneva, ILO).

Statham, J.; Mooney, A. 2003. *Around the clock: Childcare services at atypical times* (Bristol, The Policy Press).

Statistics South Africa. 2007a. *Labour Force Statistics, September 2007* (Pretoria).

—. 2007b. *Mid-year population estimates 2007* (Pretoria).

Sudarshan, R.M.; Bhattacharya, S. 2008. *Through the magnifying glass: Women's work and labour force participation in urban Delhi* (New Delhi, ILO Subregional Office for South Asia).

Sure Start. 2003. *Full-day care: National standards for under 8s day care and childminding* (Nottingham, UK, Department for Education and Skills).

—. 2006. *Supporting childcare makes good business sense.* Available at http://www.dcsf. gov.uk/everychildmatters/publications/leaflets/1396 [11 June 2009].

—; National Childminding Association. 2005. *Childminding networks work!* Available at http://www.ncmaccf.org.uk/shared_asp_files/uploadedfiles/1ef3a04e-57e6-4ffc-9acf-07982d46b039_networks_work.pdf [11 June 2009].

Tabarot, M.; Lépine, C. 2008. *Rapport au premier Ministre sur le développement de l'offre d'accueil de la petite enfance* (Paris, La Documentation Française).

Thailand, Ministry of Education, Office of the Education Council. 2004. *[Strategy for the development of 3–5-year-old children]* (in Thai) (Bangkok). Available at http://www.onec.go.th/publication/47029/sara_47029.htm [16 June 2009].

Thailand, National Statistical Office; UNICEF. 2006. *Monitoring the situation of children and women: Thailand multiple indicator cluster survey, December 2005–February 2006, final report* (Bangkok).

Trades Union Congress (TUC). 2006. *Who's looking after the children? A trade union guide to negotiating childcare* (London).

Umayahara, M. 2006. *Early childhood education policies in Chile: From pre-Jomtien to post-Dakar* (Paris, UNESCO).

UNESCO. 2005. *Policy review report: Early childhood care and education in Kenya*, Early Childhood and Family Policy Series (Paris).

—. 2006. *Education for all, global monitoring report: Strong foundations: Early childhood care and education* (Paris).

UNESCO, International Bureau of Education (IBE). 2006a. "Brazil: Country profile", paper prepared for the *Education for All Global Monitoring Report 2007* (Geneva, UNESCO).

—. 2006b. *South Africa: Early childhood care and education (ECCE) programmes* (Geneva, UNESCO).

—. 2006c. *Thailand: Early childhood education and care (ECCE) programs* (Geneva, UNESCO).

UNESCO; OECD. 2007. *Summary review of the UNESCO/OECD early childhood policy review project for Brazil, Indonesia, Kazakhstan and Kenya* (Paris).

UNISON. 2004. *Bargaining support guide: Bargaining for childcare* (London).

United Kingdom, Department for Education and Skills. 2006a. *Supporting childcare makes good business sense* (London).

—. 2006b. *Choice for parents, the best start for children: Making it happen: An action plan for the ten year strategy: Sure Start children's centre, extended schools and childcare* (London).

—. 2007. *Provision for children under five years of age in England: January 2007* (London).

United Kingdom, HM Revenue and Customs. 2007a. *Help with the costs of childcare information for parents and childcare providers* (London).

—. 2007b. *Paying for childcare: Getting help from your employer* (London).

United Kingdom, National Audit Office. 2006. *Sure Start children's centre: Report by the Comptroller and Auditor General* (London).

United Nations Development Programme (UNDP). 2006. *Kenya national human development report 2006: Human security and human development: A deliberate choice* (Nairobi).

United States Bureau of Labor Statistics. 2007. *National compensation survey: Employee benefits in private industry in the United States* (Washington, DC).

—. 2008a. *Employment characteristics of families summary* (Washington, DC).

—. 2008b. *Career guide to industries, 2008–09 edition: Child day care services* (Washington, DC).

—. 2009. *Occupational outlook handbook, 2008–09 edition* (Washington, DC).

United States Census Bureau. 2005. *Who's minding the kids? Child care arrangements: Spring 2005, detailed tables* (Washington, DC).

United States Department of Health and Human Services. 2007. *Early child care linked to increases in vocabulary, some problem behaviours in fifth and sixth grade* (United States, National Institutes of Health).

—. 2008. *Child Care and Development Fund fact sheet* (Washington, DC).

United States Government Accountability Office. 2005. *Means-tested programs: Information on program access can be an important management tool* (Washington, DC).

—. 2007. *Women and low-skilled workers: Other countries' policies and practices that may help these workers enter and remain in the labor force* (Washington, DC).

United States Internal Revenue Service. 2008. *Claiming the child and dependent care tax credit* (Washington, DC).

Valdejão, R.; Purvinni, L. 2008. "Poucos e bons", in *Pais e Filhos*, 3 June. Available at http://www.revistapaisefilhos.com.br/htdocs/index.php?id_pg=109&id_txt=700 [19 June 2009].

Viganego, J.P. 2008. *Présentation de l'experience du Centre Charlie Chaplin* (unpublished document), April.

Wallet, P. 2006. "Pre-primary teachers: A global analysis of several key education indicators", background paper prepared for the *Education for All Global Monitoring Report 2007* (Geneva, UNESCO).

Wanjek, C. 2005. *Food at work* (Geneva, ILO).

Washington State Child Care Resource and Referral Network. 2008. *Tax credits for employers: U.S. Economic Growth and Tax Reconciliation Act of 2001* (Washington, DC).

Wazir, R. 2001. "Early childhood care and development in India: Some policy issues", in M. Daly (ed.): *Care work: The quest for security* (Geneva, ILO).

Whitehouse, G. et al. 2007. *Reassessing the "family-friendly workplace": Trends and influences in Britain, 1998–2004*, Employment Relations Research Series, No. 76 (London, Department for Business, Enterprise and Regulatory Reform).

Williams, T.; Samuels, M.L. 2001. *Nationwide audit of ECD provisioning in South Africa* (Pretoria, Department of Education).

Winston, P. 2007. *Meeting responsibility at work and home: Public and private support* (Washington, DC, The Urban Institute).

Woolley, P. 2007. *Is workplace daycare a workable solution?* 13 December. Available at http://www.straight.com/article-124530/is-workplace-daycare-a-workable-solution [11 June 2009].

Working Families. 2006. *Childcare options: Guidance for SMEs, Working Families Factsheet* (London). Available at http://www.parentsatwork.org.uk/asp/employer_zone/e_fs_childcare.asp [16 August 2008].

World at Work. 2007. *Attraction and retention: The impact and prevalence of work-life and benefit programs*. Available at http://www.worldatwork.org/waw/adimLink?id=21945 [16 June 2009].

World Health Organization (WHO). 2002. *World report on violence and health* (Geneva).

Zepeda, E. 2007. "Addressing the employment–poverty nexus in Kenya: Comparing cash transfer and job creation programmes", in *International Poverty Centre*, No. 40.

Index